ALPHABETICAL LIST
OF THE OFFICERS OF THE
MADRAS ARMY

WITH THE DATES OF THEIR RESPECTIVE PROMOTION,
RETIREMENT, RESIGNATION OR DEATH,
WHETHER IN INDIA OR IN EUROPE,

FROM THE YEAR 1760
TO THE YEAR 1834 INCLUSIVE
(CORRECTED TO SEPTEMBER 30, 1837).

COMPILED AND EDITED BY MESSRS. DODWELL AND MILES,
East India Army Agents

The Naval & Military Press Ltd

Published by
The Naval & Military Press Ltd
Unit 10, Ridgewood Industrial Park,
Uckfield, East Sussex,
TN22 5QE England
Tel: +44 (0) 1825 749494
Fax: +44 (0) 1825 765701
www.naval-military-press.com
www.military-genealogy.com
© The Naval & Military Press Ltd 2007

In reprinting in facsimile from the original, any imperfections are inevitably reproduced and the quality may fall short of modern type and cartographic standards.

Printed and bound by Lightning Source

THE OFFICE OF GENERAL AGENCY

TO THE

EAST INDIA COMPANY'S CIVIL AND MILITARY SERVICE,

No. 69, CORNHILL:

MESSRS. DODWELL AND MILES.

An OFFICE of GENERAL AGENCY (with EAST INDIA READING AND SUBSCRIPTION ROOM), for the purpose of rendering assistance to OFFICERS in the HON. EAST INDIA COMPANY'S CIVIL and MILITARY SERVICE, is established at No. 69, Cornhill.

The business of this Office is conducted by MR. EDWARD DODWELL (late Chief Clerk in the Civil and Military Pay Department at the East India House), and by MR. JAMES S. MILES (late Assistant to MR. DODWELL in the above Department), who have quitted the Company's Service, agreeably to the plan of Reduction consequent on the altered circumstances of the Company.

MR. DODWELL having been thirty years, and MR. MILES twenty years, in the Civil and Military Department of the Hon. Company's Home Establishment, and thus become conversant with the rules and regulations of the Military and Civil Services, their Office (under the firm of DODWELL and MILES) will be found an easy medium through which annual Subscribers of one pound (payable at Lady-day in each year) may obtain the most recent intelligence from India, as well as accurate information on the following points:

1. The names of all CIVIL SERVANTS retired on the ANNUITY FUNDS from the three Presidencies, with the dates of admission thereto.

2. The names of Civil Servants in the receipt of ABSENTEE ALLOWANCE.

3. The names of OFFICERS on the OFF-RECKONING FUNDS at the three Presidencies, with those who stand next in Succession thereto, with the amount of PAST SHARES of Off-Reckonings in any one year, from the date of their first institution.

4. FURLOUGH PAY due to Officers, according to their Certificates received from India.

5. RETIRED PAY, and CIVIL PENSIONS.

6. ALL CASUALTIES, whether Civil or Military, Promotions, Retirements, Removals, Posting to Regiments, and appointments to Civil Stations in India.

7. REGULATIONS respecting the Bengal, Madras, and Bombay Military Funds, with amount of Monthly stoppages on account thereof.

8. REGULATIONS respecting FAMILY REMITTANCES, and the annual amount allowed to be remitted by each Officer, and to whom payable in England, according to the Rolls received from India.

9. INDIAN LOAN PROPERTY.

10. EFFECTS OF DECEASED PERSONS according to schedules received from the Registrar's Office in India.

11. DISTRIBUTION OF PRIZE PROPERTY.

12. ADDRESSES OF CIVIL AND MILITARY SERVANTS.

*** Passages engaged to India and the colonies, with detailed lists of the necessary Outfits, &c., without charge to the parties.

BAGGAGE SHIPPED AND CLEARED.

Messrs. DODWELL and MILES will assist, through the forms of the Court, WRITERS, CADETS, and ASSISTANT SURGEONS, proceeding to India. They will also supply forms of application, and conduct any correspondence with the Court, connected with the interests of the Company's Civil or Military Servants.

ALPHABETICAL LIST

OF THE

OFFICERS OF THE INDIAN ARMY;

WITH

THE DATES OF THEIR RESPECTIVE
PROMOTION, RETIREMENT, RESIGNATION, OR DEATH,
WHETHER IN INDIA OR IN EUROPE;

FROM

THE YEAR 1760, TO THE YEAR 1834 INCLUSIVE,
CORRECTED TO SEPTEMBER 30, 1837.

———o✦o———

COMPILED AND EDITED BY MESSRS. DODWELL AND MILES,

East India Army Agents, 69, Cornhill.

DEDICATED BY PERMISSION

TO THE

HONOURABLE COURT OF DIRECTORS

OF

The East India Company.

———

LONDON:
LONGMAN, ORME, BROWN, AND CO.,
PATERNOSTER ROW;
W. H. ALLEN, & Co., 7, LEADENHALL STREET; J. M. RICHARDSON, 28, CORNHILL;
AND W. THACKER, & Co., ST. ANDREW'S LIBRARY, CALCUTTA.

SOLD ALSO BY DODWELL AND MILES, 69, CORNHILL.

———

1838.

Entered at Stationers' Hall.

BENSLEY, PRINTER, PHIPPS-BRIDGE, MITCHAM.

TO THE HONOURABLE

THE COURT OF DIRECTORS

OF THE

EAST INDIA COMPANY.

Honourable Sirs,

We undertook the Work now submitted to the Public from a persuasion of its utility; and we send it to the Press encouraged by the permission to inscribe it to your Honourable Court, our kind and generous Patrons.

Engaged from early youth in the business of your Home Establishment, especially in the Military branch of it, we naturally feel much interest in matters connected with the Indian Army, and we doubt not that the List which we publish of the Individuals to whom, under wise councils, Great Britain is mainly indebted for the vast extension and stability of her Eastern Empire, will be received by the Public with much approbation.

This List includes the Periods of Service, the Promotions, Retirements, or Deaths, whether in India or in Europe, of nearly Fifteen Thousand Officers in your Honourable Company's Army, from the Year 1760 to the present time: it has been prepared with minute and untiring research; and no name is inserted, rank appended, nor date stated, the accuracy of which is not sanctioned by Documents of indisputable authority.

Though we may attach undue importance to our unostentatious but elaborate Performance, Your Honourable Court will, we trust, yet deign to accept of this Dedication as a sincere Testimony of Respect for your Public Character, and of Gratitude for many Acts of personal Kindness and Condescension, from

Honourable Sirs,

Your obliged and obedient Servants,

EDWARD DODWELL,
JAMES SAMUEL MILES.

69, CORNHILL, *December*, 1837.

SUBSCRIBERS IN ENGLAND

TO

MESSRS. DODWELL AND MILES'S

ALPHABETICAL LIST OF THE INDIAN ARMY.

THE HONOURABLE

COURT OF DIRECTORS OF THE EAST INDIA COMPANY,

Forty Copies.

GENERAL.
Robert Bell.

LIEUTENANT-GENERALS.
Samuel Bradshaw.
Sir Hector Maclean, K. C. B.
Charles Corner.
Lambert Loveday.
St. George Ashe.
Sir Thomas Dallas, G. C. B.
Tredway Clarke.
Sir Thomas Brown, K. C. B.
John Dighton.
W. H. Blachford.
Sebright Mawbey, H. M. Service.

MAJOR-GENERALS.
James Price.
Sir Henry Worsley, K. C. B.
Donald Macleod, C. B.
William Blackburne.
William Roome.
George Wahab.
Edward Boardman.
William Farquhar.
Sir Hugh Fraser, K. C. B.
Alexander Fair, C. B.
Sir Charles Deacon, K. C. B.
Arthur Molesworth.
Thomas Whitehead, C. B.
William Croxton.
Henry Roome.
Sir George M. Cox, Bart.
Jeffery Prendergast.
Richard Podmore.
William Munro.
Sir James Russell, K. C. B.
G. R. Kemp.
Alexander Limond.
W. D. Cleiland, 2 copies.
J. F. Dyson.
William C. Fraser.

SUBSCRIBERS.

COLONELS.

James Ahmuty.
Augustus Andrews, C. B.
Alfred Richards, C. B.
W. P. Price.
Andrew Aitchison.
S. Goodfellow.
Adam Hogg.
W. S. Heathcote.
W. G. Pearse.
T. H. Smith.
William Hull.
Peter De la Motte.
James Durant.
C. S. Fagan, C. B.
S. H. Tod.
Sir Robert H. Cunliffe, Bart.
William Sandwith.
C. A. Walker.
Frederick Bowes.
William Gordon.
Robert Home.
Richard Whish.
Lechmere C. Russell.
S. R. Strover.

LIEUTENANT-COLONELS.

William Cuninghame.
Robert Barnewell,   2 copies.
W. H. L. Frith.
C. M. Bird.
William Franklin.
Joseph Garner.
H. I. Bowler.
John Sutherland.
J. A. Kelly.
John Ward.
John Rodber.
John Nixon.
P. M. Hay.
Edward L. Smythe.

MAJORS

James C. Hyde.
J. Walsh, H. M. Service.
William Yule.
James Fagan.

CAPTAINS.

Sir John Campbell, K.C.H. & K.L.S.
R. M. Grindlay,   2 copies.
J. H. Robley.
T. C. S. Hyde.
H. G. White, H. M. Service.
J. S. Iredell.
James Grant Duff.

LIEUTENANTS.

W. F. Curtis.
D'Ormieux Von Streng, H. M. Service.
John William Kaye.
Henry Jackson.
C. A. Sinclair, H. M. Service.
Richard Samuel M. Sprye.
William Loveday.
Thomas Brown.

ENSIGN.

Charles Richard Woodhouse.

SURGEONS.

John Dean, E. I. C. Service.
John Brown, E. I. C. Service.

A

Alexander, Josias Dupre, Esq., E. I. H.
Alexander, R., Esq.

B

Brock, Irving, Esq.
Bach, Adolphus, Esq.
Barclay, J., Esq.
Barber, James, Esq.

C

Chapman, Rev. S. T.
Clarke, Francis, Esq., E I. H.   5 copies
Campbell, Thomas, Esq., ditto
Crawford, Charles Venner, Esq.
Chapman, John Kemble, Esq.
Carr, Rowland, Esq.

SUBSCRIBERS.

D
Daviniere, G. T., Esq., E. I. H.
Dodwell, William, Esq., C. S.
Drysdale, W. C., Esq.
Dodwell, Mrs.

F
Franks, W. A., Esq., E. I. H.

G
Grissell, T. D., Esq.
Guyon, Gardiner Guion, Esq.

H
Hill, David, Esq., E. I. H.
Hornidge, Marmaduke, Esq., E. I. H.
Holgate, — Esq.
Hodgson, John, Esq., C. S.

J
Jenkins, Edward, Esq., E. I. H.
Johnson, Mrs. Charles Conwell

K
Keith, William, Esq., E. I. H.
Keith, Thomas Hilton, Esq., E. I. H.

L
Loveday, The Rev. Thomas
Loveday, Arthur, Esq.
Lulham, Edward, Esq.
Ludlow, — Esq.
Longley, Mrs. M.
Longley, Miss Emma.

M
Melvill, James Cosmo, E. I. H.
Melvill, Philip, Esq., E. I. H.
Mills, Henry, Esq., E. I. H.
Morris, William, Esq.
Masson, John, Esq.

N
Nicolson, Alfred, Esq.

O
Owen, William, Esq.

P
Peacock, Thomas L., Esq. E. I. H.
Phillipart, Sir John

R
Roberts, Mrs. Colonel
Ricketts, Mordaunt, Esq., C. S.
Rundall, James, Esq.
Ryle, Charles, Esq., E. I. H.

S
Shillito, James F., Esq., E. I. H.
Scott, William, Esq.,   2 copies

T
Thornton, Edward, Esq., E. I. H.

V
Vaughan, the Venerable Archdeacon.
Vincent, J. R. Esq., E. I. H.
Vansittart, Robert, Esq., C. S.
Vaughan, Petty, Esq.

W
Wright, William, Esq., late Auditor General to the E. I. C.
Webster, James, Esq.
Winfield, C. H., Esq.
Watts, William, Esq.

Bruce, Shand, & Co., Messrs.
Cockburn, J., & Co., Messrs.
Gladstanes, Kerr, & Co., Messrs.
Haviside, T., & Co., Messrs.
Maynard, Robert, & Co., Messrs.
Whittaker & Co., Messrs.

Asylum Life Office,   2 copies.
Clerical, Medical, and General Life Office.
Metropolitan Life Assurance Society
Universal Life Office.
National Loan Fund and Life Insurance Society.
Jersey Athenæum.

THE NAMES WITH DATES OF APPOINTMENT

OF THE

COMMANDERS IN CHIEF IN INDIA,

FROM THE YEAR 1770, TO THE YEAR 1837.

Appointed	NAMES.	Assumed Command.	Quitted Command.
	Brigadier-General Sir ROBERT BARKER	Mar. 24, 1770	
	Colonel CHARLES CHAPMAN	Dec. 22, 1773	Jan. 18, 1774
	Colonel ALEXANDER CHAMPION	Jan. 18, 1774	Dec. 29, 1774
Feb. — 1774	Lieutenant-General JOHN CLAVERING	1774	Aug. 30, 1777
	(Died Aug. 30, 1777. On the death of General Clavering, the duties of Commander-in-Chief were carried on by the Military Board; but on Oct. 16, 1777, Brigadier-General Giles Stibbert, who was appointed provincial Commander-in-Chief, assumed the Command of the Army, which he held till the arrival of Sir Eyre Coote.)		
	Lieutenant-General Sir EYRE COOTE, K. B. . . .	Mar. 25, 1779	Apr. 27, 1783
	(Brigadier-General Stibbert again assumed the Chief Command, and held the same until Lieutenant-General Sloper arrived.)		
	Lieutenant-General ROBERT SLOPER	July 21, 1785	Sep. 12, 1786
Apr. 11, 1786	LORD CORNWALLIS, (Governor General) . . .	Sep. 12, 1786	Oct. 28, 1793
	(Colonel Mackenzie and Colonel Ahmuty were appointed to the Chief Command during the absence of Lord Cornwallis, in the years 1790 and 1793.)		
Sep. 19, 1792	Major-General Sir R. ABERCROMBY	Oct. 28, 1793	Apr. 30, 1797
	(Major General Morgan held the chief Command during General Abercromby's absence.)		
Oct. 4, 1797	Lieutenant-General Sir A. CLARKE, K. B. . . .	May 17, 1798	July 31, 1801
	(Having held the provincial Command from April 30, 1797.)		
Aug. 13, 1800	Lieutenant-General GERARD LAKE . . . . . . (afterwards Lord Lake.)	July 31, 1801	July 30, 1805

Appointed.	NAMES.	Assumed Command.	Quitted Command.
Mar. 20, 1805	Marquis CORNWALLIS (Governor General) . . (Died Oct. 5, 1805. Lord Lake held the provincial command during the absence of Lord Cornwallis.)	July 30, 1805	Oct. 5, 1805
Feb. 19, 1806	Lieutenant-General Lord LAKE . . . . (Lord Lake had held the Command from the death of Lord Cornwallis in his capacity of provincial Commander in Chief.)	Oct. 10, 1805	Oct. 17, 1807
Dec. 23, 1806	Lieutenant-General Sir GEORGE HEWITT	Oct. 17, 1807	Dec. 18, 1811
Mar. 13, 1811	Lieutenant-General Sir GEORGE NUGENT . . . . (On the arrival of Lord Moira, Sir George Nugent assumed the provincial command, agreeably to the Court's Resolution of Nov. 18, 1812.)	Jan. 14, 1812	Oct. 4, 1813
Nov. 18, 1812	General the Earl of MOIRA . . . . (Afterwards Marquis of Hastings, Governor General.)	Oct. 4, 1813	Jan. — 1823
Jan. 2, 1822	Lieutenant-General the Honourable Sir EDWARD PAGET, G. C. B.	Jan. 13, 1823	Oct. 7, 1825
Feb. 9, 1825	General Lord COMBERMERE, G. C. B. & G. C. H.	Oct. 7, 1825	
Feb. — 1829	General the Earl of DALHOUSIE, G. C. B. . . .	Jan. 1, 1830	
Oct. — 1830	General Sir EDWARD BARNES, G. C. B. . . .	Jan. 10, 1832	
May — 1833	General Lord WILLIAM C. BENTINCK, G. C. B. . .	. . . 1834	
Feb. — 1835	Lieutenant-General Sir HENRY FANE, G. C. B. . .	Sep. 5, 1835	

ALPHABETICAL LIST OF THE OFFICERS

OF THE

BENGAL ARMY,

WITH THE DATES OF THEIR RESPECTIVE PROMOTION, RETIREMENT, RESIGNATION OR DEATH, WHETHER IN INDIA OR IN EUROPE,

FROM THE YEAR 1760 TO THE YEAR 1834 INCLUSIVE
(CORRECTED TO SEPTEMBER 30, 1837).

THE NAMES WITH DATES OF APPOINTMENT

OF THE

COMMANDERS IN CHIEF IN BENGAL,

FROM THE YEAR 1777, TO THE YEAR 1837.

Appointed.	NAMES.	Assumed Command.	Quitted Command.
...1777....	Lieutenant-General GILES STIBBERT	Oct. 16, 1777	Mar. 25, 1779
	,, ,, ...	Oct. 6, 1780	July 25, 1785
	(General Stibbert held the provincial command during the absence of Sir Eyre Coote, at Madras, and continued to hold the command after Sir Eyre Coote's death, till the arrival of General Sloper.)		
Dec. 6, 1790	Colonel MCKENZIE. . . . . (During absence of Lord Cornwallis.)	Dec. 6, 1790	Aug. 1, 1792
Aug. 15, 1793	Colonel AHMUTY. . . . . (During absence of Lord Cornwallis.)	Aug. 15, 1793	Oct. 5, 1793
Sep. 19, 1792	Major-General SIR R. ABERCROMBY. . . . . . (Oct. 28, 1793, assumed chief command in India.)	Oct. 5, 1793	Oct. 28, 1793
Jan. 17, 1797	Major-General MORGAN. . . . . (During absence of General Abercromby.)	Jan. 17, 1797	Apr. 30, 1797
April 6, 1796	Lieutenant-General Sir A. CLARKE, K.B. . . . (May 17, 1798, assumed chief command in India.)	Apr. 30, 1797	May 17, 1798
Apr. 11, 1805	Lieutenant-General Gerard Lord LAKE. . . . . (Oct. 5, 1805, assumed chief command in India.)	July 30, 1805	Oct. 5, 1805
Nov. 18, 1812	Lieutenant-General Sir GEORGE NUGENT. . . .	Oct. 9, 1813	Dec. 28, 1814

LIST

OF

The Officers in the East India Company's Service,

ON

THE BENGAL ESTABLISHMENT,

WHO HAVE RECEIVED THE HONOUR

OF

THE ORDER OF THE BATH,

WITH THE DATE OF THEIR RESPECTIVE APPOINTMENTS.

NAMES.	Rank when first admitted.	Companions.	Knights Commanders.	Knights Grand Cross.
John Macdonald	Lt.-General		April 7, 1815	
Robert Blair	Major-Gen.		,,	
George Wood	,,		,,	
John Horsford	,,		,,	
Henry White	,,		,,	
Gabriel Martindell	,,		,,	
George S. Browne	,,		,,	
David Ochterlony	,,		,,	Dec. 10, 1816
Robert Haldane	Colonel	June 4, 1815	,,	
William Toone	,,	,,	Nov. 26, 1819	
Lewis Thomas	,,	,,		
Robert Gregory	,,	,,		
Richard Doveton	,,	,,		
Henry A. O'Donnel	Lt-Colonel	,,		
J. W. Adams	,,	,,	Sep. 26, 1831	Mar. 10, 1837
Henry Worsley	,,	,,	,,	
Samuel Wood	,,	,,		
George Raban	,,	,,		
Udney Yule	,,	,,		
William Casement	,,	,,	Mar. 10, 1837	
Thomas Wood	Major	,,		
William Elliot	,,	,,		
Michael Keating	,,	,,		
W. A. Thompson	Lt.-Colonel	Dec. 8, 1815		
John Ludlow	Major	,,		
Robert Paton	,,	,,		
William Innis	,,	,,		
Thomas Lowrey	,,	,,		
John Burnet	Lt.-Colonel	Dec. 21, 1816		
Joseph O'Halloran	,,	,,	Mar. 10, 1837	
John Arnold	Colonel	Feb. 3, 1817	Jan. 2, 1827	

NAMES.	Rank when first admitted.	Companions.	Knights Commanders.	Knights Grand Crosses.
William H. Cooper	Lieut.-Col.	Feb. 3, 1817	....	....
Alexander Caldwell	,,	,,	Mar. 10, 1837	....
Robert Houstoun	,,	,,	,,	....
John Shapland	,,	,,	....	....
George Mason	Major	,,	....	....
Alexander Macleod	,,	,,	....	....
Dyson Marshall	Major-Gen.	....	Oct. 14, 1818	....
Robert Gahan	Lieut.-Col.	Oct. 14, 1818	....	....
Donald Macleod	,,	,,	....	....
Thomas Anburey	Major	Oct. 24, 1818	....	....
Thomas Brown	Major Gen.	....	July 23, 1823	....
James Dewar	Lieut.-Col.	July 23, 1823	....	....
William G. Maxwell	,,	,,	....	....
George M. Popham	,,	,,	....	....
Robert Hetzler	,,	,,	....	....
Richard Clarke	,,	,,	....	....
Lucius R. O'Brien	,,	,,	....	....
Edward J. Ridge	Major	,,	....	....
Robert Stevenson	Lieut.-Col.	Dec. 26, 1826	Mar. 10, 1837	....
William Richards	,,	,,	....	....
Thomas Whitehead	,,	,,	....	....
Clements Brown	,,	,,	....	....
Christopher S. Fagan		,,	....	....
Alfred Richards	,,	,,	....	....
Stephen Nation	,,	,,	....	....
John Delamain	,,	,,	....	....
Thomas Wilson	,,	,,	....	....
George Pollock	,,	,,	....	....
Henry S. Pepper	,,	,,	....	....
William C. Baddeley	,,	,,	....	....
James Skinner	,,	,,	....	....
Cornelius Bowyer	,,	,,	....	....
William L. Watson	,,	,,	....	....
George Hunter	Major	,,	....	....
Alexander Knox	Major-Gen.	....	Sep. 26, 1831	....
John Rose	Colonel	Sep. 26, 1831	....	....
Gervaise Pennington	,,	,,	....	....
Robert Pitman	,,	,,	....	....
William C. Faithful	,,	,,	....	....
Alexander Lindsay	,,	,,	....	....
Henry J. Roberts	Lieut.-Col.	,,	....	....
James Caulfield	,,	,,	....	....
Richard Tickell	,,	,,	....	....
Charles Fitzgerald	,,	,,	....	....
Robert Smith	,,	,,	....	....
J. N. Jackson	Major	,,	....	....
Archibald Irvine	,,	,,	....	....

ALPHABETICAL LIST OF THE OFFICERS
OF THE
MADRAS ARMY,
WITH THE DATES OF THEIR RESPECTIVE PROMOTION, RETIREMENT, RESIGNATION
OR DEATH, WHETHER IN INDIA OR IN EUROPE.

FROM THE YEAR 1760 TO THE YEAR 1834 INCLUSIVE
(CORRECTED TO SEP. 30, 1837).

THE NAMES WITH DATES OF APPOINTMENT

OF THE

COMMANDERS IN CHIEF AT MADRAS,

FROM THE YEAR 1784, TO THE YEAR 1837.

Appointed.	NAMES.	Assumed Command.	Quitted Command.
Oct. 7, 1784	Lieutenant-General ROBERT SLOPER . . . . . (July 21, 1785, assumed Chief Command in India.)	June - - 1785	July 21, 1785
Dec. 7, 1784	Lieutenant-General Sir J. DALLING	July 21, 1785	April 6, 1786
Apr. 11, 1786	Lieutenant-General Sir ARCHIBALD CAMPBELL . . (Governor.)	April 6, 1786	Feb. 7, 1789
July 7, 1789	Major-General Sir W. MEDOWS . . . . . . (Governor. The Command having been held by the Senior Officer, until the arrival of General Medows.)	Feb. 20, 1790	Aug. 1, 1792
Apr. 28, 1795	Major-General Sir ALURED CLARKE . . . . . (March 6, 1797, proceeded to assume Command in Bengal. The Command was held by the Senior Officer until the arrival of Sir Alured Clarke.)	Jan. 15, 1796	Mar. 6, 1797
	Major-General GEORGE HARRIS	Mar. 27, 1797	Jan. 22, 1800
Dec. 10, 1800	Lieutenant-General JOHN STUART	Aug. 1, 1801	Oct. 17, 1804
Dec. 21, 1803	Major-General Sir J. F. CRADOCK	Oct. 17, 1804	Sep. 17, 1807
May 29, 1797	Lieutenant-General H. McDOWALL	Sep. 17, 1807	Apr. 10, 1810
	Lieutenant-General GEORGE HEWITT	Apr. 10, 1810	Sep. 27, 1810
Feb. 14, 1810	Major-General Sir S. AUCHMUTY.	Sep. 27, 1810	May 21, 1813
Feb. 12, 1812	Lieutenant-General Hon. J. ABERCROMBY. . . (Governor.)	May 21, 1813	May 25, 1814
Dec. 3, 1813	Lieutenant-General Sir THOMAS HISLOP	May 25, 1814	June 15, 1821
Dec. 6, 1820	Lieutenant-General Sir A. CAMPBELL, Bart., K.C.B. (Died Dec. 11, 1824, after which General Bowser the Senior Officer, took the Command.)	June 15, 1821	Dec. 11, 1824
May 11, 1825	Lieutenant-General Sir G. T. WALKER, G.C.B. . .	Mar. 3, 1826	. . . .
Oct. — 1830	Lieutenant-General Sir R. W. O'CALLAGHAN, K.C.B.	May 11, 1831	. . . .
Apr. — 1836	Lieutenant-General Sir PEREGRINE MAITLAND, K.C.B.	Oct. 11, 1836	. . . .

LIST

OF

The Officers in the East India Company's Service,

ON

THE MADRAS ESTABLISHMENT,

WHO HAVE RECEIVED THE HONOUR

OF

THE ORDER OF THE BATH,

WITH THE DATE OF THEIR RESPECTIVE APPOINTMENTS.

NAMES.	Rank when first admitted.	Companions.	Knights Commanders.	Knights Grand Cross.
Hector Maclean	Major-Gen.	....	April 7, 1815	....
Thomas Dallas	,,	....	,,	Aug. 1, 1833
John Chalmers	,,	....	,,	....
Sir John Malcolm	Colonel	....	,,	Nov. 26, 1819
Augustus Floyer	,,	....	,,	....
Robert Barclay	,,	....	,,	....
W. H. Hewitt	,,	June 4, 1815	....	....
Colin Mackenzie	Lieut-Col.	,,	....	....
J. L. Caldwell	,,	,,	Mar. 10, 1837	....
John Colebrooke	,,	,,	....	....
Alexander Grant	,,	,,	....	....
John Noble	Major	,,	....	....
William Dickson	,,	,,	....	....
Thomas Munro	Colonel	Oct. 14, 1818	Nov. 26, 1819	....
John Doveton	,,	,,	Nov. 26, 1819	....
Hopetoun, S. Scott	Lieut-Col.	,,	Sep. 27, 1831	....
Robert Scot	,,	,,	,,	....
Andrew McDowall	,,	,,	,,	....
John Crosdill	,,	,,	....	....
Samuel Dalrymple	,,	,,	....	....
James Russell	,,	,,	Mar. 10, 1837	....
Henry F. Smith	,,	,,	....	....
Henry Bowen	,,	,,	....	....
Valentine Blacker	,,	"	....	....

NAMES.	Rank when first admitted.	Companions.	Knights Commanders.	Knights Grand Crosses.
T. H. S. Conway	Lieut.-Col.	Oct. 14, 1818		
Henry Munt	Major	,,		
J. L. Lushington	,,	,,	Mar. 10, 1837	
Joseph Knowles	,,	,,		
John Mackenzie	,,	,,		
Patrick Vans Agnew	,,	,,		
William Morison	Lieut.-Col.	Sep. 4, 1821		
Charles Deacon	,,	July 23, 1823	Mar. 10, 1837	
Thomas Pollock	,,	,,		
David Newall	,,	,,		
Augustus Andrews	,,	,,		
Charles Macleod	,,	,,		
John Ford	Major	,,		
Thomas Bowser	Lieut.-Gen.		Dec. 26, 1826	
James Brodie	Lieut.-Col.	Dec. 26, 1826		
Alexander Fair	,,	,,		
Edward W. Snow	,,	,, —		
B. B. Parlby	,,	,,		
Charles Hopkinson	,,	,,		
James Wahab	,,	,,		
R. L. Evans	Major	,,		
J. D. Greenhill	Colonel	Sep. 26, 1831		
John Doveton	,,	,,		
H. M. Kelly	,,	,,		
F. W. Wilson	,,	,,		
Hugh Fraser	Major-Gen.	Apr. 7, 1832		
David Foulis	,,	Mar. 5, 1835		

INDIAN ARMY LIST.

MADRAS.

NOTE.

The Editors beg to intimate that, in the following List, they have adopted the Alphabetical plan only as far as the first letter, deeming it in every respect preferable to adhere as nearly as possible to *the Seasons of Appointment*, by which means increased facility will be given for tracing and comparing the relative ranks and periods of service of those who have entered the army in the same season.

They beg also to advise their Subscribers that, in their Army List, they have invariably adhered, as far as has been practicable, and except where it is otherwise stated, to the date of *Regimental* Rank up to the Rank of Lieut.-Colonel inclusive.

⁎ Where the Corps is not specially stated against each Officer's name, it is to be concluded that such Officer belongs to the Infantry.

ALPHABETICAL

OFFICERS OF THE

AT THE MADRAS

FROM THE YEAR 1760 TO 1834 INCLUSIVE

NAMES.	Cadet.	Cornet, Ensign, or Second Lieutenant.	Lieutenant.	Captain.	Major.
Alcock, H. R.	1762	....	....	May 4, 1768	....
Abbott, Noble S. Wm.	1769	Sep. 1, 1780	....	Jan. 14, 1782	....
Anderson, Walter	1770	June 29, 1771	Apr. 26, 1777	Nov. 2, 1783	....1794...
Aubrey, George	1771	Nov. 9, 1773	....	Dec. 21, 1783	....
Agnew, Alexander P.	....	Apr. 20, 1774	Oct. 7, 1780	Apr. 12, 1785	June 1, 1796
Adams, Knightly	....	Aug. 5, 1778	Nov. 14, 1782	....	....
Askill, Francis	1778	Apr. 10, 1779	Dec. 10, 1783	June 1, 1796	Dec. 10, 1799
Allan, Sir Alexander, Bt.*	1779	Aug. 27, 1780	Apr. 17, 1786	June 1, 1796	Aug. — 1803
Allison, Charles	1780	Oct. 7, 1781	....	....	....
Armstrong, Charles	1783	Sep. 7, 1783	Aug. 21, 1790	Dec. 10, 1799	....
Annesley, Wm.	1790	June 8, 1791	June 6, 1793	....	....
Ahier, Joshua	,,	June 30, 1791	June 15, 1793	June 17, 1800	....
Aldridge, Charles	,,	July 24, 1791	Jan. 1, 1794	Aug. 14, 1800	Sep. 29, 1808
Aiskill, F. Kirkpatrick	1793	....	Mar. 18, 1795	May 9, 1802	....
Andrews, Augustus (C. B.)	,,	....	Apr. 14, 1795	Apr. 13, 1801	July 23, 1814
Ahmuty, Thos. A. S.	1795	Mar. 19, 1796	Nov. 29, 1797	Sep. 21, 1804	Jan. 5, 1814
Arthur, Thomas—*engineers*	,,	April 8, 1796	Oct. 14, 1802	Nov. 15, 1810	....
Addison, Charles	1797	Sep. 7, 1798	Dec. 26, 1798	Dec. 12, 1804	Brevet, June 5, 1814
Acton, Thomas	,,	Aug. 24, 1798	Dec. 26, 1798	....	....
Agnew, P. Vans (C. B.)†..	,,	Sep. 6, 1798	Dec. 26, 1798	Jan. 1, 1807	Jan. 19, 1816
Anderson, Peter—*cavalry*..	1798	Sep. 4, 1799	June 28, 1800	....	....
Agar, Henry	1799	....	Dec. 15, 1800	....	....
Armstrong, John	,,	....	Dec. 15, 1800	....	....
Andrews, John	1800	July 20, 1801	Dec. 15, 1802	....	....

* Chosen Director of the E. I. C. at the Gen. Elec. in 1814.
† Chosen Director of the E. I. Company, May 14, 1833.

LIST OF THE

INDIAN ARMY

PRESIDENCY;

CORRECTED TO THE YEAR 1837.

Lieut.-Colonel.	Colonel.	Major General.	Lieut.-General.	Date of Resignation, Retirement, or Death.
May 29, 1783	....	....	....	Resigned May — 1784.
....	....	....	....	Died July — 1789.
June 1, 1796	....	....	....	Died Oct. 24, 1797.
....	....	....	....	King's Service, 1789.
Oct. 4, 1798	Sep. 21, 1804	June 4, 1811	....	Died Jan. 7, 1813, at Bath.
....	....	....	....	King's Service, Jan. 30, 1793.
May 1, 1804	Jan. 1, 1812	June 4, 1814	....	Died Nov. 24, 1821, at St. Thomas's Mount.
....	....	....	....	Resigned Nov. 14, 1804. Died Sep. 14, 1820.
....	....	....	....	Died 1791.
....	....	....	....	Killed July 10, 1806, at Vellore.
....	....	....	....	Died July 30, 1795, at the Presidency.
....	....	....	....	Died Nov. 14, 1804.
....	....	....	....	{ Died March 15, 1813, on board the "Ingram" Packet, Madras Roads.
....	....	....	....	Dismissed April 5, 1810.
Nov. 8, 1820	Commt. May 13, 1827 Col. June 5, 1829.	....	....	
Feb. 28, 1819	....	....	....	Retired May 19, 1824.
....	....	....	....	Died May 1, 1817, at Quilon.
....	....	....	....	Died Dec. 24, 1817.
....	....	....	....	Died July 1, 1799, at Seringapatam.
Feb. 15, 1822	....	....	....	Retired July 1, 1825.
....	....	....	....	Died Nov. 14, 1805.
....	....	....	....	Died May 19, 1811, near Samulcottah.
....	....	....	....	Died March 10, 1804, at Bombay.
....	....	....	....	Died Dec. 20, 1808.

MADRAS

NAMES.	Cadet.	Cornet, Ensign, or Second Lieutenant.	Lieutenant.	Captain.	Major.
Ashe, Hoadly, William....	1800	....	July 20, 1801	....	....
Ardagh, John R.	,,	July 20, 1801	May 16, 1803	Feb. 19, 1819	Feb. 18, 1830
Allen, George	1802	April 17, 1803	Sep. 24, 1803	....	....
Aubrey, George William ..	1803	....	Sep. 21, 1804	Feb. 28, 1819	....
Ash, William	1804	....	July 17, 1805	....	....
Agnew, David............	,,	....	July 17, 1805	Jan. 1, 1819	Sep. 20, 1826
Alves, Charles George	,,	....	July 17, 1805	Dec. 2, 1820	June 2, 1831
Anderson, John	,,	....	July 17, 1805	Dec. 25, 1822	Apr. 17, 1826
Anderson, Alexander......	,,	....	Sep. 14, 1805	Jan. 1, 1819	....
Alves, Nathaniel..........	,,	....	Sep. 20, 1805	Aug. 13, 1820	Sep. 10, 1830
Adkin, Alexander	1805	July 21, 1808	....	....	....
Abbey, William	,,	....	Oct. 22, 1807	....	....
Adair, Thomas — *cavalry*..	,,	Oct. 9, 1806	....	....	....
Anstruther, Robert John ..	,,	June 27, 1806	....	....	....
Asher, James	,,	....	....	....	....
Armstrong, James	,,	June 27, 1806	Sep. 9, 1808	....	....
Allen, David —*cavalry*....	,,	July 7, 1807	Sep. 13, 1813	Sep. 1, 1818	....
Alexander, John..........	1806	July 3, 1807	....	....	....
Auchinback, William	,,	....	....	....	....
Addison, Campbell........	,,	July 3, 1807	....	....	....
Addison, John............	,,	July 3, 1807	Mar. 18, 1809	....	....
Armstrong, William	,,	July 3, 1807	June 7, 1809	....	....
Abdy, James N.—*artillery*	,,	....	Nov. 5, 1806	Sep. 1, 1818	Mar. 14, 1829
Alston, Thomas	,,	July 3, 1807	....	....	....
Ainslie, William..........	,,	July 3, 1807	....	....	....
Allan, William	,,	July 3, 1807	Sep. 17, 1812	....	....
Allan, Richard	,,	July 3, 1807	Oct. 30, 1812	Oct. 23, 1824	....
Aldwinkle, Fred.—*artillery*	,,	....	Mar. 25, 1808	....	....
Austen, Nath. Lawrence ..	,,	May 20, 1808	Aug. 4, 1810	May 1, 1824	....
Aveline, C. O.— *cavalry* ..	1807	Nov. 23, 1809	Sep. 1, 1818	....	....
Anderson, James	,,	Mar. 1, 1809	June 17, 1811	....	....
Anthony, Joseph	,,	Oct. 5, 1808	Oct. 2, 1812	Jan. 20, 1824	....
Allen, Henry	,,	Sep. 4, 1808	....	....	....
Allan, James	,,	April 6, 1810	Mar. 23, 1816	....	....
Armstrong, David........	1808	Apr. 7, 1810	Jan. 17, 1813	....	....
Anderson, Alex.— *engineers*	1809	July 7, 1810	July 29, 1815	Dec. 9, 1821	June 5, 1829
Ashton, William—*artillery*	,,	July 7, 1810	May 19, 1814	....	....
Amiel, Henry C. — *cavalry*	1810	....	....	....	....
Abell, Edward............	,,	Apr. 24, 1811	....	....	....
Auber, James Peter	1811	June 11, 1812	June 14, 1815	....	....
Anderson, J. R. — *engineers*	1813	July 6, 1813	....	....	....
Aldret, John —*artillery* ..	1814	July 11, 1815	Oct. 14, 1818	Sep. 28, 1826	....
Agnew, William Henry....	1816	....	Dec. 25, 1817	Oct. 15, 1824	....
Anderson, John—*artillery*	1817	June 3, 1818	May 13, 1821	....	....
Adams, Francis Samuel ..	1818	....	June 13, 1819	....	....
Alexander, Robert........	,,	....	June 13, 1819	Oct. 11, 1826	Mar. 5, 1836
Alcock, Francis	,,	....	....	....	....

PRESIDENCY.   4—5

Lieut-Colonel.	Colonel.	Major-General.	Lieut.-General.	Date of Resignation, Retirement, or Death.
....	....	....	....	Resigned Nov. 20, 1804.
....	....	....	....	Retired Sep. 1, 1832, in India.
....	....	....	....	Died July 4, 1808, at Chittledroog.
....	....	....	....	Resigned June 29, 1821, in India.
....	....	....	....	Died Aug. 27, 1808.
....	....	....	....	{ Invalided March 20, 1827. Died April 7, 1827, at Verdoopetty.
July 20, 1836	....	....	....	
Aug. 20, 1831	....	....	....	
....	....	....	....	Died June 25, 1819, in camp at Itchapore.
Jan. 1, 1836	....	....	....	
....	....	....	....	Resigned Nov. 7, 1810.
....	....	....	....	Died Aug. 16, 1812.
....	....	....	....	Died Dec. 3, 1810.
....	....	....	....	Resigned Aug. 26, 1808.
....	....	....	....	Died Nov. 30, 1806.
....	....	....	....	Resigned Jan. 16, 1810.
....	....	....	....	{ Invalided Dec. 20, 1825, in India. Died March 26, 1833, at Nellore.
....	....	....	....	{ Killed by a fall from his horse, at Trinchinopoly, March 16, 1810.
....	....	....	....	Died at Masulipatam, May 19, 1808.
....	....	....	....	Died Dec. 30, 1810, at Jaulnah.
....	....	....	....	Died May 11, 1812.
....	....	....	....	Died Dec. 3, 1817, at Berhampore.
....	....	....	....	Died May 28, 1809, at Seringapatam.
....	....	....	....	Died March 24, 1810, in England.
....	....	....	....	Killed in action, Oct. 7, 1824, at Rangoon.
....	....	....	....	Died Jan. 26, 1831, at Madras.
....	....	....	....	{ Died of wounds received on board His Majesty's ship "Nereide," Aug. 24, 1810.
....	....	....	....	Retired April 24, 1834, in England.
....	....	....	....	Retired May 20, 1823, in England.
....	....	....	....	{ Died Oct. 29, 1818, in camp, at the West Bank of the Moosar River.
....	....	....	....	Died May 23, 1830, at Coimbatore.
....	....	....	....	Died June 24, 1814, at Secunderabad.
....	....	....	....	Died June 22, 1822, at Bellary.
....	....	....	....	Dismissed June 30, 1823, in India.
....	....	....	....	Retired March 3, 1832, in England.
....	....	....	....	{ Struck off, having been from India beyond the period prescribed by Act of Parliament.
....	....	....	....	{ Resigned Oct. 8, 1811. Gone into His Majesty's 2nd Light Dragoons
....	....	....	....	Resigned Dec. 23, 1816, in India.
....	....	....	....	Drowned Aug. 4, 1816.
....	....	....	....	Died Dec. 23, 1818, at Jaulnah.
....	....	....	....	Died July 17, 1832, at Frankfort.
....	....	....	....	Died Oct. 7, 1826, at Secunderabad.
....	....	....	....	Died Dec. 10, 1821, in camp at Maulligaum.
....	....	....	....	Died — 1820, in England.

MADRAS

NAMES.	Cadet.	Cornet, Ensign, or Second Lieutenant.	Lieutenant.	Captain.	Major.
Arnott, David Leith	1818	....	June 13, 1819	Sep. 10, 1830	....
Albert, Hugh Charles	,,	....	June 9, 1821		
Adam, Alexander	,,	....	June 13, 1819	July 19, 1834	
Addison, Dering	,,	....	June 13, 1819		
Alcock, G.—*artillery*	1819	April 9, 1819	May 25, 1821	July 5, 1829	
Arthur, Geo. Munro	,,	....	June 19, 1820	May 15, 1833	
Armstrong, Edward	,,	April 6, 1820	Apr. 20, 1822	Apr. 23, 1828	
Awdry, John Dea	,,	April 6, 1820	Nov. 13, 1822	Aug. 14, 1830	
Archer, David	1820	Feb. 13, 1821	May 1, 1824		
Alexander, James—*cavalry*	,,	Apr. 27, 1822	July 15, 1829		
Arbuthnot, G. B.—*cavalry*	,,	Feb. 13, 1821	May 1, 1824	May 31, 1833	
Anderson, T.—*cavalry*	,,	Feb. 13, 1821	May 1, 1824	Jan. 2, 1833	
Apthorp, East	,,	Feb. 13, 1821	July 15, 1824	Oct. 10, 1833	
Affleck, Gilbert	,,	Feb. 13, 1821	Aug. 1, 1823		
Alexander, A. Ruxton	1821	Apr. 27, 1822	Oct. 8, 1824		
Atherton, Edward	,,	Apr. 27, 1822	May 1, 1824		
Anderson, J. J. Marriott	,,	Apr. 27, 1822	July 28, 1826		
Armytage, E.—*cavalry*	,,	Apr. 27, 1822	May 20, 1824		
Allardyce, James	,,	Apr. 27, 1822	Oct. 14, 1824	Sep. 16, 1830	
Adams, Thomas John	,,	....	Apr. 23, 1825		
Atkinson, Edward	,,				
Amsinck, Eames—*artillery*	,,	May 10, 1822	May 11, 1822	Dec. 5, 1831	
Ashton, John T.—*artillery*	1823	Dec. 18, 1823	May 1, 1824		
Atkinson, Edwin Henry	,,	May 14, 1824	Sep. 8, 1826	Aug. 28, 1835	....
Abbott, Charles	,,	May 14, 1824	Mar. 10, 1826		
Anstruther, P.—*artillery*	1824	June 17, 1824	June 19, 1824		
Affleck, Robert	,,	May 6, 1825	Dec. 11, 1825		
Atkinson, W. H.—*engineers*	1825	....	Dec. 17, 1824	Sep. 2, 1836	
Annesley, Wm. Richard	1826	Feb. 28, 1827			
Amsinck, John	,,	Feb. 8, 1827			
Austen, Thomas	1827	June 21, 1828	Aug. 23, 1833		
Arrow, James Ross	,,	June 21, 1828	May 29, 1829		
Allan, Grant	,,	Nov. 27, 1828	Dec. 22, 1832		
Armstrong, R. Dalzell	,,	Oct. 28, 1828	May 20, 1831		
Ashley, F. B.—*artillery*	1828	Dec. 12, 1828	Feb. 15, 1836		
Arbuthnot, James Edward	1829	....			
Armstrong, Edward	,,	Mar. 11, 1832	Jan. 31, 1835		
Austin, Thomas—*artillery*	,,	Feb. 21, 1834			
Armstrong, H. C.—*engineers*	1831	Mar. 4, 1832			
Arbuthnot, Hon. H.—*cavalry*	,,	Mar. 17, 1834	Feb. 24, 1835		
Anderson, Wm. Wallace	1833	Dec. 22, 1832	June 2, 1837		
Allan, John Shiell	1834	June 13, 1834			
B					
Brathwaite, John	....	....	....	....	June 21, 1770
Bruce, Thomas	1762	Jan. 1, 1764	....	Brevet, June 16, 1768	....
Bridges, Thomas	....	....	....	1770	Jan. 10, 1784
Bildiffe, Joseph	1764	Jan. 27, 1766	Apr. 30, 1767	Nov. 12, 1773	May 23, 1786

PRESIDENCY.   6—7

Lieut.-Colonel.	Colonel.	Major General.	Lieut.-General.	Date of Resignation, Retirement, or Death.
				Invalided Aug. 27, 1822. Pensioned from Apr. 22, 1826, in England.
				Died March 6, 1826.
				Struck off Oct. 24, 1827, in India.
				Died May 16, 1833, at Bellary.
				Died Jan. 21, 1835, at Tavoy.
				Died June 7, 1830, at Neilgherry Hills.
				Killed Jan 7, 1826, in action, at Setorir.
				Died Aug. 20, 1822, on board the L. S. "Fort William," at the Isle of France.
				Resigned Dec. 31, 1831, in India.
				Resigned May 31, 1833, in India.
				Died July 3, 1835, at Kamptee.
				Pensioned Sep. 21, 1830, in India. Died May 3, 1832, at Vizagapatam.
				Resigned Jan. 7, 1831, in India.
Oct. 22, 1772	Dec. 17, 1779	Dec. 20, 1793		Died Aug. 23, 1803, in London.
Oct. 31, 1783	Dec. 14, 1789			Died on board "the Neptune," 1794.
Nov. 8, 1785	Jan. 30, 1791	Feb. 26, 1795		Died July 16, 1823, in London.
Apr. 27, 1795	May 3, 1796			Retired in 1803, on Off Reckoning List.

MADRAS

NAMES.	Cadet.	Cornet, Ensign, or Second Lieutenant.	Lieutenant.	Captain.	Major.
Burrowes, Thos.—*cavalry*	1766	Sep. 11, 1767	....	Nov. 22, 1776	Apr. 17, 1786
Bonnevaux, Peter	....	Jan. 15, 1768	Aug. 3, 1770	July 9, 1779	Feb. 6, 1788
Blacker, William	1767	Oct. 31, 1768	Sep. 16, 1770	July 17, 1779	....
Burr, Daniel	,,	Nov. 3, 1768	Sep. 19, 1770	July 18, 1779	Sep. 9, 1789
Baillie, John	1768	July 29, 1770	Feb. 3, 1772	Jan. 3, 1782	....
Bruce, William	1768	Aug. 16, 1770	....	Jan. 11, 1782	....
Brown, Archibald	,,	Aug. 23, 1770	July 14, 1773	Jan. 12, 1782	Aug. 6, 1794
Brounker, Robert	1769	Dec. 16, 1770	....	Nov. 2, 1783	....
Butler, James B.	....	Dec. 29, 1773	Oct. 3, 1780	May 7, 1784	.... 1794 ...
Bridges, Edward	....	July 17, 1775	Apr. 16, 1785	....	....
Beale, Anthony	....	Sep. 25, 1776	Nov. 23, 1780	Apr. 1, 1793	....
Bowser, Sir Thos. (K.C.B.)	1771	Dec. 20, 1773	Oct. 25, 1779	Nov. 17, 1783	June 1, 1796
Beatson, Alexander	1775	Nov. 21, 1776	Nov. 23, 1780	May 19, 1793	Aug. 18, 1797
Brunton, James	1776	Apr. 6, 1778	Jan. 6, 1782	Mar. 18, 1794	July 24, 1798
Bannerman, John*	,,	April 9, 1778	Jan. 8, 1782	Aug. 6, 1794	Sep. 29, 1798
Boisdane, Edward	1777	June 7, 1778	Feb. 21 1782	....	....
Bullman, Edward	,,	July 27, 1778	Mar. 17, 1782	....	....
Barclay, George	....	Aug. 10, 1778	Mar. 23, 1783	....	....
Blacker, George	1778	May 27, 1779	Mar. 19, 1786	....	....
Bell, Robert—*artillery*	1779	Sep. 15, 1779	Sep. 15, 1781	Apr. 8, 1788	Dec. 25, 1800
Byrne, James	,,	July 24, 1779	Apr. 17, 1786	....	....
Bell, John—*artillery*	,,	Dec. 3, 1780	July 13, 1782	Feb. 4, 1791	Oct. 16, 1801
Barclay, William	1780	Dec. 17, 1780	Apr. 17, 1786	Aug. 5, 1797	May 9, 1802
Brown, Alexander	,,	Dec. 20, 1780	Apr. 17, 1786	....	....
Blackmore, Thos.—*artillery*	,,	Feb. 19, 1782	Oct. 23, 1784	Feb. 12, 1796	....
Barclay, Robert	....	....	Apr. 17, 1786	....	....
Balfour, James	,,	Aug. 7, 1781	Apr. 17, 1786	....	....
Bowness, George	,,	....	June 8, 1786	Aug. 18, 1797	June 6, 1801
Butler, John	,,	Aug. 23, 1781	Jan. 23, 1787	Sep. 10, 1799	....
Blair, David	,,	Aug. 26, 1781	Jan. 23, 1787	Nov. 29, 1797	Aug. 13, 1801
Brown, Johnson	,,	Aug. 30, 1781	... 1787 ...	....	....
Beazley, William	,,	Sep. 8, 1781	Dec. 26, 1787	Nov. 29, 1797	....
Boyd, Andrew	,,	Sep. 11, 1781	Feb. 22, 1788	Nov. 29, 1797	....
Blacker, Henry	,,	Sep. 13, 1781	Mar. 25, 1788	....	....
Baillie, Thomas	,,	Sep. 21, 1781	....	....	....
Briggs, Samuel	,,	Oct. 11, 1781	Nov. 1, 1788	....	....
Back, John	1781	Oct. 6, 1782	....	....	....
Betty, John—*artillery*	,,	Feb. 21, 1782	Apr. 17, 1786	....	....
Bruce, Patrick	,,	Nov. 2, 1782	Aug. 21, 1790	Dec. 26, 1798	Sep. 21, 1804
Batchellor, Edward	,,	Nov. 28, 1782	Aug. 21, 1790	Dec. 26, 1798	Mar. 1, 1805
Burke, Ulrick—*artillery*	,,	April 1, 1783	Apr. 8, 1788	Mar. 22, 1798	....
Brodie, John	,,	Dec. 7, 1782	....	....	....
Baillie, Alexander	1782	Apr. 23, 1783	Aug. 21, 1790	May 3, 1799	May 1, 1804
Buchan, Hugh	,,	Apr. 25, 1783	Aug. 21, 1790	May 4, 1799	May 1, 1804
Brown, John	,,	May 30, 1783	Aug. 21, 1790	Dec. 10, 1799	....
Blackburne, William	,,	June 5, 1783	Aug. 21, 1790	Dec. 10, 1799	Feb. 25, 1807
Barclay, Sir R., (K.C.B.)	,,	June 18, 1783	Aug. 21, 1790	Dec. 10, 1799	Sep. 21, 1804

* Chosen Director of the E. I. Company at the General Election in 1808.

PRESIDENCY.   8—9

Lieut.-Colonel.	Colonel.	Major-General.	Lieut.-General.	Date of Resignation, Retirement, or Death.
. . . .	. . . .	. . . .	. . . .	Resigned — 1790.
Mar. 18, 1794	. . . .	. . . .	. . . .	Died July 12, 1797.
. . . .	. . . .	. . . .	. . . .	Died — 1787.
Aug. 6, 1794	July 13, 1797	Jan. 1, 1805	. . . .	Died Feb. 19, 1828, in London.
. . . .	. . . .	. . . .	. . . .	Out of the Service.
. . . .	. . . .	. . . .	. . . .	Died Aug. 12, 1794.
June 1, 1796	July 31, 1799	Oct. 30, 1805	June 4, 1813	Died May 4, 1825, in London.
. . . .	. . . .	. . . .	. . . .	Dismissed the Service, April — 1789.
. . . .	. . . .	. . . .	. . . .	Died Jan. 12, 1796.
. . . .	. . . .	. . . .	. . . .	Died — 1789, at sea.
. . . .	. . . .	. . . .	. . . .	Died Nov. 23, 1795, at Ahtoor.
Nov. 29, 1797	Jan. 1, 1803	July 25, 1810	June 4, 1814	Died July 14, 1833, in England.
Dec. 10, 1799	. . . .	. . . .	. . . .	Retired August — 1813.
May 8, 1800	. . . .	. . . .	. . . .	Died Nov. 6, 1810, in England.
June 17, 1800	. . . .	. . . .	. . . .	Retired Aug. 6, 1803.
. . . .	. . . .	. . . .	. . . .	Resigned — 1791. Died June — 1794.
. . . .	. . . .	. . . .	. . . .	Died April 6, 1795, at Cuddalore.
. . . .	. . . .	. . . .	. . . .	Died — 1791.
. . . .	. . . .	. . . .	. . . .	Died — 1790.
Sep. 26, 1801	Lieut.-Col. Commt. April 4, 1804, Col. July 25, 1810.	July 25, 1810	Aug. 12, 1819, Gen. Jan. 10, 1837.	
. . . .	. . . .	. . . .	. . . .	Not to be traced.
Sep. 21, 1804	. . . .	. . . .	. . . .	Cashiered Mar. 8, 1810, in India.
Jan. 24, 1805	. . . .	. . . .	. . . .	Died May 29, 1810, at Chatteepore.
. . . .	. . . .	. . . .	. . . .	Died — 1792. [at Vizagapatam.
. . . .	. . . .	. . . .	. . . .	Invalided — 1796. Died June 1, 1805,
. . . .	. . . .	. . . .	. . . .	Not to be traced.
. . . .	. . . .	. . . .	. . . .	Died — 1792.
Sep. 21, 1804	Jan. 9, 1818	Aug. 12, 1819	. . . .	Died July 6, 1833, in Wiltshire.
. . . .	. . . .	. . . .	. . . .	Invalided in 1800. Died Dec. 1, 1815,
. . . .	. . . .	. . . .	. . . .	Died May 15, 1803. [at Tanjore.
. . . .	. . . .	. . . .	. . . .	Died — 1792, at Damicottah.
. . . .	. . . .	. . . .	. . . .	Died — 1798.
. . . .	. . . .	. . . .	. . . .	Died Oct. 21, 1798, at Vellore.
. . . .	. . . .	. . . .	. . . .	Dismissed the Service, April — 1793.
. . . .	. . . .	. . . .	. . . .	King's Service — 1789.
. . . .	. . . .	. . . .	. . . .	Died — 1793.
. . . .	. . . .	. . . .	. . . .	Died — 1792.
. . . .	. . . .	. . . .	. . . .	Died April — 1789, at Trichinopoly.
July 21, 1808	Brevet June 4, 1814	. . . .	. . . .	Retired April 14, 1817, in England.
. . . .	. . . .	. . . .	. . . .	Retired Feb. 7, 1809.
. . . .	. . . .	. . . .	. . . .	Died Aug. 16, 1804, in camp.
. . . .	. . . .	. . . .	. . . .	Died Oct. — 1789.
. . . .	. . . .	. . . .	. . . .	Retired Jan. 16, 1810.
. . . .	. . . .	. . . .	. . . .	Died Aug. 18, 1808, at Seringapatam.
. . . .	. . . .	. . . .	. . . .	{ Killed in the attack of the Fort of Loussoolgaum, Oct. 8, 1804.
June 28, 1817	Commt. May 1, 1824. Col. June 5, 1829.	Jan. 10, 1837	. . . .	
Oct. 2, 1808	Brevet June 4, 1814	. . . .	. . . .	Retired May 30, 1816, in England.

MADRAS.——C

MADRAS

NAMES.	Cadet.	Cornet, Ensign, or Second Lieutenant.	Lieutenant.	Captain.	Major.
Bryce, Alexander	1782	June 27, 1783	Aug. 21, 1790	Dec. 10, 1799	Sep. 21, 1804
Blount, Edward	,,	June 28, 1783			
Briston, John	1783	Sep. 1, 1783			
Burton, John	,,	Sep. 2, 1783	Aug. 21, 1790		
Bose, Paul	,,	Sep. 4, 1783	Aug. 21, 1790	Dec. 10, 1799	Oct. 16, 1805
Baillie, John—*artillery*		June 10, 1775	May 10, 1780	Oct. 12, 1781	...1796...
Beirne, Andrew C.—*artillery*		Apr. 23, 1783	Sep. 6, 1788		
Banks, George—*engineers*		June 6, 1774		Aug. 14, 1778	Mar. 6, 1784
Byers, John—*engineers*				Dec. 15, 1778	
Brudenell, George—*cavalry*		Mar. 13, 1778	Jan. 20, 1782		
Bowles, Henry B.—*cavalry*			Apr. 26, 1784		
Burrowes, Thos.—*cavalry*		Apr. 21, 1784	Jan. 31, 1786	Sep. 4, 1799	June 17, 1800
Baillie, Simon		Dec. 10, 1775	Oct. 27, 1780	Feb. 21, 1786	
Baillie, John (Senr.)		Apr. 21, 1778	May 7, 1781	...1796...	
Baille, Benjamin	1780	Aug. 3, 1781	Apr. 17, 1786		
Bruce, Charles D.		Nov. 23, 1782	Aug. 21, 1790		Jan. 24, 1805
Brookesbank, John		Apr. 29, 1783			
Beauman, Michl.—*artillery*	1790	Aug. 4, 1791	Apr. 12, 1796	Oct. 22, 1801	
Bettson, John—*artillery*	1791	Sep. 13, 1791	June 1, 1796		
Barclay, Robert (Junr.)			Aug. 21, 1790		
Boles, Thomas		May 6, 1788	June 7, 1792	Dec. 10, 1797	Nov. 15, 1804
Butler, John			June 7, 1792	...1799...	
Bellew, Francis			June 7, 1792		
Baxter, William	1788		June 7, 1792		
Benn, William	,,		June 20, 1792		
Boardman, Edward	1790		April 8, 1793	June 17, 1800	July 21, 1808
Brice, Robert	,,	June 16, 1791	June 6, 1793	June 17, 1800	Sep. 21, 1804
Batwell, Walter	,,	July 25, 1791	Jan. 5, 1794		
Brown, Adam	,,	July 31, 1791	Feb. 17, 1794	Feb. 21, 1801	
Baldwin, Beasley	,,	Aug. 2, 1791			
Bodley, George	,,	Aug. 12, 1791	Feb. 19, 1794		
Barroll, Richard	,,	Aug. 18, 1791			
Baynes, Thomas	,,	Aug. 20, 1791	May 12, 1794	Dec. 14, 1802	
Bagshaw, Edward B.		Sep. 17, 1791	Aug. 6, 1794	Mar. 27, 1801	Sep. 24, 1812
Bagster, William	1791	Apr. 24, 1793	Aug. 6, 1794	Mar. 22, 1802	
Bong, George—*engineers*		Dec. 11, 1780	Apr. 17, 1786	May 25, 1792	
Blair, John—*engineers*	1788		Feb. 23, 1793	Oct. 14, 1802	Apr. 25, 1808
Blair, William—*artillery*	1792	May 24, 1793	June 8, 1796		
Blofield, J. S.	,,	June 15, 1793	Aug. 6, 1794	Apr. 16, 1801	
Broughton, Thomas		April 7, 1779			
Beecroft, Robert Shaftoe	1793		Oct. 8, 1795		
Brooke, Richard	,,		Aug. 8, 1795		
Baker, James	,,		Mar. 18, 1795		
Bowen, Henry (C. B.)	1794	Dec. 25, 1795	April 4, 1796	Jan. 1, 1803	Nov. 30, 1811
Burn, Richard	,,	Dec. 29, 1795	May 28, 1796	Sep. 21, 1804	
Barker, Henry Raymond	,,	Jan. 22, 1796	June 1, 1796		
Briggs, Gilbert	1795	Mar. 21, 1796	Nov. 29, 1797		

PRESIDENCY.

Lieut.-Colonel.	Colonel.	Major-General.	Lieut.-General.	Date of Resignation, Retirement, or Death.
Nov. 22, 1808	....	....	....	Retired Dec. 13, 1809.
....	....	....	....	Home on ill health, 1792, and retired.
....	....	....	....	King's Service — 1789.
....	....	....	....	Died Dec. — 1796.
....	....	....	....	Died June 12, 1808, at Vellore.
....	....	....	....	Not to be traced.
....	....	....	....	Not to be traced.
....	....	....	....	Retired — 1791, upon Lord Clive's
....	....	....	....	Died — 1789. [Bounty.
....	....	....	....	Invalided Jan., 1791; died April 3, 1807.
....	....	....	....	Not to be traced.
May 1, 1804	....	....	....	Invalided — 1804; retired Oct. 2, 1811.
....	....	....	....	Dismissed Service — 1793.
....	....	....	....	Died 1796, on his passage to the Cape.
....	....	....	....	Not to be traced.
Sep. 11, 1809	....	....	....	Died Jan. 24, 1813, at Fort St. George.
....	....	....	....	Home — 1790.
....	....	....	....	{ Lost March 14, 1809, in the ship "Lady Jane Dundas."
....	....	....	....	Died April 1797, at Dindigul.
....	....	....	....	Died May 5, 1799, at Seringapatam.
Mar. 18, 1809	Aug. 12, 1819	July 22, 1830	....	
....	....	....	....	Died May 12, 1799.
....	....	....	....	Died — 1797.
....	....	....	....	Died Aug. 8, 1799.
....	....	....	....	Died Jan. — 1794.
June 28, 1814	Commt. May 1, 1824 Col. June 5, 1829.	Jan. 10, 1837	....	
Mar. 1, 1809	....	....	....	Died Sep. 23, 1812, at Palamcottah.
....	....	....	....	Permitted to resign — 1800.
....	....	....	....	{ Invalided Dec. 18, 1804; died Sep. 30, 1823, at Duran Akam.
....	....	....	....	Died — 1793.
....	....	....	....	Died — 1797.
....	....	....	....	Not to be traced.
....	....	....	....	Died Jan. 14, 1807.
Jan. 27, 1819	....	....	....	{ Invalided Feb. 28, 1819, in India; died June 30, 1819, at St. Thomas's Mount.
....	....	....	....	Resigned Nov. 16, 1802.
....	....	....	....	Died March 31, 1801.
....	....	....	....	Died March 24, 1812, on board the "Europe."
....	....	....	....	Died Sep. 27, 1803, on board the "Walpole."
....	....	....	....	Died Sep. 22, 1803.
....	....	....	....	Pensioned — 1787.
....	....	....	....	Died Oct., 1796, at Columbo.
....	....	....	....	Died — 1799.
....	....	....	....	Died June, 1796, at Amboyna.
....	....	....	....	Died July 12, 1821.
April 1, 1818	....	....	....	Died June 26, 1813, on passage to
....	....	....	....	Died April 25, 1803. [England.
....	....	....	....	{ Struck off Dec. 17, 1799; appointed Assistant Surgeon.

MADRAS

NAMES.	Cadet.	Cornet, Ensign, or Second Lieutenant.	Lieutenant.	Captain.	Major.
Bradley, G.—*engineers*	1795	Feb. 19, 1796	Aug. 25, 1801	....	....
Barker, Richard	,,	Feb. 14, 1796	Jan. 13, 1797	....	....
Barclay, Robert	,,	Feb. 20, 1796	May 7, 1797	Oct. 22, 1803	....
Brown, J. D.—*artillery* ..	,,	April 3, 1796	Feb. 4, 1800	Feb. 14, 1805	Sep. 1, 1818
Bruce, James	,,	....	Jan. 8, 1796	....	....
Blair, Geo. P.—*artillery* ..	1794	Jan. 8, 1796	Mar. 22, 1798	Sep. 21, 1804	Sep. 1, 1818
Bishop, C. Thos. Geo.	1796	July 29, 1797	Dec. 21, 1797	Sep. 21, 1804	Mar. 15, 1810
Blake, Henry	,,	Aug. 9, 1797	Sep. 29, 1797	....	....
Burrow, Charles..........	,,	Aug. 29, 1797	Oct. 12, 1798	....	....
Bell, Thomas H..........	,,	Aug. 19, 1797	Oct. 12, 1798	....	....
Brown, Patrick	,,	Aug. 1, 1797	June 3, 1798	Apr. 14, 1804	....
Boyle, Thomas—*cavalry* ..	,,	Nov. 29, 1797	....	....	....
Blake, John	,,	Aug. 18, 1797	Oct. 12, 1798	....	....
Brodie, James (C.B.)	1797	Sep. 10, 1797	Oct. 12, 1798	Apr. 21, 1804	June 12, 1813
Barber, James Harvey	,,	Sep. 16, 1797	Oct. 12, 1798	June 10, 1806	April 1, 1818
Blacker, V. (C.B.)—*cavalry*	,,	Aug. 29, 1798	Sep. 4, 1799	Oct. 15, 1804	Sep. 1, 1818
Bayer, R. O. —*cavalry*	,,	May 10, 1799	May 8, 1800	Aug. 14, 1805	July 26, 1819
Bell, Charles W.—*cavalry*	,,	Aug. 2, 1798	Aug. 29, 1801	Brevet 1810	....
Bowdler, Henry	,,	Aug. 30, 1798	Dec. 26, 1798	June 30, 1808	May 28, 1820
Bryant, Robert—*cavalry* ..	1795	Dec. 11, 1799	June 17, 1800	....	....
Baker, William	1798	....	Aug. 7, 1799	....	....
Ballmer, James—*cavalry* ..	,,	....	May 8, 1800	....	....
Beauman, Edward B.......	,,	....	Aug. 7, 1800	....	....
Bell, Robert—*cavalry*	,,	Sep. 4, 1799	June 17, 1800	....	....
Bonomi, J. J. J. S.—*cavalry*	,,	Sep. 4, 1799	June 17, 1800	....	....
Birch, George	,,	....	Aug. 7, 1799	July 16, 1807	....
Barnby, A. M.—*cavalry* ..	,,	Sep. 4, 1799	Dec. 8, 1799	....	....
Bellingham, J. George	,,	....	Aug. 7, 1799	April 8, 1808	....
Blackmore, W. Firmin	,,	....	Aug. 7, 1799	July 21, 1808	....
Burton, W. M.—*artillery*..	,,	....	Jan. 8, 1803	May 21, 1818	Jan. 22, 1822
Bowen, Charles	1799	....	Dec. 15, 1800	Dec. 1, 1816	May 1, 1824
Balmain, Alexander	,,	....	Dec. 15, 1800	Feb. 3, 1808	Aug. — 1809
Brown, John	,,	....	Dec. 15, 1800	....	....
Bruce, William	,,	....	Dec. 15, 1800	....	....
Bennett, William	,,	....	Dec. 15, 1800	Brevet, June — 1810	....
Beckett, Thomas	,,	....	Aug. 7, 1800	Jan. 1, 1807	Dec. 1, 1817
Blackiston, Sir Mathew ..	,,	....	July 15, 1800	Brevet Aug. 10, 1809	....
Barrett, William	,,	....	Dec. 15, 1800	....	....
Baker, Benjamin	,,	....	July 15, 1799	Oct. 4, 1810	July 26, 1826
Brown, John Wm.........	,,	....	Dec. 15, 1800	Sep. 9, 1808	....
Brown, William	,,	....	Dec. 15, 1800	Oct. 15, 1811	....
Barlow, Henry	,,	....	Dec. 15, 1800	....	....
Bye, Robert.............	,,	....	Dec. 15, 1800	May 25, 1808	....
Barrett, Benjamin A......	,,	....	Dec. 15, 1800	....	....
Barbutt, H. S.—*cavalry* ...	,,	....	Dec. 18, 1801	....	....
Brush, John	,,	....	Dec. 15, 1800	....	....
Bray, W. J. K.	...	....	....	....	....

PRESIDENCY. 12—13

Lieut.-Colonel.	Colonel.	Major General	Lieut.-General.	Date of Resignation, Retirement, or Death.
....	....	....	....	Lost Mar. 14, 1809, in the ship "Lady Jane Dundas."
....	....	....	....	Died Dec. 14, 1803.
....	....	....	....	Died May 5, 1799, at Seringapatam.
....	....	....	....	Retired March 1, 1819, in England.
....	....	....	....	Died April 4, 1799.
....	....	....	....	Died Sep. 18, 1819, in India.
Apr. 8, 1818	Commt. May 1, 1824 Col. June 5, 1829	Jan. 10, 1837	....	
....	....	....	....	Dismissed April 6, 1802.
....	....	....	....	Died Dec. 8, 1803, at Cuttack.
....	....	....	....	Resigned the Service, Feb. 10, 1802.
....	....	....	....	Died June 26, 1811, at Bangalore.
....	....	....	....	Died May 31, 1801.
....	....	....	....	Died Sep. 5, 1799.
Oct. 16, 1818	Commt. Nov. 17, 1825. Col. June 5, 1829.	....	....	Died June 18, 1831, at Dumfries.
....	....	....	....	Invalided Apr. 30, 1819. Died Nov. 27, 1819.
Oct. 20, 1823	....	....	....	Died Mar. 4, 1826, at Calcutta.
Feb. 26, 1829	....	....	....	Retired March 19, 1831.
....	....	....	....	Retired April 8, 1815, in England.
May 10, 1824	Dec. 1, 1829	....	....	
....	....	....	....	Died June 21, 1808, at St. Helena.
....	....	....	....	Died Feb. 7, 1803.
....	....	....	....	Died May 12, 1800, at Arcot.
....	....	....	....	Died Mar. 6, 1801.
....	....	....	....	Died April 19, 1801.
....	....	....	....	Killed Sep. 23, 1803.
....	....	....	....	Died Mar. 31, 1809, at Travancore.
....	....	....	....	Died Oct. 7, 1807, at Secunderabad.
....	....	....	....	Lost Mar. 14, 1809, in the ship "Lady Jane Dundas."
....	....	....	....	Died Sep. 29, 1811, at Agoada.
May 23, 1825	Brevet, June 18, 1830.	....	....	
Oct. 11, 1828	....	....	....	Retired June 6, 1833, in England.
Jan. 8, 1826	....	....	....	Retired June 6, 1830, in England.
....	....	....	....	Killed Sep. 23, 1803.
....	....	....	....	Resigned Aug. 14, 1804, in India.
....	....	....	....	Died Nov. 16, 1812, at Chittledroog.
....	....	....	....	Died March 2, 1824, in England.
....	....	....	....	Resigned May 29, 1811.
....	....	....	....	Died Sep. 8, 1812.
....	....	....	....	Retired Sep. 5, 1829, in England.
....	....	....	....	Died Feb. 23, 1813.
....	....	....	....	Died Jan. 18, 1820, at Negulivarre.
....	....	....	....	Died July 14, 1803.
....	....	....	....	Invalided Mar. 22, 1814. Died Apr. 11, 1824, at Chingleput.
....	....	....	....	Not to be traced.
....	....	....	....	Died Sep. 3, 1805.
....	....	....	....	Died July 12, 1803.
....	....	....	....	Died Sep. 12, 1801.

MADRAS

NAMES.	Cadet.	Cornet, Ensign, or Second Lieutenant.	Lieutenant.	Captain.	Major.
Bishop, Benjamin—*artillery*	1799	....	Feb. 4, 1802	....	....
Bushby, John	1800	....	July 20, 1801	....	....
Blacker, St. John—*cavalry*	,,	Sep. 29, 1801	May 1, 1804	Jan. 1, 1819	Oct. 20, 1823
Bell, John	,,	....	July 20, 1801	Mar. 20, 1814	Mar. 12, 1823
Brooke, Charles	,,	....	July 20, 1801	May 1, 1810	Jan. 26, 1822
Bryan, William	,,	....	July 20, 1801	....	....
Beard, John	,,	....	July 20, 1801	....	....
Bowes, Frederick	,,	....	July 20, 1801	Aug. 17, 1810	Oct. 17, 1819
Bray, Wm. John Knighton	,,	....	....	....	....
Bowen, Humphry S	,,	....	July 20, 1801	....	....
Briggs, John	,,	....	July 20, 1801	Oct. 4, 1810	Mar. 17, 1822
Buchan, David—*cavalry* ..	,,	July 7, 1801	May 1, 1804	....	....
Baxter, John	,,	....	Sep. 21, 1804	May 23, 1817	Jan. 23, 1830
Bulman, Thomas	,,	....	Apr. 4, 1802	Aug. 30, 1813	....
Browne, Frederick..........	,,	....	July 20, 1801	May 10, 1816	May 6, 1824
Bertram, Archibald Nat. ..	,,	....	July 20, 1801	Apr. 6, 1810	....
Blackman, Edward..........	,,	....	Nov. 28, 1802	Jan. 1, 1819	....
Beaumont, John	,,	....	July 20, 1801	Apr. 6, 1819	....
Bourne, Richard Burrows..	,,	....	Apr. 8, 1802	....	....
Blakiston, John—*engineers*	1801	....	Jan. 1, 1806	....	....
Balmain, F. N.—*cavalry* ..	1800	Sep. 15, 1801	May 1, 1804	Sep. 1, 1818	....
Brooke, Richard John	1802	....	Jan. 19, 1804	....	....
Bowes, Wm. Johnson	,,	....	....	....	....
Binny, David	,,	....	July 3, 1803	....	....
Bower, Robert	,,	....	Jan. 19, 1804	Feb. 19, 1819	....
Bowler, Henry John	,,	....	Jan. 10, 1804	Oct. 4, 1813	July 10, 1823
Beddo, James	,,	....	Jan. 19, 1804	....	....
Blackwood, William	,,	....	May 21, 1804	....	....
Barclay, Peter	,,	Apr. 17, 1803	July 4, 1804	Sep. 1, 1818	July 14, 1827
Bertier, Elisha	,,	Apr. 17, 1803	Sep. 21, 1804	....	....
Braune, Geo. Hen..........	,,	....	Aug. 16, 1804	....	....
Berrington, Rowland	,,	Apr. 17, 1803	Sep. 21, 1812	....	....
Baillie, Wm. D.—*cavalry* ..	,,	....	Oct. 8, 1807	....	....
Burman, Fras. Leathess ..	,,	....	Sep. 21, 1804	Oct. 19, 1817	....
Bishop, Chas. Moorhouse..	,,	....	Sep. 21, 1804	....	....
Baker, Wm. Thomas......	,,	....	Sep. 21, 1804	June 25, 1814	May 1, 1824
Boggs, James Major	,,	....	Sep. 21, 1804	....	....
Best, Francis—*artillery* ..	1803	....	Sep. 4, 1804	Jan. 1, 1819	... 1825 ....
Best, William	,,	....	Sep. 21, 1804	....	....
Bonner, J. G.—*artillery* ..	,,	....	Sep. 21, 1804	Jan. 1, 1819	June 9, 1825
Birt, Thomas—*artillery* ..	,,	....	July 18, 1804	....	....
Bentley, Arthur	,,	....	Sep. 21, 1804	May 11, 1819	....
Byam, Martin Wm.	,,	....	Sep. 21, 1804	....	....
Boyle, Michael	,,	....	....	....	....
Blake, Benjamin	,,	....	Sep. 21, 1804	Sep. 1, 1818	April 5, 1829
Boyn, James—*cavalry*	,,	....	Mar. 26, 1808	....	....
Bayley, James..........	,,	....	Sep. 21, 1804	Oct. 18, 1819	June 21, 1827

PRESIDENCY.   14—15

Lieut.-Colonel.	Colonel.	Major-General.	Lieut.-General.	Date of Resignation, Retirement, or Death.
....	....	....	....	Retired in 1814, and died in 1824.
....	....	....	....	Invalided Dec. 9, 1808. Died April — 1811.
....	....	....	....	Retired Jan. 2, 1828, in England.
Oct. 4, 1825	Brevet, June 18, 1831	....	....	
Jan. 3, 1825	....	....	....	Retired May 19, 1828, in England.
....	....	....	....	Killed Dec. 5, 1804.
....	....	....	....	Died Nov. 8, 1812, in Camp near Darwar.
May 1, 1824	....	....	....	
....	....	....	....	Died Sep. 12, 1801.
....	....	....	....	Died Oct. 28, 1804.
April 4, 1825	Dec. 1, 1829	....	....	
....	....	....	....	Died Aug. 2, 1809, in Camp, at Seroor.
....	....	....	....	Died Nov. 24, 1833, at Kemedy Hills.
....	....	....	....	Died Dec. 22, 1822, at Fort St. George.
Dec. 5, 1829	....	....	....	Retired April 18, 1831, in England.
....	....	....	....	Died April 1, 1816.
....	....	....	....	Retired Oct. 27, 1819.
....	....	....	....	Died Jan. 24, 1818, at Mundium.
....	....	....	....	Died May 3, 1806.
....	....	....	....	Retired July 28, 1815, in England.
....	....	....	....	Retired Jan. 2, 1826.
....	....	....	....	Died Nov. 22, 1806, at Sea.
....	....	....	....	Resigned Aug. 21, 1803.
....	....	....	....	Died July 3, 1807.
....	....	....	....	Invalided. Died June 16, 1824, at Chingleput.
Jan. 3, 1826	....	....	....	Retired Oct. 10, 1828, in England.
....	....	....	....	Died July 4, 1805, at Poonah.
....	....	....	....	Resigned May 6, 1807.
....	....	....	....	Retired Feb. 20, 1832, in England.
....	....	....	....	Died July 23, 1815, at Madras.
....	....	....	....	Died Nov. 26, 1815, at Gooty.
....	....	....	....	{ Died Aug. 14, 1806, at Prince of Wales's Island.
....	....	....	....	Died Jan. 16, 1814.
....	....	....	....	{ Invalided Nov. 19, 1830, in India. Died July 11, 1831, on board the "Cambridge."
....	....	....	....	{ Cashiered June 3, 1812. Died on his passage to England.
June 19, 1828	....	....	....	Retired Aug. 7, 1830, in India.
....	....	....	....	Struck off, Aug. 17, 1809.
....	....	....	....	Died June 9, 1825, at Masulipatam.
....	....	....	....	Died Aug. 12, 1809, at Seringapatam.
....	...1829...	....	....	Retired July 4, 1829, in England.
....	....	....	....	Died April 7, 1810, at Masulipatam.
....	....	....	....	Died April 29, 1829, at Kamptee.
....	....	....	....	Struck off, Jan. 27, 1809.
....	....	....	....	Died Oct. 30, 1804.
....	....	....	....	Died Aug. 24, 1833.
....	....	....	....	Died Jan. 6, 1818, at Seroor.
....	....	....	....	Retired July 4, 1829, in England.

MADRAS

NAMES.	Cadet.	Cornet, Ensign, or Second Lieutenant.	Lieutenant.	Captain.	Major.
Blount, Harry Charles	1803	....	Sep. 21, 1804	....	....
Bruce, William	,,	....	Sep. 21, 1804	....	....
Blair, Gilbert James	,,	....	Sep. 21, 1804	Brevet Jan. — 1818	....
Bell, Robert	,,	....	Sep. 21, 1804	Nov. 28, 1816	....
Biss, William	,,	....	Sep. 21, 1804	Brevet, Jan — 1818	....
Burnet, Dickason Thomas..	,,	....	Sep. 21, 1804	....	....
Beauchamp, R.—*artillery*..	1804	....	July 18, 1804	....	....
Briggs, John—*artillery*....	,,	....	July 18, 1804	Sep. 6, 1810	....
Bazly, William	,,	....	July 17, 1805	....	....
Burges, Edward	,,	....	Jan. 1, 1807	....	....
Bethune, Sir H. L., Bt.....	,,	....	July 18, 1804	Sep. 8, 1813	....
Berrie, William—*artillery*..	,,	....	July 17, 1805	May 23, 1819	....
Button, Philip............	,,	....	July 17, 1805	....	....
Barnard, Reading John ..	,,	....	July 17, 1805	....	....
Bannerman, E. J.—*cavalry*	,,	July 7, 1806	....	....	....
Bruce, Archibald	,,	....	July 17, 1805	....	....
Bennett, Henry Anthony ..	,,	....	July 17, 1805	....	....
Budd, George Hayward ..	,,	....	July 17, 1805	Nov. 3, 1819	Oct. 3, 1826
Bell, Hugh Alexander	,,	....	July 17, 1805	....	....
Birkett, John	,,	....	Aug. 31, 1805	....	....
Bateman, Joseph Denman	,,	....	July 17, 1805	....	....
Bolton, John Everson	,,	....	May 4, 1806	....	....
Buchan, James	,,	....	Oct. 16, 1805	....	....
Boyne, George Skene	,,	....	Dec. 17, 1805	Sep. 1, 1818	....
Batley, Benjamin	,,	....	Jan. 1, 1807	....	....
Borthwick, William	1805	June 27, 1806	Feb. 24, 1810	Feb. 17, 1824	Aug. 23, 1834
Boles, James	,,	....	Sep. 29, 1806	....	....
Barnes, James............	,,	....	Sep. 20, 1806	....	....
Burnside, James..........	,,	June 27, 1806	Nov. 18, 1809	....	....
Brumfield, Charles........	,,	June 27, 1806	Feb. 2, 1809	....	....
Bond, Edward............	,,	June 27, 1806	July 5, 1808	Jan. 1, 1819	....
Byrn, Edward William	,,	....	Sep. 18, 1807	....	....
Brown, Patrick	,,	June 27, 1806	Nov. 22, 1808	Nov. 8, 1820	....
Baker, Benjamin	,,	June 27, 1806	Nov. 24, 1808	Jan. 2, 1821	....
Babington, Wm.—*cavalry*	,,	Jan. 21, 1807	Oct. 26, 1818	May 29, 1824	....
Baker, John Law	,,	....	Oct. 10, 1807	....	....
Binny, Alexander	,,	....	....	....	....
Boys, George	,,	Jan. 1, 1807	Sep. 29, 1808	....	....
Barwell, Osborne	,,	....	....	....	....
Brown, Wm. Paul Theodore	,,	....	....	....	....
Brett, Wm. T.—*artillery*..	,,	....	May 29, 1806	Sep. 1, 1818	July 17, 1827
Binny, William	,,	June 27, 1806	Mar. 7, 1810	May 1, 1824	....
Birch, William	,,	June 27, 1806	Oct. 20, 1808	....	....
Bullivant, Richard........	,,	June 27, 1806	....	....	....
Boydell, Edward..........	,,	June 27, 1806	....	....	....
Brown, Charles, Going	,,	June 27, 1806	April 6, 1810	....	....
Bonest, William	,,	Jan. 1, 1807	Apr. 12, 1810	....	....

PRESIDENCY.   16—17

Lieut.-Colonel.	Colonel.	Major-General.	Lieut.-General.	Date of Resignation, Retirement, or Death.
				Died Feb. 13, 1810.
				Died Aug. 13, 1816, at Malacca.
				Died April 10, 1821, at Cannanore.
				{ Cashiered Aug. 19, 1813. Restored March 28, 1815. Retired Dec. 1, 1820.
				Died Aug. 8, 1819, at Cotallum.
				Died Oct. 20, 1811, at Jaulnah.
				Died 1813, at Bangalore.
				{ Died Nov. 24, 1812, in consequence of a fall from his horse.
				Died Aug. 2, 1808.
				Retired Sep. 17, 1817, in England.
				Retired Sep. 1, 1822.
				Died Nov. 2, 1820, at Viziniagrum.
				Struck off.
				Died Sep. 16, 1811.
				{ Cashiered Dec. 14, 1810. Restored March 20, 1812. Died Oct. 25, 1813, at Nagpore.
				Died Nov. 17, 1809, at Rajahmundry.
				Resigned Jan. 10, 1812.
				Died Nov. 20, 1826, at Wallajahbad.
				Died June 26, 1812, at Madras.
				Died April 3, 1815.
				Died May 25, 1810, at Masulipatam.
				Killed Nov. 25, 1816, near Kottora.
				Died Dec. 18, 1810, at Cochin.
				Retired May 13, 1820.
				Resigned 1811.
				Died May 26, 1823, at Madras.
				Died Dec. 25, 1815, at Madura.
				Died Oct. 8, 1815, at Bungalore.
				Died April 20, 1817, at Ellichpore.
				Died Dec. 21, 1822, at Nellore.
				Died Dec. 13, 1817, at Berhampore.
				Died July 6, 1826, at Bolarum, Secunderabad.
				{ Invalided May 28, 1822. Died Oct. 24, 1831, at Guntoor.
				Died Oct. 5, 1828, at Kulladghee.
				Retired Sep. 23, 1818, in England.
				Lost April 20, 1806, in the "Lady Burgess."
				Died Oct. 7, 1813, on board the "Warley."
				Resigned Jan. 28, 1807.
				Lost Nov. 5, 1806, in the "Skelton Castle."
				Invalided March 13, 1809.
				Dismissed Dec. 14, 1826, in India.
				Died June 5, 1817, at Keragaum.
				Lost Nov. 20, 1808, in the "Glory."
				Died Feb. 23, 1809, at Madras.
				Died Feb. 27, 1813, at Madura.
				Died May 26, 1811.

MADRAS.——D

MADRAS

NAMES.	Cadet.	Cornet, Ensign, or Second Lieutenant.	Lieutenant.	Captain.	Major.
Browne, B.—*cavalry*	1806	June 4, 1807			
Bradford, William James	,,	July 3, 1807	Oct. 17, 1811	Apr. 24, 1823	May 18, 1832
Batty, Gayner Espine	,,				
Ball, Thomas P.	,,	July 3, 1807	Mar. 15, 1810	Mar. 24, 1822	
Buckworth, Horatio	,,	July 3, 1807	Jan. 8, 1810		
Blake, William Milles	,,				
Butcher, George	,,	July 3, 1807			
Blood, William	,,				
Bagot, Christopher	,,	Aug. 21, 1808	Sep. 11, 1813		
Bannatyne, James	,,	July 3, 1807	May 18, 1810		
Bonette, John Harding	,,	July 3, 1807	Jan. 2, 1812	Aug. 29, 1824	Aug. 23, 1834
Butler, Robert	,,	July 3, 1807	Apr. 23, 1812	May 1, 1824	Brevet, Jan. 10, 1837
Brown, Charles	,,	July 3, 1807			
Birch, George	,,	July 3, 1807	Apr. 30, 1814		
Brodie, James	,,	July 2, 1808	Nov. 2, 1809		
Berry, John Braithwaite	,,	Aug. 17, 1808			
Backhouse, Richard	,,	July 3, 1807	Aug. 13, 1811	May 1, 1824	
Black, Chas. W.—*artillery*	1807	Aug. 22, 1808	May 6, 1809	Sep. 14, 1819	
Bowness, Geo. W.—*cavalry*	,,	Aug. 3, 1809	Sep. 10, 1817		
Budd, W. Henry—*cavalry*	,,	Mar. 11, 1809	Jan. 13, 1816		
Bell, Alexander	,,	Mar. 18, 1809	July 27, 1813		
Borthwick, Alexander	,,	Nov. 24, 1808	Feb. 9, 1813		
Babington, Geo. Kinsley	,,		Sep. 30, 1811	Apr. 25, 1821	
Baddeley, William Holmes	,,	July 29, 1809	May 19, 1814		
Barber, Edward	,,				
Bevan, Henry	,,	Jan. 17, 1810	Nov. 30, 1816	Sep. 8, 1826	
Boulton, Henry	,,	Jan. 21, 1810	Jan. 29, 1814		
Binning, John	,,	April 6, 1809	Mar. 17, 1815		
Bruce, Eyre, Evans	,,	Mar. 15, 1810	May 26, 1814	May 1, 1824	
Buchanan, James—*cavalry*	1808	Jan. 1, 1811	Nov. 9, 1812	June 29, 1827	Nov. 9, 1835
Bourdieu, William	,,	Apr. 13, 1809	Apr. 11, 1815		
Bennett, Thomas	,,	Jan. 12, 1809	Aug. 24, 1811	July 9, 1821	
Brunton, W. C.—*cavalry*	,,	Nov. 9, 1812	Jan. 28, 1817	May 1, 1824	
Butts, Henry Owen	1809	June 25, 1810	Dec. — 1814		
Burnett, Alexander	,,	July 2, 1810	July 4, 1816		
Bowness, Henry Frederick	,,	Jan. 23, 1811	Sep. 19, 1816		
Burns, William Nicol	,,	Feb. 7, 1811	Aug. 1, 1817	Aug. 7, 1828	Mar. 31, 1836
Buck, William	1810	Apr. 20, 1811	April 2, 1817		
Barker, George—*cavalry*	,,	Nov. 9, 1812			
Biddle, Thomas—*artillery*	,,	July 27, 1811	Apr. 15, 1817	May 1, 1824	
Besley, John	,,		Dec. 29, 1813		
Bond, Frederick—*artillery*	,,	July 27, 1811	Apr. 15, 1817	May 1, 1824	
Bulmer, Henry	,,	Sep. 30, 1811	May 27, 1816		
Birch, Henry	,,	Nov. 8, 1811	Sep. 2, 1815		
Bridges, Richard—*cavalry*	,,	Nov. 9, 1812	Sep. 1, 1818	1825	
Bullock, Stanley—*cavalry*	,,	Oct. 21, 1813	Sep. 1, 1818	Mar. 12, 1826	
Bolton, Philip D.—*artillery*	,,	Feb. 2, 1812			

PRESIDENCY.

18—19

Lieut.-Colonel.	Colonel.	Major-General.	Lieut.-General.	Date of Resignation, Retirement, or Death.
				Resigned Jan. 21, 1812.
				Drowned Feb. 21, 1807, on passage to India.
				Died Dec. 20, 1829, at Ahmednuggur.
				Died Nov. 9, 1818, at Soongeer.
				Died July 21, 1810.
				Died April 20, 1808.
				Died Sep. 22, 1807.
				Died April 27, 1815, at Nattore.
				{ Struck off, having been from India beyond the period prescribed by Act of Parliament.
				Retired Aug. 6, 1835, in India.
				Died Jan. 14, 1810, at Mangalore.
				Died Nov. 29, 1816, in camp, near Seroor.
				Died July 18, 1815, at Chicacole.
				Died Aug. 14, 1811.
				Died Aug. 4, 1829, at Bolaram.
				Killed Oct. 23, 1824, at Kittoor.
				Died Oct. 5, 1818.
				Resigned Jan. 27, 1817, in India.
				{ Admitted a Pensioner, Aug. 5, 1816, on Lord Clive's Fund, in England.
				Died Jan. 23, 1817.
				Retired March 31, 1833, in India.
				Died May — 1818.
				Died Oct. 24, 1809.
				Died Oct. 27, 1818, at Mooltge.
				Died — 1817, in England.
				["Carmarthen."
				Died March 22, 1820, on board the
				{ Invalided, and died Jan. 6, 1826, at Vizagapatam.
				Cashiered May 11, 1829, in India.
				Died Feb. 23, 1818, at Sindwa.
				{ Struck off, having been from India beyond the period prescribed by Act of Parliament.
				Died Sep. 4, 1824, at Nellore.
				Died Aug. 31, 1817, at St. Thome.
				Died Aug. 27, 1814, at Bangalore.
				Dismissed Sep. 3, 1823, in India.
				Drowned Nov. 18, 1816, off Plymouth
				Died May 15, 1817, at Goomsoor.
				Died May 25, 1825, in camp, at [Belgaum.
				Died Aug. 27, 1814, at Bellary.

D 2

MADRAS

NAMES.	Cadet.	Cornet, Ensign, or Second Lieutenant.	Lieutenant.	Captain.	Major.
Barlow, William—*cavalry*	1810	Sep. 1, 1814	Sep. 1, 1818		
Blenkinsop, Hen. Bristow	,,	Dec. 29, 1811	Apr. 29, 1817		
Bose, Edward Bellew	,,	June 11, 1812			
Bird, Charles H.—*cavalry*	,,	Aug. 28, 1814			
Busby, Edward	,,	June 11, 1812			
Budd, Richard	,,	June 11, 1812	Nov. 17, 1816	Jan. 1, 1825	
Bird, Charles Maddison	,,	June 11, 1812	Nov. 17, 1816	May 5, 1824	Jan. 11, 1832
Bogle, William	,,	June 11, 1812	Sep. 2, 1818		
Baddeley, Charles Holland	,,	June 11, 1812	Nov. 26, 1816	Brevet June 11, 1827	
Boldero, Charles	,,	July 6, 1813	Feb. 8, 1816	June 13, 1830	
Biss, George—*cavalry*	,,	Oct. 28, 1816	Sep. 1, 1818		
Buttanshaw, George	,,	July 6, 1813	Apr. 30, 1816		
Burrard, Philip	1813				
Bell, Thomas	,,	July 4, 1814	Apr. 9, 1816	Aug. 10, 1824	
Brooke, Wm.—*artillery*	,,	July 4, 1814	Sep. 1, 1818	Nov. 12, 1825	
Blundell, Fred.—*artillery*	,,	July 4, 1814	Sep. 1, 1818	Aug. 3, 1825	
Briggs, James	1814		Oct. 27, 1817	July 7, 1827	
Bird, John Francis	,,		July 10, 1817	June 21, 1827	
Brody, Robert	1815		May 21, 1817		
Benn, Henry C.—*artillery*	,,	April 9, 1816	Mar. 2, 1819		
Budd, John Carruthers	1816		Dec. 3, 1817		
Bell, James	,,		Apr. 6, 1818	May 11, 1824	May 25, 1835
Beaver, John Napleton			June 4, 1818	July 12, 1824	
Bradstreet, Charles Robert			June 4, 1818	Dec. 9, 1829	Jan. 31, 1837
Bissett, James	1817		June 4, 1818		
Baker, William Way	,,		June 4, 1818	Sep. 17, 1827	
Bonham, Charles Henry	,,				
Butterworth, William John	,,		June 4, 1818	June 17, 1824	May 11, 1836
Bradford, Richard	,,		June 4, 1818		
Burgess, Henry Snell	,,		June 4, 1818	Mar. 10, 1826	
Bury, William S.—*cavalry*	,,		July 15, 1819	May 20, 1827	
Boyes, John Monson	,,		June 4, 1818	May 5, 1825	
Bell, Charles Cowen	,,	April 6, 1820	Sep. 11, 1821	Jan. 12, 1826	
Barton, Thomas Robert	,,		June 4, 1818		
Barton, Samuel Dunbar	,,				
Buchanan, H. M.—*cavalry*	,,	June 3, 1818			
Buckeridge, Charles Elliot	,,		June 4, 1818		
Bainbridge, Mathew Henry	,,		July 26, 1818	June 20, 1828	
Brady, George	,,		Sep. 22, 1818	June 6, 1827	
Bradfield, Fisher	,,		July 20, 1818		
Barnett, James Brady	1818		June 13, 1819	Sep. 13, 1829	
Brown, James	,,				
Bird, Richard Johnstone	,,		June 13, 1819		
Blaxland, Mark	,,		June 13, 1819	Dec. 15, 1832	
Barton, John	,,				
Brabazon, Dupre	,,		June 13, 1819		
Barclay, Wm. Dudingston	,,		June 13, 1819	Aug. 5, 1829	

PRESIDENCY.

Lieut.-Colonel.	Colonel.	Major-General.	Lieut.-General.	Date of Resignation, Retirement, or Death.
....	....	....	....	Retired Sep. 3, 1821.
....	....	....	....	Died Sep. 15, 1823.
....	....	....	....	Died June 27, 1815, at Gooty.
....	....	....	....	Died Mar. 15, 1819, in camp before Asseerghur.
....	....	....	....	Died Feb. — 1818.
....	....	....	....	
Dec. 27, 1836	....	....	....	
....	....	....	....	Died May 31, 1822, at Jaulnah.
....	....	....	....	Retired April 23, 1832, in England.
....	....	....	....	{ Invalided Aug. 17, 1821. Died July 25, 1823, at Cuddalore.
....	....	....	....	Died May 23, 1818, in camp.
....	....	....	....	Resigned Aug. 26, 1815, in India.
....	....	....	....	Discharged May 25, 1829, in India.
....	....	....	....	Died Aug. 5, 1827, at Fort Cornwallis.
....	....	....	....	
....	....	....	....	
....	....	....	....	Died Aug. 31, 1819, at Wallajahbad.
....	....	....	....	{ Died Aug. 9, 1817, on board the "Lady Campbell," on his passage to England.
....	....	....	....	Died Aug. 20, 1820, at Nagpoor.
....	....	....	....	
....	....	....	....	Invalided in India.
....	....	....	....	
....	....	....	....	Died April 11, 1827, at Mergui.
....	....	....	....	
....	....	....	....	Died June 8, 1821.
....	....	....	....	
....	....	....	....	Died Oct. 31, 1825, at the Mauritius.
....	....	....	....	Invalided May 27, 1834, in India.
....	....	....	....	
....	....	....	....	Died May 1, 1833, at Coimbatore.
....	....	....	....	Died May 26, 1827, at Bangalore.
....	....	....	....	Died Mar. 12, 1819, in camp at Nagpore.
....	....	....	....	Died Oct. 22, 1819, at Bombay.
....	....	....	....	Resigned Jan. 15, 1823, in England.
....	....	....	....	Died Nov. 24, 1829, at St. Thomas's Mount.
....	....	....	....	{ Died Oct. 5, 1829, on board the "Catherine," at sea from Vizagapatam.
....	....	....	....	Died Nov. 29, 1824, at Rangoon.
....	....	....	....	
....	....	....	....	Died July — 1820.
....	....	....	....	Died June 14, 1826, at Jaulnah.
....	....	....	....	
....	....	....	....	Died Aug. 20, 1820, in camp at Rajahpot.
....	....	....	....	Died July 1, 1822, at Kulludghee.
....	....	....	....	Died Sep. 15, 1830, at Pulaveram.

MADRAS

NAMES.	Cadet.	Cornet, Ensign, or Second Lieutenant.	Lieutenant.	Captain.	Major.
Barron, Pierce Donovan ..	1818	....	....		
Babington, William	,,	....	June 13, 1819		
Burton, Wm. Paton	,,	....	June 13, 1819		
Bond, Tucker Francis	,,	....	....		
Babington, John—*cavalry*	1819	....	Mar. 9, 1820		
Baird, Francis John	,,	....	June 13, 1819		
Burn, George	,,	....	April 7, 1820	Feb. 25, 1833	
Butcher, James Edward ..	,,	....	April 7, 1820	Aug. 7, 1828	
Burt, N. McD.—*cavalry* ..	,,	....	Dec. 3, 1820	Mar. 7, 1827	
Brown, James Victor	,,	....	April 7, 1820	Sep. 12, 1826	
Bishop, Hugh Arthur	,,	....	April 7, 1820		
Boyce, George Keir	,,	....	Oct. 11, 1820		
Barker, Henry Francis....	,,	....	Sep. 30, 1820	Nov. 9, 1831	
Brodie, Francis Walker ..	,,	....	Apr. 14, 1821		
Boddam, Geo. Rawson	,,	....	....		
Brodie, Geo. A.—*cavalry*..	,,	....	Mar. 1, 1821		
Bedingfield, Philip........	,,	....	Dec. 2, 1820	Dec. 24, 1835	
Buxton, C. Smith	,,	....	May 15, 1820	Oct. 22, 1827	
Bruce, David	,,	....	Aug. 21, 1820		
Bell, Oswald	,,	....	Sep. 11, 1821	April 3, 1837	
Boardman, R. Edward	,,	April 6, 1820	Aug. 12, 1821	Nov. 28, 1830	
Biscoe, John S. K.	,,	....	Feb. 11, 1823		
Bayley, James Walker	,,	April 6, 1820	Nov. 23, 1822	Aug. 15, 1834	
Bennett, Henry	,,	....	June 9, 1821		
Blanch, Robert	,,	....	July 18, 1821		
Bond, Charles............	,,	....	June 14, 1821	April 1, 1833	
Baker, Henry	,,	....	July 13, 1822		
Baillie, Geo. Alexander ..	,,	....	Mar. 17, 1822	Mar. 1, 1837	
Burchell, E. S.—*artillery* ..	,,	June 11, 1820	June 8, 1821		
Black, James	1820	April 6, 1820	Nov. 19, 1822		
Boyle, T. R.—*artillery*	,,	June 16, 1820	June 8, 1821		
Brownlow, H. Richard	,,	April 6, 1820	May 10, 1823		
Bower, Henry	,,	Feb. 13, 1821	Sep. 27, 1823	June 5, 1837	
Brooshooft, Wm. Edward..	,,	Feb. 13, 1821	May 1, 1824		
Bremner, William	,,	Feb. 13, 1821	Sep. 21, 1822	Apr. 17, 1834	
Butler, Charles	,,	....	Sep. 4, 1822	Mar. 3, 1830	
Beauchamp, Maurice......	,,	Feb. 13, 1821	July 1, 1824	Mar. 5, 1834	
Bushby, John Stewart	,,	Feb. 13, 1821	July 3, 1824		
Bushby, A. Balfour	,,	Feb. 13, 1821	....		
Bradford, Charles	,,	Feb. 13, 1821	July 23, 1823	Feb. 11, 1835	
Browne, C. Alfred	,,	Feb. 13, 1821	May 1, 1824	Oct. 9, 1830	
Booker, James—*artillery* ..	,,	Dec. 19, 1820	June 8, 1821	Mar. 16, 1831	
Byng, John—*cavalry*......	,,	Feb. 13, 1821	May 1, 1824	Oct. 19, 1831	
Blood, William	,,	Feb. 13, 1821	July 15, 1823	Feb. 9, 1832	
Bingham, R. Hippesley ..	,,	Feb. 13, 1821	May 29, 1824	May 20, 1835	
Blaxland, John	,,	Feb. 13, 1821	May 2, 1824	Brevet, Feb. 13, 1836	
Babington, David	,,	Feb. 13, 1821	June 20, 1824	Nov. 17, 1835	

PRESIDENCY.

Lieut.-Colonel.	Colonel.	Major-General.	Lieut.-General.	Date of Resignation, Retirement, or Death.
....	....	....	....	Died March 20, 1820, at Cuddalore.
....	....	....	....	Died April 2, 1826, at Rangoon.
....	....	....	....	Invalided Oct. 5, 1832, in India.
....	....	....	....	Killed Oct. 7, 1824, in action at Rangoon.
....	....	....	....	Died May 1, 1832, at Jaulnah.
....	....	....	....	Died May 24, 1824, at Vellore.
....	....	....	....	
....	....	....	....	
....	....	....	....	Retired Sep. 5, 1829, in England.
....	....	....	....	Died June 6, 1831, at Kamptee.
....	....	....	....	Resigned Jan. — 1829, in India.
....	....	....	....	Died Feb. 18, 1827, at Masulipatam.
....	....	....	....	Retired Sep. 22, 1835, in India.
....	....	....	....	Died April 16, 1834, at Edinburgh.
....	....	....	....	Died Sep. 25, 1824, at Cuddapah.
....	....	....	....	Died Nov. 23, 1826, at Madras.
....	....	....	....	
....	....	....	....	Dismissed Mar. 10, 1832, in England.
....	....	....	....	Died June 26, 1824, at Cannanore.
....	....	....	....	
....	....	....	....	{ Died Nov. 25, 1824, at sea, on board the ship "Mellish."
....	....	....	....	Died May 6, 1826, in camp, at Jaulnah.
....	....	....	....	Died Jan. 6, 1826, at Mangalore.
....	....	....	....	
....	....	....	....	Died May 7, 1824, at Bangrecottah.
....	....	....	....	
....	....	....	....	Died June 26, 1827, at Kamptee.
....	....	....	....	Died at sea, on board the "Hero of Malown."
....	....	....	....	Died Nov. 16, 1823, at St. Thomas's Mount.
....	....	....	....	Died Aug. 15, 1825, at Darwar.
....	....	....	....	
....	....	....	....	Died March 1, 1830, at Penang.
Lieut.-Colonel.	Colonel.	Major-General.	Lieut.-General.	
....	....	....	....	{ Pensioned in India, and Retired in England, 1837.
....	....	....	....	Died April 4, 1827, at Momenabad.
....	....	....	....	Died June 19, 1822, at Chittoor.
....	....	....	....	Retired Jan. 11, 1836, in England.
....	....	....	....	
....	....	....	....	Died April 4, 1834, at St. Thomas's Mount.
....	....	....	....	
....	....	....	....	
....	....	....	....	
....	....	....	....	
....	....	....	....	

MADRAS

NAMES.	Cadet.	Cornet, Ensign, or Second Lieutenant.	Lieutenant.	Captain.	Major.
Briggs, Henry—*cavalry*	1820	Feb. 13, 1821	May 1, 1824		
Brett, Jas. F. Knightley	,,	Feb. 13, 1821	July 21, 1823		
Brooks, Henry	,,	Feb. 13, 1821	May 28, 1824		
Borradaile, Alfred—*cavalry*	,,	Feb. 13, 1821	Sep. 24, 1824	Feb. 20, 1833	
Byam, A. E.—*artillery*	1821	June 9, 1821	June 10, 1821	Sep. 1, 1831	
Brown, J. Read—*cavalry*	,,	Feb. 13, 1821	May 1, 1824	May 11, 1833	
Berry, Thomas	,,		May 1, 1824		
Bennet, Charles	,,				
Boddam, Wm. T.—*cavalry*	,,	Apr. 27, 1822	May 31, 1824		
Baber, Thomas Francis	,,	Apr. 27, 1822	Feb. 23, 1825		
Budd, Wm. Henry	,,	Apr. 27, 1822	Jan. 3, 1826		
Beaver, Herbert	,,	Apr. 27, 1822	May 23, 1825	May 2, 1836	
Backhouse, Chas. Orlando	,,	Apr. 27, 1822	Dec. 26, 1825	Sep. 11, 1834	
Buchanan, Duncan	,,	April 27, 1822	May 25, 1824		
Benwell, James	,,	Apr. 27, 1822	Nov. 6, 1825	Dec. 16, 1835	
Begbie, Peter J.—*artillery*	,,	May 10, 1822	May 11, 1822	Jan. 2, 1833	
Brew, John George	,,	Apr. 27, 1822			
Baylis, Thomas—*artillery*	,,	May 10, 1822	May 11, 1822	Apr. 1, 1834	
Best, Chas. Hen.—*artillery*	1822	May 10, 1822	Sep. 2, 1822	May 28, 1834	
Bridge, Albertus Thomas	,,	Apr. 27, 1822	Oct. 18, 1825		
Beevor, Horatio Clarke	,,	May 2, 1823	July 7, 1827		
Barnard, Geo. Ashby	,,	...1823...			
Boulderson, John Carne	,,	May 2, 1824	Sep. 8, 1826		
Bell, J. G. B.—*artillery*	,,	June 6, 1823	Nov. 25, 1823		
Briggs, Charles—*artillery*	,,	June 6, 1823	Jan. 17, 1824		
Baldwin, J. T.—*artillery*	,,	June 6, 1823	June 7, 1823	Dec. 22, 1834	
Back, John—*artillery*	,,	June 6, 1823	June 7, 1823	Aug. 5, 1835	
Bayley, Stuart	1823	May 14, 1824	Sep. 10, 1830		
Burrard, Naylor	,,	May 14, 1824	Jan. 12, 1826		
Biddle, William	,,	May 14, 1824	Sep. 8, 1826	May 25, 1837	
Bayles, Thomas	,,	May 14, 1824	Oct. 9, 1826		
Bates, John	,,	May 14, 1824	Sep. 8, 1826		
Blogg, Hen. Basil—*cavalry*	,,	May 14, 1824	Feb. 7, 1832		
Bean, John Henry	,,	May 14, 1824	Sep. 19, 1826		
Beaumont, William	,,		Aug. 16, 1826	Dec. 6, 1834	
Burgoyne, Fred.—*artillery*	1824	June 17, 1824	June 25, 1824		
Brett, James T.—*cavalry*	,,	May 6, 1825	June 6, 1826	Apr. 12, 1834	
Baker, Edward	,,	May 6, 1825	Jan. 11, 1834		
Brady, Anthony	,,	May 6, 1825	Mar. 4, 1827		
Brotherton, W.H.—*artillery*	,,	Sep. 15, 1824	Sep. 16, 1824		
Briggs, Stephen Charles	,,	May 6, 1825	Jan. 11, 1832		
Brett, De, Renzie James	,,	May 6, 1825	July 13, 1831		
Begbie, Alex. J.—*artillery*	,,	Dec. 16, 1824	June 10, 1825		
Briggs, George—*artillery*	,,	Dec. 16, 1824	Dec. 17, 1824		
Brown, F. John—*artillery*	,,	Dec. 16, 1824	Aug. 31, 1825		
Baillie, A. Ewen—*artillery*	,,	Dec. 16, 1824	June 9, 1825		
Burridge, John	,,	May 6, 1825			

PRESIDENCY.   24—25

Lieut.-Colonel.	Colonel.	Major General.	Lieut.-General.	Date of Resignation, Retirement, or Death.
				Died March 20, 1834, at Coimbatore.
				Died Oct. 24, 1825, on board the "Caroline."
				Resigned May 27, 1828, in India.
				Struck off, Dec. 2, 1825, in England.
				Died Feb. 22, 1823, at Bangalore.
				{ Died Jan. 21, 1827, at Sea, on passage to England.
				Died June 2, 1837, at Kamptee.
				Died Sep. 3, 1826, at Presidency.
				Died Dec. 9, 1823, at Masulipatam.
				Died June 20, 1824, at Fort St. George.
				Died Feb. 3, 1834, at Kamptee.
				Died June 3, 1832, at Bangalore.
				Died May 29, 1833, on board the "Sesostris."
				Died Oct. 13, 1831, at Jaulnah.
				Died April 11, 1832, at Bangalore.

E

MADRAS

NAMES.	Cadet.	Cornet, Ensign, or Second Lieutenant.	Lieutenant.	Captain.	Major.
Bullock, Robert	1824	May 6, 1825	Oct. 11, 1828	....	....
Barrow, Henry Clarges ..	,,	.... 1826...	....		
Babington, William Knox..	,,	.... 1826...	Aug. 2, 1828		
Babington, Charles Stewart	,,	....	Jan. 7, 1828		
Beadnell, Alfred—*artillery*	1825	June 16, 1825	May 8, 1827		
Bayley, Daniel	,,	....	July 12, 1826		
Brooks, Alfred	,,	Jan. 8, 1826	....		
Broadfoot, George	,,	Jan. 8, 1826	June 21, 1826		
Barker, Arundel	,,	Jan. 8, 1826	May 20, 1833		
Birley, Daniel	,,	....	May 12, 1827		
Burdett, Charles Wentworth	,,	.... 1826...	June 8, 1827		
Buckley, William	,,	Jan. 8, 1826	....		
Bradstreet, Robert	,,	Jan. 8, 1826	....		
Back, Thomas	,,	Jan. 8, 1826	Nov. 26, 1828		
Butler, Charles Augustus..	,,	Jan. 8, 1826	Jan. 10, 1837		
Balfour, George—*artillery*	,,	Dec. 16, 1825	June 12, 1827		
Bell, Robert..............	,,	Jan. 8, 1827	Apr. 23, 1828		
Buckle, Edward—*engineers*	,,	....	June 17, 1825		
Budd, Richard, H. J.	,,	Jan. 8, 1826	Nov. 9, 1828		
Bryce, Robert	,,	Jan. 8, 1826	Jan. 8, 1830		
Brice, Edward—*artillery* ..	,,	June 16, 1826	Feb. 25, 1828		
Bristow, William	,,	Jan. 8, 1826	....		
Beresford, J. P.—*artillery*..	1826	June 16, 1826	Apr. 19, 1829		
Bromwick, Orlando Wm...	,,	Feb. 8, 1827	....		
Beavan, Arthur Frederick	,,	Feb. 8, 1827	July 31, 1833		
Babington, C. H. St. John..	,,	Feb. 27, 1827	....		
Browne, George Griffin	,,	Aug. 21, 1827	....		
Best, Samuel—*engineers* ..	,,	....	Dec. 17, 1825		
Berdmore, P. S.—*artillery*	,,	....	....		
Bale, Benjamin	,,	.... 1827...	....		
Blackburne, Thomas	,,	Oct. 24, 1827	....		
Beagin, William George ..	,,	May 11, 1828	Oct. 10, 1833		
Borthwick, William	1827	June 21, 1828	Mar. 13, 1833		
Brice, J. P. (15 N.I.) (now Buée.)	,,	....	Mar. 8, 1829		
Birdwood, W. J.—*engineers*	,,	....	June 5, 1829		
Bell, Jasper H.—*engineers*..	,,	....	Dec. 25, 1828		
Burton, Charles	,,	Sep. 27, 1828	Sep. 15, 1836		
Boyes, Lake Torriano	,,	Sep. 3, 1828	....		
Burleigh, Henry Langford	,,	Nov. 27, 1828	Apr. 27, 1834		
Balfour, David William ..	,,	Apr. 20, 1829	Sep. 26, 1833		
Black, Bladen W.—*artillery*	,,	Dec. 13, 1827	Jan. 2, 1833		
Bell, Wm. Cornelius	,,	Apr. 19, 1828	July 14, 1832		
Bell, Hugh H.—*artillery* ..	,,	Dec. 13, 1827	July 29, 1833		
Bridges, David Macduff ..	,,	May 2, 1828	....		
Bissett, William	,,	May 29, 1829	Feb. 20, 1836		
Brockman, H. John	,,	Oct. 28, 1828	Feb. 18, 1835		

PRESIDENCY.

Lieut.-Colonel.	Colonel.	Major-General.	Lieut.-General.	Date of Resignation, Retirement, or Death.
				Died Nov. 20, 1826, at Penang.
				Died June 1, 1831, at Munguddah.
				Died April 11, 1830.
				Died May 23, 1833, Masulipatam.
				Died Feb. 22, 1834, at Dindigul.
				Died July 6, 1832, at Balcondah.
				Died Sep. 25, 1835, at Madras.
				Died April 8, 1828, at Madras.
				Died April 28, 1830, at Madras.
				Discharged March 5, 1830, in India.
				Resigned Dec. 29, 1829, in England.
				Died Apr. 25, 1827, on his passage out.
				Re-called April 8, 1828.
				Died July 7, 1835, at Madras.
Lieut.-Colonel.	Colonel.	Major-General.	Lieut.-General.	
				Died Feb. 15, 1830, at Vellore.
				Retired 1837, in India.
				Died April 5, 1834, at Shikapore.

MADRAS

NAMES.	Cadet.	Cornet, Ensign, or Second Lieutenant.	Lieutenant.	Captain.	Major.
Bruere, C. A. S.—*artillery*	1827	June 12, 1828			
Boddington, Reginald B...	1828	May 20, 1831			
Brassey, G. Ashburne	„	Apr. 29, 1831	Aug. 6, 1835		
Birdwood, M. A.—*engineers*	„				
Birley, Hornby	„	June 9, 1831			
Beachcroft, Matthews	„	Aug. 1, 1831	Dec. 24, 1834		
Boulderson, Wm. Lovell ..	„				
Barrow, J. L.—*artillery* ..	„	Oct. 9, 1831			
Babington, John—*artillery*	„	April 6, 1831			
Babington, C. D.	„	Jan. 11, 1832			
Brown, William	1829	Sep. 12, 1834			
Bordieu, J. H.—*artillery* ..	„	May 29, 1832			
Balmain, J. G.—*artillery* ..	„	Jan. 2, 1833			
Beardmore, H. T. M.—*artillery*	„	Sep. 18, 1833			
Bishop, Fred. C...........	1830	June 24, 1832	Oct. 2, 1835		
Brooke, Arthur Edw.......	1832	Nov. 24, 1832	June 16, 1837		
Beadle, Dennis R. H.	„	Feb. 16, 1833			
Blair, David	„	Nov. 20, 1833			
Blagrave, C. A.	„	Jan. 1, 1834			
Bird, William	„	Jan. 1, 1834			
Baynes, Fred. Wm.	„	Feb. 9, 1834			
Brown, Cyril Andrews	„	Feb. 5, 1834	Feb. 5, 1836		
Bruere, Rich. Alexander ..	„	Feb. 15, 183.	July 12, 1835		
Bromley, R.—*artillery*	„				
Boswell, William Henry ..	1833	Mar. 8, 1834			
Blake, Henry William	„	Dec. 13, 1833			
Bourdillon, R. P.	„	Mar. 10, 1834	Feb. 1, 1836		
Burgoyne, John Osborne ..	1834	June 13, 1834			
C					
Chesshyre, Robert	....			1770	
Collins, Edward	....	Dec. 30, 1765	Apr. 29, 1767	Oct. 15, 1773	
Conyngham, George	1766	Dec. 2, 1766	May 6, 1768	Nov. 18, 1776	Apr. 17, 1786
Clarke, George	....		July 13, 1770	Dec. 29, 1777	Apr. 17, 1786
Cuppage, John	....		Aug. 4, 1770	July 6, 1779	
Cudmore, John	....			Mar. 31, 1782	
Crawford, Arthur	1768	Sep. 28, 1770		Dec. 22, 1782	
Croker, Robert	1769	Oct. 16, 1770	Jan. 16, 1775	Mar. 23, 1783	Oct. 15, 1794
Cox, John................	„	Nov. 8, 1770	June 27, 1775	June 13, 1783	Apr. 27, 1795
Cookson, Francis	„	Dec. 24, 1770	Sep. 18, 1776	Nov. 2, 1783	
Chase, Richard	1770	June 15, 1771	Nov. 24, 1776	Nov. 2, 1783	
Campbell, David	„	July 4, 1771	Dec. 25, 1777	Nov. 2, 1783	1794
Campbell, James	1771	Apr. 6, 1773	Nov. 9, 1778	Nov. 8, 1783	June 1, 1796
Close, Sir Barry, Bart.....	„	Sep. 3, 1773	Oct. 2, 1778	Dec. 18, 1783	June 1, 1796
Castre, Charles De	....	Dec. 19, 1775		1786	
Cammeron, Robert	....	Dec. 15, 1775	Oct. 31, 1780	Dec. 20, 1786	June 1, 1796
Coke, Thomas	1775	Jan. 19, 1776	Nov. 4, 1780	Dec. 14, 1789	June 1, 1796
Cuppage, Alexander......	„	Aug. 25, 1776	Nov. 11, 1780	May 18, 1791	June 1, 1796

PRESIDENCY.   28—29

Lieut-Colonel.	Colonel.	Major-General.	Lieut.-General.	Date of Resignation, Retirement, or Death.
				Died Jan. 7, 1833, at Penang.
				Out of the Service in 1834.
				[Mount.
				Died Feb. 6, 1832, at St. Thomas's
				Killed April 3, 1834, at Somaunahpett.
				[Goomsur District.
				Killed March 5, 1836, in action in the
Aug. 16, 1785				Died 1788.
Apr. 17, 1786	Oct. 3, 1792	Feb. 26, 1795		Died April 1808.
Nov. 23, 1787	Jan. 8, 1796	May 3, 1796		Died Nov. 8, 1821, at Bath.
Dec. 14, 1789	June 1, 1796			{ Home 1794. Allowed to retire with the pay of his rank, 1796.
Oct. 3, 1792	June 1, 1796			Retired 1798.
				Died 1790.
				Resigned Jan.—1789.
June 1, 1796	Aug. 18, 1799	Apr. 25, 1808	June 4, 1813	Died Apr. 13, 1817, at Masulipatam.
				Died June 22, 1795, at Vizianaghur.
				Died 1793.
				Resigned 1792.
June 1, 1796	Jan. 7, 1802	Oct. 25, 1809	June 4, 1813	Died Jan. 28, 1828, at St. Andrew's.
				Resigned.
Dec. 21, 1797	Aug. 24, 1803	July 25, 1810		Died April 12, 1813, in England.
				King's Service, 1789.
Dec. 26, 1798				Retired Sep.—1803.
Dec. 26, 1798				Retired Sep. 9, 1803.
May 12, 1799	Oct. 25, 1809	Jan. 1, 1812	May 27, 1825	

MADRAS

NAMES.	Cadet.	Cornet, Ensign, or Second Lieutenant.	Lieutenant.	Captain.	Major.
Chalmers, Sir John (K.C.B.)	1775	Dec. 2, 1776	Nov. 19, 1780	Oct. 3, 1792	July 27, 1796
Corner, Charles	,,	Nov. 25, 1776	Dec. 7, 1780	June 6, 1793	Nov. 29, 1797
Carlisle, Charles	1777	Nov. — 1778	....	July 12, 1782	Jan. 8, 1796
Cuppage, John	,,	Apr. 18, 1778	Jan. 12, 1782	Aug. 6, 1794	Oct. 12, 1798
Coupland, Charles	,,	May 2, 1778	Jan. 21, 1782	Aug. 6, 1794	....
Collins, William	,,	May 11, 1778	Jan. 26, 1782	Oct. 14, 1794	....
Campbell, Colin	1778	May 20, 1778	Feb. 3, 1782	May 9, 1795	Dec. 26, 1798
Clarke, Thomas	1777	July 24, 1778	Mar. 14, 1782	June 1, 1796	....
Cosby, Henry S.	....	Aug. 8, 1778	Feb. 20, 1783	June 1, 1796	....
Carey, Daniel	1778	Apr. 12, 1779	Dec. 12, 1783	June 1, 1796	Dec. 10, 1799
Cunningham, James	,,	May 5, 1779	Oct. 13, 1784	June 1, 1796	June 17, 1800
Clarke, Sommers	1799	Sep. 17, 1780	Apr. 17, 1786	....	....
Cally, Arthur Mac	1780	Dec. 6, 1780	Apr. 17, 1786	July 11, 1797	Dec. 10, 1801
Cally, Andrew Mac	,,	Dec. 7, 1780	Apr. 17, 1786	July 13, 1797	Apr. 24, 1804
Convenant, John M.	,,	Aug. 13, 1781	June 8, 1786	Aug. 20, 1797	....
Cottrell, Edward	,,	Dec. 10, 1781	....	....	....
Crane, Samuel	,,	Oct. 5, 1781	Nov. 1, 1788	Dec. 21, 1797	Mar. 11, 1804
Cooke, Arthur L.	,,	Oct. 21, 1781	....	....	....
Cunninghame, William	,,	Oct. 28, 1781	Nov. 1, 1788	Sep. 29, 1798	Jan. 2, 1804
Cruickshanks, Charles	1781	Sep. 28, 1782	....	....	....
Cheap, David	,,	Sep. 29, 1782	....	....	....
Cranston, John	,,	Nov. 17, 1782	Aug. 21, 1790	....	....
Crump, Samuel	1782	Dec. 13, 1782	Aug. 21, 1790	....	....
Culloy, Robert Mac	,,	Dec. 25, 1782	Aug. 21, 1790	Mar. 4, 1799	....
Cruikshanks, Patrick	,,	Jan. 1, 1783	....	....	....
Cresswell, P. S.	,,	May 4, 1783	Aug. 21, 1790	Brevet 1798	....
Colville, Walter	,,	May 6, 1783	....	....	....
Crue, Thomas K.	,,	May 7, 1783	Aug. 21, 1790	July 31, 1799	....
Clamant, George	,,	May 31, 1783	....	....	....
Cooke, Matthew	1783	Sep. 3, 1783	....	....	....
Cormick, M. H.	....	....	Aug. 21, 1790	....	....
Carlisle, Charles—*artillery*	...	Nov. 23, 1778	Dec. 1, 1780	July 12, 1782	June 1, 1796
Clarke, Tredway—*artillery*	1779	Oct. 20, 1780	Oct. 12, 1781	July 22, 1788	June 14, 1801
Campbell, John—*artillery*	,,	Nov. 6, 1781	Oct. 18, 1784	Apr. 22, 1793	....
Conan, N. W.—*artillery*	1780	Dec. 30, 1781	Oct. 21, 1784	....	....
Coupland, Wm.—*artillery*	,,	Jan. 5, 1783	Apr. 26, 1786	....	....
Cree, Alexander—*engineers*	,,	May 24, 1786	....	....	....
Campbell, Dugald—*cavalry*	1766	Nov. 3, 1767	Dec. 8, 1768	Nov. 25, 1776	April 6, 1784
Crutzer, Henry—*cavalry*	....	....	Apr. 21, 1784	....	....
Cosby, Montague—*cavalry*	....	Dec. 12, 1785	Nov. 28, 1792	May 1, 1804	May 23, 1807
Cosby, Sir H. A. M.	....	July 28, 1760	Nov. 16, 1763	Nov. 16, 1765	....
Cochrane, Spencer	....	....	July 25, 1770	Aug. 4, 1778	May 23, 1786
Coote, John	1778	June 8, 1779	...1784....	....	....
Currie, Thomas	....	Apr. 27, 1783	Aug. 21, 1790	May 12, 1799	....
Colebrooke, J. (C.B.)—*cavalry*	1790	June 12, 1792	Nov. 1, 1798	Sep. 13, 1800	Aug. 2, 1806
Crosdill, J. (C.B.)—*artillery*	1788	Aug. 6, 1789	Aug. 17, 1793	June 14, 1801	Nov. 5, 1806
Charleton, Rd.—*artillery*	1792	June 20, 1792	June 1, 1796	Nov. 7, 1803	....

PRESIDENCY.

Lieut.-Colonel.	Colonel.	Major General.	Lieut.-General.	Date of Resignation, Retirement, or Death.
July 31, 1799	Oct. 25, 1809	Jan. 1, 1812	....	{ Died March 31, 1818, on board the "Marquis of Wellington," on passage to England.
Dec. 10, 1799	Oct. 25, 1809	Jan. 1, 1812	May 27, 1825	
Dec. 25, 1800	Oct. 16, 1801	....	....	Died on his passage home in 1804.
June 17, 1800	July 25, 1810	June 4, 1813	May 27, 1825	Died June 17, 1828, in England.
....	....	....	....	Died May 8, 1795, at Vizia aghur.
....	....	....	....	Died 1798.
....	....	....	....	Killed April 5, 1799.
....	....	....	....	Struck off Dec. 17, 1799.
....	....	....	....	Killed May 2, 1799.
May 1, 1804	....	....	....	Invalided Dec. 11, 1804.
....	....	....	....	Retired June 24, 1803.
....	....	....	....	Retired on Lord Clive's bounty, 1788.
....	....	....	....	Died March 10, 1804, at Ajuntee.
June 27, 1805	Brevet June 4, 1813.	....	....	Died Jan. 26, 1819, at Madras.
....	....	....	....	{ Invalided July 12, 1803. Died Aug. 18, 1805, at Madras.
....	....	....	....	Died 1793.
Mar. 1, 1807	....	....	....	Retired Nov. 2, 1808.
....	....	....	....	Resigned 1788.
...1808....	....	....	....	Retired June 29, 1808.
....	....	....	....	Died 1791.
....	....	....	....	Died 1790.
....	....	....	....	Died June 13, 1795, in the Vizagapatam district.
....	....	....	....	{ Invalided July 1791. Died Jan. 20, 1819, at Royaporam.
....	....	....	....	Died Oct. 1800.
....	....	....	....	Not to be traced.
....	....	....	....	Died Feb. 20, 1804.
....	....	....	....	Died 1792.
....	....	....	....	Died Feb. 8, 1805.
....	....	....	....	Died August 1789.
....	....	....	....	Died June 23, 1789, in Cuddalore.
....	....	....	....	Killed May 4, 1799.
Dec. 25, 1800	Oct. 16, 1801	....	....	Died April 3, 1804, at Portsmouth.
Oct. 16, 1801	July 25, 1810	June 4, 1813	May 27, 1825	
....	....	....	....	Died at the Mount, 1810.
....	....	....	....	{ Lost a leg at the storming of Bangalore, in 1791, and died in consequence.
....	....	....	....	Died in 1793.
....	....	....	....	Not to be traced.
Apr. 17, 1786	Feb. 26, 1795	Jan. 1, 1798	....	Retired on off reckonings, Mar. 25, 1808.
....	....	....	....	Died June 1789.
Mar. 1, 1818	....	....	....	Died July 14, 1819, at Poonah.
Sep. 17, 1781	Aug. 16, 1785	....	....	In Europe 1787, out of the service.
....	....	....	....	At home 1788, ditto, ditto.
....	....	....	....	{ Home 1786. Pensioned 1788. Died Oct. 29, 1818.
....	....	....	....	Died Mar. 25, 1802.
July 29, 1815	....	....	....	{ Died Oct. 19, 1823, on board H. M. S. "Liffey," off the Sand Heads.
Sep. 1, 1818	....	....	....	Retired Aug. 15, 1821.
....	....	....	....	Died May 12, 1806, at Ghooty.

MADRAS

NAMES.	Cadet.	Cornet, Ensign, or Second Lieutenant.	Lieutenant.	Captain.	Major.
Cooper, Charles Thomas ..	1790	....	June 7, 1792	Brevet 1799	....
Colebrooke, James	,,	....	April 1, 1793	May 7, 1800	April 8, 1808
Cawthorne, William	,,	June 6, 1791	....	....	....
Cox, Sir John, Bart.	,,	June 15, 1791	June 6, 1793	June 17, 1800	....
Cevill, James	,,	June 27, 1791	June 12, 1793	June 17, 1800	....
Campbell, James	,,	July 14, 1791	Oct. 23, 1793	Aug. 14, 1800	May 27, 1809
Chambers, William	1790	July 30, 1791	Feb. 17, 1794	June 8, 1801	....
Coghlan, Thomas	,,	Aug. 21, 1791	May 15, 1794	Apr. 20, 1801	....
Campbell, Archibald	....	Sep. 9, 1791	Aug. 6, 1794	....	....
Campbell, Dugald	....	Sep. 12, 1791	Aug. 6, 1794	....	....
Coupland, Joseph	1791	Sep. 27, 1791	Aug. 6, 1794	....	....
Cudmore, Edw.—*engineers*	....	....	June 4, 1792	....	....
Caldwell, Sir J. L. (K.C.B.)—*engineers*	1788	....	Dec. 2, 1792	Aug. 12, 1802	Jan. 1, 1806
Castle, William — *engineers*	1791	May 1, 1793	Sep. 9, 1793	....	....
Cotgrave, John—*engineers*	,,	June 23, 1793	June 1, 1796	Jan. 1, 1806	May 9, 1821
Caruthers, John—*engineers*	,,	....	....	....	....
Campbell, John	....	Oct. 19, 1768	Sep. 7, 1770	July 13, 1779	....
Capper, Francis..........	....	Apr. 17, 1778	Jan. 11, 1782	Aug. 6, 1794	Oct. 4, 1798
Collins, Edward Henry....	1793	....	July 29, 1795	....	....
Cleghorne, J. R.—*engineers*	,,	....	Sep. 13, 1794	Jan. 1, 1806	Brevet, 1819
Conway, T. H. S. (C.B.)-*cavalry*	1798	....	Sep. 4, 1799	Jan. 27, 1810	Oct. 18, 1818
Cookesley, Thos.—*artillery*	,,	Jan. 8, 1796	Apr. 14, 1798	....	....
Custance, George	,,	Dec. 27, 1795	Jan. 8, 1796	Sep. 21, 1804	Sep. 11, 1809
Campbell, Archibald	1794	Jan. 28, 1796	....	....	....
Chitty, Edwin	1795	Mar. 7, 1796	Aug. 16, 1797	Sep. 21, 1804	Jan. 25, 1813
Campbell, Daniel	,,	Mar. 5, 1796	July 25, 1797	....	....
Cranstoun, Henry	,,	Mar. 11, 1796	Sep. 16, 1797	Sep. 21, 1804	....
Collins, James William ..	,,	Mar. 10, 1796	Aug. 20, 1797	May 16, 1803	....
Campbell, John	1797	Sep. 11, 1797	Oct. 12, 1798	July 25, 1805	....
Clarke, Charles Poyntz....	1796	Aug. 24, 1797	Oct. 12, 1798	Feb. 5, 1805	....
Clapham, William	,,	Aug. 5, 1797	Sep. 29, 1798	Sep. 21, 1804	June 4, 1817
Campbell, Mungo	,,	Aug. 13, 1797	Oct. 12, 1798	Sep. 21, 1804	....
Collett, John H.—*cavalry*	1797	Jan. 25, 1799	Sep. 4, 1799	Mar. 11, 1809	Sep. 1, 1818
Carfrae, John	,,	Sep. 9, 1798	Dec. 26, 1798	Nov. 14, 1807	Sep. 22, 1818
Craigie, C. W.—*artillery* ..	1795	Apr. 1, 1796	Feb. 4, 1800	....	....
Chitty, Samuel—*cavalry* ..	1798	....	Nov. 15, 1800	....	....
Crompton, J. Dickenson ..	,,	....	Jan. 1, 1800	Dec. 26, 1806	Sep. 1, 1819
Cleaveland, S.—*artillery* ..	,,	....	Mar. 7, 1800	Sep. 30, 1813	Aug. 16, 1821
Chitty, Frederick	,,	....	Jan. 1, 1800	....	....
Cuffley, Peter Newton	,,	....	Aug. 29, 1800	Feb. 25, 1807	....
Clason, Andrew John	,,	....	Jan. 1, 1800	Jan. 15, 1807	June 25, 1814
Cope, Henry Thomas	1796	Sep. 8, 1797	Oct. 12, 1798	....	....
Clark, James Barclay	1799	....	Dec. 15, 1800	....	....
Coombs, John Munckton ..	,,	....	Dec. 15, 1800	Mar. 5, 1808	Apr. 1, 1819
Carstairs, David..........	,,	....	Dec. 15, 1800	Mar. 18, 1809	....
Conry, Edmund	,,	....	Dec. 15, 1800	Mar. 18, 1809	Aug. 6, 1820
Close, H. J.—*cavalry*	,,	....	Apr. 24, 1803	....	....

PRESIDENCY.

Lieut.-Colonel.	Colonel.	Major-General.	Lieut.-General.	Date of Resignation, Retirement, or Death.
....	....	....	....	Invalided June 2, 1802. Died March 17, 1816, at Vizagapatam.
Jan. 5, 1814	....	....	....	Died Jan. 18, 1816, at Fort St. George.
....	....	....	....	Killed — 1793, before Pondicherry.
....	....	....	....	Not to be traced.
....	....	....	....	Died April 7, 1803.
....	....	....	....	Retired April 8, 1812.
....	....	....	....	Died Sep. 12, 1804.
....	....	....	....	Not to be traced.
....	....	....	....	Not to be traced.
....	....	....	....	Died May 16, 1799.
....	....	....	....	Retired March — 1801.
....	....	....	....	Died 1796.
Sep. 26, 1811	Commt. May 1, 1824 Colonel May 27, 1825	Jan. 10, 1837	....	
....	....	....	....	Died Aug. 24, 1801.
....	....	....	....	Died April 13, 1825, at Madras.
....	....	....	....	Struck off, Dec. 17, 1799.
....	....	....	....	Pensioned 1787. Died Feb. 22, 1808.
June 17, 1800	....	....	....	Lost Mar. 14, 1809, in the "Lady Jane Dundas."
....	....	....	....	Killed at the siege of Pand lamcourchy, Sep. 5, 1779.
....	....	....	....	Died June 6, 1825, on board the "Portland," passage to England.
Mar. 5, 1826	Brevet, June 18, 1831	....	....	Died May 13, 1837, at Nackry Kul.
....	....	....	....	Killed May 2, 1799.
....	....	....	....	Died June 24, 1814, at Samalcottah.
....	....	....	....	Died Nov. 25, 1799.
Sep. 1, 1818	....	....	....	Retired Feb. 24, 1824, in England.
....	....	....	....	Died Nov. 12, 1801.
....	....	....	....	Died June 6, 1809, at Quilon.
....	....	....	....	Died Aug. 20, 1805.
....	....	....	....	Died Dec. 3, 1809, at Bellary.
....	....	....	....	Died Aug. 1, 1813, at Bangalore.
Feb. 25, 1824	June 5, 1829	....	....	Invalided Oct. 9, 1810. Died Sep. 15, 1830, at Ramnad.
....	....	....	....	
May 1, 1824	Brevet, June 5, 1829	....	....	
May 1, 1824	May 15, 1834	....	....	
....	....	....	....	Died Sep. 11, 1804, at Poonah.
....	....	....	....	Died July 18, 1801, at sea.
....	....	....	....	Invalided Dec. 9, 1819, in India. Died Sep. 18, 1823, at Negapatam.
July 26, 1824	....	....	....	Retired Jan. 28, 1828, in England.
....	....	....	....	Died Sep. 11, 1804, in camp, near Chuilgaum.
....	....	....	....	Died Nov. 14, 1818, at Mooltye.
....	....	....	....	Killed Sep. 16, 1815, in a duel, at the Cape of Good Hope.
....	....	....	....	Died June 6, 1803.
....	....	....	....	Died Aug. 30, 1805.
May 1, 1824	....	....	....	Died Oct. 10, 1833, at Palaveram.
....	....	....	....	Died Aug. 29, 1819, at Madras.
May 20, 1824	....	....	....	Killed Jan. 7, 1826, in action, at Pegu.
....	....	....	....	Resigned Jan. 28, 1807.

MADRAS.——F

MADRAS

NAMES.	Cadet.	Cornet, Ensign, or Second Lieutenant.	Lieutenant.	Captain.	Major.
Charlesworth, John Lee ..	1799	....	Dec. 15, 1800	April 6, 1810	....
Cantwell, Joseph	,,	....	....	....	....
Court, Major H.—*artillery*	,,	....	Mar. 7, 1800	May 6, 1809	Brevet June. 4, 1814.
Cox, James	,,	....	Dec. 15, 1800	....	....
Cadell George............	,,	....	Dec. 15, 1800	Oct. 2, 1808	Aug. 1, 1817
Cole, Philip..............	,,	....	Dec. 15, 1800	....	....
Collier, George	,,	....	....	....	....
Carnac, Sir, James R. Bart.*	,,	....	July 15, 1800	Mar. 2, 1810	Mar. 14, 1822
Cumming, Alexander......	,,	....	July 15, 1800	Dec. 17, 1813	....
Cox, Robert Kilbye	1800	....	July 20, 1801	....	....
Close, Robert—*cavalry*....	,,	Sep. 29, 1801	May 1, 1804	Dec. 27, 1816	Aug. 28, 1821
Collins, Charles James	,,	....	July 20, 1801	....	....
Cracroft, Charles..........	,,	....	July 20, 1801	Mar. 19, 1817	Nov. 17, 1825
Chamberlain, Michael	,,	....	July 20, 1801	....	....
Church, William Lowther..	,,	....	April 8, 1803	Apr. 30, 1814	....
Carnegie, Patrick	,,	....	July 20, 1801	....	....
Cooper, Leonard	,,	....	May 8, 1803	Sep. 1, 1818	Aug. 10, 1824
Combe, Boyce	,,	....	July 20, 1801	May 31, 1816	....
Coote, John..............	,,	....	July 20, 1801	....	....
Cregoe, Frind	,,	....	July 20, 1801	June 18, 1815	....
Chambers, Thomas........	,,	....	May 5, 1802	Jan. 5, 1814	....
Cubbon, Mark............	,,	....	July 20, 1801	April 6, 1816	Nov. 23, 1823
Cleaveland, T. S.—*artillery*	,,	....	Mar. 7, 1800	....	....
Cuningham, Charles	,,	....	July 20, 1801	June 14, 1815	....
Campbell, Wm. C.—*cavalry*	,,	....	Aug. 11, 1801	Mar. 26, 1808	....
Chauvel, James S.	,,	....	July 20, 1801	May 31, 1816	Dec. 6, 1824
Coane, Montgomery	,,	....	July 20, 1801	....	....
Carter, Daniel Jellicoe	,,	....	....	....	....
Campbell, John—*cavalry* ..	1802	....	Oct. 15, 1804	Sep. 1, 1818	....
Cole, John Shenton	,,	....	Jan. 19, 1804	....	....
Cox, Thomas	,,	....	Jan. 19, 1804	June 12, 1819	Jan. 23, 1830
Carbery, Wm. Coleman	,,	....	Nov. 16, 1803	....	....
Cooper, Henry Massey	,,	....	Nov. 16, 1803	Sep. 17, 1815	....
Cope, Henry Jonathan	,,	....	Nov. 10, 1803	....	....
Crewe, Richard	,,	....	Sep. 13, 1804	Jan. 27, 1819	Sep. 5, 1827
Cunningham, Henry P.....	,,	....	Mar. 11, 1804	Feb. 4, 1816	Dec. 24, 1831
Chillingworth, Joseph	,,	....	May 9, 1804	....	....
Conway, Henry	,,	Apr. 17, 1803	May 26, 1804	Nov. 29, 1819	....
Chatfield, Wm.—*cavalry* ..	,,	....	Aug. 14, 1805	Oct. 31, 1818	....
Chambers, William Rodney	,,	....	Sep. 21, 1804	....	....
Cameron, Patrick—*cavalry*	,,	....	Oct. 28, 1804	Jan. 13, 1816	Sep. 1, 1818
Collings, Elias	,,	....	Sep. 21, 1804	....	....
Clubley, James K.—*cavalry*	1803	Sep. 24, 1804	Sep. 3, 1812	Sep. 1, 1818	Mar. 12, 1826
Crowther, Robt.—*cavalry* .	,,	July 31, 1804	Sep. 10, 1808	Brevet 1818	....
Cooch, Robert............	,,	....	Sep. 21, 1804	....	....
Chavassee, William	,,	....	Sep. 21, 1804	....	....
Cullen, William—*artillery*	,,	....	June 21, 1803	May 26, 1809	May 1, 1824

* Chosen Director of the East India Company March 7, 1837.

PRESIDENCY.

Lieut.-Colonel.	Colonel.	Major-General.	Lieut.-General.	Date of Resignation, Retirement, or Death.
....	....	....	....	Died Dec. 24, 1820, in camp at Peddapore.
....	....	....	....	Died April 6, 1802.
....	....	....	....	Retired May 25, 1819.
....	....	....	....	Died April 12, 1805.
Apr. 23, 1824	....	....	....	Retired Sep. 4, 1827, in India.
....	....	....	....	Died April 30, 1802.
....	....	....	....	Died May 19, 1801.
....	....	....	....	Retired Apr. 29, 1822.
....	....	....	....	Died June 30, 1824, at Rangoon.
....	....	....	....	Resigned Mar. 4, 1808.
....	....	....	....	Retired June 5, 1826, in England.
....	....	....	....	Died Dec. 6, 1804.
....	....	....	....	Died Oct. 2, 1826.
....	....	....	....	Resigned Oct. 14, 1804.
....	....	....	....	Died April 24, 1821, at Seringapatam.
....	....	....	....	Resigned June 3, 1806.
Feb. 18, 1830	....	....	....	Retired Feb. 9, 1834, in India.
....	....	....	....	Retired Feb. 14, 1825, in England.
....	....	....	....	Died March 23, 1805.
....	....	....	....	Retired May 30, 1816, in England.
....	....	....	....	Died Jan. 19, 1824, at Cannanore.
Apr. 22, 1826	Brevet June 18, 1831	....	....	
....	....	....	....	Not to be traced.
....	....	....	....	Retired March 26, 1816, in England.
....	....	....	....	Died on his passage to England, May 19, 1813.
....	....	....	....	Retired Feb. 20, 1826, in India.
....	....	....	....	Died June 11, 1806, at Ganjam.
....	....	....	....	Died July 21, 1802, at Cuddalore.
....	....	....	....	Retired May 12, 1828, in England.
....	....	....	....	Died June 28, 1809, at Cannanore.
Dec. 6, 1834	....	....	....	
....	....	....	....	Died Dec. 24, 1815, at Ternate.
....	....	....	....	Died Feb. 16, 1824, at Cannanore.
....	....	....	....	Died May 26, 1805.
May 31, 1833	....	....	....	Died March 31, 1836, at Octacamund.
Nov. 13, 1836	....	....	....	
....	....	....	....	Died Sep. 15, 1806, at Seringapatam.
....	....	....	....	Retired Jan. 6, 1828, in England.
....	....	....	....	Died Aug. 10, 1820, at Kalladjee.
....	....	....	....	Resigned Sep. 28, 1808.
May 1, 1824	Brevet June 5, 1829	....	....	
....	....	....	....	Died April 4, 1818, at Secunderabad.
....	....	....	....	{ Invalided Aug. 1, 1828, in India. Retired July 31, 1833, in England.
....	....	....	....	Dismissed Feb. 28, 1820, in India.
....	....	....	....	Died Dec. 15, 1805, at Seringapatam.
....	....	....	....	{ Died July 20, 1814, on his journey from Mosul to Bagdad.
Jan. 29, 1828	....	....	....	

MADRAS

NAMES.	Cadet.	Cornet, Ensign, or Second Lieutenant.	Lieutenant.	Captain.	Major.
Cutcliffe, Theodore Charles	1803	…………	Sep. 21, 1804	…………	…………
Chambers, Thomas Auriol	,,	…………	Sep. 21, 1804	…………	…………
Castell, Richard John	1804	…………	July 25, 1805	…………	…………
Colberg, Ambrose Herue	,,	…………	July 17, 1805	Sep. 1, 1818	…………
Coyle, Henry	,,	…………	July 17, 1805	May 18, 1820	Feb. 11, 1835
Cooke, Arthur	,,	…………	July 17, 1805	April 8, 1818	May 5, 1825
Colman, Charles	,,	…………	July 17, 1805	…………	…………
Clode, Thomas	,,	…………	Sep. 10, 1805	…………	…………
Crisp, John Henry	,,	…………	July 17, 1805	June 30, 1821	Sep. 2, 1832
Chambers, Augustus	,,	…………	Jan. 3, 1806	…………	…………
Crichton, John	,,	…………	Apr. 24, 1806	Brevet 1819.	…………
Cecil, Isaiah	,,	…………	July 17, 1805	…………	…………
Cadogan, Edward	,,	…………	Sep. 24, 1805	Feb. 19, 1821	July 7, 1827
Crowe, Frederick	,,	…………	July 19, 1807	July 18, 1821	…………
Cotton, Richard Thomas	,,	…………	Jan. 1, 1807	…………	…………
Croasdaile, H. G. Starkey	1805	…………	Feb. 9, 1807	Brevet, Mar. 27, 1821	…………
Carmichael Thomas	,,	…………	May 23, 1806	…………	…………
Crichton, Thomas	,,	…………	Dec. 9, 1807	Apr. 8, 1822	…………
Cushney, James Forbes	,,	…………	Jan. 1, 1807	…………	…………
Cowan, Alexander	,,	…………	July 2, 1806	…………	…………
Colebrooke, John George	,,	July 27, 1806	…………	…………	…………
Christian, Brabazon	,,	…………	…………	…………	…………
Connor, Peter	,,	…………	Aug. 20, 1807	…………	…………
Cameron, John (52 N. J.)	,,	June 27, 1806	Mar. 18, 1808	May 20, 1824	June 5, 1837
Condell, Joseph A.	,,	June 27, 1806	June 20, 1811	July 10, 1823	…………
Chase, Morgan C.--*cavalry*	,,	Jan. 3, 1807	Sep. 1, 1818	June 28, 1824	Feb. 15, 1835
Crokat, James	,,	June 27, 1806	Aug. 22, 1808	Dec. 25, 1823	…………
Carr, John	,,	June 27, 1806	…………	…………	…………
Calvert, Robert	,,	June 27, 1806	Feb. 8, 1809	…………	…………
Cole George	,,	…………	…………	…………	…………
Cursham, John	,,	June 27, 1806	Mar. 18, 1809	May 29, 1822	…………
Casey, Thomas	,,	…………	Aug. 3, 1808	…………	…………
Crowther, Carlos	,,	June 27, 1806	Dec. 6, 1812	…………	…………
Crooke, George William	,,	…………	…………	…………	…………
Creswell, Estcourt	,,	…………	…………	…………	…………
Cumming, John	1806	July 3, 1807	Aug. 19, 1810	…………	…………
Clarke, Edward	,,	July 3, 1807	Feb. 11, 1811	…………	…………
Colebrook, Robert	,,	July 3, 1807	…………	…………	…………
Christie, Braithwaite	,,	…………	…………	…………	…………
Carwardine, Robert Wale	,,	Apr. 4, 1808	…………	…………	…………
Cousens, Richard	,,	Sep. 18, 1807	Jan. 29, 1810	May 1, 1824	…………
Craster, Edmund	,,	July 3, 1807	Oct. 24, 1809	Jan. 1, 1820	June 6, 1833
Charlesworth, Charles	,,	Aug. 19, 1808	…………	…………	…………
Cazalet, Henry	,,	July 5, 1808	June 1, 1814	May 1, 1824	…………
Clubbe, Thomas	,,	July 3, 1807	…………	…………	…………
Chambers, Charles	,,	July 3, 1807	Apr. 19, 1812	…………	…………
Cleland, James	,,	July 5, 1808	…………	…………	…………

PRESIDENCY.

Lieut.-Colonel.	Colonel.	Major-General.	Lieut.-General.	Date of Resignation, Retirement, or Death.
				Invalided Nov. 30, 1816, in India. Pensioned from Nov. 5, 1825, in England.
				Pensioned April 19, 1811, in India.
				Resigned Sep. 10, 1806.
				Died Oct. 15, 1827, at Chunapatam.
				Retired May 25, 1835.
April 5, 1831				
				Killed Dec. 21, 1817, in action.
				Died June 28, 1812, at Banka.
				Invalided April 1, 1833, in India.
				Died Feb. 7, 1816, at Columbo.
				Died July 31, 1823, at Wallajahbad.
				Invalided Dec. 13, 1813; died July 12, 1827, at Vizagapatam.
May 30, 1833				
				Died July 9, 1826, at Masulipatam.
				Died April 11, 1810.
				Retired June 19, 1822.
				Died June 21, 1819, in London.
				Died Nov. 1, 1827, at Paulgautcherry.
				Died May 1, 1808, at Wallajahbad.
				Resigned Feb. 22, 1821, in England.
				Died March 9, 1809, at Hydrabad.
				Resigned Oct. 9, 1807.
				Died April 29, 1821.
				Invalided Jan. 10, 1832, in India.
				Retired Nov. 9, 1835.
				Died Aug. 28, 1829, on board the "General Palmer," on passage to England.
				Died Jan. 9, 1809, at Terrakerry.
				Died Dec. 4, 1824, in camp, at Naudair.
				Resigned March 10, 1807.
				Killed Jan. 11, 1826, in action, at St. Setoun.
				Died Dec. 8, 1822, at Chittledroog.
				Admitted Pensioner Aug. 7, 1817, on Lord Clive's Fund.
				Resigned Sep. 8, 1807.
				Resigned July 7, 1807.
				Died Sep. 26, 1813, at Vizianagrum.
				Killed Nov. 27, 1817, in action, near Nagpoor.
				Died May 31, 1815.
				Dismissed May 12, 1809, having obtained his appointment by improper means.
				Died — 1813.
				Died May 24, 1831, at Masulipatam.
				Died Oct. 20, 1809, at Bangalore.
				Died Nov. 13, 1825, in camp, at
				Resigned March 10, 1809. [Jaulnah.
				Died Oct. 21, 1814.
				Died April 9, 1809, at Seringapatam.

MADRAS

NAMES.	Cadet.	Cornet, Ensign, or Second Lieutenant.	Lieutenant.	Captain.	Major.
Clarke, Marshall	1807	Aug. 27, 1808	Apr. 24, 1811		
Coxe, George	„	Mar. 10, 1809			
Carter, Henry	„	Dec. 10, 1808	Nov. 13, 1813		
Cleveland, John Wheeler	„	Sep. 29, 1808	Nov. 17, 1810	Nov. 13, 1823	April 5, 1831
Cocke, Richard	„	Mar. 18, 1809	May 9, 1812	Aug. 7, 1824	
Chrichton, Thos. Alexander	„	Nov. 16, 1809	May 24, 1814		
Chrichton, A. C.—*artillery*	„	Jan. 12, 1809	Aug. 25, 1810		
Campbell, Alexander	„	Oct. 10, 1809	May 21, 1814		
Corbet, Patrick	„	May 27, 1809	Apr. 16, 1812	May 1, 1824	April 3, 1837
Clemons, James	„	Mar. 18, 1809	June 9, 1817	Sep. 23, 1823	
Cuxton, Richard	„	Dec. 14, 1809	Oct. 18, 1812	Nov. 19, 1824	
Curry, John Gilmore	„	Mar. 7, 1810			
Crawford, Arch.—*artillery*	1808	Jan. 12, 1809	May 26, 1809	Nov. 1, 1819	Aug. 8, 1830
Chadwick, William	„				
Campbell, A. M.—*cavalry*	„	Sep. 7, 1811	Sep. 1, 1818	Sep. 22, 1830	
Croft, Samuel—*cavalry*	„	Nov. 9, 1812			
Coventry, John—*engineers*	1809	July 7, 1810	Feb. 8, 1815		
Cuningham, William	„	June 29, 1810	Oct. 21, 1815	Oct. 11, 1828	
Calder, Alexander	„	Dec. 19, 1810	Dec. 25, 1815	Aug. 15, 1824	Mar. 27, 1832
Chauvel, Thomas Arthur	1810	Mar. 30, 1811	Jan. 24, 1817	June 18, 1825	
Cookson, Christ.—*cavalry*	„	Nov. 9, 1812			
Conran, George—*artillery*	„	July 27, 1811	May 19, 1814	May 21, 1823	May 1, 1833
Campbell, Edward Charles	„	June 27, 1811	Dec. 1, 1816		
Cosnahan, James Mark	„	June 17, 1811			
Coull, Alex. D.—*artillery*	„	July 27, 1811	Sep. 21, 1818		
Currie, James	„				
Cooke, Richard	„	Dec. 2, 1811	Oct. 22, 1814		
Crowther, Lewis	„		Jan. 15, 1813		
Chisholm, John—*artillery*	1811	June 11, 1812	Sep. 1, 1818	July 26, 1824	
Chisholm, Wm.—*artillery*	„	June 11, 1812			
Carter, R. Thomas Hannah	„	June 11, 1812			
Corbould, John Warren	„	June 11, 1812	Nov. 28, 1817		
Claridge, Thomas Michael	1812	July 6, 1813	Dec. 1, 1816	July 10, 1826	May 24, 1832
Clemons, Thomas	„	July 6, 1813	June 9, 1817		
Cussans, Thomas—*artillery*	1813	July 4, 1814	Sep. 1, 1818		
Carew, Wm. S.—*artillery*	1816	June 26, 1817	Sep. 19, 1819	Mar. 14, 1829	
Carruthers, W. Carpenter	„		April 5, 1818		
Cotton, H. C.—*engineers*	„	Dec. 5, 1817	Dec. 9, 1821	May 21, 1825	
Campbell, Sir J. N. Robert, K.C.H., K.L.S.—*cavalry*	1817		Sep. 1, 1818	Dec. 8, 1826	
Clemons, John Samuel	„		June 4, 1818		
Charleton, Wm. Edward	„		June 4, 1818		
Clarke, Augustus	„		Sep. 15, 1818	Dec. 21, 1829	
Campbell, J. C. Harris	„		June 4, 1818	May 26, 1829	
Campbell, Robert Calder	„		Oct. 2, 1818	Oct. 3, 1826	Apr. 28, 1836
Chauvel, Charles George	„		July 10, 1818	May 18, 1832	
Cotton, C. Wm.—*cavalry*	„	June 3, 1818	Dec. 15, 1819		
Cheape, George—*cavalry*	„	June 3, 1818	Dec. 8, 1819		

PRESIDENCY.

Lieut.-Colonel.	Colonel.	Major General	Lieut.-General.	Date of Resignation, Retirement, or Death.
. . . .	. . . .	. . . .	. . . .	Retired Sep. 30, 1823, in England.
. . . .	. . . .	. . . .	. . . .	Resigned Jan. 21, 1815, in India.
. . . .	. . . .	. . . .	. . . .	{ Invalided June 1, 1817. Died June 6, 1818 at Sankerrydroog.
May 11, 1836	. . . .	. . . .	. . . .	
. . . .	. . . .	. . . .	. . . .	Died Aug. 24, 1826, at Madras.
. . . .	. . . .	. . . .	. . . .	{ Died Feb. 18, 1823, on board the "Catharine," at Sea.
. . . .	. . . .	. . . .	. . . .	Pensioned on Lord Clive's Fund, May 18, 1814.
. . . .	. . . .	. . . .	. . . .	Died Nov. 19, 1819, at Ryacottah.
. . . .	. . . .	. . . .	. . . .	Died Dec. 8, 1833, in Camp near Bannewar.
. . . .	. . . .	. . . .	. . . .	Died Oct. 7, 1829, at Tavoy.
. . . .	. . . .	. . . .	. . . .	Struck off in England.
. . . .	. . . .	. . . .	. . . .	Resigned Oct. 24, 1809.
. . . .	. . . .	. . . .	. . . .	{ Died at Arnee, from a fall from his horse, Dec. 30, 1813.
. . . .	. . . .	. . . .	. . . .	Died Dec. 8, 1821, at Masulipatam.
. . . .	. . . .	. . . .	. . . .	Invalided in India.
. . . .	. . . .	. . . .	. . . .	Resigned Sep. 11, 1818, in England.
. . . .	. . . .	. . . .	. . . .	Died Dec. 25, 1820, at Taggapet.
. . . .	. . . .	. . . .	. . . .	Died Sep. 11, 1812.
. . . .	. . . .	. . . .	. . . .	Died Nov. 5, 1818, at Masulipatam.
. . . .	. . . .	. . . .	. . . .	Resigned Jan. 14, 1812, in India.
. . . .	. . . .	. . . .	. . . .	Died Oct. 22, 1821, at Nellore.
. . . .	. . . .	. . . .	. . . .	{ Invalided Sep. 12, 1816, in India. Died Aug. 26, 1816, at Berhampore.
. . . .	. . . .	. . . .	. . . .	Killed in action Jan. 1, 1818, near Seroor
. . . .	. . . .	. . . .	. . . .	Died Sep. 10, 1813, at Madras.
. . . .	. . . .	. . . .	. . . .	Struck off July 7, 1820.
. . . .	. . . .	. . . .	. . . .	Died April 28, 1836, at Ellore.
. . . .	. . . .	. . . .	. . . .	Died at Rangoon, Oct. 15, 1824.
. . . .	. . . .	. . . .	. . . .	Struck off Jan. 23, 1823, in England.
. . . .	. . . .	. . . .	. . . .	Died June 9, 1830, in Devonshire.
. . . .	. . . .	. . . .	. . . .	{ Invalided Jan. 3, 1826, in India. Died May 2, 1827, at Rayacottah.
. . . .	. . . .	. . . .	. . . .	{ Died at sea, Oct. 20, 1824, on his passage to Calcutta from Rangoon.
. . . .	. . . .	. . . .	. . . .	Died Dec. 19, 1819, at Mhow
. . . .	. . . .	. . . .	. . . .	Invalided July 12, 1831, in India.
. . . .	. . . .	. . . .	. . . .	Died Nov. 15, 1821, at Sholapore.
. . . .	. . . .	. . . .	. . . .	Died June 7, 1825, at Arcot.

MADRAS

NAMES.	Cadet.	Cornet, Ensign, or Second Lieutenant.	Lieutenant.	Captain.	Major.
Coffin, Isaac Campbell....	1817	....	Nov. 9, 1818	July 26, 1828	....
Currie, Benjamin Harris ..	,,	....	Oct. 31, 1818	....	....
Chisholme, Archibald......	,,	....	Oct. 31, 1818	April 8, 1833	....
Cockburne, William	,,	....	Dec. 30, 1818	....	....
Croft, Wm. Thorney......	,,	....	June 13, 1819	....	....
Calvert, John Teer........	,,	....	June 13, 1819	....	....
Cameron, Thos. Macknight	,,	....	June 13, 1819	June 19, 1831	....
Clendon, Thomas	,,	....	June 13, 1819	....	....
Clayhills, George Dunbar..	,,	....	June 13, 1819	June 19, 1828	....
Coxe, Wm. Boucher	1818	....	June 13, 1819	Nov. 21, 1826	....
Campbell, James..........	,,	....	June 13, 1819	July 7, 1827	Feb. 14, 1836
Clarke, Edward Thomas ..	,,	....	June 13, 1819	Mar. 3, 1830	....
Campbell, Robert Nutter..	,,	....	June 13, 1819	Sep. 6, 1829	....
Cotton, William	,,	....	June 13, 1819	May 24, 1828	....
Charleton, Richard John ..	1819	....	June 13, 1819	....	....
Chauvel, John Edward....	,,	....	June 13, 1819	Mar. 7, 1829	....
Carter, Robert Cooke	,,	....	June 13, 1819	....	....
Clemons, Clement	,,	....	April 7, 1820	....	....
Clough, John	,,	....	April 7, 1820	Jan. 10, 1829	....
Cocker, Frederick W.	,,	....	April 7, 1820	....	....
Cook, Philip	,,	...1819....	April 7, 1820	....	....
Claridge, Thomas S.	,,	....	Feb. 19, 1821	June 21, 1826	....
Campbell, Archibald Alex.	,,	....	April 7, 1820	....	....
Campbell, John	,,	....	April 7, 1820	Jan. 23, 1830	....
Codrington, Robert	,,	....	April 7, 1820	May 31, 1833	....
Cuppage, William	,,	....	July 13, 1820	Apr. 10, 1837	....
Chalon, Thomas Burnard..	,,	....	Feb. 23, 1822	....	....
Carroll, Coote Alexander..	,,	....	May 5, 1821	....	....
Campbell, John Archibald	,,	April 6, 1820	July 14, 1822	....	....
Carpenter, Thos. David....	,,	....	Feb. 23, 1821	Sep. 12, 1829	....
Coningham, Hen.—*cavalry*	,,	April 6, 1820	Aug. 28, 1821	Nov. 30, 1828	....
Colebrooke, J. Ulrick	,,	April 6, 1820	Aug. 20, 1821	....	....
Currie, Henry	,,	April 6, 1820	Feb. 21, 1823	....	....
Cragie, William	,,	....	July 17, 1821	Nov. 26, 1834	....
Church, Charles	,,	April 6, 1820	Feb. 25, 1824	....	....
Campbell, M.—*artillery* ..	,,	June 16, 1820	June 8, 1821	June 10, 1830	....
Cameron, Alex. D.........	1820	April 6, 1820	Dec. 22, 1822	....	....
Cumberlege, B. W.—*cavalry*	,,	April 6, 1820	May 1, 1824	May 4, 1836	....
Chifney, A. R.—*cavalry* ..	,,	Feb. 13, 1821	....	....	....
Coventry, Andrew	,,	Feb. 13, 1821	May 1, 1824	Feb. 16, 1833	....
Cramer, John Henry......	,,	....	Mar. 8, 1825	Mar. 19, 1831	....
Carthew, Morden	,,	Feb. 13, 1821	Apr. 19, 1823	Brevet, Feb. 13, 1836	....
Cranston, William........	,,	....	Jan. 30, 1823	....	....
Chalmers, Fred. S. C.	,,	Feb. 13, 1821	Feb. 17, 1824	Brevet, Feb. 13, 1836	....
Campbell, Alexander......	,,	Feb. 13, 1821	....	....	....
Chambers, Philip	,,	Feb. 19, 1821	Apr. 23, 1823	June 6, 1831	....
Cotton, A. T.—*engineers* ..	,,	....	May 1, 1824	June 5, 1829	....

PRESIDENCY.

40—41

Lieut.-Colonel.	Colonel.	Major-General.	Lieut.-General.	Date of Resignation, Retirement, or Death.
				Died June 20, 1826, on passage from Rangoon.
				Died Oct. 13, 1821, at Fort St. George.
				{ Invalided Dec. 5, 1826, in India. Retired June 11, 1832, in England.
				Died July 23, 1821, in Camp, at Maulligaum.
				Died June 26, 1826, at Belgaum.
				Resigned Aug 15, 1830, in India.
				Died Jan. — 1835.
				Died Sep. 11, 1826, at Masulipatam.
				Died May 30, 1831, at Shamul.
				Died Jan. 19, 1824, near Goa.
				Died Oct. 15, 1824, at Rangoon.
				{ Died Feb. 27, 1827, on board the "Eliza," off Augenweel Fort.
				Died Feb. 19, 1825, at Chittagong.
				Died Oct. 7, 1824, at Rangoon.
				Died Nov. 6, 1823, at Masulipatam.
				Died Mar. 24, 1825, at Madras.
				{ Died in 1828, on board the "Alfred," on passage to England.
				Died Nov. 7, 1831, at Royacottah.
				Died May 5, 1827, at Capperpaud.
				Died Dec. 4, 1831, on board the "York."
				{ Struck off, April 26, 1825, having been absent from India more than five years.
				Died July — 1822.
				Died June 14, 1825, at Courtullum.
				Died Mar. 20, 1822, at St. Thomas's Mount.

MADRAS.——G

MADRAS

NAMES.	Cadet.	Cornet, Ensign, or Second Lieutenant.	Lieutenant.	Captain.	Major.
Clarke, Francis Anthony ..	1820	....	May 6, 1824	Brevet Feb. 13, 1836.	....
Carmichael, Robert Grant	,,	Feb. 13, 1821	June 17, 1824	Brevet Feb. 13, 1836.	....
Campbell, Henry Foster ..	1821	....	....	....	....
Clifford, William Henry ..	,,	Apr. 27, 1822	Aug. 15, 1824	....	....
Cameron, George Paulett..	,,	Apr. 27, 1822	Nov. 14, 1825	....	....
Considine, Danl. Hifferman	,,	Apr. 27, 1822	Apr. 24, 1826	....	....
Coxe, Robert Taylor	,,	Apr. 27, 1822	Aug. 31, 1824	....	....
Crozier, Francis Rawson ..	,,	Apr. 27, 1822	Oct. 13, 1824	April 1, 1835	....
Carr, Samuel	,,	Apr. 27, 1822	Nov. 26, 1824	....	....
Cole, Charles James	1822	Apr. 27, 1822	Sep. 8, 1826	....	....
Clay, Herbert Pelham	,,	May 2, 1823	....	....	....
Coles, Thomas	,,	May 2, 1823	Feb. 20, 1825	....	....
Clutterbuck, Edward	,,	May 2, 1823	June 17, 1824	Brevet Feb. 13, 1836.	....
Clerk, Frederick Joseph ..	1823	May 14, 1824	Sep. 20, 1826	Mar. 11, 1832	....
Cowie, Edward	,,	....	Aug. 6, 1825	July 20, 1836	....
Cotes, William Gee	,,	May 14, 1824	....	....	....
Campbell, John (21 N. I.)	,,	May 14, 1824	April 7, 1835	....	....
Chinnery, Wm. Charles ..	,,	May 14, 1824	Sep. 8, 1826	Apr. 10, 1836	....
Cuppage, Adam	,,	May 14, 1824	Sep. 8, 1826	....	....
Congden, John Henry B...	,,	May 14, 1824	June 29, 1825	Mar. 29, 1835	....
Cross, William	,,	May 14, 1824	May 1, 1826	....	....
Croggon, Jn. W.—*artillery*	,,	Dec. 18, 1823	May 1, 1824	....	....
Cooke, William	,,	....	July 21, 1825	....	....
Clayhills, Charles	1824	May 6, 1825	June 21, 1826	....	....
Cottrell, Clemt. C.—*cavalry*	,,	May 6, 1825	July 29, 1826	....	....
Congdon, James Jos. Gold	,,	May 6, 1825	Apr. 18, 1827	....	....
Coles, James	,,	May 6, 1825	Feb. 10, 1828	....	....
Cameron, Jn. St. Vincent M.	,,	May 6, 1825	Sep. 29, 1826	....	....
Colbeck, Henry	,,	May 6, 1825	Aug. 1, 1831	....	....
Cosby, Charles A.	,,	Feb. 2, 1826	Sep. 8, 1826	June 2, 1837	....
Campbell, D. A.—*artillery*	1825	June 16, 1825	Dec. 2, 1825	....	....
Christie, Thomas Milligan .	,,	Jan. 8, 1826	Apr. 24, 1834	....	....
Church, John Alexander ..	,,	Jan. 8, 1826	Aug. 15, 1834	....	....
Cherry, Peter T.—*cavalry* .	,,	Jan. 8, 1826	Feb. 26, 1829	....	....
Cazalet, William W.	,,	..1827....	....	....	....
Cooke, Thomas William ..	,,	....	Oct. 31, 1828	....	....
Cannan, James	,,	Jan. 8, 1826	....	....	....
Coates, John Wilson	,,	Jan. 8, 1826	Feb. 3, 1832	....	....
Cooke, William Fothergill .	,,	Jan. 8, 1826	....	....	....
Cantis, William	,,	Jan. 8, 1826	Jan. 1, 1829	....	....
Campbell, John (38 N. I.)..	,,	Jan. 8, 1826	June 15, 1834	....	....
Cottrell, Lucius F.—*cavalry*	,,	Jan. 21, 1828	Apr. 13, 1833	....	....
Charteris, John Maxwell ..	,,	Jan. 8, 1826	Oct. 28, 1833	....	....
Childers, George Leonard..	,,	Jan. 8, 1826	Jan. 7, 1833	....	....
Clarke, Geo. Bartholomew	,,	Jan. 8, 1826	....	....	....
Carr, George	,,	Jan. 8, 1826	Oct. 10, 1836	....	....
Curre, John..............	1826	Jan. 8, 1826	Nov. 24, 1827	....	....

PRESIDENCY.

Lieut.-Colonel.	Colonel.	Major General.	Lieut.-General.	Date of Resignation, Retirement, or Death.
....	....	....	....	
....	....	....	....	
....	....	....	....	Died at Chicacole, Oct. 6, 1824.
....	....	....	....	Cashiered Aug. 18, 1828, in India.
....	....	....	....	
....	....	....	....	
....	....	....	....	Died Aug. 23, 1833, at Jaulnah.
....	....	....	....	
....	....	....	....	Died March 2, 1833, at Weybridge.
....	....	....	....	Died Feb. 2, 1832, at Madras.
....	....	....	....	Died Nov. 10, 1826, at Presidency.
....	....	....	....	
....	....	....	....	
....	....	....	....	
....	....	....	....	Died Oct. 31, 1825, in Bombay.
....	....	....	....	
....	....	....	....	
....	....	....	....	
....	....	....	....	
....	....	....	....	
....	....	....	....	Died Oct. 21, 1831, at Jaulnah.
....	....	....	....	Lost at sea, Oct. 10, 1836.
....	....	....	....	Invalided May 25, 1832, in India.
....	....	....	....	Died May 28, 1830, at Palaveram.
....	....	....	....	Died July 14, 1831, at Cuddapah.
....	....	....	....	Died Jan. 30, 1830, at Bombay.
....	....	....	....	
....	....	....	....	Died May 7, 1829, at Moulmein.
....	....	....	....	Died at Madras, Sep. 23, 1836.
....	....	....	....	
....	....	....	....	{ Relinquished his appointment in England, Oct. 10, 1827.
....	....	....	....	Died March 17, 1829, at Madura.
....	....	....	....	Resigned Feb. 18, 1833, in England.
....	....	....	....	
....	....	....	....	Died May 3, 1836, at Pisa, in Italy.
....	....	....	....	
....	....	....	....	Died Feb. 21, 1835.
....	....	....	....	Died March 3, 1829, at Veidaputty.
....	....	....	....	
....	....	....	....	Died April 12, 1833, at Vingottam.

G 2

MADRAS

NAMES.	Cadet.	Cornet, Ensign, or Second Lieutenant.	Lieutenant.	Captain.	Major.
Caruthers, David—*artillery*	1826	June 16, 1826	Sep. 1, 1831	....	....
Carter, Sherman John	,,	Jan. 8, 1826	Mar. 29, 1835	....	....
Cooke, C. John—*artillery* ..	,,	May 3, 1827	Oct. 14, 1831	....	....
Cotton, F. C.—*engineers* ..	,,	....	Dec. 17, 1825	....	....
Cannan, Robert	,,	Feb. 27, 1827	May 26, 1830	....	....
Coxwell, Joseph Atwell S.	,,	Jan. 5, 1828	May 27, 1834	....	....
Cotton, Edward Gutterson	,,	Oct. 21, 1827	Feb. 9, 1832	....	....
Compton, Charles Francis	,,	Nov. 10, 1827	Nov. 17, 1831	....	....
Crawford, John Albert	,,	Jan. 5, 1828	....	....	....
Christie, James	,,	Feb. 26, 1828	....	....	....
Campbell, James	,,	May 23, 1827	Dec. 21, 1834	....	....
Cotter, George S.—*artillery*	,,	June 15, 1827	May 23, 1832	....	....
Croft, S. William—*artillery*	,,	Dec. 15, 1826	Oct. 9, 1831	....	....
Church, William James ..	1827	July 19, 1828	Nov. 17, 1835	....	....
Cockburn, Archd. Keir	,,	Aug. 2, 1828	June 9, 1833	....	....
Cox, Edward Thomas	,,	Sep. 3, 1828	May 2, 1836	....	....
Collingridge, Samuel	,,	... 1828	....	....	....
Clarke, James W.	,,	Oct. 28, 1828	....	....	....
Congreve, Harry—*artillery*	,,	Dec. 13, 1827	Apr. 1, 1834	....	....
Campbell, Duncan Charles	,,	June 2, 1829	Oct. 31, 1835	....	....
Carden, W. McGrath	,,	June 2, 1829	....	....	....
Colt, John Hamilton	,,	June 2, 1829	....	....	....
Cotton, Robert	1828	Oct. 9, 1830	Feb. 14, 1833	....	....
Cooper, F. Yates—*cavalry*	,,	Mar. 28, 1829	Feb. 20, 1833	....	....
Carruthers, F. J.—*cavalry*	,,	May 7, 1829	May 13, 1837	....	....
Cooper, M. Beale	1829	Apr. 12, 1832	Apr. 3, 1837	....	....
Coffin, Sealright S.	,,	Apr. 12, 1832	... 1837	....	....
Cazalet, Peter Grenville ..	,,	May 16, 1832	Feb. 15, 1836	....	....
Caulfield, John—*artillery* ..	,,	May 28, 1834	....	....	....
Corfield, Septimus I.	1830	July 4, 1832	....	....	....
Conolly George Stuart	1831	....	....	....	....
Cumine, George—*cavalry*	,,	Jan. 2, 1833	May 3, 1836	....	....
Campbell, T. Hay—*artillery*	,,	June 22, 1836	....	....	....
Cotton, Wm. E. Prescott	,,	Nov. 24, 1832	Nov. 28, 1836	....	....
Chapman, R. H.—*engineers*	1832	Sep. 2, 1836	....	....	....
Crowe, Robert	,,	Feb. 24, 1833	....	....	....
Cooke, William John	,,	June 11, 1833	....	....	....
Crewe, Richard	,,	Dec. 13, 1833	Feb. 12, 1836	....	....
Cotton, John S.—*cavalry* ..	,,	Feb. 15, 1834	Jan. 17, 1837	....	....
Cook, Walter	1833	Feb. 15, 1834	Oct. 30, 1836	....	....
Cameron, John—*cavalry* ..	,,	Mar. 11, 1834	Feb. 24, 1836	....	....
Corsar, John H.—*cavalry* ..	,,	Mar. 1, 1834	....	....	....
Carr, George, 2 Rt.	,,	Dec. 13, 1833	April 3, 1836	....	....
Carter, Charles	1834	June 13, 1834	....	....	....
Chester, Robert	,,	June 13, 1834	Mar. 31, 1836	....	....
Case, C. H.	,,	Jan. 13, 1835	....	....	....
Cooke, C.	,,	Dec. 12, 1834	Feb. 14, 1836	....	....

PRESIDENCY.   44—45

Lieut.-Colonel.	Colonel.	Major General.	Lieut.-General.	Date of Resignation, Retirement, or Death.
....	....	....	....	Died June 4, 1836, at Kamptee.
....	....	....	....	
....	....	....	....	
....	....	....	....	
....	....	....	....	
....	....	....	....	
....	....	....	....	
....	....	....	....	
....	....	....	....	Dismissed Jan. 25, 1832, in India.
....	....	....	....	{ Pensioned April 2, 1831, on Lord Clive's Fund, in England.
....	....	....	....	
....	....	....	....	
....	....	....	....	
....	....	....	....	
....	....	....	....	
....	....	....	....	
....	....	....	....	Died Sep. 1, 1828, at the Isle of France.
....	....	....	....	Died April 20, 1833, at Kamptee.
....	....	....	....	
....	....	....	....	Killed May 15, 1836, at Vellore.
....	....	....	....	
....	....	....	....	Resigned Sep. 15, 1832, in England.
....	....	....	....	
....	....	....	....	
....	....	....	....	
....	....	....	....	
....	....	....	....	
....	....	....	....	
....	....	....	....	Died Aug. 28, 1832, at Madras.
....	....	....	....	
....	....	....	....	
....	....	....	....	Died Sep. 9, 1837, in England.
....	....	....	....	
....	....	....	....	
....	....	....	....	
....	....	....	....	
....	....	....	....	
....	....	....	....	
....	....	....	....	
....	....	....	....	
....	....	....	....	

MADRAS

NAMES.	Cadet.	Cornet, Ensign, or Second Lieutenant.	Lieutenant.	Captain.	Major.
Curtis, E. C.—*cavalry*	1834	Mar. 23, 1835	Apr. 20, 1837	....	....
Cooper, Richard	,,	Dec. 12, 1834	....	....	....
Cadell, J. G. S.—*cavalry* ..	,,	Feb. 24, 1835	....	....	....
Cadell, A. T.—*artillery*	,,	....	....	....	....
D					
Durand, John James	....	Apr. 15, 1763	Mar. 13, 1768	June 8, 1776	....
Dupont, John	....	....	July 31, 1770	Dec. 6, 1778	....
Dunwoody, Thomas	1769	Oct. 13, 1770	Nov. 1, 1774	Feb. 2, 1783	Aug. 6, 1794
Dawes, Nathaniel	,,	Nov. 13, 1770	Dec. 26, 1775	Nov. 2, 1783	....
Dalrymple, James	1770	Feb. 22, 1772	July 4, 1778	Nov. 2, 1783	Mar. 1, 1794
Doveton, Gabriel	1775	May 7, 1776	Nov. 9, 1780	Dec. 29, 1789	June 1, 1796
Dyce, Alexander..........	,,	Nov. 18, 1776	Nov. 25, 1780	Apr. 10, 1793	Aug. 18, 1797
Durand, John James	1776	April 2, 1778	Jan. 4, 1782	Feb. 17, 1794	Dec. 21, 1797
Desse, Peter C.	1777	May 10, 1778	Jan. 25, 1782	Oct. 3, 1794	Oct. 12, 1798
Dodds, James	1778	Apr. 17, 1779	Jan. 20, 1784	....	....
Darley, John	,,	May 3, 1779	May 20, 1784	June 1, 1796	June 17, 1800
Dallas, Peter	,,	May 29, 1779	Mar. 20, 1786	June 1, 1796	June 17, 1800
Dougherty, Foster O.	1779	Aug. 3, 1780	Apr. 17, 1786	....	....
Denton, Alexander	,,	Aug. 5, 1780	Apr. 17, 1786	June 1, 1796	....
Davidson, William........	,,	Aug. 11, 1780	Apr. 17, 1786	June 1, 1796	Feb. 6, 1801
Dowse, William	1781	Oct. 4, 1782	July 27, 1789	Oct. 12, 1798	Sep. 21, 1804
Dunbar, Robert	,,	Oct. 30, 1782	....	....	....
Davidson, George	1782	Apr. 10, 1783	....	....	....
Dingwall, William........	,,	May 22, 1783	....	....	....
Dickson, Joseph..........	,,	June 9, 1783	Aug. 21, 1790	Jan. 1, 1800	Sep. 18, 1807
Davidson, John—*artillery*	1779	Oct. 21, 1780	Oct. 13, 1781	....	....
Darke, Richard—*artillery*	1780	Jan. 2, 1783	Apr. 17, 1786	Apr. 28, 1797	....
Donaldson, C.—*artillery* ..	....	Mar. 8, 1784	May 19, 1789	Feb. 26, 1800	....
Darley, Henry—*cavalry* ..	1771	Sep. 9, 1773	....	Dec. 19, 1783	Feb. 19, 1788
Delmonte, B.—*cavalry*	....	Nov. 25, 1784	Feb. 2, 1786	Brevet, Jan. 7, 1796	....
Deas, Alexander—*cavalry*	1780	June 16, 1785	Oct. 23, 1787	Sep. 4, 1799	May 20, 1801
Dunn, James—*cavalry*	,,	Dec. 1, 1785	Dec. 10, 1791	June 17, 1800	May 1, 1804
Doveton, Sir Jno. (G.C.B.)-*cavalry*	1782	Dec. 5, 1785	June 12, 1792	May 8, 1800	Sep. 2, 1801
Dallas, Charles—*cavalry* ..	....	Mar. 25, 1784	July 22, 1793	May 20, 1801	....
Darell, John	....	....	July 23, 1770	Aug. 3, 1778	....
Dallas, Sir T. (G. C. B.)-*cavalry*	1778	Apr. 25, 1778	Jan. 15, 1782	June 1, 1786	Dec. 18, 1794
Dalrymple, Simon	....	June 30, 1778	Jan. 2, 1782	Dec. 11, 1793	Nov. 29, 1797
Dighton, John	1778	Apr. 26, 1779	May 20, 1784	June 1, 1796	Feb. 14, 1800
Dunbar, William Duff	,,	Apr. 25, 1779	May 20, 1784	....	....
Dring, William	....	Aug. 4, 1779	....	....	....
Daniell, Fras. A...........	1792	June 16, 1793	June 6, 1799	Sep. 24, 1803	Feb. 15, 1805
Dalrymple, S. (C.B.)—*artillery*	1788	Aug. 8, 1789	Oct. 13, 1793	Sep. 26, 1801	July 4, 1807
Daly, M.—*artillery*	1791	Sep. 15, 1791	....	....	....
Davis, James	1790	June 20, 1791	June 6, 1793	....	....
Desborough, John Henry..	,,	July 5, 1791	Aug. 24, 1793	June 17, 1800	....
Dodd, Broughton	,,	July 13, 1791	Oct. 2, 1793	Jan. 23, 1802	June 13, 1808
D'Ormieux, Philip	,,	Sep. 3, 1791	Aug. 6, 1794	....	....

PRESIDENCY.

Lieut-Colonel.	Colonel.	Major-General.	Lieut.-General.	Date of Resignation, Retirement, or Death.
....	....	....	....	Died June 20, 1837, at Kamptee.
....	....	....	....	
....	....	....	....	
....	....	....	....	
July 22, 1786	....	....	....	{ Invalided Dec. 11, 1793. Died Dec. 31,1805, at Vizagapatam.
Sep. 24, 1790	....	....	....	Invalided Aug. 17, 1791. Died Sep. 28, 1807.
....	....	....	....	Died Aug. 4, 1795, at Vizagapatam.
....	....	....	....	Died 1791.
June 1, 1796	....	....	....	Died Dec. 9, 1800, at Hyderabad.
May 4, 1799	Oct. 25, 1809	Jan. 1, 1812	....	Died April 9, 1824, in London.
Aug. 18, 1799	Oct. 25, 1809	Jan. 1, 1812	May 27, 1825	Died Dec. 24, 1835, at Cheltenham.
Dec. 10, 1799	Oct. 25, 1809	Jan. 1, 1812	....	Died Dec. 24, 1822, at Fort St. George.
Aug. 27, 1800	....	....	....	Died Jan. 23, 1805.
....	....	....	....	Died Sep. 29, 1795. [Howe."
May 26, 1804	....	....	....	Died Apr. 3, 1808, on board the "Earl
Oct. 13, 1804	....	....	....	Died Jan. 26, 1806, at Seringapatam.
....	....	....	....	Died 1791.
....	....	....	....	Died April 17, 1799, at Samulcottah.
....	....	....	....	Dismissed Mar. 26, 1806, in England.
Apr. 8, 1808	June 4, 1814	....	....	Died June 27, 1814, at Bangalore.
....	....	....	....	Died June — 1789.
....	....	....	....	Died Dec. 4, 1799, at Masulipatam.
....	....	....	....	Not to be traced.
....	....	....	....	Died Jan. 23, 1808.
....	....	....	....	Died 1788, at Tanjore.
....	....	....	....	Retired 1798, on the Non-effective List.
....	....	....	....	Died June 20, 1803, at Seringapatam.
....	....	....	....	Resigned 1791.
....	....	....	....	Died Dec. 7, 1799.
May 1, 1804	....	....	....	Retired June 3, 1807.
Nov. 25, 1805	....	....	....	Retired Jan. 21, 1812.
Oct. 15, 1804	June 4, 1813	Aug. 12, 1819	Jan. 10, 1837	
....	....	....	....	Retired 1803.
....	....	....	....	Died 1789, in Europe.
May 7, 1799	Oct. 25, 1809	Jan. 1, 1812	May 27, 1825	
Dec. 10, 1799	....	....	....	Died Jan. 1, 1804.
Jan. 2, 1804	June 4, 1813	Aug. 12, 1819	Jan. 10, 1837	
....	....	....	....	Home, out of the Service, 1789.
....	....	....	....	Resigned 1788.
Jan. 1, 1812	....	....	....	Retired July 28, 1820.
Sep. 1, 1818	....	....	....	Died May 12, 1821, at Madras.
....	....	....	....	Died Nov.—1794. [1797.
....	....	....	....	Invalided Mar. 3, 1795. Died Sep. 13,
....	....	....	....	Died Oct. 10, 1804.
Apr. 30, 1814	....	....	....	{ Invalided July 31, 1817, in India. Retired Nov. 30, 1823, in England.
....	....	....	....	{ Killed Sep. 5, 1799, at the Siege of Pandalam Courchy.

MADRAS

NAMES.	Cadet.	Cornet, Ensign, or Second Lieutenant.	Lieutenant.	Captain.	Major.
Davidson, John	1791	Sep. 6, 1791	....	....	....
Davis, William, Senr.	1791	Oct. 1, 1791	Aug. 6, 1794	....	....
Davis, William, Junr.	....	Apr. 28, 1793	Aug. 6, 1794	Mar. 21, 1802	....
Douglas, Thomas	....	Oct. 22, 1770	Feb. 2, 1775	April 2, 1783	....
Doveton, W.—*engineers* ..	1792	Sep. 24, 1793	....	....	....
Deacon, Sir C. (K.C.B.)..	1793	....	April 2, 1795	Jan. 27, 1803	Mar. 25, 1807
Day, Henry	1794	Jan. 23, 1796	June 1, 1796	....	....
Davis, Edward F.	1795	Feb. 27, 1796	May 10, 1797	Sep. 21, 1804	....
Dillon, Joseph............	,,	Mar. 26, 1796	Nov. 29, 1797	May 9, 1804	....
Dymock, John	,,	Feb. 25, 1796	May 8, 1797	Sep. 21, 1804	Dec. 1, 1816
Duncan, James	1794	Jan. 17, 1796	June 1, 1796	May 1, 1804	....
Dandrige, Samuel—*cavalry*	1797	Nov. 1, 1798	Sep. 4, 1799	....	....
Dawson, Richard	1796	Aug. 23, 1797	Oct. 12, 1798	....	....
Dickson, W. (C.B.)—*cavalry*	1795	....	Sep. 4, 1799	June 27, 1804	Sep. 1, 1818
Dickson, Thomas	1796	Sep. 2, 1797	Oct. 12, 1798	....	....
Davidson, A. H.—*cavalry*..	,,	Nov. 1, 1798	Sep. 4, 1799	Feb. 15, 1805	Feb. 22, 1812
Duggan, T. Frederick	1797	July 25, 1798	Oct. 26, 1798	April 1, 1805	....
Doveton, J. (C.B.)—*cavalry*	,,	Oct. 31, 1798	Sep. 4, 1799	Nov. 25, 1805	Sep. 6, 1810
Davis, R. William	1795	Mar. 28, 1796	Nov. 29, 1797	Sep. 21, 1804	....
Darke, Thomas—*cavalry* ..	1797	....	Dec. 2, 1800	....	....
Dade, George—*cavalry*	1798	....	June 17, 1800	....	....
Dalrymple, Hugh	,,	July 7, 1801	May 1, 1804	....	....
Douglas, Thomas	,,	....	Jan. 21, 1800	June 18, 1807	....
Degravers, Henry	1799	....	Dec. 15, 1800	April 6, 1810	May 1, 1824
Davie, Peregrine	,,	....	Dec. 15, 1800	Apr. 16, 1812	....
Davie, Henry	,,	....	Dec. 15, 1800	....	....
Dalley, F. Charles	,,	....	....	....	....
Davis, Richard	,,	....	Dec. 15, 1800	Jan. 1, 1807	Jan. 27, 1819
Downes, Henry	,,	....	Dec. 15, 1800	April 6, 1810	....
Durand, Horace..........	1794	....	Nov. 29, 1797	Sep. 21, 1804	May 19, 1817
De Crez, John James	1800	....	Mar. 22, 1802	....	....
Dering, Charles	,,	....	July 20, 1801	Apr. 30, 1814	....
Denton, John	,,	....	April 6, 1802	....	....
Duncombe, John..........	,,	....	July 20, 1801	Jan. 29, 1815	....
Desveaux, Arthur	,,	....	July 20, 1801	....	....
Dalziel, John	,,	....	July 20, 1801	Jan. 8, 1816	Sep. 6, 1829
Dalgairns, Robert	,,	....	July 20, 1801	....	....
Darby, C. Barrett—*cavalry*	1802	....	May 23, 1807	Oct. 31, 1817	Dec. 3, 1820
Decarteret, Charles	,,	Apr. 17, 1803	June 1, 1804	June 13, 1816	....
Dawson, T. Walter	,,	....	Mar. 11, 1804	....	....
Duncan, Charles	,,	Jan. 14, 1804	Nov. 15, 1805	....	....
Dauvenant, Wm. Henry ..	,,	Apr. 17, 1803	Sep. 21, 1804	....	....
Donne, Charles	,,	Apr. 17, 1803	May 4, 1804	....	....
Douglas, A. Sholto	,,	Apr. 17, 1803	Sep. 21, 1804	....	....
Davenport, E. Ormis......	,,	Apr. 17, 1803	Sep. 21, 1804	....	....
Dunn, John..............	,,	....	Feb. 22, 1804	....	....
Delamain, T. L. H........	,,	....	Sep. 21, 1804	....	....

PRESIDENCY.

48—49

Lieut.-Colonel.	Colonel.	Major General.	Lieut.-General.	Date of Resignation, Retirement, or Death.
....	....	....	....	Not to be traced.
....	....	....	....	Died Dec. — 1795.
....	....	....	....	Died May 26, 1806.
....	....	....	....	Pensioned — 1787.
....	....	....	....	Died July 14, 1795, at Fort St. George.
Jan. 25, 1813	Commt. May 1, 1824. Col. June 5, 1829.	Jan. 10, 1837	....	
....	....	....	....	Died Sep. 1, 1802.
....	....	....	....	{ Dismissed by sentence of a General Court Martial, 1806.
....	....	....	....	Died April 18, 1805, in England.
....	....	....	....	Died Apr. 18, 1823, in camp, at Kulladjee.
....	....	....	....	Died May 22, 1804, at Noosum.
....	....	....	....	Died Nov. 15, 1800.
....	....	....	....	Died July 7, 1799, at Madras.
July 7, 1823	June 5, 1829	....	....	
....	....	....	....	Died July 16, 1805, in the Wynaad.
....	....	....	....	Died Mar. 31, 1812, on his journey to the Coast.
....	....	....	....	Died April 11, 1813, at Cork.
July 15, 1819	Commt. May 1, 1824 Col. June 5, 1829.	Jan. 10, 1837	....	
....	....	....	....	Died Dec. 16, 1805, at Ghooty.
....	....	....	....	Killed Dec. 26, 1816, in action.
....	....	....	....	Died Dec. 25, 1801.
....	....	....	....	Died Jan. 22, 1810, at Ballasore.
....	....	....	....	Died Oct. 21, 1819, at Fort St. George.
May 13, 1827	....	....	....	Invalided Oct. 8, 1830, in India.
....	....	....	....	Died May 1, 1824, at Madras.
....	....	....	....	{ Lost on board the "Jane, Duchess of Gordon," March 14, 1809.
....	....	....	....	Died Oct. 25, 1800, at Fort William.
....	....	....	....	{ Invalided Mar. 31, 1819. Pensioned Sep. 16, 1828, in India.
Sep. 8, 1826	....	....	....	Died July 3, 1832, at Courtallum.
Nov. 23, 1823	Mar. 3, 1830	....	....	Died Nov. 26, 1834, at Madras.
....	....	....	....	Died Sep. 10, 1804.
....	....	....	....	Died Feb. 14, 1821, at Seringapatam.
....	....	....	....	Died Dec. 14, 1806.
....	....	....	....	Retired April 10, 1821.
....	....	....	....	Pensioned Sep. 25, 1804.
....	....	....	....	Retired March 10, 1831, in India.
....	....	....	....	Died June 28, 1810.
Mar. 20, 1831	....	....	....	Died May 27, 1833, in England.
....	....	....	....	Died May 5, 1824, at Bellary.
....	....	....	....	Died May 18, 1812.
....	....	....	....	Died June 26, 1808, at Pondicherry.
....	....	....	....	Died April 23, 1811, at Banda.
....	....	....	....	{ Admitted a Pensioner on Lord Clive's Fund, Jan. 22, 1819, in England.
....	....	....	....	Died — 1813.
....	....	....	....	Died Oct. 30, 1815, at Negapatam.
....	....	....	....	Died Sep. 4, 1806.
....	....	....	....	Lost Mar. 14, 1809, in the "Bengal."

MADRAS

NAMES	Cadet.	Cornet, Ensign, or Second Lieutenant.	Lieutenant.	Captain.	Major.
Dynely, William	1803	....	Sep. 21, 1804	....	....
Dunmore, George	,,	....	Sep. 21, 1804	....	....
Dixon, Henry	,,	....	Sep. 21, 1804	....	....
Drew, George	,,	....	Sep. 21, 1804	Sep. 1, 1818	July 6, 1827
Duff, James	,,	....	Sep. 21, 1804	....	....
Domvile, Christopher	,,	....	Sep. 21, 1804	....	....
Dalgairns, James	,,	....	Sep. 21, 1804	Aug. 12, 1821	June 17, 1829
Duffin, Robt. W.—*cavalry*	,,	Mar. 19, 1805	....	....	....
Dumas, Henry	,,	....	Sep. 21, 1804	....	....
Driffield, E. J. A.—*artillery*	,,	July 18, 1804	Aug. 17, 1804	....	....
Donald, Thomas	1804	....	....	....	....
Dumaresq, William Cooke	,,	....	July 17, 1805	....	....
Dun, Charles Denis	,,	....	July 17, 1805	May 10, 1820	Aug. 8, 1833
Davidson, Michael H.	,,	....	Sep. 9, 1805	Mar. 3, 1824	....
Dunn, John	,,	....	....	....	....
Dun, George	1805	....	Jan. 15, 1807	....	....
Dore, G. Willoughby	,,	Jan. 1, 1807	Aug. 17, 1808	....	....
Dowton, Lewis	,,	Jan. 1, 1807	May 2, 1808	....	....
Denny, Arthur	,,	....	Nov. 23, 1806	....	....
Du Heaume, Edward	,,	June 27, 1806	Aug. 14, 1812	....	....
Dowden, Henry	,,	June 27, 1806	Sep. 4, 1808	May 5, 1821	....
Douglas, Hugh	,,	June 27, 1806	Oct. 27, 1808	....	....
Daker, William Jones	,,	June 27, 1806	Apr. 28, 1809	....	....
Dodgson, Joseph	,,	....	....	....	....
Dalyell, John	1806	July 3, 1807	....	....	....
Donaldson, David	,,	July 3, 1807	Apr. 5, 1810	....	....
Doveton, F. L.—*cavalry*	,,	Mar. 26, 1808	Oct. 21, 1813	Sep. 1, 1818	Aug. 2, 1828
Dixon, Henry	,,	July 3, 1807	Feb. 19, 1812	....	....
Dickinson, T. Gustavus	,,	....	....	....	....
Dodwell, George	,,	July 3, 1807	....	....	....
Dale, Thomas	,,	July 3, 1807	Nov. 7, 1810	....	....
Darby, William John	1807	Mar. 1, 1809	July 13, 1813	....	....
Dowden, Charles	,,	Aug. 7, 1809	....	....	....
Dawes, Robert Blanch	,,	Oct. 24, 1809	May 7, 1813	....	....
Dukinfield, Charles E.	,,	Jan. 17, 1810	Sep. 1, 1818	May 1, 1824	....
Dinwiddie, Lawrence	,,	Mar. 15, 1810	Mar. 18, 1814	....	....
Dew, Samuel	,,	....	....	....	....
Derville, Fred.—*artillery*	,,	Feb. 11, 1809	April 6, 1810	Oct. 19, 1820	Aug. 15, 1832
Doveton, H. B.—*cavalry*	1808	Nov. 9, 1812	....	Sep. 24, 1824	....
Drake, William	,,	May 1, 1810	June 22, 1814	Jan. 2, 1826	....
Davies, Thomas—*engineers*	,,	....	April 6, 1810	....	....
Dighton, John	1809	....	....	....	....
Dunmore, R. (now Napier.)	,,	June 27, 1810	July 16, 1817	....	....
D'Esterre, Samuel Yeates	,,	Nov. 12, 1810	Dec. 14, 1814	....	....
Daviniere, Charles	1810	Nov. 30, 1811	July 10, 1817	Feb. 24, 1828	....
Dods, George	,,	Jan. 11, 1812	Sep. 15, 1813	June 15, 1824	....
Dalzell, William Denholm	1811	June 11, 1812	May 19, 1817	Jan. 26, 1825	....

PRESIDENCY.

Lieut.-Colonel.	Colonel.	Major-General.	Lieut.-General.	Date of Resignation, Retirement, or Death.
. . . .	. . . .	. . . .	. . . .	Invalided March 19, 1814. Died Sep. 4, 1814, in India.
. . . .	. . . .	. . . .	. . . .	Died Oct. 20, 1818, at Venery.
. . . .	. . . .	. . . .	. . . .	Invalided June 7, 1814. Died Sep. 6, 1814, at Jaulnah.
. . . .	. . . .	. . . .	. . . .	Invalided July 6, 1827, in India. Died Aug. 27, 1827, at Chinnapatam.
. . . .	. . . .	. . . .	. . . .	Lost March 14, 1809, in the "Jane, Duchess of Gordon."
. . . .	. . . .	. . . .	. . . .	Died July 13, 1808.
May 15, 1834	. . . .	. . . .	. . . .	
. . . .	. . . .	. . . .	. . . .	Died May 24, 1805, at Nellore.
. . . .	. . . .	. . . .	. . . .	Cashiered Feb. 10, 1813.
. . . .	. . . .	. . . .	. . . .	Died Aug. 28, 1811, of wounds received at Java.
. . . .	. . . .	. . . .	. . . .	Resigned Jan. 28, 1806.
. . . .	. . . .	. . . .	. . . .	Died Jan. 1, 1812, at Madras.
. . . .	. . . .	. . . .	. . . .	
. . . .	. . . .	. . . .	. . . .	Died June 12, 1828, at Madras.
. . . .	. . . .	. . . .	. . . .	Resigned April 14, 1807.
. . . .	. . . .	. . . .	. . . .	Died April — 1820.
. . . .	. . . .	. . . .	. . . .	Died June 24, 1821.
. . . .	. . . .	. . . .	. . . .	Pensioned Sep. 13, 1815, on Lord Clive's Fund.
. . . .	. . . .	. . . .	. . . .	Died Aug. 12, 1811.
. . . .	. . . .	. . . .	. . . .	Died June 8, 1813, at Seringapatam.
. . . .	. . . .	. . . .	. . . .	Died Jan. 13, 1826, in camp, at Ava.
. . . .	. . . .	. . . .	. . . .	Died May 27, 1810, at Cochin.
. . . .	. . . .	. . . .	. . . .	Died Dec. 13, 1814, at Banda.
. . . .	. . . .	. . . .	. . . .	Died Feb. 21, 1807, on passage to India.
. . . .	. . . .	. . . .	. . . .	Lost March 14, 1809, in the ship "Jane, Duchess of Gordon."
. . . .	. . . .	. . . .	. . . .	Died Dec. 10, 1818, at Madras.
May 31, 1833	. . . .	. . . .	. . . .	
. . . .	. . . .	. . . .	. . . .	Died Dec. 26, 1812.
. . . .	. . . .	. . . .	. . . .	Resigned Oct. 4, 1808.
. . . .	. . . .	. . . .	. . . .	Died June 27, 1810.
. . . .	. . . .	. . . .	. . . .	Died June 4, 1822, at Masulipatam.
. . . .	. . . .	. . . .	. . . .	Killed Aug. 20, 1815, at Hyderabad.
. . . .	. . . .	. . . .	. . . .	Died April 15, 1813, at Trichinopoly.
. . . .	. . . .	. . . .	. . . .	Died Feb. 21, 1819, in camp, near Belgaum.
. . . .	. . . .	. . . .	. . . .	Retired from Dec. 20, 1826, in England.
. . . .	. . . .	. . . .	. . . .	Died March 28, 1823, at Bellary.
. . . .	. . . .	. . . .	. . . .	Died Aug. 12, 1809, at Cuddalore.
. . . .	. . . .	. . . .	. . . .	Died April 8, 1830, at Wallajahbad.
. . . .	. . . .	. . . .	. . . .	Killed May 18, 1818, at the siege of Malegaum.
. . . .	. . . .	. . . .	. . . .	Died — at sea.
. . . .	. . . .	. . . .	. . . .	Resigned Aug. 30, 1824, in England.
. . . .	. . . .	. . . .	. . . .	Invalided Nov. 29, 1822.
. . . .	. . . .	. . . .	. . . .	
. . . .	. . . .	. . . .	. . . .	Retired April 26, 1829, in England.

MADRAS

NAMES.	Cadet.	Cornet, Ensign, or Second Lieutenant.	Lieutenant.	Captain.	Major.
Dickson, Edward	1811	June 11, 1812	Mar. 2, 1818	May 1, 1824	....
Dormer, Robert	,,	June 1, 1812	June 2, 1816	....	....
Dickenson, John—*artillery*	1812	July 6, 1813	Sep. 1, 1818	Nov. 18, 1824	....
De Paiba, John James	1813	July 4, 1814	....	....	....
Dowker, Howard	,,	July 4, 1814	Jan. 24, 1817	July 15, 1824	Oct. 10, 1833
Drewry, Wm. T.—*engineers*	1814	July 4, 1814	May 9, 1821	Apr. 14, 1825	....
Dyce, Archibald Brown	1816	....	June 4, 1817	July 16, 1827	Mar. 19, 1831
Derville, Adolphus	,,	....	April 6, 1818	June 2, 1825	Dec. 27, 1826
Dighton, D. B.—*artillery*	1817	June 3, 1818	Oct. 19, 1820	....	....
Dallas, Thomas	,,	....	June 4, 1818	Sep. 20, 1826	....
Doveton, Edward	,,	....	....	....	....
Drever, James	,,	....	Oct. 14, 1818	Dec. 5, 1826	Aug. 6, 1835
Douglas, Archibald	,,	....	Nov. 8, 1818	May 25, 1831	....
Davison, Valentine Orlando	1818	....	....	....	....
Dowell, Richard	,,	....	June 13, 1819	Apr. 24, 1832	....
Deane, John	,,	....	June 13, 1819	June 6, 1833	....
Dusantoy, Edward John	,,	....	June 13, 1819	....	....
Dyer, Edward	,,	....	June 13, 1819	Sep. 5, 1827	....
Dennett, John Jordaine	,,	....	June 13, 1819	....	....
Dennett, Christopher	,,	....	June 13, 1819	Brevet June 12, 1834	....
Downing, George	,,	....	June 13, 1819	Nov. 26, 1828	....
De Montmorency, H.F.-*cavalry*	1819	....	July 29, 1820	....	....
Disney, Lambert B.	,,	....	July 24, 1820	July 14, 1832	....
Duff, Daniel	,,	....	April 7, 1820	June 17, 1830	....
De Lannoy, Geo. Frederick	,,	....	May 14, 1820	....	....
Davidson, James	,,	....	May 16, 1820	Jan. 11, 1832	....
Duff, John Andrew	,,	....	Aug. 21, 1820	....	....
Dixon, John Beachcroft	,,	April 6, 1820	June 22, 1822	....	....
Darby, Frederick	,,	April 6, 1820	Oct. 23, 1821	Aug. 23, 1834	....
Deacon, Robert	,,	....	May 14, 1821	....	....
Douglas, Geo. Norval	1820	Feb. 13, 1821	May 27, 1823	....	....
Donaldson, A. G.—*cavalry*	,,	Feb. 13, 1821	May 1, 1824	....	....
Dudgeon, Francis	,,	Feb. 13, 1821	Oct. 21, 1824	Brevet Feb. 13, 1836	....
Dallas, Henry John	,,	Feb. 13, 1821	May 1, 1824	....	....
Duke, Thomas	,,	Feb. 13, 1821	Nov. 30, 1822	Feb. 9, 1834	....
Dewes, John	,,	....	....	....	....
Duncan, William	,,	Feb. 13, 1821	....	....	....
Douglas, Wm. Newman	,,	....	....	....	....
Dyce, Andrew	1821	Apr. 27, 1822	Sep. 5, 1824	....	....
Doveton, Fred. Brickdale	,,	Apr. 27, 1822	June 4, 1825	....	....
Duval, Lewis Emanuel	,,	Apr. 27, 1822	Feb. 26, 1826	....	....
Davies, Michael	,,	Apr. 27, 1822	May 1, 1824	Apr. 27, 1834	....
Dale, Thomas	,,	Apr. 27, 1822	June 27, 1826	....	....
Daniell, George Noble	,,	....	....	....	....
Daniell, Frederick	,,	Apr. 27, 1822	June 20, 1824	Apr. 12, 1835	....
Davidson, Geo. Kearsley	,,	....	....	....	....
Du Pasquier, Wm. F.	,,	Apr. 27, 1822	July 10, 1826	....	....

PRESIDENCY.

Lieut.-Colonel.	Colonel.	Major-General.	Lieut.-General.	Date of Resignation, Retirement, or Death.
....	....	....	....	Invalided May 7, 1830, in India. Died April 7, 1831.
....	....	....	....	Died Jan. 16, 1821, at Belgaum.
....	....	....	....	Struck off May 5, 1834.
....	....	....	....	Died Dec. 4, 1817, at Berhampore.
....	....	....	....	Died March 5, 1835, on board the "Elphinstone."
Apr. 10, 1836	....	....	....	
....	....	....	....	
....	....	....	....	Killed at Kittoor, Oct. 23, 1824.
....	....	....	....	Dismissed Dec. 10, 1826.
....	....	....	....	Died Sep. 17, 1823, at Calcutta.
....	....	....	....	
....	....	....	....	
....	....	....	....	Died Sep. 2, 1819, at Madras.
....	....	....	....	
....	....	....	....	Died Oct. 2, 1836, at Secunderabad.
....	....	....	....	Died Sep. 22, 1832, in England.
....	....	....	....	Retired Dec. 16, 1835, in England.
....	....	....	....	Struck off the Army List, in 1821.
....	....	....	....	Pensioned 1837, in India.
....	....	....	....	Died April 2, 1834, at Mangalore.
....	....	....	....	Retired Oct. 17, 1832, in England.
....	....	....	....	Died Dec. 24, 1834, at Secunderabad.
....	....	....	....	
....	....	....	....	Died Sep. 21, 1829, at Madras.
....	....	....	....	
....	....	....	....	Resigned March 16, 1824, in India.
....	....	....	....	
....	....	....	....	Died Feb. 4, 1833, in Salem.
....	....	....	....	Died Nov. 21, 1831, at Cannanore.
....	....	....	....	Died May 14, 1825, at Trichinopoly.
....	....	....	....	
....	....	....	....	Died Feb. 23, 1827, in camp, at Kamptee.
....	....	....	....	
....	....	....	....	Struck off in England.
....	....	....	....	Died July 21, 1824, at Belgaum.
....	....	....	....	Died Feb. 20, 1823, at Seringapatam.
....	....	....	....	Died July 31, 1833, at Jaulnah.
....	....	....	....	
....	....	....	....	Retired Aug. 9, 1836, in England.
....	....	....	....	
....	....	....	....	Died Dec. 16, 1826, at Kamptee.
....	....	....	....	Died Jan. 21, 1823, at Vellore.
....	....	....	....	Invalided.
....	....	....	....	Cashiered in India, Aug. 19, 1824.
....	....	....	....	

MADRAS

NAMES.	Cadet.	Cornet, Ensign, or Second Lieutenant.	Lieutenant.	Captain.	Major.
Deas, Wm. Pat.—*cavalry*	1822	May 2, 1823	Sep. 30, 1825	Oct. 12, 1833	
Dunbar, W. G. C.—*cavalry*	,,				
Dickson, James	,,	May 2, 1823	Sep. 8, 1826	Dec. 27, 1832	
Denman, C. J.—*artillery*	,,	June 6, 1823	Nov. 17, 1823		
Dalzell, J. G.—*artillery*	,,				
Ditmas, Thomas—*artillery*	,,	June 6, 1823	June 11, 1823	June 22, 1836	
Du Vernet, James Smith	,,	May 2, 1823	Jan. 11, 1829		
Dickinson, R. Beachcroft	1823	May 14, 1824	May 7, 1826		
Deck, James George	,,	May 14, 1824	Jan. 2, 1826		
Dardell, James Colin	,,	May 14, 1825	Sep. 8, 1826		
Dixon, Henry	,,				
De Blaquiere, George	1824		Sep. 8, 1826		
Donaldson, Robert	,,	May 6, 1825	Feb. 24, 1827		
Dunsmure, Geo.—*cavalry*	,,	May 6, 1825	July 22, 1826	Oct. 29, 1833	
Davie, Calma	,,		Jan. 5, 1828		
Durant, Edwin L.	1825	Jan. 8, 1826	Oct. 11, 1827		
Dearsley, Wm. Henry	,,	Jan. 8, 1826			
Durdis, Hen. Richard	,,	...1826...			
Davies, Joseph—*cavalry*	,,	...1827...			
Dawson, Henry	,,	Jan. 8, 1826			
Dyce, J. N.—*cavalry*	,,				
Dawney, Robert	,,	...1826...			
Darby, William	,,	Jan. 8, 1826	April 5, 1829		
Douglas, John	,,	Jan. 8, 1826	Aug. 14, 1830		
Durant, A. E. B.	,,		Oct. 8, 1829		
Down, Edward—*cavalry*	,,		June 12, 1827		
Deacon, Nelson Wavell	,,	Jan. 8, 1826			
Dunlop, Wm. Wallace	,,	Jan. 8, 1826	Mar. 30, 1828	Jan. 27, 1837	
De Butts, A.—*engineers*	,,		June 17, 1825		
Denman, E. H. F.—*artillery*	1826	June 16, 1826	May 8, 1829		
Donaldson, H. Montgomerie	,,	Jan. 16, 1827	Nov. 23, 1831		
Douglas, A.—*engineers*	,,		Dec. 17, 1825		
Dods, Joseph	,,	Mar. 5, 1827	May 16, 1832		
Durand, Jno. Chas. Aylmer	,,	July 5, 1827			
Davis, George	,,	Mar. 10, 1827	Aug. 15, 1832	Oct. 16, 1836	
Drew, William	,,	Sep. 19, 1827	Sep. 11, 1830		
Dobbs, Richard Stewart	,,	Mar. 12, 1828	Dec. 8, 1833		
Doratt, Augustus Frederick	,,	...1828...			
Drought, Justin. Raynsford	,,	May 27, 1828			
Drysdal, William	1827	Mar. 7, 1829	June 2, 1831		
Ditmas, Fred.—*engineers*	,,		July 23, 1829		
Dundas, David H.	1828				
Dancer, George—*artillery*	,,	Oct. 9, 1831	Sep. 1, 1831		
Douglas, Wm.—*engineers*	1830				
Dorid, Alexander	1833	May 27, 1834			
Davies, Arthur	1834				
Dobbie, H. M.	,,	Mar. 23, 1835			

PRESIDENCY.

Lieut.-Colonel.	Colonel.	Major-General.	Lieut.-General.	Date of Resignation, Retirement, or Death.
				Died Nov. 27, 1824, at Trichinopoly.
				Died Aug. 28, 1824, at Madras.
				Died May 18, 1824, at St. Thomas's Mount.
				Died May 16, 1834, at Mangalore.
				Died May 2, 1831, at Ragonautpooruns.
				Died June 6, 1825, at Wallajahbad.
				Died Jan. 15, 1834, at Vizianagrum.
				Died Dec. 20, 1830, at Octacamund.
				Died April 27, 1830, at Kamptee.
				Retired Oct. 18, 1833, on Lord Clive's Fund in England.
				Died Dec. 12, 1826, at Gooty.
				Struck off, June 29, 1827, in India.
				Pensioned Oct. 14, 1828, in India. Died Aug. 19, 1830, at Cochin.
				Pensioned April 23, 1832, on Lord Clive's Fund in England.
				Died Oct. 17, 1826, at Vellore.
				Lost Oct. 17, 1836, at Sea.
				Retired April 21, 1836, in England.
				Pensioned Jan. 7, 1830, on Lord Clive's Fund in England.
				Died April 23, 1830, at Mangalore.
				Died Feb. 15, 1836, in England.
				Died April 18, 1829, at Jaulnah.
				Died Dec. 24, 1833, at Vizianagrum.
				Died June 10, 1828, at Bangalore.
				Died May 28, 1831, at Wallamgahady.
				Died Mar. 14, 1833, at Chiracole.
				Died Feb. 18, 1832, at Laulpett.
				Died Aug. 16, 1835, at Bangalore.

MADRAS

NAMES.	Cadet.	Cornet, Ensign, or Second Lieutenant.	Lieutenant.	Captain.	Major.
Doria, R. A.	1834	Feb. 24, 1835	....	....	....
Dumergue, E.	,,	Apr. 6, 1835	....	....	....
E					
Eidington, James	....	....	....	.... 1770...	May 7, 1784
Edmondes, Edward........	1764	Nov. 14, 1765	Nov. 12, 1766	May 17, 1773	....
Eagle, Archibald	1769	Nov. 10, 1770	Aug. 7, 1775	Sep. 1, 1783	....
Eastland, Richard	,,	Nov. 26, 1770	Feb. 6, 1776	Nov. 2, 1783	....
Evans, John Tindal	....	July 18, 1775	Oct. 20, 1780	Aug. 16, 1785	June 1, 1796
English, John	1779	Oct. 21, 1780	Apr. 17, 1786	Mar. 7, 1797	Mar. 27, 1801
Evans, Henry	1782	May 26, 1783	Aug. 21, 1790	Jan. 1, 1800	Aug. 27, 1807
Everett, George	,,	June 22, 1783	....	....	....
Everall, Thomas..........	....	Sep. 9, 1783	Aug. 21, 1790	....	....
Elliott, William—*cavalry*..	....	Mar. 25, 1784	Jan. 30, 1786	May 7, 1799	May 8, 1800
Evans, John..............	1792	May 9, 1793	Aug. 6, 1794	....	....
Egan, Michael	1793	....	July 14, 1795	....	....
Evans, Francis	1795	Feb. 16, 1796	Mar. 4, 1797	....	....
Edwards, Edward	1796	Aug. 11, 1797	Oct. 4, 1798	Sep. 21, 1804	Sep. 1 1818
Elliott, William	1797	Aug. 9, 1798	Dec. 26, 1798	....	....
Edmonds, John	1798	....	Dec. 15, 1800	Sep. 20, 1806	....
Elphinstone, Charles	1799	....	Dec. 15, 1800	June 7, 1809	May 1, 1824
Evans, Rich. Lacey, (C. B.)	1800	....	July 20, 1801	May 30, 1810	May 1, 1824
Edmonds, Richard	1802	....	June 30, 1804	July 10, 1817	....
Erskine, James	,,	....	Sep. 21, 1804	....	....
Erskine, G. F. W.—*cavalry*	,,	....	April 6, 1810	....	....
Ewing, John	,,	Apr. 17, 1803	Dec. 15, 1803	Nov. 30, 1817	Jan. 13, 1825
Elam, John	,,	....	....	....	....
Ellis, William Fane	1803	....	Sep. 21, 1804	....	....
Eckersall, John James	,,	....	Sep. 21, 1804	....	....
Elderton, Charles Augustus	1804	....	July 17, 1805	Dec. 18, 1817	Oct. 4, 1825
Evans, Lacey	1805	....	....	....	....
Eccles, Gilbert William ..	,,	June 27, 1806	Mar. 18, 1809	....	....
Edye, Charles	1806	July 3, 1807	Jan. 15, 1811	....	....
Ennis, Francis Geo. Boyd..	,,	July 3, 1807	May 12, 1810	....	....
Eyles, William	,,	July 3, 1807	May 27, 1809	....	....
Ellaway, Edward Jones....	1807	Apr. 28, 1809	June 24, 1814	....	....
Egan, George.............	,,	Apr. 6, 1810	July 9, 1814	....	....
Eastment, Thomas........	1810	Jan. 15, 1812	Aug. 5, 1816	Oct. 1, 1829	....
Ewing, Humphrey	1812	July 6, 1813	Mar. 30, 1816	....	....
Eades, Charles Horatio....	1814	July 11, 1815	Sep. 24, 1817	....	....
Evans, Charles	1815	....	Sep. 29, 1817	....	....
Ely, Francis Howe........	1816	....	Dec. 5, 1817	Oct. 25, 1826	....
Elliott, Charles	1817	....	....	....	....
Elliott, Wm. Edw. Alured .	1818	....	June 13, 1819	May 8, 1829	....
Eaton, David Hunter	1819	....	April 7, 1820	July 18, 1832	....
Eames, Richard Fairfax ..	,,	....	July 2, 1820	Oct. 6, 1829	....
Edie, Alexander	,,	....	....	....	....
Eades, Francis............	,,	....	Nov. 29, 1821	Sep. 26, 1825	....

PRESIDENCY.

Lieut-Colonel.	Colonel.	Major-General.	Lieut.-General.	Date of Resignation, Retirement, or Death.
....	....	....	....	
....	....	....	....	
Feb. 7, 1786	....	....	....	Out of the service, 1789.
....	....	....	....	At home 1786. Out of the service —
....	....	....	....	Died Sep. — 1789.
....	....	....	....	In King's service 1789.
Oct. 12, 1798	....	....	....	Died May 18, 1799. [1805.
Sep. 21, 1804	....	....	....	Invalided Dec. 11, 1804. Died Nov. 23,
....	....	....	....	Died Aug. 16, 1810, at Ganjam.
....	....	....	....	Not to be traced.
....	....	....	....	Died Dec. 18, 1795.
....	....	....	....	Died Sep. 1, 1801.
....	....	....	....	Died Sep. — 1799, at St. Helena.
....	....	....	....	Killed Mar. 31, 1801.
....	....	....	....	Died July 1, 1803, at Poonah.
May 1, 1824	June 5, 1829	....	....	
....	....	....	....	Died Aug. 8, 1803.
....	....	....	....	Died Nov. 10, 1818, in camp at Nowagur.
....	....	....	....	Died Aug. 19, 1831, at Secunderabad.
May 31, 1827	....	....	....	
June 21, 1827	Brevet, June 18, 1823	....	....	Retired Oct. 2, 1822.
....	....	....	....	Died Nov. 12, 1819, at Bombay.
....	....	....	....	Died June 18, 1814, at Arcot.
....	....	....	....	Died April 1, 1828, in London.
....	....	....	....	Died May 28, 1804.
....	....	....	....	Died Nov. 9, 1816, near Nagpore.
....	....	....	....	{ Invalided Apr. 6, 1810, in India. Died Jan. 17, 1815, at Sankerrydroog.
June 18, 1831	....	....	....	Died April 4, 1807.
....	....	....	....	Died April 22, 1812.
....	....	....	....	Died Dec. 26, 1812, at Jaulnah.
....	....	....	....	Died Oct. 13, 1821, at Cuddalore.
....	....	....	....	Died Dec. 31, 1819, in camp at Kunner.
....	....	....	....	{ Died April 23, 1823, on board the " David Scott," off the Cape of Good Hope.
....	....	....	....	Killed May 29, 1818, at Mallegaum.
....	....	....	....	Died Feb. 7. 1825, at Mangalore.
....	....	....	....	Died Nov. 3, 1818, in camp near [Mooltye.
....	....	....	....	
....	....	....	....	Killed May 13, 1819, at Copaul Droog.
....	....	....	....	Died Jan. 16, 1834, in camp at ['Teeryherry.
....	....	....	....	Died Feb. 25, 1825, at Madras.

I

MADRAS

NAMES.	Cadet.	Cornet, Ensign, or Second Lieutenant.	Lieutenant.	Captain.	Major.
Ewing, Robert Boyd	1819				
Edgar, John	,,	April 6, 1820	Feb. 26, 1823		
Elphinstone, Rich^d. Stephen	1820	Feb. 13, 1821			
Edwards, Hen. Molesworth	1821				
Elliot, George—*cavalry*	,,	Apr. 27, 1822	June 22, 1825	Nov. 18, 1836	
Everest, John	,,	Apr. 27, 1822	June 22, 1825		
Elliott, James Shortreed	,,	Apr. 27, 1822			
Ensor, Frederick	,,	Apr. 27, 1822	Sep. 8, 1826		
Elliott, Robert	1823				
Elliott, James Forbes	,,	May 14, 1824	Dec. 9, 1825		
Elsey, William	,,	Mar. 14, 1824	Nov. 17, 1825	May 24, 1832	
Evelyn, Wm. Edgar Little	,,	Apr. 14, 1824	Sep. 8, 1826		
Edwards, Geo. R.—*cavalry*	1825	...1828....	May 12, 1829		
Emery, Heberdew Finden	1826	Jan. 5, 1827	May 13, 1831		
Eykyn, James	1828	June 3, 1831			
Erskine, Wm. D.—*cavalry*	1829	Feb. 7, 1831	Sep. 24, 1833		
Eaton, G. P.—*artillery*	,,	Oct. 14, 1831			
Elliott, Chs. M.—*engineers*	1832	Oct. 2, 1836			
Eden, William Frederick	,,	June 11, 1833	Nov. 4, 1836		
Eckford, G. H.	1834	Mar. 4, 1835			
F					
Fraser, Charles				....1770...	
Flint, William	1769	Sep. 30, 1770	May 5, 1774	Nov. 23, 1782	
Fotheringham, George	,,	Oct. 31, 1770	Mar. 27, 1775	Mar 3, 1783	...1794....
Forbes, John	1770	July 10, 1771		Nov. 2, 1783	
Forbes, William		Dec. 11, 1775		Mar. 12, 1786	
Fergusson, Edward	1775	Sep. 24, 1776	Nov. 22, 1780	Jan. 16, 1793	Mar. 18, 1797
Forbes, James		Feb. 10, 1777	Mar. 20, 1781	Sep. 18, 1793	
Foulis, Alexander	1777	May 9, 1778	Jan. 24, 1782	Sep. 8, 1794	
Frank, James	,,	June 13, 1778	Feb. 24, 1782	Feb. 13, 1796	
Fenwick, William		Aug. 27, 1778	June 25, 1783	June 1, 1796	
Fen, Thomas	1778	Apr. 29, 1779	May 20, 1784	June 1, 1796	May 7, 1800
Fraser, Peter	1780	Dec. 18, 1780	Apr. 17, 1786		
Freer, Richard Hall	,,	Sep. 3, 1781			
Farlane, Alexander Mac	,,	Sep. 14, 1781	April 1, 1788	Nov. 29, 1797	May 26, 1804
Fletcher, Robert			Aug. 21, 1790	Dec. 10, 1799	Sep. 21, 1804
Foote, George		May 4, 1785	Aug. 21, 1790		
Friend, Benjamin—*artillery*	1781	April 2, 1783	Apr. 30, 1788		
Fennell, Baker—*artillery*	1783	Oct. 27, 1784	Apr. 11, 1791	Mar. 1, 1800	
Freese, John W.—*artillery*	1785	Dec. 7, 1785	Aug. 11, 1792	Mar. 1, 1800	Sep. 21, 1804
Forrest, Arthur—*engineers*		May 23, 1786		Sep. 3, 1793	
Fie, John Mac—*cavalry*			Apr. 23, 1784		
Fonblanque, Thos.—*cavalry*	1780	Oct. 20, 1783	Jan. 28, 1786		
Floyer, Sir A. (K.C.B.)—*cavalry*		Dec. 20, 1783	Jan. 29, 1786	Nov. 1, 1798	April 8, 1802
Fry, Edmund—*cavalry*		June 20, 1785	Mar. 6, 1791		
Forbes, George—*cavalry*	1781	Dec. 31, 1782	June 4, 1792		
Forsyth, Charles	,,	Nov. 5, 1782			

PRESIDENCY.

Lieut.-Colonel.	Colonel.	Major General	Lieut.-General.	Date of Resignation, Retirement, or Death.
....	....	....	....	Died April 18, 1821, at Gooty.
....	....	....	....	Died Dec. 26, 1832, at Masulipatam.
....	....	....	....	Died May 14, 1822, at Vizianagrum.
....	....	....	....	Died at Madras, Dec. 28, 1824.
....	....	....	....	
....	....	....	....	Died Mar. 7, 1832, at Madras.
....	....	....	....	Resigned April 4, 1826, in India.
....	....	....	....	Resigned May 23, 1835, in England.
....	....	....	....	Died at Wallajahbad, Nov. 26, 1824.
....	....	....	....	
....	....	....	....	Retired Nov., 1836.
....	....	....	....	Died Aug. 22, 1833, at Vizagapatam.
....	....	....	....	
....	....	....	....	
....	....	....	....	
....	....	....	....	
....	....	....	....	
....	....	....	....	
....	....	....	....	
....	....	....	....	
May 7, 1784	Sep. 24, 1790	....	....	Died May 5, 1795.
June 1, 1796	....	....	....	Retired June 1798.
June 1, 1796	Dec. 10, 1799	....	....	Invalided Jan. 6, 1802. Died Dec. 12, 1802.
....	....	....	....	Died 1790.
....	....	....	....	Died 1793.
....	....	....	....	Retired May 25, 1804.
July 31, 1799	....	....	....	Died Aug. 1797.
....	....	....	....	{ Home 1792. Died March 17, 1796, at Presidency.
....	....	....	....	Died July 10, 1797.
....	....	....	....	Died January 1797.
....	....	....	....	Invalided Apr. 21, & died Dec. 2, 1801.
....	....	....	....	Died Nov. 1796.
....	....	....	....	Died May 1789.
....	....	....	....	Died Sep. 11, 1807, in England.
Nov. 22, 1806	June 4, 1814	....	....	Cashiered July 18, 1817, in India.
....	....	....	....	Died Aug. 28, 1799.
....	....	....	....	Died 1796, at the Mount.
....	....	....	....	Died June 8, 1801, on his passage home
July 19, 1809	May 1, 1821	....	....	{ Died on board the H. C. S. "Duke of York," at sea, July 25, 1824.
....	....	....	....	Died Oct. 13, 1802.
....	....	....	....	Died 1790.
....	....	....	....	Killed (date not known).
Feb. 15, 1805	June 4, 1813	....	....	Died Oct. 17, 1818, at Hydrabad.
....	....	....	....	Died 1793.
....	....	....	....	Not to be traced.
....	....	....	....	Out of the Service.

MADRAS

NAMES.	Cadet.	Cornet, Ensign, or Second Lieutenant.	Lieutenant.	Captain.	Major.
Forbes, Nathaniel	1781	.... 1782...	Aug. 21, 1790	Dec. 26, 1798	July 11, 1802
Foulis, D. (C. B.)—*cavalry*	1790	Dec. 23, 1791	Nov. 1, 1798	Sep. 2, 1801	Jan. 22, 1812
Farran, Charles	1788	....	June 7, 1792	Sep. 21, 1804	June 30, 1808
Fraser, T. Augustus	1790	July 3, 1791	July 14, 1793	June 17, 1800	Feb. 24, 1808
Fraser, Sir Hugh (K. C. B.)	„	July 29, 1791	Feb. 17, 1794	Feb. 11, 1801	Mar. 16, 1805
Fotheringham, J.—*engineers*	„	June 24, 1793	June 1, 1796	Jan. 1, 1806	....
Fotheringham, R. H.—*engineers*	„	May 8, 1792	Sep. 3, 1793	Jan. 1, 1806	Mar. 24, 1812
Fortune, John	„	Sep. 14, 1791	Aug. 6, 1794	Sep. 21, 1804	Jan. 25, 1813
Fitzpatrick, John	„	Sep. 16, 1791	Aug. 6, 1794	Dec. 10, 1800	....
Frith, Arthur	1791	Sep. 25, 1791	Aug. 6, 1794	Feb. 20, 1802	Feb. 1, 1809
Farquhar, W.—*engineers*	1790	July 10, 1791	Aug. 11, 1793	Jan. 1, 1803	Sep. 26, 1811
Fowler, R. T.—*artillery*	1792	June 18, 1793	June 17, 1797	....	....
Fraser, William	„	June 11, 1793	Aug. 6, 1794	....	....
Freeman, Charles	....	....	April 5, 1783	....	....
Fair, Alexander (C. B.)	1792	Oct. 1, 1793	Oct. 16, 1794	Sep. 21, 1804	Apr. 30, 1810
Forbes, Gordon James	1793	....	Dec. 19, 1795	....	....
Fraser, Pasley Weir	1794	Jan. 10, 1796	June 1, 1796	....	....
Fraser, Thomas—*engineers*	„	Jan. 2, 1796	Aug. 6, 1800	July 14, 1808	....
Fish, John	1795	Feb. 26, 1796	May 9, 1797	....	....
Foster, Bayntun	1796	Aug. 30, 1797	Oct. 12, 1798	....	....
Falconer, John	„	Aug. 27, 1797	Oct. 12, 1798	....	....
Fraser, Edward	1797	Sep. 5, 1798	Dec. 26, 1798	Jan. 27, 1806	....
Farrell, Thomas	1798	....	....	....	....
Forbes, David	„	....	Dec. 15, 1800	April 6, 1810	....
Forster, Richard	„	....	June 17, 1800	....	....
Fraser, Wm. Charles	1797	Aug. 27, 1798	Dec. 26, 1798	Feb. 25, 1807	Jan. 4, 1815
Ferrior, Charles	„	....	Jan. 1, 1800	Aug. 19, 1808	Apr. 19, 1823
Frank, J. C.—*artillery*	„	Sep. 29, 1798	Mar. 1, 1800	July 28, 1808	Mar. 2, 1819
Forbes, Robert	1799	....	Dec. 15, 1800	....	....
Fraser, James Stewart	„	....	Dec. 15, 1800	Nov. 16, 1809	Dec. 10, 1819
Ford, John (C. B.)	„	....	Dec. 15, 1800	May 27, 1809	May 16, 1822
Fernyhough, Wilson	„	....	Dec. 15, 1800	Oct. 10, 1810	....
Fair, William	„	....	Dec. 15, 1800	....	....
Franks, Joseph Bridges	„	....	Dec. 15, 1800	....	....
Fraser, Donald	1800	....	....	....	....
Foster, Edgar Moody	„	....	July 20, 1801	Feb. 25, 1812	....
Fenwick, Robert	„	....	Apr. 15, 1802	Jan. 24, 1815	Sep. 8, 1826
Fitzpatrick, Edward	1802	....	Nov. 16, 1803	Apr. 15, 1817	Sep. 8, 1826
Fenoulhet, Peter	„	Apr. 17, 1803	June 1, 1804	....	....
Fair, Thomas	„	....	Jan. 19, 1804	May 19, 1817	....
Forward, Hugh	„	Apr. 27, 1803	May 1, 1804	....	....
Fraser, Pringle	„	Apr. 17, 1803	Dec. 17, 1803	Mar. 1, 1815	....
Finch, Charles E.—*cavalry*	„	....	....	....	....
Fagan, John	„	Apr. 17, 1803	Mar. 1, 1804	....	....
Fielder, Wm. Henry	„	Apr. 17, 1803	Jan. 11, 1804	....	....
Forbes, Charles	„	....	Jan. 2, 1804	Feb. 9, 1818	....

PRESIDENCY.

Lieut.-Colonel.	Colonel.	Major General.	Lieut.-General.	Date of Resignation, Retirement, or Death.
Feb. 5, 1805	June 4, 1813	Aug. 12, 1819	Jan. 10, 1837	
July 26, 1819	June 5, 1829	Jan. 10, 1837	....	
May 26, 1814	Commt. May 1, 1824 Col. June 5, 1829.	Jan. 10, 1837	....	
Sep. 18, 1813	....	....	....	Died Feb. 14, 1822, at Secunderabad.
Dec. 14, 1809	Aug. 12, 1819	July 22, 1830	....	
....	....	....	....	Died Aug. 3, 1821, at Trichinopoly.
....	....	....	....	Retired Oct. 7, 1815, in India.
....	....	....	....	Died Jan. 9, 1815, at Trichinopoly.
....	....	....	....	Died April 29, 1810.
June 18, 1815	....	....	....	Died April 22, 1824, at Bolghatty, near Cochin.
May 9, 1821	Commt. Sep. 8, 1824 Col. June 5, 1829	Jan. 10, 1837	....	
....	....	....	....	Killed Sep. 23, 1803, at the battle of Assaye.
....	....	....	....	Died May 26, 1801.
....	....	....	....	{ Pensioned 1787. Died Dec. 1, 1804, at Masulipatam.
July 17, 1819	Commt. July 28, 1826 Col. June 5, 1829	Jan. 10, 1837	....	
....	....	....	....	Not to be traced.
....	....	....	....	Struck off, Dec. 17, 1799.
....	....	....	....	Retired March 1, 1819, in England.
....	....	....	....	Killed April 20, 1799.
....	....	....	....	Died Oct. 16, 1801.
....	....	....	....	Died Oct. 28, 1804.
....	....	....	....	Retired June 29, 1810.
....	....	....	....	Resigned Nov. 4, 1801.
....	....	....	....	Died April 18, 1815, at Banda.
....	....	....	....	Died Feb. 11, 1803, at sea.
Oct. 17, 1819	Commt. Sep. 8, 1826 Col. June 5, 1829	Jan. 10, 1837	....	
Nov. 17, 1825	....	....	....	Retired Feb. 17, 1830, in England.
....	....	....	....	{ Invalided Oct. 31, 1819, in India. Died Apr. 14, 1833, at Trichinopoly.
....	....	....	....	Died Oct. 27, 1804.
May 1, 1824	June 5, 1829	....	....	
June 29, 1825	....	....	....	Died Jan. 2, 1826, at Bycullah.
....	....	....	....	Retired Aug. 13, 1818, in England.
....	....	....	....	Died Jan. 14, 1811.
....	....	....	....	Died Dec. 17, 1803, at Aurungabad.
....	....	....	....	Died July 14, 1801.
....	....	....	....	Died Jan. 13, 1815, in India.
Apr. 3, 1832	....	....	....	
....	....	....	....	Retired June 16, 1829, in England.
....	....	....	....	Died Jan. 7, 1810, at Quilon.
....	....	....	....	Died Dec. 24, 1822, at Goa.
....	....	....	....	Cashiered Oct. 13, 1806.
....	....	....	....	Died July 21, 1820, at Bombay.
....	....	....	....	Died Feb. 9, 1804.
....	....	....	....	Died Dec. 8, 1805.
....	....	....	....	Died Nov. 2, 1805.
....	....	....	....	Died March 26, 1825, at Masulipatam.

MADRAS

NAMES.	Cadet.	Cornet, Ensign, or Second Lieutenant.	Lieutenant.	Captain.	Major.
Forbes, James	1802	....	Sep. 21, 1804	....	....
Flint, George—*cavalry*....	,,	Mar. 4, 1803	....	....	....
French, Andrew	1803	....	Sep. 21, 1804	Jan. 25, 1818	....
Frith, James H.—*artillery*	,,	....	July 18, 1804	Feb. 28, 1810	Sep. 4, 1824
Fotheringham, A.—*cavalry*	,,	....	July 21, 1804	....	....
Fothergill, C. Octavius	,,	....	Sep. 21, 1804	Oct. 14, 1818	Apr. 11, 1829
Foote, Edward James	,,	....	Sep. 21, 1804	Aug. 25, 1819	....
Faris, George—*cavalry*	,,	Mar. 7, 1805	Oct. 31, 1818	May 1, 1824	Oct. 9, 1833
Fitzgerald, Wm. Elliott ...	1804	....	July 17, 1805	Aug. 13, 1818	....
Farquharson, Peter	,,	....	July 17, 1805	Apr. 30, 1822	....
Ferns, John St. George....	,,	....	July 17, 1805	....	....
Forsyth, George	,,	....	Jan. 27, 1806	....	....
Freswell, James	,,	....	Nov. 24, 1805	Jan. 24, 1823	....
Farmer, Maurice	,,	....	July 17, 1805	....	....
Field, George	,,	....	July 2, 1806	Sep. 1, 1818	June 18, 1828
Fowke, Francis—*cavalry*..	1805	Oct. 9, 1806	Mar. 11, 1809	....	....
Field, George	,,	June 27, 1806	Oct. 19, 1808	....	....
Fenwick, William	,,	June 27, 1806	July 19, 1808	Oct. 23, 1820	....
Fiott, Edward	,,	June 27, 1806	Aug. 28, 1808	....	....
Fyfe, John	,,	....	Oct. 22, 1806	June 10, 1820	....
Flyn, Edmond	,,	....	....	....	....
Fergusson, John	,,	June 27, 1806	Jan. 21, 1809	....	....
Fatio, Ellis John—*cavalry*	,,	Apr. 13, 1807	....	....	....
Fell, James	1806	July 3, 1807	....	....	....
Fullarton, H. E.—*cavalry*	,,	Aug. 15, 1807	May 20, 1813	....	....
Fenoulhet, William	,,	July 3, 1807	Mar. 14, 1813	....	....
Frew, Robert	1807	Jan. 25, 1809	Jan. 10, 1815	May 1, 1824	....
Farquharson, Andrew	,,	Dec. 21, 1809	....	....	....
Festing, John Green	,,	Oct. 21, 1809	June 12, 1813	....	....
Fergusson, Charles	,,	Mar. 2, 1810	Sep. 27, 1815	....	....
Fenning, D. A.—*cavalry* ..	,,	Dec. 9, 1810	Sep. 1, 1818	Aug. 15, 1829	....
Fosberry, Francis	1808	May 5, 1810	Sep. 24, 1814	May 9, 1825	....
Fullarton, Henry—*engineers*	1809	....	Sep. 26, 1811	Mar. 2, 1819	....
Fitzgerald, Edward	,,	Oct. 10, 1810	....	....	....
Fulton, John	,,	....	Aug. 17, 1810	Mar. 17, 1823	....
Fletcher, Charles	1810	Oct. 11, 1811	....	....	....
Fraser, Andrew	1811	June 11, 1812	Sep. 14, 1815	Sep. 8, 1826	....
Forrest, James............	,,	June 11, 1812	Oct. 19, 1817	Aug. 25, 1826	....
Fergusson, Robert........	,,	June 11, 1812	Jan. 29, 1817	....	....
Friday, T. W—*artillery* ...	1815	Apr. 9, 1816	Nov. 13, 1818	....	....
Foord, Henry S.—*artillery*	1816	June 26, 1817	May 26, 1819	Jan. 29, 1828	....
Fox, Stephen Warden	,,	....	April 6, 1818	....	....
Fullarton, James	1817	....	June 4, 1818	Aug. 2, 1828	....
Flemyng, William	,,	....	....	....	....
Fitzgibbon, R. B.—*cavalry*	,,	....	Sep. 15, 1819	June 27, 1830	....
Fraser, James	,,	....	Nov. 11, 1818	....	....
Farran, Charles	,,	....	Nov. 15, 1818	Jan. 26, 1830	....

PRESIDENCY.

Lieut.-Colonel.	Colonel.	Major-General.	Lieut.-General.	Date of Resignation, Retirement, or Death.
				Died Jan. 28, 1818, at Hindiah.
				Died Sep. 6, 1811, at Jaulnah.
				Killed Mar. 29, 1825, in action at Arracan.
Sep. 13, 1829				
				Killed April — 1810, in Persia.
				Invalided May 25, 1830, in India.
				Died Dec. 24, 1823, at Bangalore
				Died Feb. 14, 1835, at Kamptee.
				Died June 12, 1820.
				Retired Dec. 15, 1832, in India.
				Died May 10, 1813, at Bellary.
				Resigned April 18, 1810.
				Died June 19, 1824, at Rangoon.
				Resigned Aug. 11, 1812.
				{ Invalided Jan. 9, 1829, in India. Died Sep. 15, 1831, at Coimbatore.
				Resigned Nov. 22, 1809.
				Died July 12, 1813.
				Retired Sep. 15, 1826, in England.
				Died Nov. 18, 1824, in England.
				{ Died Nov. 17, 1830, on board the "Lord William Bentinck."
				Resigned Feb. 20, 1807.
				Killed Aug. 26, 1811, at Java.
				Died May 20, 1812, at Pondicherry.
				{ Lost March 14, 1809, in the "Jane, Duchess of Gordon."
				Died Oct. 27, 1816, in Camp near Ellichpore.
				{ Resigned Sep. 26, 1815, in India. Died July 16, 1823, at Arnee.
				Retired July 9, 1834, in England.
				Died June 21, 1814.
				Died July 9, 1817, at Ellore.
				{ Invalided Nov. 30, 1816, in India. Died Nov. 13, 1817, at Vizianagrum.
				{ Invalided Nov. 23, 1827, in India. Retired June 7, 1830.
				Died Jan. 23, 1825, at Negapatam.
				Died Nov. 7, 1814, at Madras.
				Retired Feb. 24, 1833, in India.
				Cashiered April 7, 1815, in India.
				{ Died May 7, 1829, on board the "James Patterson," on passage to England.
				Died June 6, 1818, at Jaulnah.
				Died May 27, 1821.
				Died Jan. 22, 1822, at Chittledroog.
				Resigned April 18, 1823, in India.
				Dismissed Nov. 18, 1836.
				Died Oct. 20, 1827.

MADRAS

NAMES.	Cadet.	Cornet, Ensign, or Second Lieutenant.	Lieutenant.	Captain.	Major.
French, St. John Bogle	1818	....	Dec. 11, 1818	Feb. 25, 1826	....
Fryer, George	,,	....	June 13, 1819	Dec. 11, 1824	....
Francklyn, Edward	,,	....	June 13, 1819	Jan. 12, 1826	....
Fladgate, Charles	,,	....	June 13, 1819	Feb. 13, 1829	....
Francis, Robert	,,	....	June 13, 1819	April 5, 1829	....
Fitzgerald, Maurice G.	,,	....	June 13, 1819	....	....
Forster, Thomas B.	,,	....	June 13, 1819	May 13, 1827	....
Fairbrass, Frederick W.	,,	....	June 13, 1819	....	....
Floyer, G. M.—*cavalry*	1819	....	June 13, 1821	....	....
Forster, Claudius—*cavalry*	,,	....	Nov. 16, 1821	....	....
Fletcher, Philip	,,	....	July 18, 1820	....	....
Faunce, Edm. Burrell	,,	April 6, 1820	Sep. 17, 1823	Aug. 3, 1830	....
Foskett, Wm. Reynolds	1820	Feb. 13, 1821	May 1, 1824	Brevet Feb. 13, 1836.	....
Freeman, W. R. A.	,,	Feb. 13, 1821	Feb. 14, 1826	Feb. 12, 1836	....
Fuller, Henry—*cavalry*	,,	Feb. 13, 1821	May 1, 1824	....	....
Fitzgerald, James	,,	Feb. 13, 1821	July 16, 1824	June 25, 1836	....
Flyter, Duncan	,,	Feb. 13, 1821	Dec. 5, 1824	....	....
Forbes, James	1821	Apr. 27, 1822	June 18, 1825	....	....
Flint, C. R.—*cavalry*	1822	May 2, 1823	Feb. 19, 1825	....	....
Fennell, John R.	1823	May 14, 1824	Dec. 5, 1825	....	....
Forbes, F.—*cavalry*	,,	May 14, 1823	May 26, 1825	Mar. 12, 1833	....
Fish, N. H.—*artillery*	,,	Dec. 18, 1823	May 1, 1824	....	....
Fisher, Thomas Jas.	,,	Sep. 14, 1824	Sep. 8, 1826	....	....
Favell, J. C. N.—*cavalry*	1824	May 6, 1825	Aug. 28, 1826	Nov. 9, 1835	....
Faunce, Robert N.	,,	May 6, 1825	June 18, 1828	April 3, 1836	....
Forster, George	,,	May 6, 1825	Jan. 19, 1833	....	....
Faber, C. E.—*engineers*	,,	....	May 1, 1824	Dec. 29, 1830	....
Farran, Charles Jas.	,,	May 6, 1825	May 18, 1831	....	....
Freeman, Edward N.	,,	May 6, 1825	Feb. 21, 1827	....	....
Furlonge, Wm. Townley	,,	....	June 21, 1826	....	....
Fraser, Hugh—*cavalry*	,,	....	Mar. 21, 1827	....	....
Frith, Charles Harris	1825	May 20, 1826	....	....	....
Fyfe, William	,,	....	Sep. 8, 1826	....	....
Fortescue, John Charles	,,	....	Apr. 12, 1827	....	....
Ferrers, C. C.—*cavalry*	,,	....	....	....	....
French, F. F.—*cavalry*	,,	Jan. 8, 1826	Oct. 6, 1828	....	....
Fortescue, Wm. Neynoe	,,	....	Apr. 21, 1827	....	....
Farran, J. O. C.	,,	Jan. 8, 1826	Jan. 10, 1829	....	....
French, George Edw.	,,	Jan. 8, 1826	....	....	....
Foot, C. C.	1826	Jan. 8, 1826	June 13, 1836	....	....
Freese, George	,,	Jan. 8, 1826	Sep. 14, 1831	....	....
Freeman, Charles H.	,,	....	....	....	....
Forsyth, James	,,	June 21, 1827	Sep. 12, 1834	....	....
Freese, Chas. Robert	,,	Mar. 28, 1828	....	....	....
Farquhar, Robert	1827	June 21, 1828	Jan. 4, 1832	....	....
Forster, Joseph	,,	Aug. 9, 1828	....	....	....
Falconer, G. A. H.	,,	Nov. 27, 1828	July 13, 1835	....	....

PRESIDENCY.

Lieut.-Colonel.	Colonel.	Major General.	Lieut.-General.	Date of Resignation, Retirement, or Death.
....	....	....	....	Retired Sep. 6, 1836, in England.
....	....	....	....	
....	....	....	....	
....	....	....	....	
....	....	....	....	Invalided Feb. 12, 1836.
....	....	....	....	Died June 7, 1827, at Kamptee.
....	....	....	....	{ Died July 9, 1826, on board the "Neptune," for England.
....	....	....	....	Died Nov. 23, 1827, at Hydrabad.
....	....	....	....	Resigned Jan. 23, 1827, in India.
....	....	....	....	{ Retired Jan. 11, 1834, on Lord Clive's Fund, in England.
....	....	....	....	
....	....	....	....	
....	....	....	....	[Dorking.
....	....	....	....	Died May 10, 1837, at Holcomb, near
....	....	....	....	
....	....	....	....	Died March 31, 1831, at Chicacole.
....	....	....	....	
....	....	....	....	Resigned June 17, 1828, in England.
....	....	....	....	
....	....	....	....	
....	....	....	....	
....	....	....	....	Died May 28, 1837, at Nagpore.
....	....	....	....	
....	....	....	....	
....	....	....	....	
....	....	....	....	Died Oct. 1, 1836, at Rathgon, Dublin.
....	....	....	....	
....	....	....	....	Died Nov. 25, 1828, at Chicacole.
....	....	....	....	
....	....	....	....	Died June 7, 1834, at Poondy.
....	....	....	....	Resigned Aug. 13, 1829, in England.
....	....	....	....	
....	....	....	....	Discharged Aug. 30, 1829, in India.
....	....	....	....	Resigned June 16, 1832, in England.
....	....	....	....	Invalided Mar. 22, 1831, in India.
....	....	....	....	
....	....	....	....	Cashiered Sep. 6, 1832, in India.
....	....	....	....	Died Sep. 15, 1836, at Kamptee.
....	....	....	....	Died Feb. 24, 1836, on board "Bolton."
....	....	....	....	Died Apr. 9, 1827, on his passage out.
....	....	....	....	
....	....	....	....	Died Dec. 9, 1829, at Cannanore.
....	....	....	....	
....	....	....	....	Died Aug. 16, 1829, at Vizianagrum.
....	....	....	....	

MADRAS.——K

MADRAS

NAMES.	Cadet.	Cornet, Ensign, or Second Lieutenant.	Lieutenant.	Captain.	Major.
Ferrier, Hay	1827	Jan. 28, 1829	Dec. 19, 1831		
Freshfield, J. S.—*cavalry* ..	,,	Sep. 3, 1828	Jan. 8, 1835		
Fothergill, John Wm.	,,	June 2, 1829	June 24, 1832		
Fletcher, Robert........	1828	Jan. 19, 1836			
Fleetwood, Willoughby ..	,,				
Fair, Peter	,,	Nov. 9, 1831	Nov. 24, 1833		
Free, Henry George	1830	June 24, 1832			
Fowler, Jonathan—*cavalry*	,,	May 26, 1832	Jan. 20, 1835		
Foulis, Archibald—*artillery*	1831				
Fast, R. F. G.—*engineers*..	1833				
G					
Grant, Cornelius	1768	Oct. 16, 1768	Sep. 5, 1770	July 11, 1779	
Geils, Thomas—*artillery* ..	1767	...1767....	...1768....	June — 1777	July 8, 1781
Gowdie, Francis.........	,,	Nov. 4, 1768	Sep. 20, 1770	July 19, 1779	Dec. 14, 1789
Godfrey, William	....	Dec. 31, 1773	Oct. 15, 1780	May 8, 1784	Apr. 30, 1802
Gordon, Thomas.........	1775	Jan. 19, 1776	Nov. 8, 1780	Dec. 20, 1789	June 1, 1796
Greene, John	....	Aug. 23, 1776	Nov. 10, 1780	May 12, 1791	
Gibbings, Arthur	1777	Nov. 15, 1778	Jan. 29, 1782	Oct. 15, 1794	Oct. 12, 1798
Graham, James	....	Mar. 31, 1778	Feb. 8, 1782	July 30, 1795	Dec. 26, 1798
Gomond, Richard	1777	June 17, 1778	Feb. 26, 1782	...1796....	May 19, 1799
Gordon, Henry	....	July 6, 1778	Mar. 8, 1782		
Grant, Alexander	1777	July 26, 1778	Mar. 16, 1782		
Gray, Thomas G.	,,	July 29, 1778	Nov. 9, 1782	June 1, 1796	Dec. 10, 1799
Goodsman, John.........	....	Aug. 6, 1778	Feb. 2, 1783		
Gahagan, Robert	....	Aug. 14, 1778	April 2, 1783		
Godfrey, Samuel.........	1778	Aug. 25, 1778	May 20, 1783	...1796....	
Gee, Middleton Mac	,,	Apr. 23, 1779	May 8, 1784		
Gepp, Edward M. T......	,,	June 6, 1779	Apr. 17, 1786	June 1, 1796	June 17, 1800
Gillum, Thomas	1779	Aug. 20, 1780	Apr. 17, 1786	June 1, 1796	
Green, Thomas	,,	Sep. 20, 1780	Apr. 17, 1786	July 27, 1796	June 8, 1801
Greenhill, Alexander.....	,,	Oct. 10, 1780	Apr. 17, 1786	Jan. 13, 1797	Feb. 21, 1801
Gorry, John.............	,,	Oct. 20, 1780	Apr. 17, 1786		
Gibbons, Sloan	....	Oct. 23, 1780	Apr. 17, 1786	May 8, 1797	
Grant, Robert M.	1780	Aug. 7, 1781	Apr. 17, 1786	Aug. 16, 1797	Jan. 27, 1803
Graham, James George....	,,	Aug. 20, 1781	Jan. 23, 1787	Nov. 29, 1797	May 19, 1803
Godfrey, Charles	,,	Sep. 16, 1781	May 6, 1788	Nov. 29, 1797	Sep. 8, 1803
Grant, Allan	,,	Oct. 19, 1781	Nov. 1, 1788	Sep. 18, 1798	
Geraud, Wm. Thomas	1781	Oct. 19, 1782	April 3, 1790	Oct. 12, 1798	
Goonan, Denis	1782	Dec. 19, 1782			
Gurnell, Thomas	,,	Dec. 21, 1782	Apr. 21, 1790	Jan. 15, 1799	Jan. 1, 1807
Grace, William	,,	Dec. 30, 1782			
Groce, Onslow	,,	May 13, 1783	Aug. 21, 1790	July 31, 1799	
Gordon, James	,,	May 15, 1783			
Graham, John...........	,,	May 27, 1783	Aug. 21, 1790		
Goldsworthy, John	,,	June 16, 1783	Aug. 21, 1790	Dec. 10, 1799	Apr. 30, 1805
Gordon, Alexander	,,	June 24, 1783	Aug. 21, 1790		
Geoghagan, Fras.--*artillery*	....	Oct. 23, 1784	April 7, 1791		

PRESIDENCY.

Lieut.-Colonel.	Colonel.	Major-General.	Lieut.-General.	Date of Resignation, Retirement, or Death.
				Died May 14, 1833, at Dublin.
				Died Nov. 28, 1836, at Vizagapatam.
				Died Sep. 4, 1835, at Palaveram.
				Not to be traced.
Apr. 17, 1786	Jan. 8, 1796	May 3, 1796		Died Oct. 24, 1815, in Scotland.
Apr. 27, 1795	Nov. 29, 1797	Jan. 1, 1805		On the Retired List, Feb. 19, 1813.
				Invalided March — 1791. Died Jan. 13, 1809.
				Died Sep. 17, 1798, at Madras.
				Died June 29, 1795, at the Presidency.
Dec. 10, 1800				Retired 1803.
				Died Jan. 31, 1802.
				Retired March — 1800.
				Resigned 1788, on account of ill health.
				Died 1793.
				Killed June 7, 1801.
				Military Fund Jan. 30, 1793.
				Died 1792.
				Died Aug. 15, 1799.
				Not to be traced.
				Died Jan. 10, 1802, at Munsoorcottah.
				Died Aug. 12, 1801.
Sep. 21, 1804				{ Invalided Mar. 21, 1805. Retired July 6, 1808.
Sep. 21, 1804				Retired Sep. 9, 1807.
				King's Service 1789.
				Retired Aug. 4, 1801.
Feb. 5, 1805				Retired Oct. 3, 1810.
Mar. 1, 1805	June 4, 1813	Aug. 12, 1819		Died April 22, 1828, at Dieppe.
Sep. 18, 1807				Retired June 20, 1809.
				Died May 3, 1804, at Madras.
				Not to be traced.
				Died 1791.
Dec. 29, 1811				{ Invalided Jan. 4, 1814. Died Nov. 25, 1816, at Vellore.
				Died 1792.
				Died 1800.
				Not to be traced.
				Died July — 1794.
				Retired Mar. 4, 1808.
				Died 1793.
				Died June — 1797.

MADRAS

NAMES.	Cadet.	Cornet, Ensign, or Second Lieutenant.	Lieutenant.	Captain.	Major.
Gent, William—*engineers* ..	1772	Jan. 20, 1775	Aug. 14, 1778	Nov. 11, 1781	Feb. 23, 1793
Grant, John—*cavalry*	1782	....	June 29, 1785	....	....
Grant, Alexander—*cavalry*	....	....	Jan. 26, 1786	....	Sep. 4, 1799
Gregor, Wm. Mc—*cavalry*	....	Dec. 9, 1785	Oct. 24, 1792	June 17, 1800	....
Gibbings, Edward	....	May 6, 1774	Oct. 9, 1780	Aug. 16, 1785	June 1, 1796
Griffin, D. Fitzgerald	....	June 13, 1778	Feb. 23, 1782	Feb. 12, 1796	May 12, 1799
Guthrie, John—*engineers* ..	....	Sep. 25, 1781	Apr. 13, 1786	....	....
Geekie, James —*cavalry* ..	....	Apr. 22, 1784	Feb. 1, 1786	Sep. 4, 1799	....
Gourlay, John—*artillery* ..	....	Feb. 3, 1789	Aug. 6, 1793	June 9, 1801	....
Geils, Andrew—*artillery* ..	1790	July 9, 1791	Feb. 12, 1796	....	....
Geils, Thomas—*artillery* ..	1791	Apr. 27, 1793	June 1, 1796	....	....
Gericke, George Frederick	....	....	June 7, 1792	Dec. 10, 1799	....
Gibson, Thomas Samuel ..	....	Nov. 13, 1788	June 7, 1792	....	....
Gordon, John Duff	1790	June 11, 1791	Sep. 19, 1793	June 17, 1800	....
Graham, Thomas	„	July 17, 1791	Oct. 24, 1793	....	....
Grant, Peter	„	Aug. 25, 1791	July 1, 1794	June 9, 1801	....
Grant, Alexander (C. B.) ..	„	Aug. 28, 1791	Aug. 6, 1794	May 17, 1801	Mar. 1, 1809
Gardiner, George	1792	Sep. 29, 1793	....	....	....
Grant, James—*cavalry*	1793	May 9, 1799	Mar. 18, 1795	Aug. 2, 1806	Sep. 1, 1818
Gordon, Wills Hill	„	....	Aug. 5, 1795	....	....
Gibbs, Charles	„	....	June 23, 1795	....	....
Greenhill, Jas. David (C. B.)	1794	Jan. 19, 1796	June 1, 1796	Feb. 21, 1804	April 6, 1810
Gregson, Robert	1795	Mar. 17, 1796	Oct. 21, 1797	....	....
Gennys, John	„	Mar. 15, 1796	Oct. 21, 1797	June 27, 1804	Mar. 8, 1810
Grant, Duncan—*cavalry* ..	„	Mar. 2, 1796	....	....	....
Grange, Rich. G. *cavalry*—	1789	....	Aug. 5, 1796	....	....
Grand, George Robert	1796	Aug. 17, 1797	Oct. 12, 1798	Sep. 21, 1804	Nov. 6, 1811
Garrard, William—*engineers*	„	Aug. 7, 1797	Jan. 1, 1803	Sep. 26, 1811	....
Gibson, George Milson	„	Aug. 14, 1797	Oct. 12, 1798	Sep. 21, 1804	Apr. 13, 1813
Gellie, James— *artillery* ..	„	Aug. 22, 1797	Mar. 1, 1800	....	....
Gabriel, John Edward	1795	....	Nov. 29, 1797	Sep. 5, 1804	Nov. 6, 1811
Gordon, Lewis	1796	Aug. 8, 1797	Sep. 29, 1798	....	....
Gibson, Alured—*artillery*	1797	Sep. 18, 1797	Mar. 1, 1800	July 4, 1807	....
Gillespie, George —*cavalry*	„	Sep. 8, 1798	Sep. 4, 1799	April 6, 1810	Sep. 1, 1818
Griffith, Charles—*artillery*	„	Aug. 18, 1798	Mar. 1, 1800	....	....
Gordon, Thomas Cosmo ..	„	July 27, 1798	Nov. 27, 1798	July 17, 1805	....
Gilchrist, Edward	„	Aug. 11, 1798	Dec. 26, 1798	....	....
Goodall, Lawrence	1795	Mar. 30, 1796	Oct. 29, 1797	....	....
Grant, Peter—*artillery*	1790	....	Aug. 9, 1797	Sep. 21, 1804	....
Grensell, Joseph	1798	....	Jan. 1, 1800	July 11, 1806	....
Grant, James—*cavalry*	....	....	Sep. 4, 1799	Aug. 2, 1806	Sep. 1, 1818
Gahagan, Charles—*artillery*	1799	....	Apr. 19, 1800	May 11, 1806	....
Green, John	„	....	Dec. 15, 1800	Apr. 6, 1810	Apr. 23, 1824
Geph, George Edward	„	....	Dec. 15, 1800	....	....
Grant, Alexander	„	....	July 20, 1801	Aug. 12, 1809	Jan. 24, 1823
George, John	„	....	Dec 15, 1800	....	....
Greaves, James Bexwith ..	„	....	....	....	....

PRESIDENCY.

Lieut.-Colonel.	Colonel.	Major General.	Lieut.-General.	Date of Resignation, Retirement, or Death.
Aug. 16, 1793	May 3, 1796	Apr. 29, 1802	....	Retired Aug. 11, 1802.
....	....	....	....	Died 1791.
....	....	....	....	Died Aug. 20, 1801.
....	....	....	....	Died Oct. 1, 1803.
Oct. 12, 1798	....	....	....	Retired 1803.
Jan. 27, 1803	....	....	....	Died July 3, 1804.
....	....	....	....	At home. Pensioned —
....	....	....	....	Invalided Oct. — 1800. Retired — Pensioned —
....	....	....	....	Resigned April — 1798.
....	....	....	....	Resigned April — 1798.
....	....	....	....	Died May 16, 1801.
....	....	....	....	Died 1793.
....	....	....	....	Died April 19, 1801.
....	....	....	....	Died Aug. 8, 1795, at Masulipatam.
....	....	....	....	Died Feb. 27, 1810.
Jan. 19, 1816	Commt. May 1, 1824. Col. June 5, 1829.	....	....	Died Dec. 6, 1834, in Scotland.
....	....	....	....	Died May 17, 1808, at Vellore.
....	....	....	....	Died Dec. 14, 1819, at Ellichpore.
....	....	....	....	Died Mar. 14, 1799, at Trincomalee.
....	....	....	....	Struck off Dec. 17, 1799.
Nov. 7, 1818	Commt. Oct. 14, 1824. Col. June 5, 1829.	Jan. 10, 1837	....	
....	....	....	....	Died in England (date not known).
....	....	....	....	Died Feb. 23, 1818, at Mangalore.
....	....	....	....	Died May 21, 1799.
....	....	....	....	Retired 1796, on Half Pay, in Europe.
....	....	....	....	{ Invalided Nov. 7, 1811, in India. Struck off, Sep. 25, 1823, in England.
April 1, 1825	Brevet, Dec. 1, 1829	....	....	Died Sep. 2, 1836, at Octacamund.
....	....	....	....	Died May 24, 1814, at Vizagapatam.
....	....	....	....	Died May 20, 1803.
....	....	....	....	Died Mar. 23, 1815, at Nundy Droog.
....	....	....	....	Died Dec. 5, 1801.
....	....	....	....	Retired Sep. 2, 1813.
May 1, 1824	....	....	....	{ Died Dec. 17, 1826, on board the "Recovery," for England.
....	....	....	....	Killed Sep. 23, 1803, at Assaye.
....	....	....	....	Died Oct. 9, 1809, at Mangalore.
....	....	....	....	Died — 1800.
....	....	....	....	Cashiered April 14, 1800.
....	....	....	....	Died Feb. 27, 1810.
....	....	....	....	Died June 3, 1808, at Sadras.
....	....	....	....	Died Dec. 14, 1819, at Ellichpore.
....	....	....	....	Died April 14, 1817, at Ellichpore.
Sep. 8, 1826	Brevet, June 18, 1831	....	....	
....	....	....	....	Invalided Dec. 8, 1807. Died June 30, 1811.
Aug. 1, 1825	....	....	....	{ Died June 20, 1827, on board the "Sophia," on passage to England.
....	....	....	....	Died June 28, 1803.
....	....	....	....	Died Jan. 22, 1802.

MADRAS

NAMES.	Cadet.	Cornet, Ensign, or Second Lieutenant.	Lieutenant.	Captain.	Major.
Godfrey, Frederick	1799		Dec. 15, 1800		
Gape, Charles	1800				
Gwynne, Edward Matthew	,,				
Griffenhoofe, William	,,		May 26, 1802	Mar. 23, 1814	
Gwynne, Rowland	,,		July 20, 1801	Nov. 1, 1809	
Gummer, Stephen Stone	,,		July 20, 1801	Sep. 29, 1808	Mar. 3, 1824
Green, Francis	,,		July 20, 1801		
Gordon, Charles	,,		July 20, 1801		
Guille, Richard	,,		May 9, 1802	Apr. 14, 1817	
Gibson, John Thomas	,,		July 20, 1801	Apr. 11, 1815	May 1, 1824
Grut, Thomas	,,		July 20, 1801		
Goreham, G. J.—*artillery*	,,		Dec. 12, 1800	Apr. 20, 1810	Brevet, June 4, 1814
Goodbehere, Edmond	1802		Jan. 19, 1804		
Green, Samuel	,,		Jan. 19, 1804	June 13, 1816	
Grant, John	,,				
Gooch, William	,,				
Graham, Nicholas	,,	Apr. 17, 1803	Nov. 16, 1803		
Godley, William	,,	Apr. 17, 1803	May 29, 1804	Dec. 1, 1817	July 28, 1826
Gorton, James—*cavalry*	,,		Oct. 31, 1804	Sep. 1, 1818	
Guinness, John Grattan	,,		Sep. 5, 1804		
Grehan, Patrick	1803		Sep. 21, 1804		
Garling, James	,,		Sep. 21, 1804		
Goble, Francis Methold	,,		Sep. 21, 1804		
Gore, Ralph	,,		Sep. 21, 1804		
Gordon, William	,,		Sep. 21, 1804	May 16, 1822	1828
Gowland, T. Beach Jarrett	1804		July 17, 1805		
Gibson, John Roebuck	,,		July 17, 1805		
Glenholme, John	,,		July 25, 1805		
Goodrich, Thomas	1805	Jan. 1, 1807	Mar. 5, 1808		
Godfrey, John Race	,,		June 23, 1808	Oct. 14, 1821	Jan. 15, 1833
Golding, John	,,		June 27, 1806		
Grant, George	,,	Jan. 1, 1807	Mar. 1, 1809		
Gilbert, Charles James	,,	June 27, 1806	Oct. 22, 1809		
Grinsted, David	,,				
Graves, Philip	,,	June 27, 1806	Jan. 23, 1808		
Gwynne, John	,,	June 27, 1806	May 5, 1810	May 1, 1824	
Gray, Robert, Senr.	,,	June 27, 1806	Dec. 21, 1809	May 24, 1821	
Gray, Robert, Junr.	,,	June 27, 1806	Jan. 13, 1808		
Greenhill, Thomas—*cavalry*	,,	Apr. 13, 1807	June 19, 1814	June 21, 1822	
Gill, Glencairn	,,	Jan. 1, 1807	Oct. 10, 1810	May 1, 1824	
Grant, George Mackenzie	1806	July 3, 1807	Mar. 1, 1810		
Grant, Archibald	,,	July 3, 1807	Aug. 18, 1809		
Green, Harry	,,	July 3, 1807	Oct. 9, 1811		
Gwynne, Iltid	,,	July 3, 1807	Apr. 13, 1813	Apr. 19, 1823	Nov. 21, 1826
Gordon, Alexander	,,	July 3, 1807	Apr. 6, 1810	May 1, 1824	Mar. 3, 1830
Greaves, W. T. N.—*cavalry*	,,	July 10, 1807	Apr. 9, 1815	May 1, 1824	
Grierson, Alexander	,,	July 3, 1807	Oct. 21, 1811		

PRESIDENCY.

Lieut.-Colonel.	Colonel.	Major-General.	Lieut.-General.	Date of Resignation, Retirement, or Death.
....	....	....	....	Resigned March 9, 1807.
....	....	....	....	Died at Chingleput, Jan. 18, 1802.
....	....	....	....	Resigned Sep. 6, 1803.
....	....	....	....	{ Invalided June 1, 1816, in India, Died Oct. 28, 1817, at Negapatam.
....	....	....	....	Died July 20, 1823, at Madras.
July 28, 1826	Brevet June 18, 1831	....	....	
....	....	....	....	Died at Masulipatam, Aug. 29, 1813.
....	....	....	....	Died at Ellichpore, May 25, 1804.
....	....	....	....	Retired in England, July 14, 1824.
Dec. 12, 1828	Brevet Jan. 22, 1834.	....	....	
....	....	....	....	Lost in the ship "Glory," Nov. 20, 1808.
....	....	....	....	Died May 20, 1818, in camp, near Chandah.
....	....	....	....	Died at Cochin, Nov. 11, 1810.
....	....	....	....	Died Sep. 14, 1818, at Fort St. George.
....	....	....	....	Died Jan. 6, 1805. "Union."
....	....	....	....	Died on his passage out in the
....	....	....	....	Died Nov. 2, 1804.
....	....	....	....	Retired Apr. 4, 1829, in England.
....	....	....	....	{ Invalided Feb. 9, 1827, in India. Died March 28, 1827, at St. Thomé.
....	....	....	....	Struck off.
....	....	....	....	Died April 12, 1807.
....	....	....	....	Died June 4, 1820.
....	....	....	....	Died Feb. 14, 1813.
....	....	....	....	Died at sea, Jan. 30, 1813.
....	....	....	....	Retired Nov. 25, 1828, in England.
....	....	....	....	Resigned Aug. 25, 1810.
....	....	....	....	Resigned Oct. 6, 1809.
....	....	....	....	Died Jan. 4, 1810.
....	....	....	....	Died Dec. 28, 1813.
....	....	....	....	Retired Feb. 10, 1836, in India.
....	....	....	....	Died Mar. 30, 1811, at Seringapatam.
....	....	....	....	Killed in action, near Nagpore, Nov. 27, 1817.
....	....	....	....	{ Invalided Aug. 3, 1810, Died Dec. 31, 1816, at Berhampore,
....	....	....	....	Died June 25, 1807.
....	....	....	....	Died at Goa, July 4, 1812.
....	....	....	....	Retired Sep. 30, 1829, in England.
....	....	....	....	{ Invalided in India, Jan. 25, 1825. Died June 7, 1829, at Vizagapatam.
....	....	....	....	{ Admitted a Pensioner on Lord Clive's Fund, Oct. 30, 1817.
....	....	....	....	Died Feb. 18, 1825, in camp, at Belgaum.
....	....	....	....	{ Invalided Aug. 13, 1830, in India. Retired Jan. 15, 1832, in England.
....	....	....	....	Died 1811.
....	....	....	....	Died April 6, 1816.
....	....	....	....	Died June 2, 1821.
....	....	....	....	Died May 31, 1833, in Ellore.
....	....	....	....	Retired March 26, 1832, in India.
....	....	....	....	Died in England, Mar. 6, 1827.
....	....	....	....	Died Aug. 30, 1815, at Madras.

MADRAS

NAMES.	Cadet.	Cornet, Ensign, or Second Lieutenant.	Lieutenant.	Captain.	Major.
Grant, Charles St. John ..	1806	July 3, 1807	Apr. 12, 1813	Sep. 8, 1826	Brevet Jan. 10, 1837
Gray, Andrew............	,,	July 21, 1808	Jan. 14, 1815	May 1, 1824	....
Glass, James	,,	July 3, 1807	Jan. 25, 1811	Aug. 1, 1823	May 30, 1833
Greig, Hector	,,	July 3, 1807	Apr. 23, 1812	....	....
Gordon, Robert—*cavalry*..	1807	Nov. 28, 1808	Oct. 31, 1817	Nov. 6, 1824	....
Graham, John............	,,	....	....	....	....
Gordon, John—*cavalry*....	,,	....	....	....	....
Gore, Henry H.—*artillery*	,,	Feb. 11, 1809	Mar. 9, 1810	....	....
Gifford, Thomas..........	,,	May 2, 1809	June 21, 1812	....	....
Garrard, George—*cavalry*	1808	Dec. 15, 1810	....	....	....
Gale, Humphry Senhouse	,,	May 23, 1810	July 23, 1814	....	....
Gordon, Robert	,,	June 27, 1810	Jan. 29, 1815	Mar. 13, 1825	....
Gleig, Alexander	1809	Nov. 17, 1810	Apr. 19, 1815	....	....
Grimshaw, John..........	,,	June 28, 1810	Dec. 11, 1813	....	....
Gibb, Charles Henry......	,,	June 17, 1810	Dec. 29, 1815	....	....
Gibbings, Robert	,,	Aug. 19, 1809	April 2, 1816	May 1, 1824	....
Gibbings, John	,,	Aug. 4, 1810	Nov. 11, 1814	....	....
Glover, William..........	,,	Oct. 4, 1809	....	....	....
Gamage, John J.—*artillery*	,,	July 7, 1810	Nov. 25, 1812	Oct. 17, 1821	....
Gregory, Henry—*artillery*	,,	July 7, 1810	Sep. 3, 1813	Feb. 1, 1822	....
Graham, William	,,	Nov. 12, 1810	June 6, 1817	....	....
Grant, Alex.—*engineers* ..	,,	July 7, 1810	May 2, 1817	....	....
Garnault, Joseph	1810	May 23, 1811	Mar. 17, 1814	May 2, 1824	Apr. 17, 1834
Gordon, Francis..........	,,	June 5, 1811	....	....	....
Goodrich, James—*cavalry*	,,	Dec. 11, 1812	....	....	....
Griffinhoofe, George	,,	Nov. 6, 1811	April 9, 1815	....	....
Gahagan, E. Price—*cavalry*	,,	June 19, 1814	....	....	....
Gordon, Peter............	1811	June 11, 1812	Jan. 17, 1815	....	....
Gem, Henry.............	,,	June 11, 1812	....	....	....
Glen, W. John David	1812	July 6, 1813	April 4, 1816	....	....
Gray, George	,,	July 6, 1813	Mar. 30, 1816	Sep. 8, 1826	....
Gomonde, R. J.—*artillery*	1814	....	....	....	....
Gordon, William Grant ..	1817	....	June 4, 1818	May 16, 1822	June 1828
Greene, Geo. Burnaby	,,	....	Aug. 9, 1818	....	....
Groves, Edward	1818	....	June 13, 1819	.... 1829 ...	....
Gray, Edmund Charles....	,,	....	June 13, 1819	....	....
Gunning, John	,,	....	June 13, 1819	Dec. 31, 1828	....
Grant, Alex.—*cavalry*	,,	....	Jan. 28, 1820	Oct. 29, 1833	....
Gordon, John	,,	....	June 13, 1819	....	....
Graham, Charles Henry ..	,,	....	....	....	....
Goolde, Henry	1819	....	April 7, 1820	May 8, 1830	....
Gilby, William B.	,,	....	April 7, 1820	Oct. 28, 1834	....
Gray, William	,,	....	April 7, 1820	Mar. 18, 1832	....
Goodrich, Samuel B.......	,,	....	April 7, 1820	....	....
Gardiner, William P.	,,	....	April 7, 1820	....	....
Glover, Philip D.	,,	....	April 7, 1820	Dec. 25, 1833	....
Gompertz, William	,,	....	April 7, 1820	....	....

PRESIDENCY.

Lieut.-Colonel.	Colonel.	Major-General.	Lieut.-General.	Date of Resignation, Retirement, or Death.
				Died Jan. 3, 1832. ["Morley."
				Died June 21, 1835, on board the
				Resigned Sep. 9, 1813, in England.
				Died June 11, 1827, at Kamptee.
				Died Sep. 24, 1808.
				Died Sep. 31, 1809. [Mount.
				Died Sep. 20, 1818, at St. Thomas's
				Admitted a Pensioner on Lord Clive's Fund.
				{ Invalided Nov. 30, 1816, in India; died Jan. 23, 1818, at Bombay.
				Died Aug. 9, 1818, in camp, at Ajunta.
				Died Sep. 3, 1817, at Darwar.
				Died May 18, 1819, near Copaul Droog.
				Died Aug. 15, 1826, at Cheltenham.
				Died April 12, 1826, at Mangalore.
				{ Died Jan. 9, 1818, of wounds received in action, Dec. 21, at Maheidpoor.
				Died Sep. 11, 1812, at Guzzlehutty Pass.
				Died Sep. 27, 1826, at Penang.
				{ Died Mar. 15, 1831, on board the "Lady Macnaghten," on passage to England.
				Died Jan. 29, 1823, at Fort St. George.
				Died May 26, 1825, at Prome.
				Died July 12, 1814, at Jaulnah.
				Retired Jan. 22, 1816, in England.
				Died Oct. 27, 1817, in England.
				Died Dec. 4, 1818, at St. Thomé.
				Died April 16, 1824, at Seringapatam.
				Died Jan. 19, 1818.
				Killed Dec. 21, 1817, in action.
				[Mount.
				Died March 20, 1816, at St. Thomas's
				Retired Nov. 25, 1828, in England.
				{ Died Aug. 22, 1825, on board the "William Money."
				Retired Oct. 16, 1830, in England.
				Died Sep. 20, 1822, at Berhampore.
				Died April 28, 1831.
				Died Nov. 9, 1824, at Cannanore.
				Resigned June 15, 1834, in England.
				Died April 10, 1837, at Chichacole.
				Died Nov. 10, 1826, at Morgue.
				Died Nov. 8, 1831, at Madras.
				Died April 7, 1836, at Goomsoor.

MADRAS.——L

MADRAS

NAMES.	Cadet.	Cornet, Ensign, or Second Lieutenant.	Lieutenant.	Captain.	Major.
Griffiths, Frederick Benj...	1819	....	April 7, 1820	....	....
Garraway, Robert	,,	....	June 18, 1820	....	....
Guppy, Edward	,,	....	June 12, 1821	....	....
Glover, John Campbell....	,,	....	April 7, 1820	Nov. 13, 1830	....
Grant, Robert	,,	....	....	....	....
Gordon, Robert Huntley ..	,,	April 6, 1820	May 16, 1822	....	....
Grubb, John	,,	April 6, 1820	May 29, 1822	....	....
Geoghegan, Nicholas......	,,	April 6, 1820	July 2, 1822	Sep. 15, 1832	....
Green, Thomas Littleton ..	1820	April 6, 1820	Jan. 5, 1824	Oct. 9, 1830	Jan. 27, 1837
Garstin, Robert—*cavalry*..	,,	Feb. 13, 1821	May 1, 1824	May 13, 1837	....
Gould, Edw. B.—*cavalry*..	,,	April 6, 1820	May 1, 1824	....	....
Gray, David	,,	Feb. 13, 1821	....	....	....
Goldsworthy, Josiah Webbe	,,	Feb. 13, 1821	Oct. 14, 1823	June 15, 1833	....
Gibson, George	,,	....	Mar. 24, 1822	....	....
Gibb, James.............	,,	....	....	....	....
George, John Moore	,,	Feb. 13, 1821	June 19, 1824	....	....
Græme, Chs. H.—*cavalry* .	,,	Feb. 13, 1821	May 1, 1824	Oct. 27, 1834	....
Gledstanes, Ralph Skinner	,,	Feb. 13, 1821	Apr. 24, 1823	Aug. 20, 1831	....
Green, John Geo.—*cavalry*	,,	Feb. 13, 1821	May 1, 1824	....	....
Gordon, John	,,	Feb. 13, 1821	June 2, 1825	Brevet, Feb. 13, 1836	....
Gaitskell, Edward—*cavalry*	,,	Feb. 13, 1821	May 15, 1825	....	....
Grant, Samuel A.	1821	Feb. 13, 1821	Jan. 25, 1824	Oct. 10, 1836	....
Gregory, Arthur W.—*cavalry*	,,	Feb. 13, 1821	Nov. 24, 1826	....	....
Graham, John Robert	,,	Apr. 27, 1822	April 3, 1826	Mar. 27, 1835	....
Gordon, George	,,	Apr. 27, 1822	Dec. 14, 1825	....	....
Gascoigne, Evelyn John ..	,,	Apr. 27, 1822	Sep. 8, 1826	....	....
Gosling, Henry Charles ..	,,	Apr. 27, 1822	April 6, 1826	....	....
Gordon, James W.........	,,	Apr. 27, 1822	....	....	....
Grant, William	,,	Apr. 27, 1822	....	....	....
Gordon, James	,,	Apr. 27, 1822	Sep. 8, 1826	....	....
Gordon, William	,,	Apr. 27, 1822	July 12, 1824	....	....
Gibson, George	,,	Apr. 27, 1822	Sep. 8, 1826	....	....
Gerrard, John............	,,	Apr. 27, 1822	Sep. 8, 1826	....	....
Grant, Charles—*artillery* ..	,,	May 10, 1822	May 11, 1822	Nov. 17, 1831	....
Geils, Thos. Edm.—*artillery*	1822	May 10, 1822	May 11, 1822	May 1, 1833	....
Gibb, William Edward	,,	May 2, 1823	July 14, 1827	....	....
Greaves, Joseph Nelson ..	,,	May 2, 1823	....	....	....
Grantham, George........	1823	....	Mar. 2, 1826	Aug. 15, 1832	....
Goldingham, G. A.—*artillery*	,,	Feb. 7, 1824	May 1, 1824	....	....
Griffith, Henry	,,	Sep. 14, 1824	Oct. 21, 1827	June 7, 1836	....
Gunthorpe, J. H.—*artillery*	,,	June 17, 1824	June 28, 1824	....	....
Glas, Arch^d. Mac Laghlan	1824	Mar. 10, 1825	Sep. 23, 1832	....	....
Gill, Robert.............	,,	May 6, 1825	Sep. 8, 1826	....	....
Gordon, Henry (18 N. I.)..	,,	May 6, 1825	June 20, 1828	....	....
Green, Chs. Jas.—*engineers*	,,	....	May 1, 1824	Mar. 4, 1831	....
Grant, James—*cavalry*	,,	May 6, 1825	Jan. 24, 1827	....	....
Green, Henry	,,	Feb. 2, 1826	Aug. 8, 1826	....	....

PRESIDENCY.

Lieut.-Colonel.	Colonel.	Major-General.	Lieut.-General.	Date of Resignation, Retirement, or Death.
....	....	....	....	Died Feb. 20, 1827, at Gooty.
....	....	....	....	Died July 8, 1827, at Masulipatam.
....	....	....	....	Resigned Nov. 22, 1822, in India.
....	....	....	....	
....	....	....	....	Died April 16, 1821, at Belgaum.
....	....	....	....	{ Invalided Aug. 13, 1830, in India. Retired Feb. 23, 1833, in England.
....	....	....	....	Died June 3, 1825, at Donnabue.
....	....	....	....	
....	....	....	....	
....	....	....	....	
....	....	....	....	Resigned Nov. 19, 1830, in England.
....	....	....	....	Died Mar. 13, 1822, in camp, at Nalgood
....	....	....	....	{ Died Jan. 26, 1830, at sea, on board the "Providence."
....	....	....	....	Died Nov. 29, 1821, at Trichinopoly.
....	....	....	....	Died Mar. 13, 1829, at Pallamcottah.
....	....	....	....	
....	....	....	....	
....	....	....	....	Struck off April 25, 1829, in India.
....	....	....	....	
....	....	....	....	Invalided March 20, 1827, in India.
....	....	....	....	
....	....	....	....	Died Nov. 11, 1833.
....	....	....	....	
....	....	....	....	
....	....	....	....	
....	....	....	....	Died Aug. 20, 1825, at Masulipatam.
....	....	....	....	Died Aug. 22, 1826, in Edinburgh.
....	....	....	....	{ Died Jan. 10, 1829, on board the "Mount Stuart Elphinstone."
....	....	....	....	{ Pensioned on Lord Clive's Fund, Mar. 10, 1833, in England.
....	....	....	....	Died May 28, 1834, at Bellary.
....	....	....	....	
....	....	....	....	Died Oct. 30, 1830, in London.
....	....	....	....	
....	....	....	....	Died Oct. 11, 1831, in England.
....	....	....	....	
....	....	....	....	
....	....	....	....	Died May 27, 1834, at Berhampore.
....	....	....	....	
....	....	....	....	
....	....	....	....	
....	....	....	....	Died May 6, 1832, at Simla.
....	....	....	....	

MADRAS

NAMES.	Cadet.	Cornet, Ensign, or Second Lieutenant.	Lieutenant.	Captain.	Major.
Gibbings, Arthur B.	1824	May 6, 1825	...1828...		
Girand, Byng Thomas	,,	Jan. 8, 1826	Apr. 27, 1834		
Glynn, John Edmund	1825	....	July 16, 1827		
Greenwell, James Sheridan	,,	...1826....	....		
Gordon, Robert (37 N. I.)	,,	....	June 17, 1826		
Gray, Frederick	,,	Jan. 8, 1826	May 24, 1833		
Gove, Arthur Saunders....	,,	Jan. 8, 1826	....		
Gros, James Richard......	,,	Oct. 25, 1826	....		
Gottreux, Frederick	,,	Jan. 8, 1826	April 2, 1828		
Gardner, W. D. F.—*artillery*	,,	Mar. 23, 1826	....		
Grant, Francis	,,	Jan. 8, 1826	Oct. 5, 1831		
Gomm, James	,,	Jan. 8, 1826	April 1, 1833		
Groube, G. B. B.—*cavalry*	,,	Jan. 8, 1826	May 2, 1832		
Gordon, Charles	,,	Jan. 8, 1826	Mar. 8, 1832		
Grimes, John	1826	Jan. 8, 1826	Dec. 15, 1827		
Gordon, Henry (38 N. I.)..	,,	Jan. 7, 1827	April 5, 1831		
Gunthorpe, Wm. Munton..	,,	Jan. 8, 1826	Mar. 14, 1832		
Garrow, William	,,	Mar. 10, 1827	Nov. 8, 1831		
Goodenough, Edmund	,,	....	....		
Gordon, W. C.—*artillery* ..	,,	June 15, 1827	Nov. 17, 1831		
Godfrey, T. A. C.—*artillery*	1827	June 18, 1827	Dec. 5, 1831		
Green, Edward	,,	June 18, 1828	Mar. 4, 1834		
Germon, John Pinsent	,,	July 26, 1828	Mar. 5, 1836		
Glascock, Wm. Matthew ..	,,	....	....		
Groube, Dodson—*cavalry* ..	,,	....	....		
Garrard, Wm.—*engineers*..	,,	....	Dec. 29, 1830		
Gumm, Geo. M.—*artillery*	,,	Dec. 13, 1827	Aug. 15, 1832		
Gordon, Robert (32 N. I.)..	,,	Mar. 8, 1829	Oct. 28, 1834		
Gabbett, W. M.—*artillery*	1828	Dec. 12, 1828	June 4, 1836		
Glascott, Gifford	,,	Dec. 7, 1831	Feb. 11, 1835		
Gunthorpe, J. A.—*artillery*	,,	Oct. 12, 1831	....		
Garmir, Henry—*cavalry* ..	1829	Jan. 8, 1831	Mar. 12, 1833		
Gompertz, Sampson	,,	Feb. 3, 1832	July 5, 1836		
Gustard, Henry F........	,,	Mar. 10, 1832	Dec. 13, 1836		
Grubb, Wm. H.—*artillery*	,,	April 1, 1834	....		
Gould, Alex. B.—*artillery*	,,	May 1, 1833	....		
Goad, John W.—*artillery*..	1830	Feb. 15, 1836	....		
Gardner, Robert Ogilvie ..	1831	Nov. 24, 1832	Aug. 2, 1836		
Gabb, Frederick Secretan..	1832	Nov. 24, 1832	....		
Gibbon, Charles J.	,,	June 11, 1833	....		
Goodwyn, Walter F.......	,,	June 11, 1833	....		
Goolden, John	,,	....	....		
Gill, Charles	,,	Dec. 13, 1833	....		
Gall, G. L. H.—*cavalry* ..	1833	May 5, 1834	Nov. 18, 1836		
Grant, Wm. D.	,,	June 13, 1834	Jan. 27, 1837		
Greenlaw, A. J.	1834	Jan. 25, 1835	....		
Gore, A. K.	,,	Jan. 25, 1835	July 18, 1836		
Gordon, C. F.............	,,	Feb. 24, 1835	....		

PRESIDENCY.

Lieut.-Colonel.	Colonel.	Major-General.	Lieut.-General.	Date of Resignation, Retirement, or Death.
....	....	....	....	Died Sep. 2, 1828, at Vellore.
....	....	....	....	Died April 15, 1836, at Ellore.
....	....	....	....	
....	....	....	....	Died Jan. 21, 1827, at Kamptee.
....	....	....	....	
....	....	....	....	
....	....	....	....	Died June 9, 1829, at Coimbatore.
....	....	....	....	Died June 1, 1832, at Shemoga.
....	....	....	....	
....	....	....	....	Died Jan. 12, 1828, at Bolarum.
....	....	....	....	
....	....	....	....	
....	....	....	....	
....	....	....	....	
....	....	....	....	
....	....	....	....	
....	....	....	....	
....	....	....	....	
....	....	....	....	Resigned June 27, 1830, in India.
....	....	....	....	
....	....	....	....	
....	....	....	....	
....	....	....	....	Died Dec. 20, 1836, at Singapore.
....	....	....	....	{ Pensioned Feb. 4, 1831, on Lord Clive's Fund in England.
....	....	....	....	Died Sep. 27, 1829, at Jaulnah.
....	....	....	....	Died Oct. 2, 1836, at Octacamund.
....	....	....	....	
....	....	....	....	
....	....	....	....	
....	....	....	....	
....	....	....	....	
....	....	....	....	
....	....	....	....	
....	....	....	....	
....	....	....	....	
....	....	....	....	Killed March 5, 1836, in action at Goomsoor.
....	....	....	....	
....	....	....	....	Died June 9, 1834, at Madras.
....	....	....	....	
....	....	....	....	
....	....	....	....	
....	....	....	....	
....	....	....	....	Died Sep. 21, 1837, on his passage to Europe.

MADRAS

NAMES.	Cadet.	Cornet, Ensign, or Second Lieutenant.	Lieutenant.	Captain.	Major.
H					
Horne, Mathew—*artillery*	....	June 15, 1758	June 14, 1759	Oct. 1, 1764	Nov. 17, 1771
Hope, Robert	1769	Nov. 11, 1770	Sep. 5, 1775	Oct. 31, 1783	....
Haliburton, John	1771	Nov. 13, 1773	Sep. 25, 1780	Dec. 22, 1783	June 1, 1796
Hall, James S.	....	Dec. 14, 1775	Oct. 30, 1780	....	....
Hammond, William	....	....	Nov. 9, 1780	Mar. 21, 1791	....
Higginbotham, Thomas	1776	Mar. 15, 1778	Jan. 1, 1782	....	....
Hughes, Abraham	1777	Apr. 21, 1778	Jan. 14, 1782	....	....
Hart, Thomas	1778	May 18, 1778	Feb. 1, 1782	....	Dec. 26, 1798
Hill, Joseph Gulston	1777	July 21, 1778	Mar. 14, 1782	June 1, 1796	July 31, 1799
Home, John	,,	July 31, 1778	Nov. 11, 1782	June 1, 1796	Dec. 10, 1799
Harding, Richard	1778	May 18, 1779	Jan. 19, 1786	June 1, 1796	June 17, 1800
Helass, John	,,	June 4, 1779	Apr. 17, 1786	June 1, 1796	....
Hunt, John	1779	July 28, 1779	Apr. 17, 1786	June 1, 1796	Feb. 1, 1802
Howland, Robert	,,	Aug. 4, 1780	Apr. 17, 1786	....	....
Hall, John	,,	Sep. 3, 1780	Apr. 17, 1786	July 20, 1796	....
Henderson, Thomas	,,	Oct. 14, 1780	Apr. 17, 1786	....	....
Haddow, George	1780	Sep. 19, 1781	July 14, 1788	Nov. 29, 1797	Jan. 19, 1804
Harris, Benjamin	,,	Sep. 24, 1781	July 26, 1788	Nov. 29, 1797	July 4, 1804
Hewitson, Christopher	1781	Jan. 6, 1782	....	....	....
Hall, Hamilton	,,	Jan. 7, 1782	Dec. 7, 1788	Oct. 12, 1798	Sep. 21, 1804
Holford, Denis M.	,,	Oct. 1, 1782	June 20, 1789	Oct. 12, 1798	....
Horner, Thomas	....	Dec. 5, 1782	....	....	....
Heatland, William P.	1782	Dec. 14, 1782	Aug. 21, 1790	Dec. 26, 1798	...1806....
Haycock, Richard	1782	Dec. 23, 1782	....	....	....
Heber, Charles O.	,,	Dec. 29, 1782	....	....	....
Hope, Archibald	,,	June 2, 1783	....	....	....
Haven, William G.	,,	June 8, 1783	....	....	....
Huill, William L.	,,	June 12, 1783	....	....	....
Holland, John	,,	June 20, 1783	Aug. 21, 1790	....	....
Hunter, Samuel	,,	June 26, 1783	....	....	....
Hall, George—*artillery*	,,	July 25, 1778	Nov. 29, 1780	Feb. 18, 1782	Mar. 18, 1791
Howley, Richard—*artillery*	1780	Nov. 29, 1780	Feb. 18, 1782	June 11, 1789	Sep. 26, 1801
Humphreys, T.—*artillery*	....	Nov. 30, 1780	Feb. 18, 1782	....	....
Hayes, Thomas—*artillery*	1781	Feb. 18, 1782	Oct. 22, 1784	May 6, 1793	May 15, 1806
Hammond, John—*artillery*	1782	May 6, 1783	Nov. 27, 1788	Feb. 4, 1800	....
Haynes, Christian—*artillery*	....	Oct. 24, 1784	....	....	....
Hemming, Jacob—*engineers*	....	Sep. 29, 1781	Apr. 17, 1786	Dec. 2, 1792	....
Huddleston, R. J.—*cavalry*	1782	Sep. 20, 1783	Jan. 27, 1786	Nov. 1, 1798	June 17, 1800
Hargrave, James—*cavalry*	....	June 18, 1785	May 12, 1788	Sep. 4, 1799	Dec. 21, 1803
Hill, Thomas—*cavalry*	....	....	June 19, 1785	....	....
Hughes, James	....	Mar. 4, 1765	Aug. 3, 1766	Nov. 26, 1772	....
Haffey, Burges J.—*cavalry*	1789	May 3, 1790	Aug. 1, 1796	....	....
Haffey, Thomas—*cavalry*	1790	July 5, 1792	....	....	....
Hall, James—*artillery*	1789	May 20, 1790	Feb. 2, 1795	....	....
Hathway, James—*artillery*	1790	Sep. 4, 1791	June 1, 1796	....	....
Hallcott, Thomas	....	Nov. 21, 1772	Sep. 19, 1778	Nov. 2, 1783	June 1, 1796

PRESIDENCY.

Lieut.-Colonel.	Colonel.	Major-General.	Lieut.-General.	Date of Resignation, Retirement, or Death.
....	Oct. 11, 1772	....	....	Died Dec. 14, 1789.
....	....	....	....	Died Nov. — 1793.
July 24, 1798	....	....	....	Died 1805.
....	....	....	....	Resigned Feb. —1790. [1798.
....	....	....	....	Invalided Sep. — 1791. Died Apr. 17,
....	....	....	....	Died Dec. 1793.
....	....	....	....	Invalided Aug. 1791. Died Jan. 31, 1804.
....	....	....	....	Invalided Feb. 18, 1798.
Jan. 1, 1803	....	....	....	Died Apr. 15, 1812, at Seringapatam.
....	....	....	....	Not to be traced.
....	....	....	....	Died Feb. 21, 1801, at Trincomalee.
....	....	....	....	Died January — 1797.
....	....	....	....	Invalided May 8, 1802. Died Dec. 11, 1803.
....	....	....	....	Died July — 1788.
....	....	....	....	Died Dec. 1, 1799.
....	....	....	....	{ Invalided July — 1791. In Europe, for health, 1795.
July 11, 1806	....	....	....	Retired July 15, 1807.
Sep. 10, 1807	....	....	....	Retired Sep. 7, 1808.
....	....	....	....	{ Retired 1792, on Lord Clive's bounty. Died 1795.
Sep. 18, 1807	Aug. 24, 1822	....	....	Died May 12, 1827, in Trichinopoly.
....	....	....	....	Died May 8, 1799.
....	....	....	....	Died Oct. — 1789.
....	....	....	....	Retired Aug. 26, 1807.
....	....	....	....	Pensioned Oct.—1789. Died May 27,
....	....	....	....	Died 1791. [1799.
....	....	....	....	Not to be traced.
....	....	....	....	Not to be traced.
....	....	....	....	Died 1790. [Clive's Fund.
....	....	....	....	Pensioned March 14, 1798, on Lord
....	....	....	....	Died 1792.
June 1, 1796	....	....	....	Died Oct. 17, 1797, at Madras.
April 4, 1804	....	....	....	Retired May 13, 1806.
....	....	....	....	Died May 1789.
May 29, 1806	June 4, 1814	July 19, 1821	....	Died Aug. 31, 1831, in Ireland.
....	....	....	....	Died Feb. 5, 1805, in England.
....	....	....	....	Pensioned Apr. — 1788. Died—1793.
....	....	....	....	Invalided Sep. 3, 1793. Retired 1800.
May 1, 1804	....	....	....	Retired Feb. 21, 1812.
....	....	....	....	Died May 3, 1805.
....	....	....	....	Died 1791.
Sep. — 1780	....	....	....	Died 1791.
....	....	....	....	Died (date not known).
....	....	....	....	Died 1793.
....	....	....	....	} Invalided Oct. 21, 1801. Died Mar. 4, 1803, at Ganjam.
....	....	....	....	Died Jan. 4, 1803, at Negapatam.
Mar. 18, 1797	....	....	....	Resigned Dec. 21, 1797.

MADRAS

NAMES.	Cadet.	Cornet, Ensign, or Second Lieutenant.	Lieutenant.	Captain.	Major.
Hazard, Joseph William ..	1788	....	June 7, 1792	Jan. 1, 1800	....
Hewitt, Wm. Hen. (C.B.) ..	1789	....	Oct. 2, 1792	Dec. 17, 1799	Oct. 9, 1804
Hamilton, Galbraith	1790	....	Apr. 20, 1793	June 17, 1800	Oct. 9, 1804
Haughton, William	,,	June 23, 1791	June 6, 1793	....	....
Hawes, Mathew	,,	July 4, 1791	July 17, 1793	June 17, 1800	Feb. 25, 1807
Haslewood, Joseph	,,	July 22, 1791	Dec. 11, 1793	Apr. 22, 1801	Feb. 9, 1805
Havilland, T. F. De—*engineers*	1792	May 3, 1793	June 1, 1796	Jan. 1, 1806	Oct. 8, 1815
Henderson, J. C.—*engineers*	,,	....	....	....	....
Hodson, George	....	Feb. 3, 1771	May 15, 1778	Nov. 2, 1783	....
Hay, George	1792	....	....	....	....
Haddon, P. B.—*artillery* ..	,,	Sep. 27, 1793	....	....	....
Hawkins, John	1793	....	Dec. 19, 1795	Oct. 9, 1804	....
Harding, Benjamin	1794	Dec. 23, 1795	Jan. 8, 1796	Jan. 11, 1804	....
Hampton, Thomas........	,,	Jan. 7, 1796	Jan. 8, 1796	....	....
Harris, William	1793	....	Oct. 8, 1795	....	....
Hay, Joseph	1794	Jan. 11, 1796	June 1, 1796	Sep. 21, 1804	....
Heming, Richard	1795	....	Jan. 8, 1796	Sep. 21, 1804	....
Hodgson, Charles	,,	Dec. 21, 1795	Jan. 8, 1796	June 3, 1802	June 27, 1810
Herbert, Morgan	,,	Feb. 6, 1796	July 20, 1796	....	....
Harrison, Henry	,,	Feb. 21, 1796	May 8, 1797	....	....
Hall, Lovell William......	1796	July 31, 1797	May 14, 1798	Sep. 21, 1804	....
Heath, Charles	,,	....	Nov. 29, 1797	Sep. 21, 1804	Oct. 9, 1810
Hutchins, Mathew	,,	Aug. 2, 1797	July 24, 1798	....	....
Hamilton, C.—*cavalry*	1797	May 9, 1799	Sep. 4, 1799	....	....
Hanham, John	1795	Feb. 15, 1796	Feb. 4, 1797	....	....
Hickie, William..........	,,	April 7, 1796	Nov. 29, 1797	....	....
Hurdis, J. Curtaie	1798	....	June 17, 1800	Dec. 17, 1805	....
Hughes, Robert	,,	....	Jan. 1, 1800	Jan. 1, 1807	....
Hatton, Christopher T.....	,,	....	Jan. 1, 1800	Nov. 22, 1806	....
Hankins, William	,,	....	Jan. 1, 1800	Aug. 20, 1807	Oct. 10, 1819
Hare, George	,,	Aug. 19, 1798	Dec. 26, 1798	Mar. 12, 1805	April 8, 1818
Hope, Mark	,,	....	June 17, 1800	....	....
Hay, Edward	,,	....	Jan. 1, 1800	May 28, 1806	....
Hilliard, George..........	1797	July 23, 1798	Oct. 24, 1798	....	....
Hatherley, Henry Wells ..	1799	....	Dec. 15, 1800	....	....
Harris, Wllliam	,,	....	Dec. 15, 1800	Jan. 8, 1813	....
Hicks, Thomas	,,	....	Dec. 15, 1800	Oct. 10, 1810	Feb. 11, 1823
Hawes, Charles	,,	....	Dec. 15, 1800	....	....
Hampton, James	,,	....	Dec. 15, 1800	Mar. 7, 1810	....
Hankin, James	,,	....	Dec. 15, 1800	July 22, 1807	....
Howell, J. W. Hamilton ..	,,	....	Dec. 15, 1800	Sep. 9, 1808	Oct. 17, 1819
Hamilton, A. Carroll......	,,	....	Dec. 15, 1800	....	....
Hall, John	,,	....	Dec. 15, 1800	April 6, 1810	Sep. 1, 1818
Hughes, Alex. Radford....	,,	....	Dec. 15, 1800	Oct. 10, 1809	....
Harington, Henry Lens ..	,,	....	Dec. 15, 1800	Aug. 2, 1806	....
Hay, David..............	,,	....	July 15, 1800	....	....
Hankin, George..........	,,	....	July 15, 1800	....	....

PRESIDENCY.

Lieut.-Colonel.	Colonel.	Major General.	Lieut.-General.	Date of Resignation, Retirement, or Death.
. . . .	. . . .	. . . .	. . . .	Died Sep. 16, 1804.
Dec. 27, 1808	Brevet. June 4, 1814	. . . .	. . . .	Died Apr. 16, 1826, at sea, near Bombay.
Feb. 1, 1809	. . . .	. . . .	. . . .	Died Aug. 30, 1819, in England.
. . . .	. . . .	. . . .	. . . .	Died July 25, 1797, at Amboyna.
. . . .	. . . .	. . . .	. . . .	Died Oct. 14, 1809.
Oct. 21, 1809	. . . .	. . . .	. . . .	Invalided Feb. 22, 1811.
May 1, 1824	. . . .	. . . .	. . . .	Retired April 20, 1825, in England.
. . . .	. . . .	. . . .	. . . .	Resigned — 1793.
. . . .	. . . .	. . . .	. . . .	Invalided. Died Dec. 22, 1800.
. . . .	. . . .	. . . .	. . . .	Resigned Feb. 14, 1794.
. . . .	. . . .	. . . .	. . . .	Died Aug. — 1796, at the Mount.
. . . .	. . . .	. . . .	. . . .	Died July 6, 1805, on board the "Indus."
. . . .	. . . .	. . . .	. . . .	Resigned Feb. 19, 1808.
. . . .	. . . .	. . . .	. . . .	Died May 19, 1801.
. . . .	. . . .	. . . .	. . . .	Died Dec. — 1803, at Bombay.
. . . .	. . . .	. . . .	. . . .	Lost Aug. 11, 1809, in the "True Briton."
. . . .	. . . .	. . . .	. . . .	Died Dec. 26, 1806, on board the "Diana."
Sep. 29, 1817	. . . .	. . . .	. . . .	{ Died Aug. 9, 1824, on board the "Fort William," on his passage from Rangoon.
. . . .	. . . .	. . . .	. . . .	Died — 1800.
. . . .	. . . .	. . . .	. . . .	Struck off, Oct. 10, 1801.
. . . .	. . . .	. . . .	. . . .	{ Proceeded from Balambangang, and is supposed to have been lost at sea.
Oct. 19, 1817	. . . .	. . . .	. . . .	Died Feb. 18, 1819, in camp, at Ajunta.
. . . .	. . . .	. . . .	. . . .	Died Jan. 8, 1801, at Canton.
. . . .	. . . .	. . . .	. . . .	Resigned Aug. 13, 1805.
. . . .	. . . .	. . . .	. . . .	Died Sep. 20, 1800.
. . . .	. . . .	. . . .	. . . .	Cashiered Sep. 22, 1802.
. . . .	. . . .	. . . .	. . . .	Died Aug. 8, 1819, at Cannanore.
. . . .	. . . .	. . . .	. . . .	Died Nov. 19, 1813.
. . . .	. . . .	. . . .	. . . .	Died Oct. 20, 1808.
May 1, 1824	. . . .	. . . .	. . . .	{ Invalided Dec. 4, 1829, in India. Retired Dec. 31, 1831, In England.
. . . .	. . . .	. . . .	. . . .	Died May 4, 1821, in camp at Kulladjee.
. . . .	. . . .	. . . .	. . . .	Died Dec. 11, 1803.
. . . .	. . . .	. . . .	. . . .	Retired April 29, 1814.
. . . .	. . . .	. . . .	. . . .	Struck off, July 26, 1803.
. . . .	. . . .	. . . .	. . . .	Died Nov. 3, 1804.
. . . .	. . . .	. . . .	. . . .	Retired April 24, 1816, in England.
. . . .	. . . .	. . . .	. . . .	{ Invalided March 11, 1823. Died May 23, 1833, at Cuddalore.
. . . .	. . . .	. . . .	. . . .	Died Feb. 8, 1807.
. . . .	. . . .	. . . .	. . . .	Lost Aug. 11, 1821, in the "Lady Lushington."
. . . .	. . . .	. . . .	. . . .	{ Invalided April 5, 1816, in India. Died Jan. 18, 1819, at Chicacole.
. . . .	. . . .	. . . .	. . . .	Died May 9, 1824, at Poonamallee.
. . . .	. . . .	. . . .	. . . .	Died April 1, 1803.
. . . 1824	. . . .	. . . .	. . . .	Died May 5, 1824, at Condapilly.
. . . .	. . . .	. . . .	. . . .	Died June 22, 1816, in England.
. . . .	. . . .	. . . .	. . . .	Died May 22, 1819, at Bellary.
. . . .	. . . .	. . . .	. . . .	Resigned June 6, 1802.
. . . .	. . . .	. . . .	. . . .	Died March 1, 1810.

MADRAS.—M

MADRAS

NAMES.	Cadet.	Cornet, Ensign, or Second Lieutenant.	Lieutenant.	Captain.	Major.
Hodgson, Thomas	1799		July 15, 1800	Jan. 10, 1815	
Huntley, Thomas Edward	„		July 15, 1800	Mar. 19, 1817	
Hopkinson, Sir. C. (B.B.)-*artillery*	1800		Dec. 12, 1800	Mar. 9, 1810	May 13, 1821
Hill, Percy George	„		July 20, 1801		
Hewitt, David	„		July 20, 1801		
Hume, John Unwin	„		July 20, 1801		
Home, Robert	„		July 20, 1801	Jan. 5, 1814	May 1, 1824
Hindley, Edward—*cavalry*	„	Aug. 17, 1801	Dec. 21, 1803	Sep. 1, 1818	Mar. 20, 1822
Hamilton, John Hay	„		1803		
Hunter, Robert	„		Feb. 7, 1803	Dec. 7, 1817	Apr. 3, 1832
Howden, William	„		July 20, 1801		
Henderson, Peter	„		July 20, 1801	Aug. 9, 1810	May 1, 1824
Hatherly, Narcissus Henry	„		July 20, 1801	Aug. 17, 1810	May 1, 1824
Henry, John	„		July 20, 1801	June 27, 1810	May 20, 1824
Harvey, Henry	„		July 20, 1801	July 13, 1811	
Hunter, George	„		July 20, 1801	June 27, 1810	May 1, 1824
Hunter, Patrick	„		July 11, 1802		
Hunter, Thomas	„		April 8, 1803	Mar. 14, 1813	
Herne, Edward—*cavalry*	„	Aug. 21, 1801	Sep. 24, 1803	July 29, 1815	Mar. 9, 1820
Hall, Charles	„		July 20, 1801	Jan. 8, 1813	Nov. 15, 1818
Hargrave, William	1801		July, 2, 1803	Jan. 1, 1819	
Hackett, James	1800		Dec. 15, 1800	Apr. 4, 1808	Aug. 22, 1820
Harvey, Henry Cory	1802	Apr. 17, 1803	Nov. 16, 1803	Apr. 16, 1812	
Hughes, Valentine	„		Jan. 19, 1804		
Hadgson, Samuel Irton	„		Jan. 19, 1804	Mar. 1, 1819	Feb. 27, 1827
Hassand, Richard	„				
Hill, West Tertius	„	Apr. 17, 1803	June 27, 1804		
Hamilton, David Dundas	„		May 1, 1804		
Home, William James	„	April 17, 1803	Nov. 24, 1803		
Hemming, Robert	„		June 27, 1804		
Hay, Alexander	„		Sep. 21, 1804		
Hunter, Williamson	1803		Sep. 21, 1804	Aug. 30, 1819	
Hoffstetter, John Lewis	„		Sep. 21, 1804		
Hardy, William	„		Sep. 21, 1804	Jan. 29, 1818	
Herbert, Charles	„		Sep. 21, 1804	Oct. 22, 1819	May 23, 1825
Harris, Michael John	„		Sep. 21, 1804	Sep. 1, 1818	May 6, 1824
Hollingworth, George W.	„		Sep. 21, 1804		
Hadwen, John	„		Sep. 21, 1804	May 12, 1818	
Heude, William	1804		Jan. 1, 1807	Sep. 1, 1818	
Hall, Humphry Senhouse	„		July 17, 1805	Feb. 25, 1824	
Hodgson, James	„		July 17, 1805	Dec. 10, 1819	
Hare, Hugh Charles	„				
Hancorne, Thomas	„		Oct. 29, 1805		
Hancock, Edward Young	„		Nov. 22, 1806		
Hunter, McNaughton C.	„		June 10, 1806		
Hooper, Benjamin	„		July 17, 1805	Sep. 1, 1818	
Holmes, Henry	1805		July 11, 1806	July 29, 1819	

PRESIDENCY.

Lieut.-Colonel.	Colonel.	Major-General.	Lieut.-General.	Date of Resignation, Retirement, or Death.
....	....	....	....	Retired March 18, 1817, in England.
....	....	....	....	Died May 9, 1820.
May 1, 1824	....	....	....	Retired Sep. 12, 1829, in India.
....	....	....	....	Died Sep. 21, 1806, at Palamcottah.
....	....	....	....	Died Dec. 4, 1803.
....	....	....	....	Died Dec. 28, 1804.
May 20, 1828	Brevet Jan. 23, 1834	....	....	
....	....	....	....	Retired Jan. 1, 1826, in England.
....	....	....	....	Resigned June 29, 1804.
....	....	....	....	Retired July 1, 1833, in England.
....	....	....	....	Died August 15, 1804.
Sep. 3, 1827	....	....	....	Died May 23, 1832, at Rothsay.
July 14, 1827	....	....	....	Retired Jan. 12, 1830, in India.
Feb. 6, 1830	....	....	....	
....	....	....	....	Retired Nov. 28, 1821.
July 7, 1827	....	....	....	Died April 2, 1832, in Edinburgh.
....	....	....	....	Died Feb. 29, 1804, at Bombay.
....	....	....	....	Invalided May 31, 1814. Died Nov. 2, 1814.
....	....	....	....	Died March 19, 1822, at Sholapore.
....	....	....	....	Died July 9, 1823, in England.
....	....	....	....	Died Nov. 28, 1819, at Berhampore.
Aug. 10, 1824	Dec. 1, 1829	....	....	
....	....	....	....	Died March 30, 1822, at Darwar.
....	....	....	....	Died Jan. 19, 1813.
July 4, 1832	....	....	....	Died Dec. 27, 1836, in camp at Naugaum.
....	....	....	....	Resigned the Service, 1803.
....	....	....	....	Died May 8, 1812, at Jaulnah.
....	....	....	....	Died Oct. 28, 1805, at Arcot.
....	....	....	....	Died Dec. 8, 1809.
....	....	....	....	Died April 14, 1813, at Quilon.
....	....	....	....	Struck off in England.
....	....	....	....	Died Sep. 10, 1821, at Hinghee, near Nagpore.
....	....	....	....	Invalided Sep. 30, 1816, in India.
....	....	....	....	Died Aug. 28, 1824, at Negapatam.
Apr. 19, 1831	....	....	....	
Jan. 22, 1830	....	....	....	Died Sep. 9, 1830, at Presidency.
....	....	....	....	Died July 20, 1805, in camp near Bellary.
....	....	....	....	{ Struck off in England from Apr. 17, 1822, having been absent from India more than 5 years.
....	....	....	....	Died May 18, 1824, at Masulipatam.
....	....	....	....	Died July 15, 1827.
....	....	....	....	Retired June 20, 1826, in England.
....	....	....	....	Resigned April 29, 1806.
....	....	....	....	{ Died Dec. 22, 1817, of wounds received in action on the 21st.
....	....	....	....	Struck off in England.
....	....	....	....	Died Jan. 21, 1816, at Akowla.
....	....	....	....	Died Nov. 6, 1828, at Masulipatam.
....	....	....	....	Retired Aug. 1, 1821.

MADRAS

NAMES.	Cadet.	Cornet, Ensign, or Second Lieutenant.	Lieutenant.	Captain.	Major.
Hanson, James	1805	....	Nov. 3, 1805	May 1, 1824	Feb. 15, 1832
Holmes, Edward	,,	June 27, 1806	June 27, 1810	....	....
Hamilton, David	,,	....	....	....	....
Hammond, Anthony	,,	....	July 16, 1807	....	....
Horn, George John	,,	....	July 22, 1807	....	....
Howel, Henry Augustus	,,	....	July 22, 1807	....	....
Higgins, Thomas	,,	....	Oct. 30, 1806	....	....
Henderson, Robert	,,	....	July 12, 1806	....	....
Hilton, William	,,	....	Jan. 12, 1808	....	....
Hodge, James Thomas	,,	....	July 5, 1807	....	....
Herring, William	,,	....	Aug. 21, 1808	....	....
Haultain, Arthur	,,	....	July 11, 1806	May 27, 1823	....
Hutchinson, George	,,	June 27, 1806	Mar. 18, 1809	Sep. 8, 1826	Nov. 16, 1836
Hoyes, James	,,	....	....	....	....
Hall, Matthew	,,	June 27, 1806	Aug. 7, 1809	....	....
Hammond, James John	,,	June 27, 1806	Apr. 6, 1810	May 1, 1824	....
Hoby, John	,,	June 27, 1806	Jan. 25, 1809	....	....
Harkness, Henry	,,	June 27, 1806	May 30, 1810	May 1, 1824	....
Herring, John	,,	June 27, 1806	Nov. 20, 1809	....	....
Hamilton, Walter—*cavalry*	,,	July 7, 1807	Dec. 27, 1816	....	....
Hasker, William Cottrell	,,	June 27, 1806	May 8, 1811	Aug. 2, 1821	....
Hughes, Samuel	,,	June 27, 1806	May 1, 1810	May 1, 1824	....
Hitchins, Benj. Robertson	1806	July 3, 1807	Aug. 4, 1810	Jan. 8, 1826	Brevet Jan. 10, 1837.
Harrison, John Pryce	,,	July 3, 1807	Apr. 3, 1811	....	....
Hodges, Henry William	,,	July 3, 1807	Apr. 8, 1810	Dec. 25, 1822	June 5, 1830
Harvey, Henry	,,	July 3, 1807	June 27, 1811	....	....
Hodder, Samuel	,,	July 3, 1807	Sep. 14, 1812	....	....
Haddaway, Thomas	,,	July 3, 1807	April 6, 1810	....	....
Hevey, T.	,,	June 27, 1807	July 31, 1811	....	....
Hutchinson, Charles	,,	July 2, 1807	....	....	....
Henderson, William	,,	July 3, 1806	Aug. 12, 1812	....	....
Hine, Henry Pinson	,,	July 3, 1807	Nov. 6, 1811	....	....
Hodgkinson, Roger	,,	July 3, 1807	Oct. 25, 1809	....	....
Hume, James	,,	July 3, 1807	Apr. 6, 1810	....	....
Harrison, James—*artillery*	,,	Feb. 16, 1808	Feb. 17, 1808	Sep. 1, 1818	July 5, 1829
Heath, George	,,	July 3, 1807	Nov. 17, 1810	....	....
Hansard, R. Wm. Kemeys	,,	July 3, 1807	Aug. 2, 1813	....	....
Hibgame, Edw. Thurlow	,,	Mar. 18, 1808	May 26, 1810	Dec. 22, 1822	Feb. 15, 1836
Haggard, Samuel	,,	July 3, 1807	Feb. 25, 1812	....	....
Hanmer, Graham	,,	July 3, 1807	....	....	....
Hodges, Richard Harris	,,	July 3, 1807	June 1, 1815	....	....
Hyde, Thos. Chas. Seymour	,,	July 3, 1807	Jan. 10, 1815	May 1, 1824	....
Hakewill, Charles	1807	Mar. 18, 1809	....	....	....
Harrison, Henry	,,	Sep. 9, 1808	Mar. 25, 1812	....	....
Hendrie, Andrew	,,	Oct. 2, 1808	June 27, 1812	Sep. 8, 1826	....
Hewlett, Nathaniel	,,	....	....	....	....
Harris, Henry Lucas	,,	April 7, 1809	Nov. 5, 1814	....	....

PRESIDENCY.

Lieut-Colonel.	Colonel.	Major-General.	Lieut.-General.	Date of Resignation, Retirement, or Death.
....	....	....	....	Died Oct. 28, 1817, in camp, near Darwar.
....	....	....	....	Died Feb. 15, 1807.
....	....	....	....	Resigned March 15, 1811.
....	....	....	....	Died July 18, 1820, at Bangalore.
....	....	....	....	Died Dec. 20, 1809.
....	....	....	....	Died Mar. 16, 1815, at Madura.
....	....	....	....	Died July 1, 1808.
....	....	....	....	Died Dec. 23, 1819, at Bombay.
....	....	....	....	Died Sep. 13, 1818, at Hydrabad.
....	....	....	....	Died Mar. 4, 1819, at Palamcottah.
....	....	....	....	Died May 10, 1833, at Cuddapah.
....	....	....	....	Lost in the ship "Lady Burges," April 20, 1806.
....	....	....	....	{ Died with the Field force, under Colonel Douse, Apr. 28, 1813.
....	....	....	....	Retired May 8, 1832, in England.
....	....	....	....	{ Died Apr. 7, 1810, on his way from Aleppi to Quilon.
....	....	....	....	Retired July 7, 1834, in England.
....	....	....	....	Died Oct. 26, 1817, in camp at Bassim
....	....	....	....	Retired April 12, 1834, in India.
....	....	....	....	Invalided Dec. 31, 1824.
....	....	....	....	{ Invalided Oct. 8, 1830, in India. Retired Nov. 25, 1831, in England.
....	....	....	....	Died Sep. 19, 1812, at Fort St. George.
Apr. 1, 1835	....	....	....	
....	....	....	....	Died Aug. 29, 1814, at Jaulnah.
....	....	....	....	Died May 6, 1819, at Chittledroog.
....	....	....	....	Died Nov. 16, 1819, at Bellary.
....	....	....	....	Died Sep. 18, 1816, at Masulipatam.
....	....	....	....	Died May 3, 1808, at Guntoor.
....	....	....	....	Cashiered June 8, 1813.
....	....	....	....	Died Oct. 1, 1818, in camp, near Ellichpore.
....	....	....	....	{ Invalided Nov. 1, 1809. Cashiered July 18, 1812.
....	....	....	....	Died Aug. 6, 1824, at Samulcottah.
....	....	....	....	Retired May 1, 1833, in England.
....	....	....	....	{ Died June 13, 1821, in camp, near Venkettahgurry Pettah.
....	....	....	....	Died Sep. 30, 1820, in London.
....	....	....	....	Invalided Apr., 1836, at his own request.
....	....	....	....	{ Died Jan. 29, 1818, on board the "Carmarthen," on passage to England.
....	....	....	....	Resigned Feb. 6, 1811.
....	....	....	....	Died July 7, 1820, at Masulipatam.
....	....	....	....	Invalided Sep. 21, 1830, in India, and retired.
....	....	....	....	Died July 11, 1815, at Chichacole.
....	....	....	....	Died April 19, 1815, in camp, near Amilnair.
....	....	....	....	Died Aug. 6, 1828, at Cuddalore.
....	....	....	....	Died Aug. 13, 1808, at Cuddalore.
....	....	....	....	Died Dec. 1, 1819, at Bolarum.

MADRAS

NAMES.	Cadet.	Cornet, Ensign, or Second Lieutenant.	Lieutenant.	Captain.	Major.
Herring, William	1807	Oct. 12, 1808	Apr. 30, 1814		
Howell, Thomas	,,	Aug. 18, 1809	Aug. 13, 1812	May 1, 1824	
Hockley, T. H. J.—*artillery*	,,		July 28, 1808	Mar. 2, 1819	Sep. 13, 1829
Hunt, John	,,				
Highmoor, R. L.—*cavalry*	,,	Oct. 6, 1810	Sep. 1, 1818	May 1, 1824	May 1, 1835
Hunter, F.—*cavalry*	1808	Nov. 9, 1812	Sep. 1, 1818	May 13, 1828	
Hopper, R.—*artillery*	1809	July 7, 1810	Nov. 30, 1811		
Henry, John	,,				
Hunter, N.—*artillery*	,,	July 7, 1810	June 20, 1812	Aug. 16, 1821	
Hasker, W. C.	1810		May 8, 1811		
Hodges, Henry	,,	Mar. 31, 1811	Dec. 22, 1817		
Huddleston, R. A.—*cavalry*	,,	Dec. 30, 1813			
Hyslop, Wm.—*cavalry*	,,	Jan. 17, 1814	Sep. 1, 1818		
Hutton, George (22 N. I.)	1811	June 11, 1812	Sep. 17, 1815	Jan. 15, 1826	
Hewetson, Charles	,,	June 11, 1812	Oct. 9, 1815	Feb. 27, 1827	
Harrison, George	,,	June 11, 1812			
Harris, E. G.—*cavalry*	1812	Dec. 1, 1816	Sep. 1, 1818		
Haleman, Francis	,,	July 6, 1813	Aug. 14, 1816	Sep. 19, 1826	Oct. 9, 1830
Hosmer, Charles—*artillery*	,,	July 6, 1813	Sep. 1, 1818	June 9, 1825	
Hele, W. S.—*artillery*	1813	July 4, 1814	Sep. 1, 1818	Dec. 12, 1825	
Howison, John	,,	July 4, 1814	June 13, 1816	May 6, 1824	
Hannington, J. G.	1815		Nov. 28, 1817		
Hamond, Peter—*artillery*	,,	April 9, 1816	Feb. 2, 1819	July 17, 1827	
Hyslop, A. G.—*artillery*	1816	June 26, 1817	Mar. 2, 1819	Aug. 6, 1827	
Harington, Edw. B.	,,				
Hadfield, W. Crane	1817				
Hamilton, G. J.	,,		June 4, 1818		
Hodges, W. H.	,,				
Harvey, Percy Lorenzo	,,		Aug. 12, 1818	Dec. 11, 1826	
Hodge, Peter Pender	,,		Sep. 13, 1818	Apr. 2, 1828	
Hudson, H. Wentworth	,,				
Haywood, John Lovet	1818		June 13, 1819		
Hands, Fred. Wright	,,		June 13, 1819	Jan. 14, 1826	
Hutchinson, G. F.	,,		June 13, 1819	Jan. 6, 1826	
Hart, Mont. James	,,		June 13, 1819	Apr. 14, 1826	
Hole, Joseph	,,		June 13, 1819		
Haldane, William	,,		June 13, 1819		
Humffreys, R. M.	,,		June 13, 1819	June 18, 1828	
Humffreys, John	,,		May 1, 1824		
Haig, James Russell	,,		June 13, 1819	June 4, 1826	Apr. 1, 1835
Harkness, James	,,		June 13, 1819	May 20, 1834	
Hicks, Sam. Rich.	,,		June 13, 1819	Brevet June 12, 1829	
Howard, John Biggs	1819				
Hart, George	,,		April 7, 1820		
Harwood, John	,,		May 18, 1820	...1829....	
Harding, John Ward	,,		May 10, 1820	May 21, 1833	
Hele, Philip Selby	,,		Aug. 7, 1820	...1827....	

PRESIDENCY.

Lieut.-Colonel.	Colonel.	Major-General.	Lieut.-General.	Date of Resignation, Retirement, or Death.
....	....	....	....	Struck off in England.
....	....	....	....	{ Died Aug. 9, 1825, on board the "Indianian," in Arracan River.
....	....	....	....	Retired May 4, 1833.
....	....	....	....	Resigned Oct. 24, 1809.
....	....	....	....	
....	....	....	....	
....	....	....	....	Died Dec. 30, 1811.
....	....	....	....	Died Feb.—1813, at China.
....	....	....	....	Died May 7, 1827, at St. Helena.
....	....	....	....	{ Invalided Dec. 31, 1824, in India. Retired Dec. 3, 1830, in England.
....	....	....	....	Died Sep. 9, 1822, at Musulipatam.
....	....	....	....	Died —1818, in the Straits of Sunda.
....	....	....	....	
....	....	....	....	
....	....	....	....	Resigned July 15, 1814, in India.
....	....	....	....	Died July 28, 1825, at Echodah.
Feb. 20, 1836	....	....	....	
....	....	....	....	
....	....	....	....	Retired Aug. 5, 1835, in England.
....	....	....	....	
....	....	....	....	Died Dec. 25, 1820, at Jaggepet.
....	....	....	....	
....	....	....	....	Resigned Feb. 20, 1819, in India.
....	....	....	....	Died Oct. 21, 1820, at Chanda.
....	....	....	....	Died Apr. 3, 1827, in camp, near Arcot.
....	....	....	....	Died May 4, 1819, in Camp, at Umbarepet.
....	....	....	....	Retired May 16, 1829, in England.
....	....	....	....	Died Oct. 17, 1834, at Madura.
....	....	....	....	Died June 15, 1819, at Talmore.
....	....	....	....	Dismissed Nov. 12, 1822, in India.
....	....	....	....	
....	....	....	....	Retired June 3, 1826, in England.
....	....	....	....	Died Dec. 6, 1831, at Coimbatore.
....	....	....	....	Died Dec. 3, 1819, at Wallajabad.
....	....	....	....	Died Mar. 29, 1835, at Terry Kerry.
....	....	....	....	Died Aug. 14, 1824, at Arcot.
....	....	....	....	
....	....	....	....	Died Oct. 28, 1834, at Cannanore.
....	....	....	....	
....	....	....	....	Died Aug. 31, 1822, at Chittledroog.
....	....	....	....	Died Apr. 30, 1826, at Amherst Town.
....	....	....	....	Died Sep. 11, 1829, in London.
....	....	....	....	Retired April 11, 1837, in England.
....	....	....	....	{ Invalided Dec. 14, 1827. Died May 7, 1828, at Vizagapatam.

MADRAS

NAMES.	Cadet.	Cornet, Ensign, or Second Lieutenant.	Lieutenant.	Captain.	Major.
Harden, Robert Allen	1819	....	May 28, 1820	....	....
Hall, Edward Hancock....	,,	....	Dec. 12, 1820	....	....
Hitchins, Henry Thomas ..	,,	....	Dec. 26, 1820	July 1, 1833	....
Haldane, Edward	,,	....	June 10, 1820	Mar. 11, 1831	....
Hay, Thomas Pasley......	,,	....	April 7, 1820	July 5, 1829	....
Hughes, James Victor	,,	....	Nov. 8, 1820	Dec. 7, 1831	....
Howden, James Adam	,,	....	Oct. 23, 1820	Nov. 7, 1828	....
Henderson, Patrick	,,	....	Nov. 3, 1820	Aug. 6, 1831	....
Horne, Edward......	,,	....	July 8, 1820	Oct. 2, 1836	....
Hornsby, Henry Augustus	,,	Apr. 6, 1820	Oct. 29, 1823	Brevet Apr. 6, 1835	....
Henderson, James........	,,	....	Mar. 17, 1822	....	....
Hall, Richard	,,	Apr. 6, 1820	Dec. 25, 1823	....	....
Horne, John—*artillery*	1820	June 16, 1820	May 28, 1821	Sep. 13, 1829	....
Hutt, Charles	,,	....	....	....	....
Holl, Charlton	,,	....	Mar. 14, 1822	April 5, 1831	....
Hall, Henry..............	,,	Feb. 13, 1821	May 10, 1824	Nov. 24, 1833	....
Hutchings, John..........	,,	Feb. 13, 1821	Mar. 29, 1823	Jan. 21, 1835	....
Hamond, George	,,	Feb. 13, 1821	May 1, 1824	Brevet, Feb. 13, 1836	....
Hurlock, Richard	,,	Feb. 13, 1821	Aug. 7, 1824	Feb. 15, 1836	....
Hardman, J. T.—*artillery*	,,	....	....	....	....
Harrison, Anthony	,,	Feb. 13, 1821	Nov. 7, 1823	May 11, 1836	....
Harrington, W. D.—*cavalry*	,,	Feb. 13, 1821	Mar. 12, 1826	Mar. 25, 1837	....
Halpin, William	,,	Feb. 13, 1821	May 1, 1824	Brevet Feb. 13, 1836	....
Hill, John................	,,	Apr. 27, 1822	May 8, 1824	Brevet Feb. 13, 1836	....
Harrington, H.—*cavalry* ..	,,	....	....	....	....
Harper, George Henry....	1821	Feb. 13, 1821	June 27, 1824	Feb. 11, 1835	....
Hill, William	,,	Feb. 13, 1821	Mar. 27, 1825	Sep. 22, 1835	....
Hawes, John Charles......	,,	Apr. 27, 1822	Sep. 12, 1825	Jan. 25, 1836	....
Harris, Hamlyn L.	,,	Apr. 27, 1822	May 6, 1824	Feb. 20, 1836	....
Hislop, T. M.—*cavalry*	,,	Apr. 27, 1822	Aug. 22, 1824	....	....
Holland, Erskine William	,,	....	Nov. 20, 1823	....	....
Horne, Andrew Robert....	,,	Apr. 27, 1822	Apr. 11, 1826	....	....
Hirtzel, Francis	1822	....	....	....	....
Hayne, John	,,	Apr. 27, 1822	July 3, 1826	Aug. 31, 1834	....
Heyne, Benjamin	,,	May 2, 1823	Mar. 30, 1825	....	....
Hawkshaw Edward	,,	....	....	....	....
Humffreys, T. H.—*artillery*	1823	June 6, 1823	Mar. 25, 1824	....	....
Humffrey, E. A.—*cavalry*	,,	....	April 1, 1827	Jan. 20, 1835	....
Hadfield, H. Wilbraham ..	,,	May 14, 1824	Aug. 2, 1826	Feb. 10, 1836	....
Hughes, Geo. Cumberland	,,	May 14, 1824	Oct. 16, 1827	....	....
Hoffman, Fred. William ..	,,	May 14, 1824	Dec. 9, 1825	....	....
Hopper, Frederick Henry	,,	May 14, 1824	Feb. 16, 1826	....	....
Hurrell, C. Gainsborough	,,	....	....	....	....
Hunter, John	,,	June 14, 1824	1828	....	....
Holcombe, Harcourt A.....	,,	May 14, 1824	....	....	....
Holloway, E. V. Peregrine	,,	May 14, 1824	Oct. 25, 1826	....	....
Hall, George—*artillery*	,,	....	May 19, 1824	....	....

PRESIDENCY.

Lieut.-Colonel.	Colonel.	Major General.	Lieut.-General.	Date of Resignation, Retirement, or Death.
				Resigned Nov. 26, 1829, in England.
				Died July 5, 1821, at Condapilly.
				Died May 10, 1828, at Palaveram.
				Died July 22, 1823, at Bangalore.
				Drowned — 1821, on passage out.
				Died April 22, 1823, at Coimbatore.
				Died April 13, 1833, in England.
				Resigned March 14, 1827, in England.
				Died May 2, 1830.
				Died Sep. 10, 1824, at Madras.
				{ Died April 30, 1826, on board the "Glenelg," in Rangoon River.
				Invalided from Nov. 4, 1836.
				Died Jan. 7, 1834, in Germany.
				{ Died Dec. 30, 1827, at sea, on board the "Childe Harold."
				Died May 4, 1825, at Junally, near Chittledroog.
				{ Retired May 26, 1828, on Lord Clive's Fund, in England.
				Died Nov. 16, 1825, at Mahatte.

MADRAS.——N

MADRAS

NAMES.	Cadet.	Cornet, Ensign, or Second Lieutenant.	Lieutenant.	Captain.	Major.
Hawes, John B.	1824	May 6, 1825	....		
Hodson, Charles William..	,,	May 6, 1825	May 31, 1833		
Humphreys, David Boyne..	,,	Feb. 2, 1826	Sep. 8, 1826		
Harrison, George A.	,,	May 6, 1825	Dec. 17, 1826		
Hill, Charles Thorold	1825	Jan. 8, 1826	May 8, 1829		
Hamilton, Francis	,,	Jan. 8, 1826	Dec. 12, 1828		
Heywood, Arthur	,,	Jan. 8, 1826	....		
Harriott, Henry	,,	Jan. 8, 1826	Nov. 2, 1827		
Hughes, John Edward	,,	Jan. 8, 1826	Sep. 2, 1832		
Hull, Thomas Hillman	,,	Jan. 8, 1826	Dec. 31, 1827		
Hughes, Edward..........	,,	Jan. 8, 1826	Dec. 7, 1831		
Hayes, Daniel............	,,	Jan. 8, 1826	....		
Halpin, John	,,	Jan. 8, 1826	June 6, 1833		
Humphrey, Fred. Wm.....	,,	Jan. 8, 1826	Oct. 22, 1834		
Hunter, Roger R.--*artillery*	,,	Apr. 15, 1826	June 29, 1828		
Hollis, William	,,	Jan. 8, 1826	Feb. 5, 1832		
Halpin, George	,,	Jan. 8, 1826	Apr. 30, 1829		
Horsley, Charles Henry....	,,	Jan. 8, 1826	June 23, 1832		
Hodson, Doveton	,,	Jan. 8, 1826	Apr. 7, 1836		
Henderson, Francis	1826	Jan. 8, 1826	July 6, 1833		
Hall, Edw. John—*cavalry*	,,	Jan. 8, 1826	May 19, 1832		
Haig, William............	,,	....	Nov. 30, 1828		
Hawkes, Thos. C.	,,	.... 1828...	Sep. 16, 1830		
Haly, George Thomas	,,	Jan. 16, 1827	Nov. 9, 1831		
Hadfield, Alex. James	,,	Feb. 8, 1827	Nov. 17, 1831		
Herford, William	,,	Feb. 8, 1827	May 27, 1834		
Hennah, Sam. W.—*cavalry*	,,	Feb. 8, 1827	Jan. 7, 1834		
Haines, Gregory..........	,,	Feb. 8, 1827	Mar. 24, 1835		
Hogarth, James	,,	Feb. 27, 1827	....		
Henderson, R.—*engineers*..	,,	....	Dec. 17, 1825		
Hillyard, Henry Temple ..	,,	Nov. 24, 1827	May 24, 1833		
Hewitt, P. Cornish—*cavalry*	,,	....	....		
Harding, Edmund Vincent	,,	May 29, 1828	Aug. 21, 1831		
Halsted, William Anthony	1827	June 21, 1828	Feb. 2, 1833		
Hamilton, Richard........	,,	Aug. 6, 1828	Feb. 10, 1836		
Hiern, Maurice Henry	,,	Sep. 17, 1828	....		
Hobart, Chas. Robert	,,	Oct. 28, 1828	....		
Howard, Henry	,,	Oct. 24, 1829	Jan. 21, 1835		
Hawkins, Fred. Cæsar	,,	Feb. 3, 1829	Feb. 21, 1835		
Holmes, Peter............	,,	Jan. 10, 1829	Dec. 6, 1831		
Henderson, R.-*engineers* 1st.	,,	June 15, 1827	....		
Harrison, G. W.—*artillery*	,,	June 12, 1828	....		
Hill, Henry Pix	,,	July 10, 1830	Oct. 25, 1833		
Houghton, Henry	1828	Apr. 29, 1831	June 19, 1835		
Hayman, John Briggs	,,	Apr. 29, 1831	Nov. 26, 1834		
Hacking, James..........	,,	July 13, 1831	....		
Harvey, Gardiner	,,	July 16, 1831	Aug. 31, 1834		

PRESIDENCY.

Lieut.-Colonel.	Colonel.	Major General.	Lieut.-General.	Date of Resignation, Retirement, or Death.
				{ Died Oct. 13, 1827, on board the "General Palmer."
				Discharged Apr. 1, 1836, in India.
				Died July 17, 1837, in India.
				{ Drowned Aug. 5, 1828, near Nagracoil, in Travancore.
				Resigned Sep. 18, 1827, in India.
				Resigned May 23, 1832, in England.
				Retired Dec. 16, 1833, in England.
				Died Sep. 26, 1828, at Madras.
				Died Feb. 5, 1828, at Arcot.
				Killed, Mar. 30, 1832, in action near [Malacca.
				Died Nov. 10, 1832, at Ellore.
				Died Sep. 26, 1833, at Mangalore.
				Died May 20, 1834, at Colan.
				Resigned Feb. 2, 1836.
				Died in Camp, Dec. 13, 1836, at Goomsoor.
				Died July 1, 1833, at Madras.

MADRAS

NAMES.	Cadet.	Cornet, Ensign, or Second Lieutenant.	Lieutenant.	Captain.	Major.
Harvey, Chas. C.—*artillery*	1829	May 23, 1832	....	....	....
Hutton, George—*artillery*	,,	Jan. 8, 1833	....	....	....
Hay, Samuel	1830	June 24, 1832	....	....	....
Horsley, Wm. H.—*engineers*	,,	Feb. 8, 1832	....	....	....
Hughes, Frederick—*cavalry*	1831	Dec. 9, 1832	May 4, 1836	....	....
Hervey, Albert H. A.	1832	Dec. 25, 1832	....1837...	....	....
Hoseason, Charles James ..	,,	June 11, 1833	....	....	....
Harrison, John Robinson..	,,	Jan. 29, 1834	....	....	....
Haines, Thomas..........	,,	Jan. 21, 1834	....	....	....
Hay, William Grant	1833	Mar. 1, 1834	....	....	....
Hutchinson, Charles Henry	1834	....	....	....	....
I J					
Jeanret, Samuel	1775	Sep. 1, 1776	Nov. 18, 1780	Oct. 3, 1792	July 20, 1797
Innes, James (Sen.)	,,	Feb. 5, 1777	Dec. 10, 1780	Sep. 8, 1793	Nov. 29, 1797
Innes, James (Jun.)	1777	July 4, 1778	Mar. 7, 1782	June 1, 1796	July 31, 1799
Irton, Samuel	1778	May 5, 1779	Nov. 2, 1784	June 1, 1796	June 17, 1800
Intosh, James Mac.	1779	July 26, 1779	Apr. 17, 1786	June 1, 1796	....
Jones, James	1781	Mar. 4, 1781	Nov. 14, 1788	Oct. 4, 1798	May 11, 1803
Inrath, James Mac.	,,	Oct. 17, 1782	....	....	....
Innes, John..............	,,	Oct. 23, 1782	Apr. 3, 1790	Oct. 22, 1798	....
Joyce, Patrick	1782	Dec. 18, 1782	Aug. 21, 1790	Dec. 26, 1798	....
Jervais, Abraham	....	Jan. 15, 1783	Aug. 21, 1790	....	....
Judson, John—*artillery* ..	1768	Oct. 23, 1769	Aug. 25, 1773	Dec. 3, 1780	....
Intyre, W. Mac.—*artillery*	....	Oct. 20, 1780	Dec. 30, 1781	....	....
Isaacke, Wm. B.—*artillery*	1780	Dec. 5, 1780	July 15, 1782	Mar. 7, 1791	....
Jourdan, John—*artillery*..	1781	Feb. 23, 1782	Apr. 17, 1786	Aug. 30, 1796	....
Jennings, Daniel—*engineers*	....	Oct. 1, 1781	Apr. 17, 1786	....	....
Jourdan, Edward—*cavalry*	1768	Aug. 7, 1770	May 18, 1772	Jan. 8, 1782	Apr. 17, 1786
Jeekie, James—*cavalry*....	....	Apr. 22, 1784	Feb. 1, 1786	....	....
Jacobs, Samuel—*cavalry* ..	1771	Sep. — 1773	Oct. 28, 1779	....	....
Jones, Richard—*artillery*..	1772	May 27, 1772	July 24, 1778	....	....
James, Thomas........	....	July 1, 1778	Mar. 5, 1782	....	....
Isaacke, Fred.—*artillery* ..	1791	Apr. 25, 1793	June 1, 1796	....	....
Jones, John Lloyd........	1790	June 18, 1791	June 6, 1793	June 17, 1800	....
Johnson, John Gerraud....	,,	June 21, 1791	June 6, 1793	....	....
Johnstone, Geo.—*engineers*	....	....	June 12, 1791	Sep. 3, 1793	....
Jones, John	....	July 20, 1779	....	....	....
Johnstone, Stainforth......	1792	....	Oct. 9, 1794	Sep. 21, 1804	....
Jones, Anselm............	1795	Mar. 31, 1796	Nov. 29, 1797	Sep. 21, 1804	Apr. 11, 1815
Jones, Henry Charles	1796	Aug. 15, 1797	Oct. 12, 1798	....	....
Johnson, J. Thomas	1797	July 31, 1798	Dec. 26, 1798	Jan. 1, 1807	....
Ives, James..............	,,	Sep. 1, 1798	Dec. 26, 1798	May 23, 1806	Apr. 30, 1814
Jones, William Ireland....	,,	Aug. 17, 1798	Dec. 26, 1798	June 27, 1805	Sep. 1, 1818
James, Francis	1795	Mar. 4, 1796	July 16, 1797	Aug. 24, 1803	....
Jolly, Walter	1798	....	Feb. 19, 1800	Nov. 9, 1805	Feb. 25, 1824
Jones, Richard—*cavalry* ..	,,	....	Mar. 14, 1800	....	....
Jones, Edward	1799	....	....	....	....

PRESIDENCY.

Lieut-Colonel.	Colonel.	Major-General.	Lieut.-General.	Date of Resignation, Retirement, or Death.
....	....	....	....	
....	....	....	....	
....	....	....	....	
....	....	....	....	
....	....	....	....	
....	....	....	....	Died Sep. 5, 1835, at sea.
....	....	....	....	
....	....	....	....	
....	....	....	....	
....	....	....	....	
....	....	....	....	
				[1806.
July 31, 1799	....	....	....	Invalided Dec. 9, 1801. Died Mar. 10,
Dec. 10, 1799	....	....	....	Died April 23, 1804, at Madras.
Jan. 1, 1803	Jan. 1, 1812	June 4, 1814	....	Died Sep. 21, 1818, at Fort St. George.
June 6, 1804	....	....	....	Died Mar. 13, 1813, in England.
....	....	....	....	Died 1798, on board the "Osterley."
....	....	....	....	Invalided Apr. 13, 1804. Died Sep. 19,
....	....	....	....	Died 1791. [1811.
....	....	....	....	Died Mar. 21, 1802.
....	....	....	....	Died Feb. 2, 1808, at Bellary.
....	....	....	....	Died Nov. — 1793.
....	....	....	....	Not to be traced.
....	....	....	....	Died 1789.
....	....	....	....	Died June 7, 1801, at Chittledroog.
....	....	....	....	Killed May 4, 1799, at Seringapatam.
....	....	....	....	Died 1792.
....	....	....	....	Resigned 1788.
....	....	....	....	Not to be traced.
....	....	....	....	Not to be traced.
....	....	....	....	Invalided 1779.
....	....	....	....	Not to be traced.
....	....	....	....	Died 1800, at Trincomalee.
....	....	....	....	Retired Nov. 10, 1813.
....	....	....	....	Died 1796.
....	....	....	....	Dismissed 1800.
....	....	....	....	Pensioned 1787. Died Oct. 5, 1792.
....	....	....	....	Lost Nov. 20, 1808, in the "Glory."
....	....	....	....	{ Invalided June 1, 1816, in India. Died Apr. 30, 1817, at Cochin.
....	....	....	....	Died Dec. 29, 1798, at Vellore.
....	....	....	....	Died Jan. 23, 1815, at Cuddalore.
June 12, 1819	....	....	....	Died Oct. 16, 1819, at Darampoory.
....	....	....	....	Retired April 3, 1825, in England.
....	....	....	....	Died Feb. 2, 1813, in camp near Hurighur.
....	....	....	....	Died Sep. 6, 1826, in London.
....	....	....	....	Died 1800.
....	....	....	....	{ Drowned June 13, 1800, on his passage out on board the "Rockingham."

MADRAS

NAMES.	Cadet.	Cornet, Ensign, or Second Lieutenant.	Lieutenant.	Captain.	Major.
Jenkins, Thomas	1799	....	Dec. 15, 1800	....	....
Jeffreys, George	,,	....	Dec. 15, 1800	Aug. 4, 1812	....
James, William	....	....	Dec. 15, 1800	July 27, 1813	....
Jones, Hon. R. Montgomery	1800	....	....	....	....
Johnston, John	,,	....	....	....	....
Jobson, James	,,	....	July 20, 1801	Dec. 11, 1813	....
Jones, William (13 N. I.)	,,	....	July 20, 1801	Mar. 27, 1816	May 1, 1824
Jackson, Ranjot	....	Aug. 1, 1775	Oct. 22, 1780	....	....
Jeffries, Rowland—*cavalry*	1801	Feb. 10, 1802	June 27, 1804	Oct. 18, 1818	Jan. 1, 1827
Jackson, George	,,	....	May 26, 1803	Aug. 2, 1813	May 1, 1819
Jackson, Gregory	1800	....	Dec. 15, 1800	Feb. 3, 1808	April 1, 1824
Jolly, James	1799	....	Jan. 1, 1800	....	....
Johnston, Cornwallis Chas.	1802	....	May 9, 1804	Mar. 23, 1816	....
Johnston, A. H.—*cavalry*	,,	....	Oct. 19, 1804	July 7, 1823	....
Jobson, Robert	,,	Apr. 17, 1803	May 9, 1804	....	....
Innes, John	1803	....	Sep. 21, 1804	....	....
Irwin, Hudleston	,,	Mar. 7, 1805	....	....	....
Jones, Henry	,,	July 31, 1804	Jan. 23, 1810	Sep. 1, 1818	....
Isacke, William B.	,,	....	Sep. 21, 1804	Sep. 1, 1818	Nov. 13, 1829
Jolly, George	,,	....	Sep. 21, 1804	....	....
Jenkins, Robert	,,	....	Sep. 21, 1804	....	....
James, Richard—*cavalry*	1804	July 7, 1806	Nov. 28, 1808	Sep. 1, 1818	Sep. 22, 1830
Isacke, Geo. Hutchinson	,,	....	July 25, 1805	....	....
Jourdan, Henry George	,,	....	July 17, 1805	May 14, 1821	May 24, 1828
Jones, George	,,	....	Aug. 16, 1806	Sep. 14, 1819	....
Jeffery, Wm. Williams	,,	....	July 17, 1805	....	....
Johnstone, Ch. Blayney M.	,,	....	Sep. 25, 1805	....	....
Jameson, James	,,	....	Feb. 10, 1806	....	....
Janson, Louis Thos. James	1805	....	....	....	....
Jackson, Thomas	,,	....	Nov. 22, 1806	....	....
Inglis, Archibald	,,	June 27, 1806	Jan. 9, 1808	May 1, 1824	Oct. 17, 1830
Jones, Theophilus Bolton	,,	June 27, 1806	Nov. 9, 1812	Aug. 20, 1821	....
Inverarity, Robert	,,	....	June 4, 1807	Brevet, May 23, 1821	....
James, John	,,	Jan. 1, 1807	Sep. 11, 1809	....	....
James, Michael	,,	....	....	....	....
Jones, Henry	,,	June 27, 1806	....	....	....
Jamieson, James	,,	....	Dec. 4, 1809	....	....
Jones, Ellis N. Owen	,,	Sep. 27, 1806	Aug. 12, 1809	....	....
James, John Polglase	1806	July 3, 1807	May 2, 1809	July 1, 1824	Nov. 26, 1828
Irvie, Thomas	,,	July 3, 1807	Dec. 28, 1811	....	....
Jobson, Graham John	,,	....	....	....	....
Jackson, William John	,,	July 3, 1807	April 6, 1810	....	....
Johnstone, Richard	1807	....	....	....	....
J'Anson, John	,,	Sep. 11, 1809	....	....	....
James, John Irving	1808	April 8, 1810	Mar. 1, 1815	....	....
Jop, Jas. Barclay—*artillery*	1810	July 27, 1811	....	....	....
Johnson, Edwin Julius	1811	June 11, 1812	May 1, 1815	Nov. 2, 1824	....

PRESIDENCY.

Lieut.-Colonel.	Colonel.	Major General	Lieut.-General.	Date of Resignation, Retirement, or Death.
....	....	....	....	Died Sep. 13, 1813, at Ellore.
....	....	....	....	Retired Feb. 9, 1818, in England.
....	....	....	....	Died Jan. 17, 1826, at Masulipatam.
....	....	....	....	Died Dec. 21, 1803.
....	....	....	....	Died Nov. 23, 1803.
....	....	....	....	Died June 3, 1818, at Berhampore.
....	....	....	....	Died June 18, 1824, at Terrimun-
....	....	....	....	Died 1791. [galum.
....	....	....	....	{ Invalided Sep. 11, 1827, in India. Retired April 18, 1831, in England. }
May 1, 1824	June 5, 1829	....	....	
Sep. 8, 1826	....	....	....	Died April 1, 1835, at Penang.
....	....	....	....	Died Dec. 12, 1802, at Sea.
....	....	....	....	Died Oct. 14, 1817, at Hydrabad.
....	....	....	....	Died May 19, 1824, at Saloo, near Jaulnah.
....	....	....	....	Lost Feb. — 1807, in the brig "William Kennedy."
....	....	....	....	Died Jan. 28, 1817, in Europe.
....	....	....	....	Died Dec. 8, 1810.
....	....	....	....	{ Struck off, having been absent from India more than five years, from Feb. 20, 1825, in England. }
Sep. 11, 1834	....	....	....	
....	....	....	....	Died July 10, 1806, at Vellore.
....	....	....	....	{ Died Feb. 23, 1818, on board the "Richmond," on passage to England. }
May 4, 1836	....	....	....	
....	....	....	....	Cashiered March 7, 1810.
July 6, 1833	....	....	....	Retired Feb. 15, 1836, in India.
....	....	....	....	Died Mar. 22, 1834, at the Cape.
....	....	....	....	Died Nov. 19, 1809, at Santa Bednor.
....	....	....	....	Retired May 6, 1821.
....	....	....	....	Died Dec. 15, 1820, at Masulipatam.
....	....	....	....	Lost in the "Glory," Nov. 20, 1808.
....	....	....	....	Died Jan. 7, 1823, at Cochin.
Mar. 5, 1836	....	....	....	Retired April 3, 1837.
....	....	....	....	Retired July 9, 1834, in England.
....	....	....	....	Retired June 14, 1824, in England.
....	....	....	....	Died Nov. 10, 1819, at Nagpore.
....	....	....	....	Lost Nov. 20, 1808, in the "Glory."
....	....	....	....	Died June 22, 1808.
....	....	....	....	Pensioned Dec. 4, 1809, on Lord Clive's Fund.
....	....	....	....	Retired Sep. 5, 1821.
Oct. 10, 1833	....	....	....	
....	....	....	....	Died June 17, 1812, at Negapatam.
....	....	....	....	Died Jan. 10, 1808, on passage to India.
....	....	....	....	Died Jan. 28, 1817.
....	....	....	....	Resigned Nov. 16, 1810.
....	....	....	....	Died Sep. 10, 1812.
....	....	....	....	Died April 5, 1826, at Rangoon.
....	....	....	....	Died Aug. 17, 1812.
....	....	....	....	Died Nov. 8, 1828, at Cawnpore.

MADRAS

NAMES.	Cadet.	Cornet, Ensign, or Second Lieutenant.	Lieutenant.	Captain.	Major.
Jones, John	1811	June 11, 1812	Apr. 26, 1814	....	....
Jackson, Edw.—*cavalry* ..	,,	....	....	....	....
Jackson, Samuel	1812	July 6, 1813	July 8, 1815	....	....
Jenkins, Geo.—*engineers* ..	1815	May 2, 1817	....	....	....
Justice, William	1818	....	June 13, 1819	Apr. 19, 1831	....
Johnston, William	,,	....	June 13, 1819	Oct. 21, 1829	....
Jardine, Edward	1819	....	....	....	....
Johnson, Nicholas	,,	....	Apr. 7, 1820	June 3, 1831	....
Joseph, Michael	,,	....	Apr. 7, 1820	Sep. 12, 1834	....
Johnstone, T. J. M.	,,	Apr. 6, 1820	Oct. 14, 1821	Brevet, April 6, 1835	....
James, Edward	,,	....	Feb. 13, 1821	....	....
Jobling, George	,,	....	Apr. 11, 1821	....	....
Jones, John—*cavalry*	,,	Apr. 6, 1820	Oct. 20, 1823	Feb. 26, 1829	....
Impey, J. S.	,,	April 6, 1820	May 1, 1824	....	....
Johnston, George Rich. ..	,,	....	Aug. 2, 1821	Brevet April 6, 1835.	....
Irvine, John—*cavalry*	,,	April 6, 1820	Mar. 20, 1822	....	....
Jackman, J. I.	,,	Apr. 6, 1820	May 1, 1824	....	....
James, Thomas R.	,,	....	May 7, 1822	Brevet April 6, 1835	....
Jefferies, Alex. Hoy	,,	Apr. 6, 1820	July 1, 1823	Apr. 3, 1833	....
Inglis, Hugh—*cavalry*	1820	Apr. 6, 1820	May 1, 1824	Mar. 18, 1833	....
Jones, John	,,	Feb. 13, 1821	Sep. 8, 1826	Brevet Feb. 13, 1836	....
Johnstone, John	,,	Feb. 13, 1821	Nov. 2, 1824	Mar. 14, 1830	....
Joy, R. A.	,,	Feb. 13, 1821	June 15, 1825	....	....
Irving, W. J.	,,	....	....	....	....
Jones, John Lloyd	1821	Apr. 27, 1822	Feb. 24, 1828	....	....
Jackson, H. Felix	1824	May 6, 1825	....	....	....
Jones, Thos. Walker	,,	Jan. 8, 1826	Oct. 14, 1827	....	....
Johnston, Adam Blair	1825	Jan. 8, 1826	Sep. 5, 1827	....	....
James, Richard H.	,,	Jan. 8, 1826	May 18, 1832	....	....
Jackson, Henry	,,	Jan. 8, 1826	June 13, 1828	....	....
Jones, Alfred Burnell	,,	Jan. 8, 1826	Oct. 22, 1827	....	....
Johnstone, W. G.	,,	Jan. 8, 1826	Feb. 3, 1832	....	....
Jones, James	,,	....	Apr. 20, 1829	....	....
Johnson, Ralph S.	1826	June 6, 1827	....	....	....
Jenkins, Thos. Askwith ..	,,	Feb. 27, 1827	May 30, 1833	....	....
Junor, William	,,	May 23, 1828	Jan. 16, 1834	....	....
Johnston, J. McMahon	1827	Aug. 31, 1828	April — 1836	....	....
Ireland, Charles	,,	Apr. 10, 1829	Aug. 7, 1835	....	....
Johnstone, David	,,	....	....	....	....
Jones, A. B.—*cavalry*	1829	....	May 31, 1833	....	....
Jacson, Roger	1831	July 14, 1832	Nov. 29, 1836	....	....
Inverarity, J.—*engineers* ..	,,	Apr. 5, 1834	....	....	....
Jenkins, W. G. P.	1832	Nov. 24, 1832	Mar. 27, 1836	....	....
Irby, Claude Fred.	,,	Nov. 24, 1832	May 15, 1836	....	....
Impey, Edw. H.	,,	Feb. 14, 1833	Dec. 27, 1836	....	....
Johnson, Patrick H.	,,	June 11, 1833	June 5, 1837	....	....
Jackson, W. Bayley	,,	Feb. 15, 1834	....	....	....

PRESIDENCY.

Lieut.-Colonel.	Colonel.	Major-General.	Lieut.-General.	Date of Resignation, Retirement, or Death.
				Died March 11, 1821, at Vellore.
				Died May 31, 1814, at Arcot. [stone."
				Died Apr. 19, 1826, on board " Elphin-
				Died Dec. 4, 1817, at Akowla.
				Invalided Feb. 16, 1830, in India.
				Dismissed Sep. 9, 1823, in India.
				Died June 16, 1831, at Tanjore.
				Invalided
				Retired Nov. 5, 1832, in England.
				{ Invalided Dec. 22, 1829, in India. Died Sep. 2, 1831, at Vizagapatam.
				{ Died Nov. 23, 1836, in the Traveller's Bungalow, at Rompechandad, near Guntoor.
				Died June 21, 1825, at Negapatam.
				Invalided in 1825, in India.
				Died Jan. 9, 1836, at Mangalore.
				Invalided
				Died Apr. 7, 1822, at Wallajabad.
				Died Sep. 12, 1831, at Vellore.
				Died Oct. 19, 1829, at St. Thomas's [Mount.
				Died Nov. 26, 1828, at Vepery.
				Died Sep. 12, 1834, at Vizianagrum.
				Died May 13, 1830, at Trichinopoly.
				Died Dec. 22, 1830, at Madras.
				Killed April 3, 1834, in Coorg.
				Resigned Jan. 5, 1836, in India.

MADRAS.——O

MADRAS

NAMES.	Cadet.	Cornet, Ensign, or Second Lieutenant.	Lieutenant.	Captain.	Major.
Isaacke, William (51 N. I.)	1833	Mar. 10, 1834	....	....	....
Johnston, J. G.—*engineers*	,,	....	....	....	....
Innes, Henry David	1834	Feb. 9, 1835	....	....	....

K

NAMES.	Cadet.	Cornet, Ensign, or Second Lieutenant.	Lieutenant.	Captain.	Major.
Kelly, Robert	....	Oct. 6, 1760	....	Nov. 27, 1765	Oct. 12, 1780
Keating, William	1762	Oct. 9, 1764	....	June 20, 1770	....
Kinnon, Laughlan Mac....	1769	Oct. 17, 1772	....	April 1, 1783	....
Knox, Thomas............	,,	Nov. 3, 1772	Apr. 27, 1775	Apr. 15, 1783	....
Kinsey, William..........	1771	May 8, 1773	July 13, 1779	Dec. 14, 1783	June 1, 1796
Kennedy, Johnson	....	May 5, 1774	....	Apr. 12, 1785	June 1, 1796
Kennet, John	1777	July 16, 1778	Mar. 12, 1782	June 1, 1796	July 31, 1799
Kerras, James Mac	,,	July 28, 1778	Nov. 8, 1782	June 1, 1796	Sep. 24, 1799
Kirkpatrick, James Achilles	1779	Oct. 18, 1780	Apr. 17, 1786	Mar. 18, 1797	Dec. 10, 1800
Keay, P. H..............	1780	Aug. 25, 1781	Jan. 23, 1787	Oct. 21, 1797	....
Kingston, Strictland	1781	Nov. 14, 1782	Aug. 21, 1790	Dec. 26, 1798	Sep. 21, 1804
King, William............	1782	May 5, 1783	Aug. 21, 1790	July 31, 1799	....
Kennedy, Daniel—*artillery*	1770	Mar. 8, 1772	....	Sep. 16, 1781	....
Kennedy, Timy.—*artillery*	....	....	June 11, 1789	....	....
Kenzie, K. Mac—*artillery*	....	July 1, 1786	....	....	....
Kissleback, J. A.—*engineers*	....	Oct. 12, 1780	Sep. 10, 1783	....	....
Kipper, George—*cavalry*..	1782	Dec. 8, 1785	Oct. 24, 1792	June 17, 1800	....
Kenny, William	....	Sep. 28, 1776	Dec. 8, 1780	July 14, 1793	Nov. 29, 1797
Kelly, Geo. Robt. Abraham	1790	....	Feb. 22, 1793	May 19, 1803	Apr. 13, 1813
Kae, Hugh Mac	....	....	June 7, 1792	April 8, 1802	....
Keasberry, John Palmer ..	1790	Aug. 3, 1791	Feb. 17, 1794	July 1, 1800	May 23, 1808
Kelso, Archibald—*engineers*	1792	....	....	....	....
Kirkbride, David	....	Oct. 31, 1783	....	....	....
Kenny, Daniel Courtney ..	1793	....	May 9, 1795	Jan. 27, 1802	Mar. 20, 1809
Knowles, Joseph (C. B.) ..	1795	Mar. 12, 1796	Sep. 19, 1797	Sep. 21, 1804	Sep. 24, 1812
Kingsley, William—*artillery*	1796	Aug. 4, 1797	Mar. 1, 1800	Feb. 16, 1807	....
Keir, Thomas	,,	Aug. 26, 1797	Oct. 12, 1798	....	....
Keene, Henry George	,,	Sep. 6, 1797	Oct. 12, 1798	....	....
Keats, George	1795	Mar. 18, 1796	Nov. 23, 1797	Sep. 21, 1804	Mar. 7, 1810
King, John	1798	....	Jan. 1, 1800	....	....
Kelly, Hastings M. (C. B.)	1797	July 24, 1798	Oct. 24, 1798	Sep. 21, 1804	April 5, 1810
Kinsey, Miles Bassett	1798	Aug. 21, 1798	Dec. 26, 1798	....	....
Kelly, James Amos	1799	....	Dec. 15, 1800	Aug. 5, 1812	Sep. 8, 1818
King, Thomas............	,,	....	Dec. 15, 1800	June 13, 1808	May 1, 1824
Kennedy, Robert—*cavalry*	,,	....	Aug. 11, 1801	....	....
Kirwan, James	,,	....	Dec. 15, 1800	Mar. 5, 1808	....
Kinsey, Thomas—*artillery*	1800	....	Dec. 12, 1800	....	....
Kenny, Wolfenden........	,,	....	July 20, 1801	....	....
Kennedy, David	,,	....	....	....	....
Kingdon, Christopher	,,	....	May 1, 1802	....	....
King, Penford............	,,	....	July 20, 1801	Sep. 18, 1813	....
Kettle, James Tillary	,,	....	July 20, 1801	Feb. 2, 1814	....
Kennet, John	,,	....	July 20, 1801	Mar. 3, 1813	....

PRESIDENCY.

Lieut.-Colonel.	Colonel.	Major General.	Lieut.-General.	Date of Resignation, Retirement, or Death.
	Nov. 8, 1785			Died 1790.
Nov. 16, 1783				Died 1788.
				Died 1793.
				Died 1794.
Nov. 29, 1797	Jan. 1, 1803	July 25, 1810	June 4, 1814. Gen. Jan. 10, 1837.	Died April 6, 1837, in England.
				Died June, 1796, at Amboyna.
				Died June 23, 1803.
Oct. 13, 1804				Died July 10, 1806, at Vellore.
Dec. 14, 1804				Died Oct. 15, 1805.
				{ Invalided Oct. 15, 1799. Died April 16, 1823, on board the L. S. "Moira," on his passage to England
Aug. 19, 1808				Retired May 25, 1814.
				Died April 12, 1801.
				Invalided at Cuddalore 1788. Died 1792.
				Not to be traced.
				Not to be traced.
				Died 1792.
				{ Pensioned Oct. 1800. Died at Nellore, Apr. 21, 1812.
Dec. 10, 1799				Died at Elitchpore, April 30, 1804.
				Died May 29, 1818.
				Killed in the battle of Assaye, Sep. 23, 1803.
Sep. 29, 1813				Died April 29, 1814, at Java.
				Resigned the service, 1793.
				Pensioned, 1787. Died Dec. 2, 1799.
Mar. 23, 1816	Commt. May 1, 1824 Colonel June 5, 1829			
Sep. 22, 1818				Died Nov. 1, 1824, at Bombay.
				Died at Seringapatam, July 27, 1808.
				Died at Vellore, July 12, 1801.
				Struck off Aug. 16, 1801.
				Died Dec. 9, 1817, at Mangalore.
				Died Nov. 17, 1804.
Mar. 24, 1822	June 5, 1829			{ Died Feb. 14, 1832, on board "La Belle Alliance," at sea.
				Died May 8, 1803.
May 1, 1824				Retired in England, Jan. 12, 1825.
Sep. 8, 1826	Brevet, June 18, 1831			
				King's service Apr. 24, 1814. 19 Rt. L. D.
				Died Sep. 8, 1808, at Secunderabad.
				Died at Madras, Aug. 5, 1805.
				Cashiered Oct. 17, 1803.
				Died Feb. 29, 1804.
				Died June 10, 1816, in England.
				Died June 12, 1816.
				{ Invalided July 31, 1817, in India. Died Oct. 21, 1819, at San Kerrydroog.
				Died July 7, 1815, at Bangalore.

MADRAS

NAMES.	Cadet.	Cornet, Ensign, or Second Lieutenant.	Lieutenant.	Captain.	Major.
Kutzleben, William Baron	1800	....	Sep. 21, 1804	Sep. 1, 1818	Oct. 11, 1828
Kent, Henry Young	1799	....	Dec. 15, 1800	Oct. 24, 1809	....
Kelson, W. M.—*cavalry*	1802	....	....	....	....
Kelty, John Macro	,,	....	May 1, 1804	....	....
Knott, John	,,	Apr. 17, 1803	Feb. 26, 1804	....	....
Kempster, George Forth	,,	....	....	....	....
Kemble, Matthew—*cavalry*	,,	....	July 10, 1807	July 26, 1819	....
Kennedy, William	1803	....	Sep. 21, 1804	....	....
Kelso, William	,,	....	Sep. 21, 1804	Apr. 8, 1819	Mar. 13, 1825
Kitson, James	1804	....	July 17, 1805	Aug. 6, 1820	Feb. 6, 1830
Kinsey, Charles	,,	....	July 17, 1805	....	....
Kyd, Hugh	,,	....	July 17, 1805	Sep. 8, 1818	Dec. 12, 1828
Keating, Henry	,,	....	Mar. 14, 1807	July 13, 1821	....
Kitchen, James—*artillery*	,,	....	May 11, 1806	Sep. 1, 1818	Nov. 12, 1825
Kinnin, Oswald	1805	....	Mar. 5, 1807	....	....
Kippen, Campbell	,,	....	Aug. 2, 1806	....	....
King, John	,,	....	June 30, 1808	....	....
Keir, George	1806	....	....	....	....
King, Henry Rice	1807	Dec. 27, 1808	June 8, 1814	....	....
Kerr, Archibald—*cavalry*	,,	Feb. 14, 1809	Mar. 26, 1815	Feb. 16, 1824	May 4, 1836
Kitt, Henry	,,	Oct. 25, 1809	Feb. 9, 1813	....	....
Kinsey, James Strange	,,	Oct. 21, 1809	Jan. 22, 1815	....	....
Kelly, Thomas	,,	....	....	....	....
Kay, Charles	,,	....	....	....	....
Kaye, John H.—*cavalry*	1808	Nov. 9, 1812	Oct. 31, 1818	....	....
Kerr, James (33 N. I.)	1809	Nov. 17, 1809	June 2, 1816	July 2, 1825	....
Kennan, T. Y. B.—*artillery*	,,	July 7, 1810	May 24, 1813	Jan. 26, 1822	....
Keighly, H. P.—*cavalry*	1810	Nov. 9, 1812	Oct. 13, 1817	Mar. 1, 1821	Brevet, Jan. 10, 1837
Kelly, John T.—*artillery*	,,	Feb. 2, 1812	....	....	....
King, Edward—*artillery*	1811	June 11, 1812	Sep. 1, 1818	....	....
Kellett, George Housten	1818	....	June 13, 1819	....	....
Keating, Christopher	1819	....	June 13, 1819	....	....
Kirby, Hickman R.	,,	....	April 7, 1820	June 24, 1830	....
Kerr, James (2 Eur. Reg.)	,,	....	Oct. 22, 1820	May 20, 1833	Sep. 6, 1836
Kenny, Thomas G. E. G.	1820	Feb. 13, 1821	July 14, 1823	Brevet, Apr. 6, 1835.	....
Kenny, Henry Evans	,,	....	May 1, 1824	Brevet Apr. 6, 1835.	....
Kingston, William W.	,,	....	Jan. 26, 1822	....	....
Kerr, Claudius A.—*cavalry*	,,	Feb. 13, 1821	May 1, 1824	....	....
Kinloch, David	,,	Feb. 13, 1821	Oct. 1, 1823	....	....
Knox, James—*cavalry*	,,	Feb. 13, 1821	May 1, 1824	....	....
Key, John Binney	1823	May 14, 1824	Jan. 6, 1826	....	....
Kynaston, Charles Thomas	1824	May 6, 1825	Dec. 24, 1826	....	....
Killitt, James Feker	,,	May 6, 1825	....	....	....
Kennedy, John Hamilton	,,	Jan. 8, 1826	July 13, 1831	....	....
Knyvett, Frederick	1825	Jan. 8, 1826	July 18, 1832	....	....
Kennedy, Hugh Alexander	,,	Jan. 8, 1826	May 21, 1833	....	....
Kinloch, Æneas Mackintosh	,,	....	Oct. 25, 1827	....	....

PRESIDENCY.

Lieut.-Colonel.	Colonel.	Major-General.	Lieut.-General.	Date of Resignation, Retirement, or Death.
Aug. 8, 1833				Died Oct. 10, 1836, at Berhampore.
				Died April 2, 1813.
				Died May 20, 1804.
				Lost in the "Prince of Wales," 1805.
				{ Invalided March 24, 1812. Struck off 1819, in England.
				Not to be traced.
				Died June 27, 1824, at Belgaum.
				Killed May 29, 1818, at Mallegaum.
Sep. 10, 1830				Retired June 9, 1833.
Dec. 6, 1834				
				Retired Feb. 7, 1816, in England.
Feb. 9, 1834				Retired March 5, 1836.
				{ Invalided Nov. 8, 1831, in India. Retired Oct. 7, 1832, in India.
Sep. 1, 1831				
				Died 1818.
				Died July 30, 1819, at Cannanore.
				{ Died Oct. 29, 1812, in the "Duncan," on his passage to Persia.
				Resigned July 7, 1807.
				Died May 20, 1823, in camp.
				Died Aug. 20, 1816, at Pondicherry.
				Died Sep. 14, 1824, at Negapatam.
				{ Dismissed May 12, 1809. Appointment obtained by improper means. Re-appointed 1809. Died June 8, 1809, at Bangalore.
				Died April 18, 1809, at Cuddalore.
				Died Dec. 16, 1819, at Mhow.
				Retired Jan. 22, 1835, in England.
				Died June 11, 1827, at Mysore.
				Died June 29, 1818, in camp near Jaulnah.
				Died Nov. 12, 1818, at Pyspore.
				Died May 22, 1832, at Stirling (N. B.)
				Died April 17, 1827, at Penang.
				Died March 27, 1836, in camp, near Rutnapore.
				{ Retired on Lord Clive's Fund, Feb. 26, 1828, in England.
				Resigned Feb. 23, 1835, in India.
				Died Oct. 31, 1828, at Bangalore.
				Lost Oct. 12, 1833, on board the "Lady Munro."
				Resigned Dec. 31, 1832, in India.
				Died Aug. 13, 1829, at Moulmein.
				Died Jan. 22, 1832, at Nagpore.
				Retired Sep. 8, 1837, in India.
				Died Aug. 13, 1831, at Condapilly.

MADRAS

NAMES.	Cadet.	Cornet, Ensign, or Second Lieutenant.	Lieutenant.	Captain.	Major.
Kempthorne, James	1825	Jan. 8, 1826	Nov. 3, 1835		
Kennedy, Hugh Scott	,,	....	Jan. 12, 1827		
Kenworthy, E. Wilson	,,	Jan. 8, 1826	Mar. 3, 1830		
Kenny, James W. G.	,,	Jan. 8, 1826	May 25, 1833		
Kerr, Alexander Boyd	1826	Jan. 8, 1826	June 2, 1832		
Kenedy, Geo. P. Carr	,,	....	May 17, 1829		
King, Edward	1827	Jan. 10, 1829	May 31, 1831		
King, H. R. C.—*cavalry*	1828	July 6, 1830	June 17,1832		
Kirby, C. Foveaux	1829	Apr. 12, 1832	May 25, 1833		
Kinkead, R.—*artillery*	,,	Aug. 15, 1832	....		
Kelso, A. John—*cavalry*	1830	May 7, 1832	Nov. 11, 1833		
Kevin, Edward	1832	Feb. 19, 1833	....		
Keating, James	,,	Dec. 13, 1833	....		
Kitson, John (45 N. I.)	1834	June 3, 1834	Oct. 17, 1836		
Kempt, R. J.	,,	....	Mar. 1, 1836		

L

NAMES.	Cadet.	Cornet, Ensign, or Second Lieutenant.	Lieutenant.	Captain.	Major.
Langley, A. Alfred	1767	Nov. 10, 1768	Sep. 26, 1770	Nov. 24, 1780	Sep. 24, 1790
Leighton, Thomas	1769	Nov. 21, 1770	Jan. 29, 1776	Nov. 2, 1783	Mar. 1, 1794
Lalande, Carey	,,	Dec. 19, 1770	Sep. 21, 1776	Nov. 2, 1783	Mar. 1, 1794
Little, Joseph	1771	May 18, 1773	Nov. 27, 1778	Dec. 13, 1783	June 1, 1796
Livingstone, Thomas	1775	Aug. 27, 1776	Nov. 13, 1780	....	....
Lee, John	1776	Feb. 11, 1777	Mar. 21, 1781	Nov. 14, 1793	....
Lang, Ross	1777	Aug. 28, 1778	Jan. 17, 1782	Aug. 6, 1794	Oct. 12, 1798
Lindsay, Adam	,,	May 5, 1778	Jan. 23, 1782	Sep. 8, 1794	Oct. 12, 1798
Long, John	,,	Mar. 16, 1778	Jan. 30, 1782	Oct. 15, 1794	Dec. 26, 1798
Limerick, W. S. Somerville	1778	Apr. 14, 1779	Dec. 13, 1783	June 1, 1706	Dec. 10, 1799
Loughlin, James O.	,,	Apr. 18, 1779	Jan. 21, 1784	....	....
Lawrence, John C.	,,	July 20, 1779	Apr. 17, 1786	....	....
Ley, George	1779	Oct. 6, 1780	Apr. 17, 1786	....	....
Leith, James	1781	Oct. 28, 1782	Aug. 21, 1790	Dec. 26, 1798	Sep. 21, 1804
Lysaught, Christopher	,,	Nov. 8, 1782	....		
Logan, Dawson	,,	Dec. 4, 1782	Aug. 21, 1790	....	....
Logan, James	1782	Dec. 27, 1782	Aug. 21, 1790	....	....
Lalor, Richard	1785	Sep. 2, 1786	....		
Lloyd, Wm. L.—*artillery*	1767	Dec. 3, 1768	Sep. 18, 1772	Dec. 2, 1780	July 22, 1786
Lennon, W. C.—*engineers*	1782	Oct. 19, 1782	Apr. 17, 1786	Aug. 16, 1793	May 1, 1804
Leonard, John—*cavalry*	1780	....	June 20, 1785	Jan. 7, 1796	Sep. 4, 1799
Leslie, B.—*cavalry*	....	Aug. 29, 1785	....		
Lantwar, Wm.—*artillery*	1778	Mar. 1, 1779	May 5, 1781	Oct. 13, 1784	....
Lane, Thomas	....	Nov. 15, 1765	Nov. 13, 1766	May 18, 1773	....
Lewis, William—*cavalry*	1789	Mar. 17, 1792	Nov. 1, 1798	May 1, 1804	Mar. 5, 1806
Lloyd, Thomas—*artillery*	1792	....	....		
Lyon, Robert	....	Jan. 20, 1789	June 7, 1792	Dec. 10, 1799	....
Lindsay, John	1788	....	June 7, 1792	Jan. 1, 1800	June 27, 1805
Leigh, Richard	1789	....	Aug. 27, 1792	Dec. 17, 1799	....
Lawder, George	1790	June 28, 1791	June 13, 1793	June 17, 1800	....
Lorani, John	,,	June 29, 1791	June 14, 1793	June 17, 1800	....

PRESIDENCY.

Lieut.-Colonel.	Colonel.	Major General.	Lieut.-General.	Date of Resignation, Retirement, or Death.
....	....	....	....	
....	....	....	....	Died Nov. 12, 1832, at sea.
....	....	....	....	
....	....	....	....	
....	....	....	....	{ Drowned in 1832-3, having fallen overboard from the "Red Rover."
....	....	....	....	
....	....	....	....	
....	....	....	....	
....	....	....	....	
....	....	....	....	
....	....	....	....	
....	....	....	....	
....	....	....	....	
....	....	....	....	
June 1, 1796	....	....	....	Retired Aug. — 1797.
June 1, 1796	May 8, 1800	....	....	Died May 22, 1808.
June 1, 1796	June 17, 1800	Apr. 25, 1808	June 4, 1813	Died Sep. 7, 1824, at Madras.
....	....	....	....	Retired June — 1798.
....	....	....	....	Died Mar. 29, 1790.
....	....	....	....	Died May — 1794. [Districts.
June 17, 1800	July 25, 1810	June 4, 1813	....	Died Aug. 23, 1822, in the Ceded
June 17, 1800	....	....	....	Retired June 26, 1805.
Mar. 27, 1801	....	....	....	Retired Oct. 1, 1808.
May 1, 1804	....	....	....	Retired July 24, 1805.
....	....	....	....	Not to be traced.
....	....	....	....	Died 1792.
....	....	....	....	Died 1788.
June 30, 1808	June 4, 1814	May 27, 1825	....	Died Nov. 12, 1829, at Madras.
....	....	....	....	Not to be traced.
....	....	....	....	Died Jan. — 1794.
....	....	....	....	Died July — 1798, at Amboyna.
....	....	....	....	Dismissed the Service.
....	....	....	....	Retired on Lord Clive's Bounty, 1788.
Jan. 1, 1806	....	....	....	Retired Nov. 14, 1810.
....	....	....	....	Died Dec. 16, 1803.
....	....	....	....	{ On leave to China for health, July 4, 1789. Returned from thence in Jan. — 1790. Died — 1790.
....	....	....	....	Died — 1789, at the Mount.
....	....	....	....	Not to be traced.
Sep. 13, 1813	....	....	....	Died Feb. 28, 1817.
....	....	....	....	{ Dismissed the Service May 28, 1793, by sentence of a Court Martial.
....	....	....	....	Died Nov. 17, 1802.
May 30, 1810	Aug. 12, 1819	....	....	Died Jan. 30, 1821, at Cannanore.
....	....	....	....	Died Oct. 17, 1801.
....	....	....	....	Died Feb. 10, 1801.
....	....	....	....	Died May 12, 1803.

MADRAS

NAMES.	Cadet.	Cornet, Ensign, or Second Lieutenant.	Lieutenant.	Captain.	Major.
Long, Edmond Perry	1790	July 18, 1791	Nov. 5, 1793	June 17, 1800	Nov. 16, 1809
Lang, George	,,	Aug. 15, 1791	Mar. 18, 1794	Jan. 7, 1802	July 25, 1805
Lucas, Charles	,,	Aug. 31, 1791	Aug. 6, 1794	Jan. 1, 1803	Mar. 18, 1809
Lanauze, Charles Guy A.	1792	Sep. 26, 1793	Oct. 14, 1794	....	....
Limond, Sir J.—*artillery*	,,	Sep. 24, 1793	Sep. 28, 1797	Sep. 21, 1804	Oct. 21, 1814
Laing, George	1794	Jan. 4, 1796	June 1, 1796	....	....
Little, Thomas	,,	Dec. 30, 1795	June 1, 1796	May 1, 1804	June 27, 1810
Le Mesurier, John Perchard	1795	Feb. 23, 1796	July 13, 1797	....	....
Langford, Robert Henry	1796	....	Nov. 29, 1797	Sep. 21, 1804	Jan. 10, 1815
Longan, Thomas	,,	....	Nov. 29, 1797	Nov. 15, 1804	....
Limond, Alexander	,,	....	Nov. 29, 1797	Oct. 20, 1804	April 9, 1812
Lester, Charles R.	1795	....	Nov. 29, 1797	Sep. 21, 1804	....
Lushington, Sir J. L. (K.C.B.)*	1796	Aug. 6, 1797	Sep. 4, 1799	May 1, 1804	Feb. 22, 1812
Lyne, Edward—*cavalry*	1795	Dec. 27, 1799	July 30, 1800	Jan. 22, 1812	....
Leigh, John	1797	....	....	....	....
Lindsay, John	1798	Sep. 15, 1797	Oct. 12, 1798	Nov. 22, 1806	Feb. 19, 1819
Lambert, George Lattin	,,	Aug. 31, 1798	Dec. 26, 1798	Sep. 21, 1804	Sep. 29, 1817
Lutwidge, Skeffington	1797	Aug. 4, 1798	Dec. 26, 1798	Oct. 11, 1804	Brevet June 4, 1814
Lecouteur, Peter	1798	....	Jan. 1, 1800	....	....
Lindsay, Henry—*artillery*	1797	June 29, 1797	Mar. 1, 1800	....	....
Lewis, Samuel	1799	....	Dec. 15, 1800	....	....
Lawless, Peter	,,	....	Dec. 15, 1800	Aug. 5, 1812	Nov. 8, 1820
Loftie, William Henry	,,	....	Dec. 15, 1800	Mar. 15, 1810	....
Lucas, John	,,	....	Dec. 15, 1800	Dec. 27, 1808	....
Lea, John	,,	....	Dec. 15, 1800	Apr. 30, 1810	....
Langley, Frederick	1800	....	July 20, 1801	....	....
Lee, Price Wakeford	,,	....	July 20, 1801	Sep. 11, 1809	Mar. 2, 1819
Lamb, John	,,	....	Mar. 22, 1802	April 2, 1816	July 2, 1825
Lott, Edwin	,,	....	July 20, 1801	....	....
Lee, Henry Shute	,,	....	July 20, 1801	Feb. 16, 1815	....
Livesmore, Richard	,,	....	....	....	....
Leonard, Francis—*cavalry*	1801	Feb. 10, 1802	May 1, 1804	....	....
Lynn, Charles Seymour	,,	....	Jan. 19, 1804	Jan. 4, 1815	....
Lynch, Nicholas	,,	....	....	....	....
Lock, James—*cavalry*	1802	....	April 7, 1807	....	....
Langton, Charles	,,	....	May 1, 1804	....	....
Lowther, James	,,	....	Oct. 9, 1804	....	....
Leggatt, Gerrard	,,	....	Sep. 21, 1804	Sep. 1, 1818	....
Leach, William	,,	Apr. 17, 1803	Feb. 21, 1804	....	....
Leith, Ernest Hepburn	1803	....	Sep. 21, 1804	Sep. 1, 1818	....
Lindsay, Hon. Edwin	1802	....	June 27, 1804	....	....
Loste, Frederick Alphonso	,,	....	Sep. 21, 1804	....	....
Laurie, David	1800	....	July 20, 1801	....	....
Laurens, Charles—*cavalry*	1803	July 31, 1804	Jan. 28, 1809	Aug. 11, 1820	....
Lindesay, (now Bethune) H.—*artillery*	,,	....	July 18, 1804	Sep. 3, 1813	....
Lawson, Spottiswoode	,,	....	Sep. 21, 1804	....	....
Leighton, James	,,	....	Sep. 21, 1804	Jan. 19, 1820	....

* Chosen Director of the E. I. Company July 25, 1827.

PRESIDENCY.

Lieut.-Colonel.	Colonel.	Major-General.	Lieut.-General.	Date of Resignation, Retirement, or Death.
. . . .	. . . .	. . . .	. . . .	Died at Fort St. George, Aug. 3, 1812.
June 27, 1810	. . . .	. . . .	. . . .	Died Mar. 19, 1814, at Jaulah.
. . . .	. . . .	. . . .	. . . .	{ Invalided June 26, 1810. Died Nov. 25, 1816, at Vizagapatam.
. . . .	. . . .	. . . .	. . . .	Died Dec. 15, 1799.
May 13, 1821	June 5, 1829	. . . .	. . . .	
. . . .	. . . .	. . . .	. . . .	Struck off October 10, 1801.
. . . .	. . . .	. . . .	. . . .	Died April 30, 1815, at Nattore.
. . . .	. . . .	. . . .	. . . .	Died March 27, 1801.
. . . .	. . . .	. . . .	. . . .	Died Nov. 30, 1816.
. . . .	. . . .	. . . .	. . . .	Died May 10, 1807.
Sep. 1, 1818	Commt. Aug 10, 1824. Col. June 5, 1829.	Jan. 10, 1837	. . . .	
. . . .	. . . .	. . . .	. . . .	Died Nov. 23, 1812.
Oct. 1, 1819	Commt. May 1, 1824 Col. June 5, 1829.	Jan. 10, 1837	. . . .	
. . . .	. . . .	. . . .	. . . .	Died Oct. 30, 1818, at Ellichpore.
. . . .	. . . .	. . . .	. . . .	Died Dec. 16, 1798.
May 1, 1824	. . . .	. . . .	. . . .	{ Invalided Jan. 22, 1830, in India. Died Feb. 19, 1830, at Bangalore.
. . . .	. . . .	. . . .	. . . .	Died Jan. 23, 1820, at Trichinopoly.
. . . .	. . . .	. . . .	. . . .	Retired March 29, 1816, in England.
. . . .	. . . .	. . . .	. . . .	Died Oct. 14, 1807, at St. Thomé.
. . . .	. . . .	. . . .	. . . .	Killed Sep. 23, 1803.
. . . .	. . . .	. . . .	. . . .	Invalided Dec. 3, 1813.
. . . .	. . . .	. . . .	. . . .	Retired June 28, 1825.
. . . .	. . . .	. . . .	. . . .	Died March 22, 1816, in England.
. . . .	. . . .	. . . .	. . . .	Died Nov. 18, 1822, at Ryepore.
. . . .	. . . .	. . . .	. . . .	{ Died on board the "City of London." Mar. 30, 1813.
. . . .	. . . .	. . . .	. . . .	Resigned Apr. 5, 1804.
May 1, 1824	. . . .	. . . .	. . . .	Retired Feb. 5, 1830, in India.
. . . .	. . . .	. . . .	. . . .	{ Invalided June 5, 1827, in India. Died at Dindigul, Sep. 9, 1828.
. . . .	. . . .	. . . .	. . . .	Died Sep. 12, 1805.
. . . .	. . . .	. . . .	. . . .	Died Feb. 15, 1818, at Vizagapatam.
. . . .	. . . .	. . . .	. . . .	{ Died on his passage, in the "Monarch," Oct. 21, 1801.
. . . .	. . . .	. . . .	. . . .	Retired Oct. 20, 1813.
. . . .	. . . .	. . . .	. . . .	Invalided.
. . . .	. . . .	. . . .	. . . .	Died Apr. 17, 1804, at Nundydroog.
. . . .	. . . .	. . . .	. . . .	Died Sep. 2, 1812.
. . . .	. . . .	. . . .	. . . .	Died at Tellicherry, Aug. 6, 1809.
. . . .	. . . .	. . . .	. . . .	Not to be traced.
. . . .	. . . .	. . . .	. . . .	Died Apr. 16, 1828, at Madras.
. . . .	. . . .	. . . .	. . . .	Died at Tripassore, May 21, 1804.
. . . .	. . . .	. . . .	. . . .	Died Aug. 19, 1821, at Bangalore.
. . . .	. . . .	. . . .	. . . .	Struck off.
. . . .	. . . .	. . . .	. . . .	Died Feb. 20, 1806.
. . . .	. . . .	. . . .	. . . .	Died May 26, 1803.
. . . .	. . . .	. . . .	. . . .	Retired from June 28, 1827, in England.
. . . .	. . . .	. . . .	. . . .	Retired Sep. 1, 1822.
. . . .	. . . .	. . . .	. . . .	Died at Onore, Jan. 11, 1808.
. . . .	. . . .	. . . .	. . . .	Died July 1, 1829, at Octacamund.

MADRAS

NAMES.	Cadet.	Cornet, Ensign, or Second Lieutenant.	Lieutenant.	Captain.	Major.
Little, John	1803		Sep. 21, 1804		
Lethbridge, Christopher	1804		July 17, 1805	Oct. 3, 1822	July 5, 1829
Low, John	,,		July 17, 1805	Dec. 25, 1820	Dec. 31, 1828
Lofft, Christopher Jebb	,,				
Lambert, Latin	,,		July 17, 1805		
Lewis, George	1805		Aug. 27, 1807		
Leigh, Edward	,,	June 27, 1806	Aug. 19, 1808		
Le Page, John	,,	June 27, 1806	Mar. 16, 1811		
Logan, John—*cavalry*	,,	July 3, 1807	Sep. 1, 1818	Sep. 30, 1825	
Logan, Henry	,,	June 27, 1806			
Locke, Thomas	1806	June 8, 1810	Sep. 1, 1818		
Lyon, James—*cavalry*	,,	Sep. 10, 1808	Mar. 1, 1817		
Lawlor, Michael	1807	Dec. 2, 1809	May 18, 1814	Brevet April 9, 1823	
Low, William	,,	Nov. 20, 1809	Jan. 8, 1813	July 3, 1824	May 5, 1833
Lighton, Samuel	,,	Feb. 24, 1810	May 17, 1814		
Logan, James Hodge	,,	Mar. 7, 1810	April 6, 1816		
Little, Simon	,,	May 28, 1810	May 22, 1813		
Leggett, Joseph	1808	May 28, 1810	Jan. 31, 1813	June 19, 1824	Dec. 22, 1832
Lee, George	,,	May 12, 1810	Aug. 21, 1816	Sep. 8, 1826	
Laurie, John	1809	July 29, 1810	July 24, 1815	Nov. 20, 1824	Oct. 31, 1835
Lonsdale, Mark	,,	Nov. 8, 1810	Aug. 5, 1816		
Ley, J. Morgan—*artillery*	1810	July 27, 1811	Sep. 1, 1818	June 19, 1824	
Lamb, John—*artillery*	,,	July 27, 1811	Aug. 3, 1817	May 1, 1824	
Lewis, Wm. F.—*artillery*	,,	July 27, 1811	Mar. 29, 1815	Jan. 17, 1824	
Limond, Thos. K.—*cavalry*	,,	Nov. 9, 1812	Oct. 28, 1816	June 17, 1820	May 31, 1833
Lys, Geo. Wm.—*artillery*	1811	June 11, 1812	Sep. 1, 1818		
Low, James	,,	June 11, 1812	Dec. 1, 1817	May 6, 1826	
Lockhart, John—*cavalry*	,,	July 9, 1815	Sep. 12, 1818		
Langford, William	1813		Nov. 10, 1816	May 2, 1829	
Lowe, Jeremiah—*artillery*	1814	July 11, 1815	Sep. 21, 1818		
Lake, Edward—*engineers*	1816	May 30, 1818	May 1, 1824	Aug. 9, 1825	
Lawe, Alex.—*engineers*	,,	May 19, 1818	May 6, 1824	June 7, 1825	
Lindesay, Alexander Trotter	1817		June 4, 1818		
Lewis, Wensley—*cavalry*	,,		Oct. 1, 1819		
Lewis, Charles Wilkins	,,		July 26, 1819		
Lynch, Henry Cormick	,,		Aug. 1, 1818	Sep. 27, 1826	
Lewis, John, (1st.) (24 N.I.)	,,		Oct. 27, 1818	Jan. 1, 1833	
Lodington, Henry John	1818		June 13, 1819	May 29, 1827	
Logan, Wm. Home	,,		June 13, 1819		
Lockhart, Wm. C.—*cavalry*	,,		Jan. 28, 1820		
Loveridge, John Edward	,,				
Luard, John Kynaster	,,		July 13, 1820	July 21, 1825	Oct. 10, 1836
Leslie, Charles	,,		June 13, 1819		
Lane, Thomas Mills	,,		Jan. 28, 1820		
Lawrence, A. W.	,,		Feb. 29, 1820	Aug. 1, 1833	
Langley, Edw. A.—*cavalry*	1819	April 6, 1820	Aug. 18, 1821	Oct. 18, 1832	
Lloyd, Oliver	,,		April 1, 1820		

PRESIDENCY.

Lieut.-Colonel.	Colonel.	Major-General.	Lieut.-General.	Date of Resignation, Retirement, or Death.
....	....	....	....	Died April 8, 1816.
Aug. 23, 1834	....	....	....	
Feb. 21, 1834	....	....	....	
....	....	....	....	Struck off, June 10, 1806.
....	....	....	....	Died April 12, 1810, at Madras.
....	....	....	....	Died June 22, 1811, at Seringapatam.
....	....	....	....	Died 1820.
....	....	....	....	Died Mar. 28, 1813, in India.
....	....	....	....	Died June 6, 1829, at St. Thomé.
....	....	....	....	Died Oct. 8, 1809, at Cudapah.
....	....	....	....	Invalided April 17, 1827, in India.
....	....	....	....	Retired April 20, 1819, in England.
....	....	....	....	Died Mar. 30, 1824, at Seringapatam.
....	....	....	....	
....	....	....	....	Died Nov. 10, 1815, at Bombay.
....	....	....	....	Died April 1, 1817, at Chittoor.
....	....	....	....	Died Mar. 10, 1815, at Bangalore.
....	....	....	....	
....	....	....	....	
....	....	....	....	
....	....	....	....	Died Oct. 29, 1823, at Gooty.
....	....	....	....	
....	....	....	....	Died Aug. 1824.
....	....	....	....	Died Dec. 11, 1825, at Prome.
....	....	....	....	
....	....	....	....	Died May 24, 1821.
....	....	....	....	
....	....	....	....	Died Dec. 3, 1819, in camp, at Jaulnah.
....	....	....	....	
....	....	....	....	Died May 20, 1822, at St. Thomas's Mount.
....	....	....	....	Died in 1832 (place and date not known).
....	....	....	....	
....	....	....	....	Died June 8, 1824, at Rangoon.
....	....	....	....	Died Dec. 29, 1825, at Kolapore.
....	....	....	....	Died Oct. 27, 1819, in camp, at Bejapore.
....	....	....	....	{ Invalided Jan. 27, 1829, in India. Retired June 28, 1831, in England.
....	....	....	....	Invalided in 1829.
....	....	....	....	Died Sep. 14, 1828, at Jaulnah.
....	....	....	....	Died Aug. 7, 1821, at Arcot.
....	....	....	....	Died May 14, 1820, at Jaulnah.
....	....	....	....	{ Invalided — June 1828. Pensioned Sep. 10, 1830, in India.
....	....	....	....	{ Pensioned Dec. 4, 1826, on Lord Clive's Fund in England.
....	....	....	....	Discharged Mar. 25, 1837, in India.
....	....	....	....	Died Feb. 26, 1823, at Ryacottah.

P 2

MADRAS

NAMES.	Cadet.	Cornet, Ensign, or Second Lieutenant.	Lieutenant.	Captain.	Major.
Leacock, George	1819	....	April 7, 1820	Brevet, April 6, 1835	....
Longworth, Theo. A. I. I...	,,	....	April 7, 1820	Oct. 25, 1833	....
Logan, George	,,	....	Aug. 21, 1821	Jan. 27, 1831	....
Logan Archibald S.	,,	....	Sep. 6, 1820	Sep. 11, 1832	....
Lindesay, John	,,	....	April 7, 1820	....	....
Lally, William Michael....	,,	....	May 5, 1820	....	....
Lyons, Coverdale	,,	....	April 7, 1820	....	....
Litchfield, Wm. E.—*cavalry*	,,	April 6, 1820	July 7, 1823	Oct. 6, 1828	....
Luard, Charles George	,,	....	July 13, 1820	....	....
Lushington, J. S.—*cavalry*	,,	April 6, 1820	Oct. 16, 1823	June 7, 1829	....
Lardner, Henry Wilson....	,,	....	Apr. 30, 1821	....	....
Lane, Charles	,,	....	Dec. 11, 1821	....	....
Lucas, Francis Blaney	,,	April 6, 1820	Jan. 16, 1823	Dec. 15, 1827	....
Lewis, William George T.	,,	April 6, 1820	Sep. 4, 1823	July 13, 1835	....
Laing, John— *cavalry*	,,	....	Sep. 9, 1822	....	....
Lee, Henry	1820	April 6, 1821	Mar. 12, 1823	Jan. 20, 1830	....
Le Hardy, Chas. Francis ..	,,	Feb. 13, 1821	Apr. 7, 1824	Apr. 12, 1837	....
Lys, William De Monte ..	,,	Feb. 13, 1821	Dec. 23, 1822	Brevet Feb. 13, 1836	....
Leatherdale, Wm.—*artillery*	,,	Dec. 14, 1820	June 8, 1821	....	....
Leslie, James F.	,,	Feb. 13, 1821	May 1, 1824	Brevet Feb. 13, 1836.	....
Littlejohn, Duncan........	,,	Feb. 13, 1821	May 1, 1824	Mar. 5, 1836	....
Lewis, W. Geo.—*artillery*..	,,	....	June 8, 1821	....	....
Loader, William	,,	....	....	....	....
Lang, Richard William....	,,	Feb. 13, 1821	Oct. 14, 1824	....	....
Lambert, Richard	1821	Apr. 27, 1822	Dec. 6, 1824	Brevet Feb. 13, 1836	....
Liardet, Charles Frederick	,,	Apr. 27, 1822	June 27, 1825	....	....
Lyons, Edward	,,	Apr. 27, 1822	Oct. 15, 1824	Mar. 4, 1834	....
Lugard, John Trewman....	,,	Apr. 27, 1822	Dec. 18, 1824	....	....
Lindsey, Chas. B.—*cavalry*	1822	May 2, 1823	Aug. 2, 1828	....	....
Lewis, John (2d.) (48 N. I.)	1823	May 14, 1824	Sep. 27, 1826	....	....
Losh, John Joseph	,,	Sep. 14, 1824	June 21, 1828	....	....
Lockhart, William E.	1824	May 6, 1825	Mar. 3, 1827	....	....
Lavie, Tudor—*artillery*	,,	Oct. 13, 1824	Oct. 24, 1824	....	....
Lord, Hugh Fred.—*cavalry*	,,	....	Feb. 10, 1827	....	....
Loyd, W. Kirkman--*artillery*	1825	Dec. 16, 1825	Aug. 6, 1827	....	....
Lys, Frank Brian	,,	....	Sep. 15, 1828	....	....
Lang, James Strachan	,,	....	Aug. 7, 1828	....	....
Lancaster, Chas.—*artillery*	,,	June 16, 1826	Mar. 14, 1829	....	....
Lamphier, William Henry..	1826	Jan. 16, 1827	April 1, 1833	....	....
Leathem, John Gay	,,	Feb. 8, 1827	....	....	....
Lawford, Edward—*engineers*	,,	....	Dec. 17, 1825	....	....
Lascelles, F. G. J.—*cavalry*	,,	Sep. 4, 1827	Jan. 30, 1834	....	....
Littlehales, Wm. Benjamin	,,	Aug. 15, 1827	July 31, 1833	....	....
Layard, John Beville......	,,	Oct. 14, 1827	Apr. 15, 1836	....	....
Lushington, R. H.—*cavalry*	,,	Aug. 19, 1828	....	....	....
Leader, William	,,	June 13, 1828	July 18, 1834	....	....
Lowe, Thomas............	,,	Oct. 24, 1827	Mar. 27, 1835	....	....

PRESIDENCY.

108—109

Lieut.-Colonel.	Colonel.	Major-General.	Lieut.-General.	Date of Resignation, Retirement, or Death.
				Died Aug. 3, 1837, at Madras.
				Died Oct. 12, 1824, at Rangoon.
				Died July 15, 1828, at Belgaum.
				Died July 12, 1824, at Rangoon.
				Died June 19, 1822, at the Presidency.
				{ Died Oct. 19, 1831, on board the "Baretto, Junr."
				Died Oct. 12, 1833, on board the "Lady Munro."
				{ Died Nov. 22, 1822, on board the "Triumph," on his passage to England.
				Resigned April 27, 1830, in India.
				Invalided.
				Died March — 1824.
				Died Nov. — 1823.
				Died Nov. 26, 1821, at Wallajahbad.
				Died Oct. 11, 1831, at Nagpore.
				Died April 3, 1836, at Mangalore.
				Retired Dec. 19, 1836, in England.
				Died Oct. 28, 1830, at Bompilly.
				Died Nov. 3, 1830, at St. Thomé.
				Invalided Aug. 17, 1832, in India.

MADRAS

NAMES.	Cadet.	Cornet, Ensign, or Second Lieutenant.	Lieutenant.	Captain.	Major.
Lloyd, Evan	1827	Dec. 4, 1829	Nov. 15,1834		
Lake, Henry A.—*engineers*	,,	....	Mar. 4, 1831		
Light, John Alexander....	1828	Dec. 23,1828	Dec. 24, 1833		
Lawford, Henry—*artillery*	,,	Dec. 12, 1828	June 22, 1836		
Lacon, John Edmund	,,	Aug. 1, 1831			
Luscombe, W. Pinsent....	1829				
Lethbridge, G. M.-*artillery*	1830				
Lamb, Charles	,,	July 18, 1832	Jan. 11, 1836		
Lautour, Peter A.........	,,	July 7, 1832			
Ludlow, S. E. O.—*engineers*	1831	May 20, 1834			
Little, R. R.—*artillery*....	1832				
Le Geyt, W. H.—*cavalry*..	,,	Oct. 23, 1834			
Ludlow, T. Haynes Browne	,,	Jan. 1, 1834			
Leycester, Ralph W. H. ..	1833	Dec. 13, 1833			
Lysaght, A...............	1834	Aug. 7, 1835	Sep. 23, 1836		

M

NAMES.	Cadet.	Cornet, Ensign, or Second Lieutenant.	Lieutenant.	Captain.	Major.
Mackay, Daniel—*artillery*	....	....	....	Aug. 6, 1770	Dec. 30, 1781
Macleod, Donald	....	Nov. 16,1767	July 29, 1769	Apr. 13, 1777	Apr. 17, 1786
Montgomery Hugh	....	....	Aug. 3, 1770	July 3, 1779	
Malcombe, Henry	1767	Nov. 7, 1768	Sep. 23, 1770	July 20,1779	Dec. 29, 1789
Muat, George	1768	Aug. 4, 1770	Mar. 14,1772	Jan. 5, 1782	Dec. 11,1793
Mayne, Philip	,,	Aug. 23,1770	July 24, 1773	June 13,1782	
Montgomery Alexander ..	1769	Sep. 24, 1770	Feb. 22, 1774	Nov. 9, 1782	
Massey, Cromwell........	,,	Dec. 26, 1770	Nov. 19,1776	Nov. 2, 1783	Mar. — 1794
Macpherson Alexander ..	1770	Jan. 21, 1772	Aug. 29, 1777	Nov. 2, 1783	Mar. — 1794
Meulch, William	,,	Feb. 3, 1772	Dec. 30, 1777	Nov. 2, 1783	
Macneile, Daniel	1771	Oct. 23, 1772	Aug. 4, 1778	Nov. 2, 1783	June 1, 1796
Mackay, James	....	Aug. 22,1774	Oct. 14, 1780		
Manoury, Isaac—*artillery*	....	....	....	June 24, 1770	
Mackay, Robert..........	....	June 4, 1775	Oct. 16, 1780	Aug. 16,1785	June 1, 1796
Moore, Thomas	....	July 24, 1775	Oct. 21, 1780	Sep. —1789	
Maclean, Sir H. (K.C.B.)..	....	Dec. 13, 1775	Oct. 29, 1780	Mar. 18, 1786	June 1, 1796
Macdonald, Donald	1775	Nov. 22,1776	Dec. 5, 1780	June 6, 1793	Oct. 21, 1797
Moore, Peter	1779	Aug. 3, 1779	Mar. 19,1781	June 1, 1796	
Moore, G.—*artillery*......	,,	Dec. 4, 1780	July 14, 1782	June 11,1789	
Maccalister, Charles......	1777	May 12, 1778	Jan. 27, 1782		
Meulth, Thomas..........	1778	May 19, 1778	Feb. 2, 1782	Apr. 27, 1795	
Macleod, Alexander, Senr.	,,	May 22, 1778	Feb. 5, 1782	June 23, 1795	Dec. 26, 1798
Moorhouse, J.—*artillery* ..	1767	Dec. 1, 1768	Feb. 16, 1772	Dec. 1, 1780	Sep. 17, 1786
Macawley, Colin	1777	July 12, 1778	Mar. 10, 1782	June 1, 1796	July 31,1799
Mandeville, F. — *artillery*	,,	Dec. 14,1778	....	Oct. 17, 1784	Sep. 28, 1797
Munro, Robert	,,	June 8, 1778	Feb. 22, 1782		
Molloy, James............	,,	June 20, 1778	Feb. 27, 1782		
Munro, John	,,	July 2, 1778	Mar. 6, 1782	June 1, 1796	June 20,1799
Miller, Blakener	,,	July 25, 1778	Mar. 15,1782		
Macgregor, Malcolme	1778	Aug. 12,1778	April 1, 1783	June 1, 1796	Dec. 10, 1799
Maccalister, Mathew......	,,	Aug. 30,1778	Sep. 1, 1783	June 1, 1796	

PRESIDENCY.

Lieut.-Colonel.	Colonel.	Major General.	Lieut.-General.	Date of Resignation, Retirement, or Death.
....	....	....	....	
....	....	....	....	
....	....	....	....	
....	....	....	....	Resigned Feb. 11, 1836, in India.
....	....	....	....	Died May 31, 1832, at Penang.
....	....	....	....	Died July 17, 1833, at Kamptee.
....	....	....	....	
....	....	....	....	Died Jan. 24, 1835, at Mangalore.
....	....	....	....	[Jan. — 1837.
....	....	....	....	Transferred to Invalid Establishment.
....	....	....	....	
....	....	....	....	
....	....	....	....	
....	....	....	....	
....	....	....	....	Died — 1783, in camp.
....	....	....	....	Resigned Oct. 16, 1787.
....	....	....	....	Died — 1792.
June 1, 1796	Jan. 1, 1798	....	....	Retired April — 1798.
June 1, 1796	May 12, 1799	....	....	Died Aug. 17, 1799, at Chittledroog.
....	....	....	....	Dismissed Service, Dec. — 1789.
....	....	....	....	Died Jan. — 1793.
June 1, 1796	Aug. 27, 1800	....	....	Retired Oct. 1, 1800.
June 1, 1796	....	....	....	Died July 23, 1798, at Amboor.
....	....	....	....	Died — 1788.
July 27, 1796	Jan. 1, 1803	July 25, 1810	June 4, 1814	Died Oct. 21, 1826, in London.
....	....	....	....	Died — 1788.
....	....	....	....	Died — 1782.
Oct. 12, 1798	Apr. 25, 1808	June 4, 1811	July 19, 1821	Died Sep. 26, 1835, in France.
....	....	....	....	Invalided — 1792, on the Military [Fund.
Dec. 26, 1798	Apr. 25, 1808	June 4, 1811	July 19, 1821	
....	....	....	....	Died June 19, 1799.
....	....	....	....	Pensioned Oct. 15, 1798.
....	....	....	....	Drowned — 1790, in the "Colbroon."
....	....	....	....	{ In Europe on Health, 1792, and no further account.
....	....	....	....	Died Oct. 17, 1797.
Dec. 10, 1801	....	....	....	Died Jan. 8, 1808, at Chittledroog.
Feb. 4, 1791	....	....	....	Killed, 1791, at the storming of Bangalore.
Jan. 1, 1803	Jan. 1, 1812	June 4, 1814	July 22, 1830	Died Feb. 21, 1836, at Clifton.
....	....	....	....	Dismissed — 1801, by Court Martial.
....	....	....	....	Died June — 1789.
....	....	....	....	Died — 1789.
....	....	....	....	Died Dec. 23, 1800.
....	....	....	....	Died — 1790.
....	....	....	....	Invalided July 10, 1802. Died Nov. 4, 1804.
....	....	....	....	Retired June — 1798.

MADRAS

NAMES.	Cadet.	Cornet, Ensign, or Second Lieutenant.	Lieutenant.	Captain.	Major.
Munro, Sir Thomas, Bart. (K.C.B.)	1778	May 20, 1779	Feb. 11, 1786	June 1, 1796	May 7, 1800
Macleod, William, Sen.	,,	May 21, 1779	Feb. 21, 1786	June 1, 1796	June 17, 1800
Mealy, Ridgeway	,,	May 31, 1779	Apr. 17, 1786	June 1, 1796	June 17, 1800
Munro, Thomas, Junr.	1779	Aug. 23, 1780	Apr. 17, 1786	....	....
Macleod, William, Junr.	,,	Sep. 7, 1780	Apr. 17, 1786	....	....
Marten, George	,,	Sep. 14, 1780	Apr. 17, 1786	July 2, 1796	Aug. 24, 1803
Monsell, John	,,	Oct. 4, 1780	Apr. 17, 1786	....	....
Maypother, Patrick	1780	Dec. 12, 1780	Apr. 17, 1786	July 25, 1797	....
Mair, Patrick	,,	Sep. 7, 1781	....	....	....
Maitland, Alexander	,,	Sep. 15, 1781	April 1, 1788	Nov. 29, 1797	June 6, 1804
Malcolm, Sir J. (G.C.B., K.L.S.)	,,	Oct. 24, 1781	Nov. 1, 1788	Sep. 29, 1798	Jan. 27, 1802
Munro, Robert, Junr.	1781	Jan. 9, 1782	Feb. 26, 1789	Oct. 12, 1798	Sep. 21, 1804
Macpherson, Andrew	1782	Apr. 27, 1783	Aug. 21, 1790	May 19, 1799	May 1, 1804
Mendham, Charles	,,	July 8, 1783	Aug. 21, 1790	....	....
Molloy, John	,,	May 5, 1783	Aug. 21, 1790	Dec. 10, 1799	....
Marlin, F. G.	1783	Aug. 28, 1783	....	....	....
Moore, Teerad—*artillery*	....	Dec. 4, 1780	July 14, 1782	....	....
Munro, James—*artillery*	....	Feb. 22, 1782	Apr. 17, 1786	....	....
Morris, Andrew—*artillery*	1782	Aug. 23, 1783	....	....	....
Murrell, L. B.—*artillery*	,,	Aug. 25, 1783	....	....	....
Maddes, B.—*artillery*	1781	Nov. 2, 1785	....	....	....
Mackie, John—*artillery*	1782	Aug. 22, 1783	Dec. 15, 1788	....	....
Mahon, R. T.—*artillery*	1784	Oct. 29, 1785	....	....	....
Maule, George—*engineers*	....	Aug. 31, 1770	Mar. 19, 1771	Aug. 24, 1773	Dec. 14, 1778
Murray, John—*cavalry*	....	....	....	April — 1784	Jan. 30, 1791
Maccalister, K.—*cavalry*	1777	May 13, 1778	....	June 1, 1796	....
Montgomery, H. C.—*cavalry*	1782	May 12, 1783	June 19, 1792	June 17, 1800	... 1804 ...
Mackay, Hugh—*cavalry*	....	Dec. 14, 1785	June 1, 1796	April 8, 1802	....
McDowall, Sir A. (K.C.B,)	1783	Sep. 5, 1783	Aug. 21, 1790	Dec. 10, 1799	Oct. 16, 1805
Mackay, Æneas	1770	June 26, 1771	Apr. 17, 1777	....	....
Muirhead, David	1765	June 8, 1766	Aug. 27, 1767	....	....
Maclean, John—*cavalry*	1788	Aug. 3, 1789	June 1, 1796	June 28, 1800	May 3, 1805
Macgill, Patrick—*cavalry*	....	June 12, 1793	Sep. 4, 1799	....	....
Mason, Henry—*cavalry*	....	June 18, 1793	Sep. 4, 1799	May 3, 1805	July 29, 1815
Mackay, Adam—*artillery*	1787	July 22, 1788	May 6, 1793	....	....
Macintire, And.—*artillery*	,,	Sep. 6, 1788	June 11, 1793	....	....
Murray, Wm.—*artillery*	1791	Oct. 2, 1791	June 1, 1796	....	....
Meulh, William	....	....	June 7, 1792	....	....
Moodie, Charles	....	....	June 7, 1792	....	....
Muirhead, Alexander	....	....	June 7, 1792	June 17, 1800	June 27, 1805
Maccally, Whitney	....	....	June 7, 1792	Jan. 1, 1800	Jan. 9, 1808
Maccally, Andrew	....	....	....	....	....
Macpherson, Greme	....	....	June 7, 1792	....	....
Morgan, John De	1788	....	July 16, 1792	Sep. 21, 1804	Aug. 20, 1807
Marricott, Thomas	1789	....	Oct. 3, 1792	May 7, 1800	Apr. 14, 1804
Maitland, John	,,	....	Dec. 5, 1792	June 17, 1800	....
Macleod, Alex. Jun.	,,	....	Jan. 16, 1793	May 7, 1800	....

PRESIDENCY.   112—113

Lieut.-Colonel.	Colonel.	Major General	Lieut.-General.	Date of Resignation, Retirement, or Death.
Apr. 24, 1804	June 4, 1813	Aug. 12, 1819	....	Died July 6, 1827, at Gooty.
Sep. 21, 1804	June 4, 1813	Aug. 12, 1819	....	Died Nov. 16, 1836, at Fulham.
Oct. 13, 1804	....	....	....	Died Sep. 19, 1805, at Nundydroog.
....	....	....	....	Died June — 1789.
....	....	....	....	Died 1791.
Mar. 23, 1805	June 4, 1813	....	....	Died June 17, 1815, at Bellary.
....	....	....	....	Died 1791.
....	....	....	....	{ Invalided July 1791. Died July 24, 1800, at Berhampore.
....	....	....	....	Died July, 1789.
Sep. 10, 1807	....	....	....	Retired May 26, 1809.
Dec. 12, 1804	June 4, 1813	Aug. 12, 1819	....	Died May 30, 1833, in London.
Jan. 9, 1808	June 4, 1814	....	....	{ Cashiered Mar. 7, 1810. Restored Jan. 28, 1814. Died May 18, 1817, at Masulipatam.
Apr. 23, 1806	....	....	....	Died May 21, 1807.
....	....	....	....	Died May 1794.
....	....	....	....	Retired Jan. 18, 1804.
....	....	....	....	Died 1790.
....	....	....	....	King's service in Jan. 1793.
....	....	....	....	Died 1791.
....	....	....	....	Died 1792.
....	....	....	....	Died Oct. 16, 1787.
....	....	....	....	Died 1792, in camp.
....	....	....	....	Died 1793, at the Mount.
....	....	....	....	Removed to King's service, 1789.
Feb. 23, 1793	....	....	....	Killed before Pondicherry, 1793.
....	....	....	....	Died at Ahtoor, May 6, 1799.
Sep. 4, 1799	Oct. 25, 1809	Jan. 1, 1812	....	Died March 9, 1820, in England.
....	....	....	....	Struck off, March 4, 1806.
....	....	....	....	Killed Sep. 23, 1803, at the battle of Assay.
Feb. 23, 1811	July 19, 1821	July 22, 1830	....	Died May 15, 1834, in India.
....	....	....	....	Not to be traced.
....	....	....	....	Not to be traced.
....	....	....	....	Died Aug. 1, 1806.
....	....	....	....	Died Dec. 15, 1800.
....	....	....	....	Died Dec. 2, 1820, at Secunderabad.
....	....	....	....	Resigned Oct. 1800.
....	....	....	....	Dismissed by Court Martial, Oct. 4, 1801.
....	....	....	....	Died in 1797, at Madras.
....	....	....	....	Died Dec. 13, 1804.
....	....	....	....	Died May 28, 1796, at the Presidency.
....	....	....	....	Died at Onore, Nov. 15, 1809.
Mar. 14, 1813	....	....	....	{ Invalided Sep. 17, 1813. Died July 9, 1814, at Chicacole.
....	....	....	....	Died in 1797.
Jan. 25, 1813	....	....	....	{ Died on board the "Larkins," on his passage to England. Nov. 27, 1816.
Dec. 27, 1806	June 4, 1814	July 19, 1821	Jan. 10, 1837	
....	....	....	....	Killed Dec. 14, 1801.
....	....	....	....	Struck off March 3, 1801.

MADRAS.—Q

MADRAS

NAMES.	Cadet.	Cornet, Ensign, or Second Lieutenant.	Lieutenant.	Captain.	Major.
Marshall, Alexander	1789	....	Feb. 4, 1793	Apr. 7, 1800	....
Morgan, Charles Stanley	1790	June 7, 1791	June 6, 1793	....	....
Mathews, R. W. Wm.	,,	June 9, 1791	June 6, 1793	June 17, 1800	....
Meyer, John Jeremiah	,,	June 13, 1791	June 6, 1793	....	....
Marshall, Josiah	,,	June 17, 1791	June 6, 1793	June 17, 1800	Mar. 18, 1809
Mackay, Robert	,,	June 19, 1791	June 6, 1793	....	....
Macintosh, Alexander	,,	July 23, 1791	Dec. 11, 1793	Feb. 21, 1802	Aug. 19, 1808
Macpherson, John	,,	July 26, 1791	Feb. 4, 1794	....	....
Macintosh, Hugh	,,	Aug. 1, 1791	Feb. 17, 1794	Aug. 27, 1800	....
Maclean, Alexander	,,	Aug. 14, 1791	Mar. 5, 1794	....	....
Macdonnell, Donald	,,	Aug. 23, 1791	June 13, 1794	Oct. 18, 1801	July 11, 1806
Munro, John	,,	Aug. 26, 1791	Aug. 6, 1794	Dec. 24, 1800	Feb. 23, 1811
Macgregor, George	,,	Sep. 5, 1791	Aug. 6, 1794	Mar. 3, 1801	June 21, 1807
Macgregor, Donald	,,	Sep. 20, 1791	Aug. 6, 1794	Dec. 8, 1801	....
Macdonald, James Reynold	,,	Sep. 21, 1791	Aug. 6, 1794	....	....
Mackenzie, C. (C.B.)—*engineers*	1781	May 16, 1783	Mar. 6, 1789	Aug. 16, 1793	Jan. 1, 1806
Monin, Anthony	1791	May 19, 1793	Aug. 6, 1794	Sep. 21, 1804	Mar. 23, 1816
Monteath, A. D.—*cavalry*	,,	June 7, 1793	Sep. 4, 1799	May 1, 1804	Mar. 11, 1809
Molesworth, Arthur	1793	....	Aug. 6, 1795	Aug. 24, 1803	Dec. 14, 1809
McMillan, Robert Gordon	,,	...1795...	Nov. 23, 1795	....	....
Marriott, Richard	,,	...1795...	Apr. 27, 1795	Apr. 24, 1804	....
Muat, George Alexander	1794	Jan. 25, 1796	June 1, 1796	June 24, 1803	May 22, 1807
Menzies, Robert	1793	....	Dec. 19, 1795	....	....
Mandeville, Charles	1794	Dec. 21, 1795	Feb. 10, 1796	Oct. 19, 1803	Dec. 27, 1808
Mainwaring, Rowland E.	1795	Dec. 28, 1795	May 18, 1796	....	....
Milward, John	,,	Jan. 13, 1796	June 1, 1796	May 1, 1804	....
Marsden, Benjamin	,,	Feb. 29, 1796	July 11, 1797	....	....
Macdougall, John	,,	Jan. 29, 1796	June 1, 1796	July 15, 1804	Aug. 17, 1810
Macleod, Charles (C.B.)	1794	Jan. 12, 1796	June 1, 1796	Sep. 21, 1804	Oct. 23, 1815
Macdonald, Charles	1795	Mar. 9, 1796	Aug. 18, 1797	....	....
Munro, William	,,	Feb. 10, 1796	Oct. 20, 1796	May 23, 1804	Nov. 7, 1810
Macdonald, John	,,	April 2, 1796	Nov. 29, 1797	....	....
Malcolm, Thomas	,,	Feb. 16, 1796	Mar. 18, 1797	....	....
Macleod, Æneas	,,	Mar. 27, 1796	Nov. 29, 1797	....	....
Macdowall, Robert	,,	April 5, 1796	Nov. 29, 1797	Jan. 1, 1807	Oct. 10, 1810
Marriott, Charles Selwood	1794	Dec. 20, 1795	Feb. 10, 1796	....	....
Man, Peter Bruels	1795	Feb. 11, 1796	Nov. 1, 1796	Sep. 21, 1804	....
Munro, George	,,	Feb. 8, 1796	July 27, 1796	....	....
Murray, William	....	....	May 5, 1795	....	....
Mackenzie, John (C.B.)	1797	Sep. 5, 1797	Oct. 12, 1798	Feb. 5, 1805	Mar. 14, 1813
Markes, Thomas	1795	....	Nov. 29, 1797	....	....
Marriott, Charles	1796	....	Nov. 29, 1797	June 27, 1804	Apr. 14, 1817
Moore, James	,,	....	Nov. 29, 1797	Sep. 21, 1804	Feb. 19, 1813
Maynard, Josiah	,,	July 30, 1797	Apr. 11, 1798	....	....
Moodie, John	,,	....	Oct. 12, 1798	Sep. 21, 1804	Sep. 18, 1813
Macdouall, Sutherland	,,	Aug. 28, 1797	Oct. 12, 1798	Jan. 31, 1805	May 26, 1814
Marriott, Charles S.	1796	Sep. 11, 1798	Dec. 29, 1798	....	....

PRESIDENCY.

Lieut.-Colonel.	Colonel.	Major-General.	Lieut.-General.	Date of Resignation, Retirement, or Death.
....	....	....	....	Retired Aug. 14, 1805.
....	....	....	....	Died Apr. 20, 1795.
....	....	....	....	Died at Amboyna, Aug. 15, 1806.
....	....	....	....	Struck off the List, in 1797.
May 31, 1816	Commt. May 1, 1824. Col. June 5, 1829.	Jan. 10, 1837	....	
....	....	....	....	Died Oct. 20, 1797.
July 28, 1814	....	....	....	Died Nov. 22, 1823, at Vellore.
....	....	....	....	Died January 1796.
....	....	....	....	Dismissed Apr. 5, 1810.
....	....	....	....	Died Aug. 18, 1795, at Chicacole.
Nov. 30, 1811	....	....	....	{ Invalided Sep. 10, 1813. Retired July 3, 1817, in England.
Feb. 9, 1818	Commt. May 1, 1824. Col. June 5, 1829.	Jan. 10, 1837	....	
....	....	....	....	Died at Seringapatam, March 7, 1810.
....	....	....	....	Died February 1, 1811.
....	....	....	....	Died May 25, 1802.
Nov. 15, 1810	Aug. 12, 1819	....	....	Died May 8, 1821, in Bengal.
May 16, 1822	June 5, 1829	....	....	
....	....	....	....	Retired September 5, 1810.
Apr. 14, 1817	Commt. May 1, 1824. Col. June 5, 1829.	Jan. 10, 1837	....	
....	....	....	....	Died Dec. 28, 1798.
....	....	....	....	Died Jan 30, 1805, at Horsham, Sussex.
Mar. 14, 1813	....	....	....	Died March 23, 1822, at St. Thomé.
....	....	....	....	Died 1796.
June 15, 1815	....	....	....	Invalided Oct. 9, 1819, in India.
....	....	....	....	Died March 20, 1801.
....	....	....	....	Died at Seringapatam, Jan. 30, 1806.
....	....	....	....	Died May 15, 1799, at Colombo.
....	....	....	....	Died in camp at Hurryghur, Mar. 2, 1813.
July 13, 1821	June 5, 1829	....	....	
....	....	....	....	Died at Malacca, 1803.
Dec. 10, 1817	Commt. May 1, 1824 Col. June 5, 1829.	Jan. 10, 1837	....	
....	....	....	....	Died at Bombay, 1801.
....	....	....	....	Resigned the Service, Sep. 26, 1797.
....	....	....	....	Died May 13, 1801.
Nov. 30, 1817	Commt. May 1, 1824	....	....	Died Nov. 16, 1825, in action, at Prome.
....	....	....	....	Struck off, Dec. 17, 1799.
....	....	....	....	Died at St. Thomé, May 7, 1811.
....	....	....	....	Died May 7, 1803.
....	....	....	....	Not to be traced.
Oct. 14, 1818	Commt. May 23, 1825	....	....	Died March 2, 1830, in London.
....	....	....	....	Died July 1, 1803.
....	....	....	....	Retired March 13, 1822.
....	....	....	....	Died June 3, 1817, at Bimlipatam.
....	....	....	....	Died Apr. 14, 1799.
....	....	....	....	Died Feb. 27, 1819, at Bombay.
Sep. 1, 1819	....	....	....	Died Nov. 7, 1820, at Madras.
....	....	....	....	Struck off, May 8, 1804, not arriving.

MADRAS

NAMES.	Cadet.	Cornet, Ensign, or Second Lieutenant.	Lieutenant.	Captain.	Major.
Maitland, Richard	1797				
Malton, Edward	1796	Sep. 9, 1797	Dec. 16, 1800	July 9, 1814	
Macbean, James	1797	Aug. 8, 1798	Dec. 26, 1798	Sep. 21, 1804	June 14, 1815
Muller, Theodore Conrad	,,	July 28, 1798	Dec. 16, 1798		
Millar, David	,,	July 22, 1798	Oct. 22, 1798	Sep. 21, 1804	
Mackay, Donald	1796	Sep. 14, 1797	Oct. 12, 1798	Oct. 22, 1807	July 17, 1819
Maddison, Henry John	1797	Aug. 28, 1798	Dec. 26, 1798		
Macdonald, John	,,	Aug. 10, 1798	Dec. 26, 1798		
Mangnall, Kay	1795	Feb. 18, 1796	May 7, 1797		
Martin, William	,,	Mar. 20, 1796	Nov. 29, 1797		
Munt, H. (C.B.)—cavalry	,,	Mar. 14, 1796	Sep. 4, 1799	Dec. 18, 1801	Jan. 17, 1810
Moore, William	1798		Jan. 1, 1800	May 5, 1810	
Monteath, William	,,				
Miller, James Isaac	,,	Aug. 14, 1798	Dec. 26, 1798	Sep. 21, 1804	
Maret, Peter Daniel	,,		Jan. 1, 1800	Jan. 1, 1807	Nov. 30, 1817
Merry, Anthony	,,	Aug. 15, 1798	Dec. 26, 1798		
Macleod, Alex.—cavalry	,,		June 17, 1800	Oct. 27, 1808	Oct. 31, 1817
Mackintosh, J. J.—artillery	,,		Apr. 19, 1800	Feb. 14, 1805	Oct. 17, 1821
Moorhouse, J.—artillery	1799		Dec. 31, 1801	July 28, 1808	
Moor, George	,,		Dec. 15, 1800	Jan. 8, 1813	
Moor, John	,,		Dec. 15, 1800	Dec. 15, 1808	May 1, 1824
Mitchell, Charles	,,		Dec. 15, 1800		
Macreith, Robert	,,		Dec. 15, 1800	June 28, 1814	
Macleod, Alexander	,,		Dec. 15, 1800	Oct. 10, 1810	Jan. 27, 1819
Mackenzie, Hume	,,		Dec. 15, 1800	Apr. — 1814	
Moore, John—cavalry	,,		Sep. 3, 1801		
Morison, W. (C.B.)—artillery	,,		Dec. 31, 1800	July 4, 1807	May 21, 1823
Morris, Wm. Henry	,,				
Mackay, John			Jan. 1, 1800		
Mackay, R. Skeene	1800				
Masterton, Dugald	,,		July 20, 1801		
Morgan, John	,,		July 20, 1801	Nov. 8, 1811	Sep. 8, 1826
Morgan, John W.—cavalry	,,	Aug. 21, 1801	Sep. 2, 1801		
Munn, Henry	,,		July 20, 1801	Feb. 24, 1818	Sep. 8, 1826
Menzies, Henry Wright	,,		July 20, 1801		
Maunsell, George	,,		July 20, 1801	May 30, 1811	Apr. 30, 1822
Maunsell, Philip Olive	,,				
Morrill, Peter	,,		Nov. 18, 1802	May 25, 1814	
Macintosh, John	,,		July 20, 1801		
Mavor, Robert	,,		July 20, 1801		
Maclaren, Alexander	,,		April 7, 1802	Mar. 20, 1814	Sep. 8, 1826
Moncrieff, M.—cavalry	,,	July 7, 1801	May 1, 1804	Sep. 13, 1813	
Mitchell, Alfred	,,				
Maitland, Gilbert	,,		July 20, 1801	Dec. 4, 1814	
Milburn, Reginald	,,		July 20, 1801		
Martin, Stephen—cavalry	,,	Feb. 10, 1802	May 1, 1804	Mar. 1, 1817	Sep. 1, 1818
Mathew, Patrick	,,	July 20, 1801			

PRESIDENCY.

Lieut.-Colonel.	Colonel.	Major General.	Lieut.-General.	Date of Resignation, Retirement, or Death.
....	....	....	....	Died Aug. 23, 1799, at Seringapatam.
....	....	....	....	Died April 9, 1816.
....	....	....	....	Died April 7, 1819, at Aurungabad.
....	....	....	....	Died June 23, 1799, at Madras.
....	....	....	....	Pensioned Apr. 30, 1810. Died
....	....	....	....	Died May 27, 1820. [Nov. 2, 1812.
....	....	....	....	Died Nov. 25, 1804.
....	....	....	....	Died Oct. 27, 1800.
....	....	....	....	Killed March 31, 1801.
....	....	....	....	Died Jan. 1, 1799, on passage to England.
Nov. 7, 1818	....	....	....	Died July 25, 1819, at Nagpore.
....	....	....	....	Died April 29, 1816.
....	....	....	....	Died Feb. 23, 1801.
....	....	....	....	Died July 10, 1806, at Vellore.
....	....	....	....	Retired Feb. 13, 1821.
....	....	....	....	Resigned March 24, 1801.
Dec. 3, 1820	....	....	....	Died May 21, 1825, at Belgaum.
Sep. 4, 1824	....	....	....	Retired in 1825.
....	....	....	....	Died May 31, 1823, at Mysore.
....	....	....	....	{ Invalided Dec. 10, 1813. Died March 29, 1820, at Nellore.
Sep. 27, 1826	....	....	....	Died Mar. 29, 1828, on board the "Parmelia," at sea.
....	....	....	....	Died Apr. 23, 1806.
....	....	....	....	Died Nov. 2, 1819, in camp, at Jaulnah.
....	....	....	....	Died Feb. 10, 1823, at St. Thomas's Mount.
....	....	....	....	Died April 27, 1814, at Tumlook.
....	....	....	....	Died July 9, 1807.
July 17, 1827	Brevet June 18, 1831	....	....	
....	....	....	....	Struck off the List, 1801.
....	....	....	....	Died Sep. 15, 1806, at Mangalore.
....	....	....	....	Died Dec. 10, 1801.
....	....	....	....	Died April 14, 1802.
Dec. 24, 1831	....	....	....	
....	....	....	....	Invalided April 5, 1811.
Feb. 15, 1832	....	....	....	Died May 25, 1833, at Masulipatam.
....	....	....	....	Resigned June 25, 1805.
May 23, 1825	....	....	....	{ Died June 17, 1828, on board the "Prince Regent," at sea.
....	....	....	....	Died Feb. 25, 1804, at Asseer Ghur.
....	....	....	....	Died July 3, 1816, at Berhampore.
....	....	....	....	Died July 8, 1815, at Akowla.
....	....	....	....	Killed Sep. 23, 1803.
....	....	....	....	Retired April 18, 1830, in England.
....	....	....	....	Retired Nov. 4, 1814, in England.
....	....	....	....	Died July 17, 1802.
....	....	....	....	Died Oct. 22, 1820, at Asseer Ghur.
....	....	....	....	Died Nov. 23, 1805, at Chittledroog.
May 22, 1825	....	....	....	Retired March 11, 1833, in India.
....	....	....	....	Died Aug. 21, 1803, at Aurungabad.

MADRAS

NAMES.	Cadet.	Cornet, Ensign, or Second Lieutenant.	Lieutenant.	Captain.	Major.
Mathew, John	1800		July 20, 1801		
Manesty, S. Gascoyne	,,		July 20, 1801		
Meredith, John I.—*cavalry*	1801	Feb. 10, 1802	Feb. 15, 1805	Sep. 1, 1818	June 6, 1826
Molesworth, R. P. Ld. Viscount	1802		Jan. 19, 1804	April 9, 1815	
Moncrieff, John	,,	Apr. 17, 1803	Jan. 10, 1804	Oct. 28, 1819	May 31, 1827
Mc Lean, Thomas	,,		Nov. 16, 1803	Dec. 25, 1815	Aug. 15, 1824
Martin, Henry Yorke	,,	Apr. 17, 1803	Nov. 16, 1803		
Macqueen, Andrew	,,	Apr. 17, 1803	Apr. 24, 1804	Feb. 10, 1818	May 1, 1824
Macleod, Allan	,,	Apr. 17, 1803	June 6, 1804		
Montgomerie, A.—*cavalry*	,,		May 1, 1804		
Marrett, Thomas	,,	Apr. 17, 1803	Sep. 17, 1804	Sep. 2, 1815	May 1, 1824
Massey, Hugh	,,	Apr. 17, 1803	Sep. 21, 1804	June 2, 1816	
Mackenzie, William	,,		June 13, 1804		
Myers, William Sibthorpe	,,		Sep. 21, 1804		
Macdonald, John	,,		Sep. 21, 1804	Apr. 14, 1818	
Macintosh, B.—*artillery*	1804		July 18, 1804	May 24, 1813	
Miller, Henry Augustus	1803		Sep. 21, 1804	Sep. 1, 1818	
Mortimer, James	,,				
Marshall, S. Gregory	,,		Sep. 21, 1804		
Manders, Isaac			Sep. 21, 1804		
Milne, William	,,		Sep. 21, 1804	Oct. 15, 1817	Oct. 14, 1824
Maquay, George—*cavalry*	,,	Mar. 7, 1805	Feb. 22, 1812	Oct. 1, 1819	
Monro, Archibald—*cavalry*	,,		June 22, 1808	Sep. 10, 1817	
Mortimer, Robert—*cavalry*	,,	Mar. 7, 1805			
Macdonald D. K.—*cavalry*	,,	Mar. 7, 1805			
Munro, E. S.—*artillery*	1804		Feb. 14, 1805		
Maxwell, John—*artillery*	,,	July 18, 1804	Sep. 12, 1804	Apr. 15, 1817	
Mackie, Lewis	1803		Sep. 21, 1804		
Macormick, James	,,		Sep. 21, 1804		
Macdonald, John	,,		Sep. 21, 1804	Aug. 14, 1818	
Moore, George	1804		Mar. 10, 1806		
Moncrief, H. Archibald	,,		July 17, 1805		
Moncrief, John William	,,		Nov. 16, 1805	May 1, 1824	
Murray, William	,,		July 17, 1805	Mar. 17, 1822	May 31, 1833
Mc Cormick, Samuel	,,		July 17, 1805		
Mallandain, John	,,		July 17, 1805	Jan. 23, 1819	May 1, 1824
Maltby, W. Shearwood	,,		Jan. 14, 1807		
Maule, Alfred	,,		July 17, 1805		
Myers, James	,,		Aug. 15, 1805	July 7, 1823	
Mackenzie, A. R.	,,		Apr. 13, 1807	May 1, 1824	
Morley, Mark	,,		Feb. 3, 1808		
Matthews, James	1805	June 27, 1806	Mar. 23, 1808	July 13, 1820	
Michael, James	,,		Mar. 11, 1807	May 14, 1820	
Mackglashan, Robert	,,		Oct. 14, 1806		
Miggison, Robert	,,				
Murcott, Robert	,,	June 27, 1806	Nov. 16, 1809	Feb. 19, 1820	Nov. 21, 1829
Mc Donald, W. Bannatyne	,,		July 11, 1806	Feb. 15, 1822	

PRESIDENCY.

Lieut.-Colonel.	Colonel.	Major-General.	Lieut.-General.	Date of Resignation, Retirement, or Death.
. . . .	. . . .	. . . .	. . . .	Lost June 1, 1804, in the "Prince of Wales."
. . . .	. . . .	. . . .	. . . .	Died March 17, 1808, on board ship.
. . . .	. . . .	. . . .	. . . .	Retired Mar. 17, 1833, in India.
. . . .	. . . .	. . . .	. . . .	Retired Feb. 18, 1820.
May 15, 1833	. . . .	. . . .	. . . .	Invalided May 1, 1834, in India.
Mar. 3, 1830	. . . .	. . . .	. . . .	
. . . .	. . . .	. . . .	. . . .	Died July 21, 1808.
. . . .	. . . .	. . . .	. . . .	{ Died Sep. 26, 1829, on board the "Catherine," from Madras, on passage to England.
. . . .	. . . .	. . . .	. . . .	Died — 1812, at Bangalore.
. . . .	. . . .	. . . .	. . . .	Died Oct. 20, 1812, at Fort St. George.
June 18, 1828	Brevet, Jan. 22, 1824	. . . .	. . . .	
. . . .	. . . .	. . . .	. . . .	Died July 25, 1818, at Bombay.
. . . .	. . . .	. . . .	. . . .	Died Aug. 10, 1805, in camp, near Hydrabad.
. . . .	. . . .	. . . .	. . . .	Died Feb. 10, 1811.
. . . .	. . . .	. . . .	. . . .	Died June 11, 1830, at Tabrez.
. . . .	. . . .	. . . .	. . . .	Died Jan. 31, 1822, at Nagpore.
. . . .	. . . .	. . . .	. . . .	Died May 8, 1825, at Cuddapah.
. . . .	. . . .	. . . .	. . . .	Died August 29, 1804, at Tripasore.
. . . .	. . . .	. . . .	. . . .	Resigned Nov. 4, 1814, in England.
. . . .	. . . .	. . . .	. . . .	{ Lost March 14, 1809, in the "Jane, Duchess of Gordon."
. . . .	. . . .	. . . .	. . . .	Died Dec. 23, 1831, in Scotland.
. . . .	. . . .	. . . .	. . . .	Retired June 20, 1823, in England.
. . . .	. . . .	. . . .	. . . .	Died Aug. 31, 1818, in camp, near Hoobly.
. . . .	. . . .	. . . .	. . . .	Died Jan. 23, 1812, at Pondicherry.
. . . .	. . . .	. . . .	. . . .	Resigned Oct. 30, 1812.
. . . .	. . . .	. . . .	. . . .	Died Jan. 16, 1814, at Masulipatam.
. . . .	. . . .	. . . .	. . . .	Died Nov. 17, 1824, on the Nillgherry [Hills.
. . . .	. . . .	. . . .	. . . .	Died Oct. 28, 1805.
. . . .	. . . .	. . . .	. . . .	Died Dec. 17, 1817, in camp, at Itchapore.
. . . .	. . . .	. . . .	. . . .	Retired Aug. 1, 1826, in England.
. . . .	. . . .	. . . .	. . . .	Died Nov. 24, 1818, at the Cape of Good Hope.
. . . .	. . . .	. . . .	. . . .	Died Aug. 12, 1820, at Secunderabad.
. . . .	. . . .	. . . .	. . . .	Invalided Aug. 4, 1829, in India.
. . . .	. . . .	. . . .	. . . .	Died Jan. 8, 1835, at Aberdeen.
. . . .	. . . .	. . . .	. . . .	Died Dec. 3, 1819, on board the "Albinia."
. . . .	. . . .	. . . .	. . . .	Retired Nov. 18, 1834, in England.
. . . .	. . . .	. . . .	. . . .	{ Invalided May 17, 1814; died May 9, 1817, at Trichinopoly.
. . . .	. . . .	. . . .	. . . .	Died May 20, 1817, at Nellore.
. . . .	. . . .	. . . .	. . . .	Died Nov. 27, 1830, at Kamptee.
. . . .	. . . .	. . . .	. . . .	Retired June 17, 1825, in England.
. . . .	. . . .	. . . .	. . . .	Died Feb. 27, 1810.
. . . .	. . . .	. . . .	. . . .	Died Dec. 8, 1829, at Kamptee.
. . . .	. . . .	. . . .	. . . .	Retired June 16, 1824, in England.
. . . .	. . . .	. . . .	. . . .	Died July 10, 1818, at Jaulnah.
. . . .	. . . .	. . . .	. . . .	Appointed a writer, Jan. 7, 1807.
. . . .	. . . .	. . . .	. . . .	Died Feb. 4, 1832, at French Rocks.
. . . .	. . . .	. . . .	. . . .	{ Died Nov. 27, 1823, at Colar, on his way to Madras.

MADRAS

NAMES.	Cadet.	Cornet, Ensign, or Second Lieutenant.	Lieutenant.	Captain.	Major.
Mathews, Solomon	1805				
Marshall, William	,,	June 27, 1806	Feb. 7, 1809		
Monk, Thos. Henry	,,	June 27, 1806	Nov. 8, 1810	Feb. 15, 1821	May 18, 1831
McKonokie, James	,,		July 2, 1808		
Muriel, George	,,		Nov. 24, 1808	May 1, 1824	May 13, 1827
Mitchell, Charles	,,	June 27, 1806	Feb. 14, 1810		
Moore, Nathaniel	,,	June 27, 1806			
Melville, Robert	,,				
McMaster, Bryce	,,		April 4, 1808	May 30, 1821	Dec. 5, 1829
Marklove, Robert	,,	June 27, 1806	Dec. 4, 1809		
Milner, John	,,		Dec. 10, 1808		
Marr, Robert John	,,	June 27, 1806	Mar. 18, 1809	Dec. 6, 1821	
Mortimer, Henry	,,	June 27, 1806			
Maxwell, George	1806	July 3, 1807	Sep. 16, 1809	May 1, 1824	
Meredith, Bridgewater	,,	July 3, 1807	June 27, 1810		
Mackintosh, Chs. Wm.	,,	July 3, 1807	Jan. 21, 1810		
Macqueen, Donald—*cavalry*	,,	June 21, 1807	Nov. 5, 1814	July 29, 1820	
Mackintosh, Alexander	,,	July 3, 1807	Dec. 2, 1811	May 1, 1824	Brevet Jan. 10, 1837
Meddowcroft, Samuel	,,	July 3, 1807	Mar. 18, 1809		
Mansfield, Robert—*cavalry*	,,	June 27, 1808	July 29, 1815	Mar. 20, 1822	Oct. 27, 1834
McCormick, Alexander	,,		July 29, 1809		
Macpherson, William	,,	July 3, 1807	Mar. 7, 1811		
Monteith, Wm.—*engineers*	,,		Mar. 18, 1809	May 2, 1817	
Malton, James	,,	July 3, 1807	Sep. 18, 1813	May 1, 1824	Brevet Jan. 10, 1837
Macleod, Alexander	,,	July 3, 1807	Nov. 17, 1812		
Moberly, Henry	,,	Aug. 9, 1806	Oct. 15, 1809	May 1, 1824	Brevet, Jan. 10, 1837
Matthews, Henry	,,	July 3, 1807	June 27, 1810		
Macdonald, Alexander	,,	July 3, 1807			
Mansell, Samuel	,,	June 30, 1808	June 27, 1810		
McCarthy, Thomas	,,	July 3, 1807	Dec. 11, 1812		
Macpherson, Evan	,,	July 3, 1807	Oct. 30, 1812	Dec. 6, 1824	June 25, 1836
McCausland, C. R.—*artillery*	,,	Feb. 16, 1808	Mar. 11, 1809		
McClelland, Alexander	,,	May 4, 1808			
Mackintosh, J.—*engineers*	,,		Jan. 4, 1808	July 29, 1815	
Macleod, Norman	,,	July 3, 1807			
Macleod, William	,,	Jan. 21, 1808	Nov. 3, 1813	May 1, 1824	Brevet Jan. 10, 1837
Milbourne, R. E.—*engineers*	1807		July 14, 1808	Oct. 8, 1815	June 7, 1825
Mercier, John Baptiste	,,	Mar. 18, 1809	July 19, 1815		
Morison, Richard	,,	Mar. 1, 1809	May 27, 1810	May 1, 1824	
Myers, John	,,	Mar. 18, 1809	Feb. 6, 1813		
Macleod, Roderick	,,	Mar. 11, 1809	Mar. 24, 1813	May 6, 1824	
Mantell, T. R. C.	,,	Mar. 20, 1809	Feb. 23, 1813	May 1, 1824	
Macdowall, Lawrence	,,	Nov. 24, 1808	Jan. 20, 1813	Oct. 14, 1824	Dec. 6, 1834
Mountford, Francis	,,	Nov. 2, 1809	Jan. 5, 1814	Brevet. Apr. 30, 1823	
McNeill, Neale	,,	June 21, 1809	May 7, 1813	May 1, 1824	
Montgomerrie, D.—*cavalry*	,,	May 3, 1811	Sep. 1, 1818	Dec. 21, 1826	
Maslen, Thomas John	,,	Oct. 15, 1809	Dec. 26, 1815		

PRESIDENCY.

Lieut.-Colonel.	Colonel.	Major-General.	Lieut.-General.	Date of Resignation, Retirement, or Death.
....	....	....	....	Died April 9, 1807.
....	....	....	....	{ Died Jan. 31, 1819, in camp, near Yellamunchilly.
....	....	....	....	Died May 18, 1832. at sea.
....	....	....	....	{ Invalided June 26, 1810. Admitted a Pensioner on Lord Clive's Fund.
May 5, 1833	....	....	....	Died Apr. 10, 1836, in camp, at Goomsoor
....	....	....	....	Resigned Oct. 7, 1814, in India.
....	....	....	....	Died Aug. 17, 1809, at Mahe.
....	....	....	....	Died Dec. 18, 1806, on board the "Monarch."
Nov. 17, 1834	....	....	....	
....	....	....	....	{ Died 1822, on board the L. S. "George Home," on passage to England.
....	....	....	....	Struck off 1820, in England.
....	....	....	....	Invalided and died May 23, 1833, at Madras.
....	....	....	....	Lost Nov. 20, 1808, in the "Glory."
....	....	....	....	{ Invalided Feb. 24, 1826, in India. Retired Jan. 3, 1832, in England.
....	....	....	....	Died Nov. 22, 1817, in camp, at Ashta.
....	....	....	....	Died June 21, 1822, at Seroor.
....	....	....	....	Died Dec. 7, 1826, at St. Thomas's [Mount.
....	....	....	....	Died Sep. 23, 1814, at Macrapilly.
....	....	....	....	Died May 2, 1835, at Neilgherries.
....	....	....	....	Died Sep. 20, 1813, at Masulipatam.
....	....	....	....	Died April 17, 1821, at Cuddapah.
Nov. 4, 1826	Brevet June 18, 1831	....	....	
....	....	....	....	
....	....	....	....	{ Invalided Nov. 30, 1816, in India. Died April 12, 1818.
....	....	....	....	Died Mar. 24, 1819, at Seringapatam.
....	....	....	....	Died May 23, 1815, at Gooty.
....	....	....	....	Died July 5, 1819, at Cannanore.
....	....	....	....	Struck off Feb. 28, 1815.
....	....	....	....	Retired Jan. 10, 1837, in England.
....	....	....	....	Died Aug. 2, 1817, near Punderpoor.
....	....	....	....	Died March 25, 1810. [France.
....	....	....	....	Died Oct. 22, 1824, in the Isle of
....	....	....	....	Died Aug. — 1811, of his wounds, at [Java.
....	....	....	....	Died Nov. 3, 1826, in the Presidency.
....	....	....	....	Died Aug. 11, 1820, at Ramghaut.
....	....	....	....	Retired April 7, 1833, in England.
....	....	....	....	Died Oct. 10, 1820, at Secunderabad.
....	....	....	....	Invalided Sep. 14, 1832, in India.
....	....	....	....	Died Nov. 16, 1831, at Prince of [Wales's Island.
....	....	....	....	Died July 11, 1824, at Madras.
....	....	....	....	Died Feb. 20, 1827, at Mangalore.
....	....	....	....	
....	....	....	....	Retired May 27, 1821.

MADRAS.—R

MADRAS

NAMES.	Cadet.	Cornet, Ensign, or Second Lieutenant.	Lieutenant.	Captain.	Major.
Macpherson, Angus	1807	Jan. 29, 1810	Mar. 16, 1813	May 1, 1824	Aug. 24, 1833
Mills, Charles	„	....	....	....	....
Mitford, Joseph George	„	April 5, 1810	July 20, 1814	July 15, 1824	....
Maitland, David Small	„	April 6, 1810	Oct. 15, 1817	....	....
Murray, A. L.—*artillery*	„	Feb. 11, 1809	July 19, 1809	June 11, 1820	Sep. 1, 1831
Morgan, Fred. Wm.	„	Mar. 17, 1810	July 8, 1815	Aug. 1, 1826	....
Maxton, Charles	1808	May 12, 1810	Apr. 28, 1815	May 1, 1824	Dec. 8, 1833
Macnaghten, W. H.—*cavalry*	„	Nov. 9, 1812	....	....	....
Milsom, George	„	Mar. 12, 1810	Dec. 10, 1817	Aug. 24, 1829	....
Morison, James—*cavalry*	1809	Nov. 9, 1812	Oct. 28, 1817	May 31, 1824	Mar. 18, 1833
Macarthur, Alexander	„	June 29, 1810	June 18, 1815	Sep. 17, 1828	....
Montgomerie, P.—*artillery*	„	July 7, 1810	Jan. 17, 1814	Sep. 2, 1822	Jan. 2, 1833
Macartney, John	„	Nov. 17, 1810	Mar. 31, 1818	Jan. 18, 1826	....
Mackintosh, William	„	Dec. 31, 1810	Dec. 26, 1815	May 1, 1824	....
Macdonald, J. (45 N. I.)	„	Jan. 15, 1811	Oct. 8, 1813	July 28, 1826	....
McGillivray, Alexander	„	....	....	....	....
Macleod, Archibald	„	Mar. 8, 1810	June 1, 1815	Nov. 17, 1825	....
Mitchell, Hugh	1810	Mar. 16, 1811	April 9, 1815	May 1, 1824	Nov. 17, 1834
Mussita, Achilles Augustus	„	June 27, 1811	Dec. 23, 1817	Dec. 14, 1825	....
Milne, Archibald	„	Oct. 25, 1811	Mar. 12, 1817	Oct. 4, 1825	....
Mathias, Vincent	„	Aug. 24, 1811	Oct. 24, 1816	July 14, 1827	May 25, 1833
Macdonald, Alexander	„	July 7, 1811	Feb. 19, 1813	....	....
McFarlane, Arthur	„	July 31, 1811	Apr. 14, 1817	Aug. 19, 1824	Aug. 20, 1831
McKenzie, D. H.—*artillery*	„	July 27, 1811	Oct. 21, 1814	June 1, 1823	....
Monke, Henry—*cavalry*	1811	....	....	....	....
Mairis, Valentine H.	„	June 1, 1812	....	....	....
Mansfield, David	„	June 1, 1812	Oct. 19, 1817	....	....
Macleod, Donald—*cavalry*	1812	Dec. 1, 1816	Sep. 1, 1818	June 6, 1826	Apr. 12, 1834
Maxtone, James	„	July 6, 1813	Oct. 1, 1816	Apr. 23, 1825	....
Metcalf, John	„	July 6, 1813	June 1, 1817	Sep. 8, 1826	....
Manners, Thomas Richard	„	July 6, 1813	May 10, 1816	Sep. 8, 1826	....
Milnes, William—*cavalry*	1816	....	Sep. 1, 1818	....	....
Munbee, Alexander	„	....	July 19, 1817	....	....
McCurdy, Wm. Alexander	1817	....	June 4, 1818	....	....
McCurdy, Edw. Archdale	„	....	June 4, 1818	Sep. 8, 1826	....
Macdonald, J. A.—*cavalry*	„	....	Mar. 16, 1819	May 9, 1830	....
Milford, Herman Joseph	„	....	June 4, 1818	....	....
McCally, Arthur	„	....	June 4, 1818	July 9, 1834	....
Monro, Edw. Francis	„	....	....	....	....
McDonald, Donald Norman	„	....	....	....	....
Millingen, Horace	1818	....	June 13, 1819	May 24, 1830	....
Mellor, James	„	....	June 13, 1819	May 31, 1827	....
Mills, John	„	....	June 13, 1819	Jan. 23, 1830	....
Mackinnon, Farquhar	„	....	June 13, 1819	....	....
Macqueen, William	„	....	June 13, 1819	....	....
Minchin, Frederick	„	....	June 13, 1819	Oct. 17, 1830	....
Montgomerie, John F.	1819	....	....	....	....

PRESIDENCY.

Lieut.-Colonel.	Colonel.	Major-General.	Lieut.-General.	Date of Resignation, Retirement, or Death.
....	....	....	....	
....	....	....	....	Died Sep. 2, 1808, on passage to India.
....	....	....	....	Retired Mar. 9, 1826, in England.
....	....	....	....	Died May 30, 1821, in camp at Chandah.
....	....	....	....	
....	....	....	....	{ Invalided Jan. 22, 1830, in India. { Retired May 18, 1832, in England.
....	....	....	....	Invalided.
....	....	....	....	{ Transferred Jan. 24, 1814, to the { Civil Establishment.
....	....	....	....	Died Oct. 25, 1833, at Cuddalore.
May 13, 1837	....	....	....	
....	....	....	....	
....	....	....	....	
....	....	....	....	Invalided Oct. 20, 1829, in India.
....	....	....	....	Died Jan. 5, 1826, at Bangalore.
....	....	....	....	{ Lost Dec. 27, 1810, in the "Elizabeth," { off Dunkirk.
....	....	....	....	Died July 10, 1826, at Anantapoor.
....	....	....	....	
....	....	....	....	Invalided Oct. 10, 1826, in India.
....	....	....	....	{ Invalided July 5, 1831, in India. { Died May 14, 1832.
....	....	....	....	Died Jan. 9, 1822, at Samulcottah.
Oct. 10, 1836	....	....	....	
....	....	....	....	Retired June 22, 1836, in England.
....	....	....	....	Removed to the Bengal Presidency.
....	....	....	....	Resigned Nov. 16, 1813.
....	....	....	....	Died Mar. 28, 1824, at Vellore.
....	....	....	....	
....	....	....	....	Died Oct. 21, 1827, at Palamcottah.
....	....	....	....	{ Invalided Aug. 17, 1827, in India. { Died June 18, 1833, at Madras.
....	....	....	....	Died Aug. 29, 1829, at Cannanore.
....	....	....	....	Died Oct. 24, 1830, at Calicut.
....	....	....	....	Died Feb. 19, 1824, at Vellore.
....	....	....	....	Died Nov. 12, 1819, at Nagpoor.
....	....	....	....	{ Died May 18, 1832, at sea, on board { the "Triumph."
....	....	....	....	Died Nov. 22, 1822, at Bushire.
....	....	....	....	Died Dec. 29, 1818, at Bombay.
....	....	....	....	{ Died Aug. 9, 1820, on board the H. C. S. "Marquis of Huntley," in the bay of Bengal.
....	....	....	....	Invalided.
....	....	....	....	{ Invalided July 13, 1832, in India. { Died Dec. 28, 1832, at Jaulnah.
....	....	....	....	Died Dec. 3, 1823, at the Cape of Good Hope.
....	....	....	....	Died Mar. 22, 1828, at Haggad Pass, in Coorg.
....	....	....	....	
....	....	....	....	Died Aug. 7, 1820, at Bellary.

MADRA

NAMES.	Cadet.	Cornet, Ensign, or Second Lieutenant.	Lieutenant.	Captain.	Major.
McNeile, Malcolm—*cavalry*	1819	April 6, 1820	Sep. 4, 1821	Sep. 12, 1827	......
Mitchell, Alexander	,,	....	Apr. 7, 1820	....	......
Minto, John McDonald	,,	....	Apr. 7, 1820	Feb. 20, 1833	......
Mimardiere, Henry John C.	,,	....	Apr. 7, 1820	Sep. 10, 1830	......
Messiter, Edward	,,	....	Apr. 7, 1820	June 7, 1830	......
McMurdo, John James	,,	....	Feb. 13, 1821	....	......
Musgrove, John Forbes ..	,,	....	Feb. 13, 1821	May 23, 1832	......
McLean, Lachlan	,,	April 6, 1820	Jan. 5, 1822	July 5, 1836	......
Massy, Edward	,,	Apr. 6, 1820	Feb. 15, 1822	Feb. 21, 1834	......
McLean, John F. Gray	,,	....	Mar. 12, 1821	....	......
Macdonald, William Pitt ..	,,	Apr. 6, 1820	Jan. 10, 1822	Nov. 9, 1831	......
Marshall, George (4 N. I.)..	,,	....	July 24, 1821	....	......
Milnes, John	,,	Apr. 6, 1820	Mar. 7, 1822	....	......
McLeay, K. Alexander	,,	Apr. 6, 1820	Sep. 17, 1823	....	......
Mills, Thomas M.	1820	....	Jan. 23, 1822	....	......
Mitchel, Robert	,,	Apr. 6, 1820	Jan. 20, 1824	Brevet, Apr. 6, 1835	......
Milnes, George Hardyman	,,	April 6, 1820	July 10, 1823	....	......
Manning, Edgar Charles ..	,,	Feb. 13, 1821	Jan. 15, 1824	....	......
Mairis, William	,,	....	Dec. 25, 1822	....	......
Morland, Henry	,,	Feb. 13, 1821	May 1, 1824	Brevet Feb. 13, 1836	......
McNair, Archibald	,,	Feb. 13, 1821	July 12, 1824	May 31, 1831	......
Mayo, Francis Charles	,,	Feb. 13, 1821	May 1, 1824	....	......
Milne, John Ogilvie	,,	Feb. 13, 1821	Feb. 19, 1823	....	......
Marshall, George Bristow	,,	Feb. 13, 1821	Nov. 28, 1823	....	......
Marshall, John H.	,,	Feb. 13, 1821	....	....	......
Macauley, William H.	,,	Feb. 13, 1821	Feb. 20, 1824	Brevet, Feb. 13, 1836	......
Maynor, Thomas	,,	Feb. 13, 1821	June 20, 1824	Brevet Feb 13, 1836	......
McClellan, Thomas	,,	....	Sep. 10, 1823	Jan. 22, 1835	......
Macleod, Alexander	,,	Feb. 13, 1821	May 1, 1824	May 2, 1835	......
Macvitie, James Stein	,,	....	Sep. 23, 1823	....	......
Mann, John	,,	Feb. 13, 1821	Sep. 18, 1825	July, 7, 1834	......
Mackenzie, Alexander	,,	Apr. 27, 1822	Sep. 19, 1824	Aug. 7, 1834	......
Macleod, William C.	,,	Apr. 27, 1822	Sep. 8, 1826	....	......
Manning, William John ..	,,	Apr. 27, 1822	Aug. 23, 1825	....	......
Miller, William Arnet	,,	....	July 26, 1826	....	......
Macleod, Coll	,,	Apr. 27, 1822	Jan. 1, 1825	Feb. 10, 1837	......
Mellish, Peter	,,	Apr. 27, 1822	Sep. 8, 1826	....	......
Mackinlay, William S.	,,	....	Mar. 13, 1825	....	......
Mackbraire, James H.	,,	Apr. 27, 1822	Mar. 25, 1825	Oct. 31, 1835	......
Middlecoat, G.—*artillery* ..	,,	May 10, 1822	May 11, 1822	May 29, 1832	......
Macleod, Leod Moira	1822	Apr. 27, 1822	Dec. 3, 1825	June 19, 1836	......
Moore, George William....	,,	May 2, 1823	Jan. 18, 1826	Sep. 11, 1830	......
Moor, Charles Page	,,	May 2, 1823	Aug. 15, 1825	....	......
Mackenzie, S. F.—*cavalry*	,,	May 2, 1823	Dec. 21, 1825	....	......
Macqueen, Æneas	,,	May 2, 1823	Feb. 27, 1827	....	......
Messiter, Charles	,,	May 27, 1823	Jan. 15, 1826	....	......
Mowatt, George Squire....	,,	May 2, 1823	Sep. 8, 1826	....	......

PRESIDENCY.

Lieut.-Colonel.	Colonel.	Major General.	Lieut.-General.	Date of Resignation, Retirement, or Death.
....	....	....	....	
....	....	....	....	Died Jan. 11, 1827, on board the "Circassian."
....	....	....	....	Died May 2, 1836, at Salem.
....	....	....	....	Retired June 24, 1832, in England.
....	....	....	....	
....	....	....	....	Died Sep. 4, 1830, at Jaulnah.
....	....	....	....	
....	....	....	....	
....	....	....	....	Died Nov. 17, 1835, at Octacamund.
....	....	....	....	Died Oct. 10, 1827, at Palamcottah.
....	....	....	....	
....	....	....	....	Cashiered March 7, 1825, in India.
....	....	....	....	
....	....	....	....	Died Feb. 18, 1830, at Yereshewale.
....	....	....	....	Died Feb. 25, 1826, at Trichinopoly.
....	....	....	....	
....	....	....	....	Died Oct. 24, 1830, at Calicut.
....	....	....	....	Died Nov. 7, 1831, in Essex.
....	....	....	....	Died in camp at Chittagong, Sep. 18, 1824.
....	....	....	....	
....	....	....	....	
....	....	....	....	Pensioned Nov. 5, 1825, in England.
....	....	....	....	Died Aug. 7, 1826.
....	....	....	....	Died May 16, 1834, at Cuddapah.
....	....	....	....	Cashiered Feb. 22, 1825, in India.
....	....	....	....	
....	....	....	....	
....	....	....	....	
....	....	....	....	Pensioned June 20, 1828, in India.
....	....	....	....	
....	....	....	....	Died June 15, 1837, at Madras.
....	....	....	....	
....	....	....	....	
....	....	....	....	Died May 15, 1832, at Palaveram.
....	....	....	....	
....	....	....	....	Discharged Nov. 9, 1827, in India.
....	....	....	....	Died Oct. 8, 1826, at Trichinopoly.
....	....	....	....	
....	....	....	....	
....	....	....	....	Died Jan. 19, 1837, at Secunderabad.
....	....	....	....	
....	....	....	....	{ Died July 11, 1826, on board the "William Money."
....	....	....	....	Retired April 17, 1835, in England.
....	....	....	....	Died April 27, 1834, at Kamptee.
....	....	....	....	{ Died Apr. 28, 1827, at Conada, near Vizianagram.

MADRAS

NAMES.	Cadet.	Cornet, Ensign, or Second Lieutenant.	Lieutenant.	Captain.	Major.
Mackenzie, George Greig	1823	May 14, 1824	Feb. 21, 1827	June 9, 1833	....
Maxwell, John—*artillery*	,,	Dec. 18, 1823	May 1, 1824	....	....
Mackenzie, Hector	,,	May 14, 1824	Apr. 13, 1826	....	....
Munsey, T. A. A.—*cavalry*	,,	May 14, 1824	Aug. 6, 1825	Oct. 9, 1833	....
Macleod, R. K.	,,	May 14, 1824	....	....	....
Miller, Wm. H.—*artillery*	,,	Dec. 18, 1823	May 1, 1824	....	....
Marshall, Herbert	,,	Sep. 14, 1824	Nov. 10, 1826	Feb. 14, 1836	....
Moore, Charles Arthur	,,	....	Aug. 10, 1825	....	....
Morgan, Edward Thomas	,,	Mar. 10, 1825	Apr. 18, 1827	Oct. 12, 1833	....
Moore, Rich. C.—*artillery*	1824	June 17, 1824	June 21, 1824	....	....
Medley, Thomas	,,	May 6, 1825	Jan. 1, 1832	June 15, 1837	....
Moore, Wm. Armitage	,,	May 6, 1825	Aug. 10, 1825	....	....
M'Nair, John C.—*artillery*	,,	Dec. 16, 1824	Dec. 17, 1824	....	....
Maitland, John—*artillery*	,,	Dec. 16, 1824	Dec. 17, 1824	....	....
Mitchell, Wm. Somerville	,,	May 6, 1825	May 9, 1832	....	....
Maclean, Thomas	,,	May 6, 1825	July 2, 1827	....	....
Molony, S. W. J.—*cavalry*	,,	Feb. 2, 1826	Jan. 1, 1827	....	....
Mathews, John Spiers	,,	Jan. 8, 1826	....	....	....
Marshall, Samuel	,,	....	Feb. 19, 1827	....	....
M'Murdo, Bryce—*artillery*	,,	June 16, 1825	June 17, 1826	....	....
M'Donnell, George Gordon	,,	....	Dec. 6, 1826	....	....
Millar, John	1825	....	Oct. 3, 1826	Jan. 24, 1835	....
Mackenzie, Colin	,,	Jan. 8, 1826	Nov. 10, 1827	....	....
Macdonald, J. K.—*cavalry*	,,	....	April 1, 1827	....	....
M'Leod, Forbes Brodie	,,	....	...1827...	....	....
Macleod, Donald M'Donald	,,	....	May 29, 1827	....	....
Macartney, James Adam	,,	....	July 9, 1827	....	....
Mortimer, Hugh H.—*artillery*	,,	Dec. 16, 1825	July 17, 1827	....	....
M'Goun, Thomas	,,	Jan. 8, 1826	Apr. 29, 1831	....	....
Macdonald, J. M.—*cavalry*	,,	....	June 29, 1827	May 28, 1837	....
Marshall, Henry O.	,,	Jan. 8, 1827	Feb. 8, 1836	....	....
Martyr, Joseph	,,	Jan. 8, 1826	July 16, 1831	....	....
Madden, John Mills	,,	Jan. 8, 1826	Dec. 15, 1832	....	....
Montgomery, H.—*artillery*	,,	Dec. 16, 1825	June 27, 1827	....	....
Macleane, Charles Moray	,,	Jan. 8, 1826	May 7, 1829	Mar. 1, 1836	....
Moore, John Stewart	,,	Oct. 25, 1826	....	....	....
Martin, Edward H.	,,	Jan. 8, 1826	Jan. 1, 1833	....	....
M'Nab, John Graham	,,	Jan. 8, 1826	Oct. 2, 1836	....	....
Moore, Lorenzo—*cavalry*	,,	Jan. 8, 1826	Oct. 29, 1830	....	....
Macdougall, John	,,	Jan. 8, 1826	May 11, 1833	....	....
Mayhew, Alfred	,,	Jan. 8, 1826	....	....	....
Manley, James Henry	,,	Feb. 12, 1827	....	....	....
M'Leod, Norman Lyttleton	,,	Jan. 8, 1826	Jan. 28, 1829	....	....
Mackenzie, J. Sutherland	,,	Jan. 8, 1826	Nov. 5, 1831	....	....
Marlett, Philip Thomas	1826	Jan. 8, 1826	....	....	....
Mackenzie, Chas. Fitzgerald	,,	Jan. 8, 1826	....	....	....
Marlay, John William	,,	Jan. 16, 1827	....	....	....

PRESIDENCY.

Lieut.-Colonel.	Colonel.	Major-General.	Lieut.-General.	Date of Resignation, Retirement, or Death.
....	....	....	....	Died June 24, 1824.
....	....	....	....	
....	....	....	....	Died Nov. 2, 1825, at Prome.
....	....	....	....	
....	....	....	....	
....	....	....	....	
....	....	....	....	
....	....	....	....	
....	....	....	....	Resigned Nov. 16, 1831, in England.
....	....	....	....	
....	....	....	....	
....	....	....	....	
....	....	....	....	
....	....	....	....	Died May 28, 1828, at Kamptee.
....	....	....	....	Died Oct. 13, 1827, at Masulipatam.
....	....	....	....	Died Sep. 4, 1830.
....	....	....	....	
....	....	....	....	
....	....	....	....	
....	....	....	....	Died Sep. 21, 1827, at Vizianagram.
....	....	....	....	{ Pensioned on Lord Clive's Fund, May 12, 1831, in England.
....	....	....	....	{ Pensioned on Lord Clive's Fund, Oct. 19, 1830, in England.
....	....	....	....	Died Mar. 4, 1830, at Secunderabad.
....	....	....	....	
....	....	....	....	
....	....	....	....	
....	....	....	....	
....	....	....	....	Resigned July 3, 1830, in England.
....	....	....	....	Died Oct. — 1836, at Secunderabad.
....	....	....	....	
....	....	....	....	
....	....	....	....	Discharged Nov. 30, 1831, in India.
....	....	....	....	Resigned Nov. 23, 1830, in India.
....	....	....	....	{ Pensioned Nov. 4, 1831, in India. Died April 24, 1834, at Cuddalore.
....	....	....	....	Died Aug. 30, 1828, at Palaveram.
....	....	....	....	{ Retired on Lord Clive's Fund, July 31, 1833, in England.
....	....	....	....	Died Oct. 27, 1828, at Palamcottah.

MADRAS

NAMES.	Cadet.	Cornet, Ensign, or Second Lieutenant.	Lieutenant.	Captain.	Major.
Master, Thomas	1826	Jan. 7, 1827	May 17, 1833		
Marriott, Edgar	,,	Jan. 7, 1827	Jan. 21, 1835		
Merritt, John	,,	Feb. 27, 1827	Aug. 22, 1833		
Macdonald, Donald	,,	Feb. 8, 1827			
Mackenzie, Robert	,,	Sep. 4, 1827	Jan. 31, 1830		
Macpherson, Sam¹. Charters	,,	Feb. 28, 1827	Mar. 31, 1831		
Mawdsley, Jn. E.—*artillery*	,,	Dec. 15, 1826	Oct. 12, 1831		
Moore, Arthur Edmund	,,	...1827....			
Maughan, Henry	,,	Sep. 5, 1827			
Mears, Thomas	,,	Jan. 5, 1828	Feb. 3, 1834		
Martin, Edward (24 N. I.)	,,	Feb. 13, 1828	Jan. 1, 1833		
Mackenzie, Charles Ross	,,	April 9, 1828	Dec. 6, 1834		
Macauley, Colin	1827	June 21, 1828			
Mackenzie, Wm. Alexander	,,	Jan. 21, 1828	May 16, 1834		
Morrill, Thomas	,,	Mar. 8, 1829			
Maitland, J. (4 L. C.)—*cavalry*	,,	Mar. 4, 1828	Jan. 2, 1833		
Moore, John—*artillery*	,,	Dec. 13, 1827	May 29, 1832		
Mac Queen, Lochlan—*cavalry*	,,	Mar. 4, 1828	Oct. 18, 1832		
Mc Dermott, J. P.—*cavalry*	,,	June 2, 1829			
Mowbray, R. H. C.—*cavalry*	,,	June 10, 1828	Oct. 9, 1833		
Marcer, William Harvey	,,	June 17, 1830	Nov. 24, 1831		
Molyneux, W. M.—*artillery*	,,	June 12, 1828			
Mylne, Robert Browne	1828	July 10, 1830	May 15, 1834		
Money, K. E. A.—*cavalry*	,,	Mar. 28, 1829	Feb. 14, 1834		
Marriott, Wilson	,,	April 2, 1830	June 13, 1832		
Miller, Edward Every	1829	Feb. 7, 1831	Feb. 14, 1835		
Mein, John D.—*artillery*	,,	Dec. 5, 1831			
Molyneux, Arthur More	,,	Jan. 11, 1832	Dec. 16, 1835		
Morgan, E. J.—*artillery*	,,	Nov. 17, 1831			
Morgell, Robert—*artillery*	1830	Dec. 22, 1834			
Marshall, George A.	,,	Apr. 12, 1835			
Marsh, Hugh	,,				
Macintire, A. W.—*artillery*	1831	June 4, 1836			
Mudie, John Jas.—*cavalry*	,,	May 26, 1832			
Mitchell, Thomas Wishart	1832	Dec. 13, 1832			
Middleton, William	,,	Nov. 24, 1832			
Mann, Charles	,,	Nov. 24, 1833	Aug. 26, 1835		
Moore, Thomas Palmer	,,	Dec. 14, 1832			
Mardall, George S.	,,	Feb. 6, 1833			
Marjoribanks, James	,,	Nov. 28, 1833	Apr. 21, 1836		
Mackinnon, Charles	,,				
Metcalfe, Howe	,,	Feb. 1, 1834	April 1, 1836		
Mason, William	,,	Feb. 15, 1834			
Man, Henry	1833	Mar. 10, 1834			
Money, Rowland Wm. T.	1834	June 13, 1834			
Moore, E. H. L.	,,	Jan. 12, 1835			
Macdonald, W. C. R.—*cavalry*	,,	Feb. 24, 1835			

PRESIDENCY.

Lieut.-Colonel.	Colonel.	Major General.	Lieut.-General.	Date of Resignation, Retirement, or Death.
....	....	....	....	
....	....	....	....	
....	....	....	....	
....	....	....	....	Died May 22, 1828, at Palaveram.
....	....	....	....	
....	....	....	....	
....	....	....	....	
....	....	....	....	{ Died on his passage to England, per " James Sibbald," Oct. 27, 1827.
....	....	....	....	Died Aug. 12, 1829, at sea.
....	....	....	....	Cashiered Feb. 1, 1835, in India.
....	....	....	....	
....	....	....	....	
....	....	....	....	Died Oct. 16, 1832, at Madras.
....	....	....	....	
....	....	....	....	Died May 16, 1831, at Anantipore.
....	....	....	....	Died Dec. 3, 1835, at Secunderabad.
....	....	....	....	
....	....	....	....	
....	....	....	....	Died July 6, 1832, at Mangalore.
....	....	....	....	
....	....	....	....	
....	....	....	....	Died Sep. 18, 1833, at Masulipatam.
....	....	....	....	
....	....	....	....	
....	....	....	....	
....	....	....	....	
....	....	....	....	
....	....	....	....	{ Name removed from the Army, Feb. 21, 1834, in England.
....	....	....	....	
....	....	....	....	Died Aug. 25, 1833, at Bangalore.
....	....	....	....	
....	....	....	....	
....	....	....	....	
....	....	....	....	
....	....	....	....	
....	....	....	....	
....	....	....	....	
....	....	....	....	Died Feb. 23, 1835, at Ongole.
....	....	....	....	Died Jan. 16, 1837, at Madras.
....	....	....	....	
....	....	....	....	
....	....	....	....	
....	....	....	....	

MADRAS

NAMES.	Cadet.	Cornet, Ensign, or Second Lieutenant.	Lieutenant.	Captain.	Major.
N					
Nixon, Sir Eccles	....	....	....	July 4, 1764	Feb. 21, 1774
North, John	1769	Sep. 6, 1770	Nov. 9, 1773	Jan. 15, 1782	....
Nash, Henry	,,	Sep. 2, 1780	Apr. 17, 1786	June 1, 1796	Aug. 7, 1803
Noble, James	1782	Dec. 22, 1782	....	....	....
Neale, William	,,	May 14, 1783	Aug. 21, 1790		
Northan, Edward—*artillery*	,,	Aug. 24, 1783	May 18, 1789		
Norris, Andrew	,,	Aug. 23, 1783	Apr. 17, 1789		
Neilson, John—*artillery*	1783	Oct. 22, 1784	Mar. 18, 1791		
Norris, John—*engineers*	....	Oct. 3, 1781	Apr. 17, 1786	May 3, 1793	Aug. 12, 1802
Nuthall, Thomas—*cavalry*	1782	Dec. 10, 1785	Nov. 28, 1792	Dec. 8, 1799	June 27, 1804
Neale, George—*cavalry*	,,	Aug. 8, 1786	June 1, 1796	July 30, 1800	Oct. 15, 1804
Nagle, James	1780	Sep. 2, 1781	Sep. 12, 1787	Nov. 29, 1797	May 20, 1804
Nail, Herman	1789	....	Jan. 23, 1793	June 17, 1800	
Nibbs, Richard	1790	July 1, 1791	June 16, 1793		
Newsome, Benjamin	,,	July 20, 1791	Nov. 14, 1793	Feb. 6, 1801	
Noble, John (C.B.)-*artillery*	1794	Jan. 8, 1796	Apr. 14, 1798	Sep. 21, 1804	Sep. 1, 1818
Newall, David (C.B.)	1795	Mar. 13, 1796	Sep. 28, 1797	May 20, 1804	Oct. 4, 1810
Nixon, John—*artillery*	,,	April 4, 1796	Mar. 1, 1800	Nov. 5, 1806	Sep. 1, 1818
Newington, Horatio	1797	July 30, 1798	May 26, 1803		
Norris, Edward	1799	....	Dec. 15, 1800		
Nixon, George Lennox	,,	....	Dec. 15, 1800	June 30, 1810	
Newall, Hugh—*cavalry*	1800	....	April 8, 1802		
Napier, Johnston	,,	....	July 20, 1801	April 9, 1812	May 1, 1824
Nixon, Joseph	,,	....	July 20, 1801	Nov. 20, 1813	Feb. 5, 1822
Norton, Harry	1802	....	July 15, 1803	May 18, 1810	
Newcome, Robert	1803	....	Sep. 21, 1804		
Newmarch, Wm.—*cavalry*	,,	....	June 27, 1808	Jan. 1, 1819	Dec. 18, 1826
Newell, Thomas George	1804	....	July 17, 1805	June 5, 1820	Feb. 4, 1832
Newman, Charles	,,	....	July 17, 1805	April 1, 1819	Apr. 19, 1830
Nickson, J. H. H.—*cavalry*	,,	Aug. 4, 1805	....		
Norton, Fletcher	,,	....	July 17, 1805	Sep. 1, 1819	
Nelthropp, Christian L.	,,	....	July 17, 1805	Brevet Jan. 8, 1819	
Norton, George	,,	....	Nov. 8, 1805	Dec. 23, 1822	
Nanney, Owen Jones E.	1805	....	Sep. 1, 1818		
Newall, John	,,	....	May 11, 1807		
Newall, Patrick Heron	,,	June 27, 1806	Oct. 2, 1808		
Norman, George	,,	Feb. 24, 1808	Sep. 6, 1820		
Noble, James	,,	June 27, 1806	April 7, 1809	Mar. 6, 1819	Sep. 10, 1830
Nash, James	,,	June 27, 1806	April 6, 1810	May 1, 1824	Aug. 6, 1831
Newland, Welbore Joseph	,,	June 27, 1806	Nov. 30, 1811		
Newman, George	,,	July 3, 1807	....		
Noble, Thomas	1806	July 3, 1807	Mar. 30, 1811		
Nicholson, Isaac	1807	Mar. 18, 1809	Aug. 25, 1811		
Noble, W. Geo. Washington	,,	June 7, 1809	Aug. 21, 1815		
Nelson, Thomas—*artillery*	,,	Feb. 11, 1809	April 6, 1810		
Nottidge, Jeremiah Brock	1808	May 12, 1810	Jan. 24, 1815	May 20, 1828	

PRESIDENCY.   130—131

Lieut.-Colonel.	Colonel.	Major General.	Lieut.-General.	Date of Resignation, Retirement, or Death.
Dec. 30, 1775	May 29, 1783	Dec. 20, 1793	....	Lost May 29, 1804, in the "Prince of [Wales."
....	....	....	....	Died 1789.
Mar. 1, 1805	....	....	....	Retired May 5, 1813.
....	....	....	....	Received Lord Clive's bounty, 1790.
....	....	....	....	{ Dismissed the service by sentence of Court Martial, Dec. 2, 1794.
....	....	....	....	Died in camp, 1795.
....	....	....	....	Died at the Mount, 1792.
....	....	....	....	Died 1793.
Jan. 1, 1803	....	....	....	Retired Sep. 25, 1811.
Jan. 17, 1810	Aug. 12, 1819	....	....	Died Aug. 14, 1829, in London.
June 4, 1811	....	....	....	Died July 28, 1815, at Akowla.
July 16, 1807	....	....	....	Retired Jan. 22, 1808.
....	....	....	....	Died Sep. 8, 1805.
....	....	....	....	Died 1794.
....	....	....	....	Died Sep. 23, 1805.
Aug. 16, 1821	....	....	....	{ Died July 16, 1827, on board the "Roxburgh Castle," in sight of Madras.
Dec. 7, 1817	Commt. May 1, 1824	....	....	Died July 30, 1827, on passage home, per "Cumberland."
May 21, 1823	....	....	....	{ Invalided Sep. 3, 1824, in India. Retired May, 15, 1827, in England.
....	....	....	....	Resigned
....	....	....	....	Resigned Dec. 23, 1802.
....	....	....	....	Died July 20, 1822, at Vellore.
....	....	....	....	Died 1813, on board the "Maitland."
Feb. 24, 1828	Brevet, Jan. 22, 1834	....	....	
Jan. 13, 1825	....	....	....	Died Apr. 10, 1826, on passage from Rangoon.
....	....	....	....	{ Died Mar. 1, 1818, at Maheidpoor, of wounds received in action, Dec. 21, 1817.
....	....	....	....	Died March 24, 1805.
....	....	....	....	Died Sep. 21, 1830, at Octacamund.
....	....	....	....	Invalided Dec. 14, 1832, in India.
....	....	....	....	Died Oct. 10, 1806.
....	....	....	....	Died April 23, 1823, at Cannanore.
....	....	....	....	Died July 16, 1821, at Chittledroog.
....	....	....	....	Died Jan. 1, 1826, near Mysore.
....	....	....	....	Retired Sep. 5, 1821, in England.
....	....	....	....	{ Admitted a Pensioner on Lord Clive's Fund, July 7, 1819.
....	....	....	....	Died April 27, 1809, at Poonamalle.
....	....	....	....	Died Aug. 23, 1829, at Secunderabad.
Feb. 15, 1836	....	....	....	Died Apr. 30, 1837, at Vishnoochuckram.
....	....	....	....	Died June 25, 1836, at Tuesa.
....	....	....	....	Died April 26, 1816.
....	....	....	....	Died March 6, 1809, at Madras.
....	....	....	....	Died March 24, 1814, at Chittledroog.
....	....	....	....	Resigned May 23, 1814.
....	....	....	....	Died Dec. 8, 1817, at Berhampore.
....	....	....	....	Died Oct. 24, 1818, at St. Thomas's [Mount.
....	....	....	....	

MADRAS

NAMES.	Cadet.	Cornet, Ensign, or Second Lieutenant.	Lieutenant.	Captain.	Major.
Nixon, John Isaac	1809				
Napier, R. D. (late Dunmore)	„	June 27, 1810	July 16, 1817		
Newport, Benjamin B.	1810	June 20, 1811			
Nattes, C. C.—*engineers*	„		Mar. 24, 1812		
Nattes, John W.—*engineers*	„	July 27, 1811	May 19, 1818		
Newman, Henry	„	Oct. 9, 1811	Dec. 1, 1816		
Noble, T. Geils—*artillery*	„	Feb. 2, 1812	Sep. 1, 1818		
Nixon, Richard James	1818		June 13, 1819	Nov. 13, 1829	
Nepean, Charles Wm.	1819		April 7, 1820	Nov. 26, 1830	
Nutt, Henry A.—*cavalry*	„	April 6, 1820	Feb. 16, 1824		
Newton, Edward	„		May 30, 1821		
Nicolson, Woodley	„	April 6, 1820	Jan. 8, 1823	Brevet, April 6, 1835	
Nixon, Harry John	„	April 6, 1820	July 3, 1823		
Newbolt, H. S.—*cavalry*	1820	Feb. 13, 1821	May 1, 1824		
Napier, Robert Sime	1819	April 6, 1820			
Neeve, John Bonnor	„		May 28, 1821	Jan. 31, 1837	
Nedham, Francis John	1820	Feb. 13, 1821	May 1, 1824	Brevet, Feb. 13, 1836	
Noble, Horatio Nelson	„	Feb. 13, 1821	Aug. 28, 1822	May 16, 1830	
Nott, George	„	Feb. 13, 1821	Aug. 29, 1824	May 15, 1834	
Nicolay, Christopher W.	„	Feb. 13, 1821	May 1, 1824		
Nicolay, Frederick Lewis	1821	Apr. 27, 1822	Aug. 25, 1826	July 18, 1836	
Neale, Henry	„	Apr. 27, 1822			
Nugent, W. G.—*engineers*	1824		May 1, 1824		
Nutting, Charles	„		Aug. 23, 1826	Sep. 6, 1836	
Newman, Henry—*artillery*	„	Dec. 16, 1824	Aug. 31, 1825		
Newsom, Clement	„	May 6, 1825	May 15, 1833		
Nisbett, Alfred E.	„	May 6, 1825	Oct. 28, 1828		
Nixon, John	„		Sep. 8, 1826		
Nixon, John William	1825	Jan. 8, 1826	Dec. 31, 1828		
North, Abraham Henry	„	Jan. 8, 1826			
Noble, James William	„	Jan. 8, 1826			
Nott, Henry	1826	Jan. 8, 1826	May 25, 1830		
Nicholls, Henry James	„	Jan. 16, 1827	Sep. 15, 1832		
Neill, James George	„		Nov. 7, 1828		
Nicolay, Thomas F.	„	June 30, 1827	June 6, 1831		
Napleton, Henry Geers	„	June 13, 1828	Jan. 12, 1834		
Newbold, Thomas John	1827	Nov. 1, 1828	Dec. 6, 1834		
North, Roger M.—*cavalry*	1828	Mar. 12, 1829	Mar. 20, 1834		
Norman, Edward	„	Dec. 7, 1831	Sep. 26, 1835		
Newby, Wm. Fletcher	1829	Mar. 27, 1832			
Norman, James—*cavalry*	1831	Feb. 17, 1834	Dec. 3, 1835		
Newland, George	„				
Nicolls, William T.	1832	Feb. 14, 1833			
Nixon, Henry	„	June 11, 1833			
Newbery, Thomas	„	Feb. 15, 1836			
Nesbitt, H. W.	1834	Feb. 9, 1835			
Nuthall, F. G.—*artillery*	„				

PRESIDENCY. 132—133

Lieut.-Colonel.	Colonel.	Major-General.	Lieut.-General.	Date of Resignation, Retirement, or Death.
				Resigned June 4, 1811.
				Resigned Aug. 30, 1824, in England.
				Died Aug. 21, 1817, at Secunderabad.
				Died Dec. 21, 1818, at Prince of Wales's Island.
				Killed May 29, 1818, at the siege of Mallegaum.
				Died March 21, 1825, at Aurungabad.
				Died Oct. 13, 1818, at Soonarah.
				Died May 25, 1837, at Vellore.
				Died April 25, 1834, at Bangalore.
				Died June 26, 1825, at Manantody.
				Pensioned Sep. 10, 1830, in India.
				Died June 14, 1830, at Trichinopoly.
				Died June 8, 1822, at Bangalore.
				Pensioned May 22, 1828, on Lord Clive's Fund, in England.
				Died Jan. 14, 1825, at Mangalore.
				Died Dec. 24, 1828, in England.
				Died Dec. 9, 1830, at Jaulnah.
				Pensioned Sep. 10, 1830, in India.
				Invalided.
				Discharged Mar. 25, 1833, in India.
				Died Feb. 16, 1836, at Secunderabad.
				Died July 4, 1837, at Arcot.
				Died Sep. 22, 1833, at Bangalore.
				Died Dec. 2, 1836, at Secunderabad.

MADRAS

O

NAMES.	Cadet.	Cornet, Ensign, or Second Lieutenant.	Lieutenant.	Captain.	Major.
Oldham, John............	1766	Oct. 24, 1767	Oct. 21, 1768	Nov. 23, 1776	Apr. 17, 1786
Oliver, James	1769	Dec. 22, 1770	Oct. 16, 1776	Nov. 2, 1783	Mar. 1, 1794
Oram, James	1771	Nov. 5, 1773	Oct. 29, 1799	Dec. 21, 1783	June 1, 1796
Ogilvie, Robert	....	May 7, 1774	....	Apr. 16, 1785	....
Orton, Pearce	1775	Nov. 19, 1776	Nov. 26, 1780	....	....
Orrock, William..........	1778	June 1, 1778	Feb. 18, 1782	Aug. 5, 1795	April 6, 1799
Ogg, Samuel William	„	June 7, 1779	Apr. 17, 1786	June 1, 1796	Jan. 7, 1802
Oliphant, William	1780	Oct. 26, 1780	Apr. 17, 1786	June 1, 1796	
Ormsby, Adam	„	Sep. 26, 1781	Aug. 16, 1788	Nov. 29, 1797	....
Orr, Alexander	„	Oct. 6, 1781	Oct. 1, 1788	July 24, 1798	Aug. 24, 1803
Ogilby, Sir David	1781	Oct. 8, 1782	Feb. 24, 1790	Oct. 12, 1798	Sep. 21, 1804
Oates, William	1782	June 17, 1783	Aug. 21, 1790	....	....
O'Brien, Francis—*artillery*	....	Aug. 2, 1779	July 31, 1781	Apr. 30, 1785	....
Ogg, Charles F.—*engineers*	....	Oct. 13, 1780	Jan. 15, 1784	....	....
Orr, John—*cavalry*	....	Aug. 18, 1777	Aug. 12, 1781	May 20, 1785	Apr. 23, 1791
Ormstone, William........	....	June 16, 1778	Feb. 25, 1782	....	....
Overend, John—*cavalry* ..	....	Sep. 1, 1791	Aug. 21, 1778	Oct. 2, 1803	Nov. 25, 1805
Ogg, Roderick	1790	....	Apr. 10, 1793	June 17, 1800	....
O'Connor, Thomas........	....	Sep. 7, 1791	Aug. 6, 1794	....	....
O'Neile, Thomas William..	....	Sep. 8, 1791	....	....	....
Ogilvie, Thomas..........	1794	....	April 8, 1795	....	....
O'Donnell, Hugh—*cavalry*	„	Jan. 14, 1796	Sep. 4, 1799	May 1, 1804	Mar. 1, 1817
O'Connell, Maurice	1795	....	Nov. 29, 1797	....	....
Ormsby, Robert—*cavalry*..	„	April 6, 1796	Nov. 29, 1797	....	....
Otto, R. B.—*cavalry*......	1797	May 10, 1799	May 8, 1800	Jan. 22, 1812	July 26, 1819
Outlaw, Robert—*cavalry* ..	1798	....	Aug. 18, 1801	May 20, 1813	....
Oliver, Wm. Charles	„	....	Jan. 1, 1800	Sep. 21, 1804	Sep. 1, 1818
Ormsby, Edward..........	1779	....	Dec. 15, 1800	....	....
O'Reilly, Thomas	„	....	Dec. 15, 1800	....	....
Osborn, Edward	„	....	Dec. 15, 1800	July 27, 1813	June 29, 1825
Oliver, Jos^h. Ward........	1800	....	Sep. 2, 1802	....	....
Oliver, William	„	....	July 20, 1801	....	....
Ogilvie, John	„	....	July 20, 1801	Sep. 17, 1812	May 1, 1824
Ormsby, William	1801	....	July 2, 1803	May 6, 1812	May 1, 1824
Ogilvie, George	1802	Apr. 17, 1803	Apr. 14, 1804	Nov. 30, 1817	Apr. 11, 1826
O'Brien, Henry—*cavalry* ..	1803	Mar. 7, 1805	Nov. 22, 1812	Aug. 28, 1821	...1832....
O'Connor, W. G.—*cavalry*	„	July 31, 1804	....	....	....
O'Donnoghue, J. J.	„	....	Sep. 21, 1804	Sep. 1, 1818	...1830....
Ogilvie, Duncan..........	1804	....	July 17, 1805	....	....
Oldnall, Edwin	„	....	July 17, 1805	Oct. 2, 1818	....
O'Reilly, William	„	....	June 4, 1806	May 1, 1824	....
O'Reilly, Godfrey	1805	June 27, 1806	Nov. 12, 1810	....	....
O'Reilly, J. T.—*cavalry* ..	„	July 7, 1807	Oct. 31, 1812	....	....
O'Hara, Henry	1806	July 3, 1807	Dec. 19, 1810	....	....
O'Dell, Robt. Deane	1811	June 11, 1812	Dec. 1, 1816	Aug. 30, 1829	....
Oliphant, James—*engineers*	1813	July 4, 1814	Mar. 2, 1819	Feb. 6, 1825	....

PRESIDENCY.

Lieut.-Colonel.	Colonel.	Major-General.	Lieut.-General.	Date of Resignation, Retirement, or Death.
Jan. 24, 1788	June 1, 1796	....	....	Allowed to retire with the pay of his Rank, 1796
June 1, 1796	June 17, 1800	....	....	Omitted in the Army Lists from 1807.
Dec. 21, 1797	....	....	....	Died Aug. 13, 1799.
....	....	....	....	Died 1792.
....	....	....	....	Died 1791.
Jan. 23, 1802	....	....	....	Died at Seringapatam, June 26, 1810.
Sep. 21, 1804	June 4, 1813	Aug. 12, 1819	....	Died Feb. 23, 1828, in London.
....	....	....	....	Died Aug. 19, 1797, on board ship.
....	....	....	....	Died Oct. 16, 1800.
July 25, 1805	....	....	....	Retired December 1809.
...1809....	....	....	....	Retired Oct. 20, 1809.
....	....	....	....	Died 1794.
....	....	....	....	Died May 1794.
....	....	....	....	Died December 1792.
Nov. 1, 1798	Apr. 29, 1802	Oct. 25, 1809	June 4, 1814	Died Nov. 26, 1835, in England.
....	....	....	....	Retired on Military Fund.
....	....	....	....	Died in Ireland, March 10, 1809.
....	....	....	....	Died March 11, 1805.
....	....	....	....	{ Pensioned Oct. 24, 1798. Died May 4, 1817, at Negapatam.
....	....	....	....	Died 1793.
....	....	....	....	Died July 5, 1801.
....	....	....	....	Killed Oct. 30, 1817, in camp at Hindah.
....	....	....	....	Retired Aug. 10, 1803, on Lord Clive's Fund.
....	....	....	....	Lost in the "Prince of Wales."
Feb. 26, 1829	....	....	....	Retired March 19, 1831, in England.
....	....	....	....	Died Oct. 25, 1819, at Fort St. George.
May 1, 1824	Aug. 8, 1833	....	....	Died Feb. 11, 1835, in England.
....	....	....	....	Died April 23, 1805.
....	....	....	....	Died at Vellore, July 10, 1806.
....	....	....	....	{ Invalided June 17, 1828, in India. Retired Dec. 8, 1828, in England.
....	....	....	....	Died at Ganjam, March 11, 1811.
....	....	....	....	Died at Seringapatam, Dec. 5, 1812.
Apr. 23, 1828	Brevet Jan. 22, 1834.	....	....	
....	....	....	....	Died March 2, 1830, at Madras.
....	....	....	....	Died Dec. 30, 1828, at Octacamund.
....	....	....	....	Retired Feb. 20, 1833, in England.
....	....	....	....	Died at Nellore, May 24, 1805.
....	....	....	....	Retired June 4, 1830, in England.
....	....	....	....	Died at St. Thomé, Oct. 14, 1824.
....	....	....	....	Died March 16, 1823, at Bangalore.
....	....	....	....	Retired June 2, 1826, in England.
....	....	....	....	Died March 29, 1816, at Juggerpet.
....	....	....	....	Struck off in England.
....	....	....	....	Died Apr. 24, 1819, in camp near Gudduck.

MADRAS

NAMES.	Cadet.	Cornet, Ensign, or Second Lieutenant.	Lieutenant.	Captain.	Major.
Owen, Charles............	1816	....	Nov. 5, 1817	....	....
O'Loughlin, John	1817	....	....	....	....
Ord, William	1818	....	June 13, 1819	....	....
Otter, Richard F.	1819	....	April 7, 1820	Jan. 4, 1832	....
Osborne, George W.......	„	Apr. 6, 1820	July 17, 1823	May 25, 1830	....
Ord, Alexander	1820	Feb. 13, 1821	....	....	....
Ormsby, Arthur John	„	Feb. 13, 1821	Apr. 23, 1824	....	....
O'Connor, Harry Edwd. C.	„	Feb. 13, 1821	Jan. 1, 1825	Brevet Feb. 13, 1836.	....
Ottley, Coghill Glendr.....	„	Feb. 13, 1821	May 1, 1824	Brevet Feb. 12, 1836.	....
Oliphant, Patrick	1821	Apr. 27, 1823	Nov. 18, 1825	....	....
Onslow, G. W. — *artillery*	„	....	May 11, 1822	Aug. 15, 1832	....
Oliver, James Dashwood ..	1823	May 14, 1824	....	....	....
O'Brien, John	„	....	....	....	....
Ogilvie, Henry Tristram ..	„	May 14, 1824	Dec. 16, 1825	May 20, 1831	....
Oakley, John—*cavalry*	„	May 14, 1824	Jan. 3, 1826	....	....
Ommanny, W. S. — *cavalry*	1824	May 6, 1825	May 20, 1827	....	....
Onslow, William Campbell	„	May 6, 1825	Jan. 22, 1827	....	....
O'Brien, Lucius	„	May 6, 1825	Feb. 26, 1828	....	....
Oakes, A. Fred.—*artillery*	„	June 16, 1825	Sep. 28, 1826	....	....
O'Neil, John D. Power....	1825	Jan. 8, 1826	Oct. 6, 1832	....	....
Onslow, Robert T.—*cavalry*	„	Jan. 8, 1826	Aug. 1, 1833	....	....
Orr, William A.—*artillery*	1826	Dec. 15, 1826	Sep. 1, 1831	....	....
Osborne, Thomas	1827	Aug. 16, 1830	May 16, 1834	....	....
Ogilvie, Patrick	1828	Dec. 6, 1831	July 11, 1834	....	....
Ottley, Mark S.—*cavalry* ..	1829	Feb. 7, 1832	May 11, 1833	....	....
Orr, Charles Alexander....	1832	Mar. 5, 1835	....	....	....
Ouchterlony, J.—*engineers*	„	....	....	....	....
Ogilvie, R. Levison James	„	June 11, 1833	June 7, 1835	....	....
Oakes, Arthur E.—*cavalry*	„	....	....	....	....
O'Grady, Richard Walter	1834	June 13, 1834	Jan. 19, 1837	....	....
Owen, William George....	„	Dec. 21, 1834	Sep. 17, 1837	....	....
P					
Patterson, John	....	....	July 5, 1770	Apr. 17, 1777	Apr. 17, 1786
Prendergrast, Thomas	....	July 10, 1770	....	Apr. 27, 1777	Apr. 17, 1786
Pringle, John	1769	Nov. 7, 1770	June 1, 1776	Nov. 2, 1783	....
Pearson, Caleb	„	Dec. 10, 1770	Aug. 26, 1776	Nov. 2, 1783	....
Parr, Thomas	1771	Feb. — 1773	Nov. 7, 1778	Nov. 6, 1783	June 1, 1796
Pictlatt, Samuel	....	Dec. 30, 1773	Oct. 4, 1780	....	....
Price, Thomas............	1775	Nov. 24, 1776	Nov. 21, 1780	....	July 27, 1796
Poole, Thomas	1776	April 7, 1778	Jan. 7, 1782	May 15, 1794	Sep. 18, 1798
Parkinson, Robert	1777	Aug. 2, 1778	Nov. 12, 1782	....	....
Parkinson, Thomas	„	Aug. 3, 1778	Nov. 13, 1782	June 1, 1796	Dec. 10, 1799
Powis, Richard	1778	Sep. 3, 1778	Nov. 1, 1783	June 1, 1796	Dec. 10, 1799
Patch, Thomas	1779	Sep. 21, 1780	Apr. 17, 1786	....	....
Peters, Thomas	„	Oct. 1, 1780	Apr. 17, 1786	June 1, 1796	....
Parley, Thomas	1780	Oct. 27, 1780	Apr. 17, 1786	....	....
Petrie, Ralph R...........	1781	Jan. 4, 1782	....	....	....

PRESIDENCY.

Lieut.-Colonel.	Colonel.	Major-General.	Lieut.-General.	Date of Resignation, Retirement, or Death.
....	....	....	....	Retired May 22, 1828, in England.
....	....	....	....	Died March 13, 1820, at Dheumawar.
....	....	....	....	Died Nov. 29, 1823, at Ryepore.
....	....	....	....	
....	....	....	....	Died March 24, 1822, at Gooty.
....	....	....	....	Died Oct. 14, 1831, in India.
....	....	....	....	
....	....	....	....	
....	....	....	....	Died Jan. 14, 1826, at Madras.
....	....	....	....	Died April 24, 1825, on board the "Boyne."
....	....	....	....	Died Dec. 30, 1835, on board the "True Briton."
....	....	....	....	Discharged Dec. 8, 1832, in India.
....	....	....	....	
....	....	....	....	Resigned Nov. 17, 1829, in England.
....	....	....	....	
....	....	....	....	Died Nov. 13, 1836, at Jaulnah.
....	....	....	....	
....	....	....	....	
....	....	....	....	
....	....	....	....	Died Oct. 18, 1834, at Bangalore.
....	....	....	....	
Feb. 19, 1788	....	....	....	Invalided Nov. 26, 1793.
....	June 1, 1796	Jan. 1, 1798	....	Died Jan. — 1799.
....	....	....	....	Died — 1788.
....	....	....	....	Invalided Sep. — 1787.
July 13, 1797	....	....	....	Died May 3, 1799.
....	....	....	....	Invalided —; died — 1789.
....	....	....	....	Invalided Sept. — 1787; died Aug. 17, 1797.
June 17, 1800	....	....	....	Retired — 1805.
....	....	....	....	Not to be traced.
Apr. 24, 1804	....	....	....	Retired March 11, 1807.
May 1, 1804	....	....	....	Died Feb. 4, 1805.
....	....	....	....	Not to be traced.
....	....	....	....	Died Aug. 5, 1798.
....	....	....	....	Dismissed the Service, Oct. — 1789.
....	....	....	....	Died — 1790.

MADRAS.———T

MADRAS

NAMES.	Cadet.	Cornet, Ensign, or Second Lieutenant.	Lieutenant.	Captain.	Major.
Phillips, George..........	1781	Oct. 25, 1782	Aug. 21, 1790	Dec. 26, 1798	Sep. 8, 1803
Prescott, William	1782	Dec. 24, 1782	Aug. 21, 1790	Oct. 12, 1798	....
Preston, William	,,	May 1, 1783	Aug. 21, 1790	Dec. 26, 1798	....
Pugh, James—*artillery*....	....	July 31, 1781	Sep. 9, 1783	April 7, 1791	....
Prescott, Fred.—*artillery*..	....	Oct. 20, 1784	Mar. 7, 1791	Mar. 1, 1800	....
Powney, C. L. S.—*artillery*	....	Sep. 6, 1786	....	....	....
Prescott, William-*engineers*	....	....	....	Mar. 31, 1782	....
Prescott, Jas. R.—*engineers*	....	Nov. 1, 1781	....	....	....
Prendergrast, M.—*engineers*	....	May 26, 1786	....	....	....
Pater, John—*cavalry*	....	....	....	Apr. 22, 1784	Nov. 19, 1790
Price, Robert—*cavalry*	1780	June 13, 1785	Oct. 23, 1787	Sep. 4, 1799	May 1, 1804
Pogson, Thomas—*cavalry*	1779	Sep. 16, 1780	June 19, 1785	Aug. 5, 1796	Sep. 4, 1799
Pierce, Frederick	....	June 18, 1786	June 7, 1792	Dec. 10, 1799	Sep. 21, 1804
Patterson, Wm. Alex.	1789	....	Nov. 1, 1792	....	....
Peacocke, William........	1790	....	April 9, 1793	....	....
Pyefinch, J. W.—*engineers*	1789	....	Mar. 6, 1793	....	....
Pittman, C. G. G.—*engineers*	,,	May 26, 1790	May 3, 1793	....	....
Pippard, George	1792	June 9, 1793	Aug. 6, 1794	....	....
Phillipson, George Burton	....	June — 1791	June 6, 1793	May 28, 1800	....
Patterson, James	1792	Sep. 28, 1793	....	June 24, 1803	....
Pollok, Thomas (C.B.)	,,	....	Oct. 28, 1794	Aug. 7, 1803	May 30, 1810
Palk, Thomas	1794	Dec. 31, 1795	June 1, 1796	April 8, 1803	....
Prendergast, Jeffrey	,,	Jan. 3, 1796	June 1, 1796	May 4, 1804	Aug. 4, 1812
Patterson, Frederick Pigou	,,	....	Dec. 19, 1795	....	....
Pollock, William	,,	Jan. 6, 1796	June 1, 1796	....	....
Powell, Chas. Harvey	1796	....	Nov. 29, 1797	Mar. 1, 1805	Sep. 1, 1818
Pereira, Manasseh Lopez ..	,,	Aug. 16, 1797	Oct. 12, 1798	Sep. 21, 1804	April 6, 1810
Pasley, Charles	,,	Aug. 10, 1797	Sep. 29, 1798	Oct. 9, 1804	....
Pearse, W. G.—*artillery* ..	1797	Aug. 5, 1797	Mar. 1, 1800	Mar. 18, 1809	Sep. 19, 1819
Ponsonby, John	,,	Sep. 3, 1798	Dec. 26, 1798	....	....
Price, John	....	....	Dec. 13, 1795	Sep. 17, 1804	....
Podmore, Richard	1795	Mar. 22, 1796	Nov. 29, 1797	Sep. 21, 1804	Oct. 15, 1809
Paschoud, John L.........	,,	Mar. 24, 1796	Nov. 29, 1797	....	....
Potter, Wm. Henry	1798	....	....	....	....
Phillips, Richard	,,	....	Dec. 15, 1800	Nov. 22, 1808	....
Preston, William	,,	Sep. 4, 1798	Dec. 26, 1798	Oct. 30, 1806	June 2, 1816
Pepper, Hercules Henry ..	1797	Aug. 23, 1798	Dec. 26, 1798	May 22, 1807	May 1, 1815
Pepper, George John	1798	....	Jan. 1, 1800	Sep. 18, 1807	....
Palin, Robert—*cavalry*....	,,	....	June 17, 1800	Feb. 22, 1812	Oct. 1, 1819
Paske, Isaac—*artillery*....	1797	July 29, 1798	Dec. 12, 1800	July 19, 1809	....
Pallmer, F. W.—*artillery*..	1799	....	Mar. 31, 1801	Mar. 18, 1809	Jan. 17, 1824
Pell, William—*artillery* ..	,,	....	....	....	....
Parminter, Richard	,,	....	Dec. 15, 1800	Aug. 27, 1807	Oct. 2, 1818
Poignand, G. W.—*artillery*	,,	....	Dec. 12, 1800	Feb. 16, 1807	....
Poignand, Lewis	,,	....	Dec. 15, 1800	Mar. 7, 1810	....
Pearson, John............	,,	....	Dec. 15, 1800	....	....
Peacock, Robert..........	,,	....	Dec. 15, 1800	....	....

PRESIDENCY.

Lieut.-Colonel.	Colonel.	Major-General.	Lieut.-General.	Date of Resignation, Retirement, or Death.
Oct. 16, 1805	....	....	....	Died 1806, near Hydrabad.
....	....	....	....	Not to be traced.
....	....	....	....	Died Mar. 21, 1802.
....	....	....	....	Died 1793.
....	....	....	....	Died Nov. 6, 1805.
....	....	....	....	King's Service 1789.
....	....	....	....	Died Nov. 14, 1797.
....	....	....	....	Died 1789.
....	....	....	....	Resigned Jan. — 1789.
Dec. 31, 1796	Jan. 1, 1798	Jan. 1, 1805	....	{ Retired on the Off-Reckoning Fund, May 13, 1813. Died Oct. 18, 1817, at Fort St. George.
....	....	....	....	Lost in the "Prince of Wales."
April 8, 1802	....	....	....	Retired Oct. 14, 1804.
Nov. 22, 1808	June 4, 1814	....	....	Died Jan. 2, 1825, at Belgaum.
....	....	....	....	Died Nov. 23, 1797.
....	....	....	....	Died 1800.
....	....	....	....	Died 1793.
....	....	....	....	Died May 27, 1798.
....	....	....	....	Died 1800.
....	....	....	....	Cashiered June 9, 1806.
....	....	....	....	Left the Service, April 5, 1810.
Aug. 1, 1817	Commt. May 1, 1824 Col. June 5, 1829	Jan. 10, 1837	....	
....	....	....	....	Died April 1, 1805.
Sep. 1, 1818	Commt. Jan. 3, 1825 Col. June 5, 1829	Jan. 10, 1837	....	
....	....	....	....	Resigned Oct. 10, 1801.
....	....	....	....	Dismissed Oct. 26, 1798.
....	....	....	....	Died Aug. 21, 1820, at Madras Roads.
July 19, 1817	Commt. May 1, 1824 Col. June 5, 1829	Jan. 10, 1837	....	
....	....	....	....	Retired Feb. 28, 1815, in England.
Jan. 17, 1824	Sep. 1, 1831	....	....	
....	....	....	....	Died Mar. 25, 1800.
....	....	....	....	{ Invalided July 1, 1806. Resigned Oct. 1, 1811.
Nov. 28, 1816	Commt. May 1, 1824 Col. June 5, 1829	Jan. 10, 1837	....	
....	....	....	....	Died Aug. 22, 1799.
....	....	....	....	Died 1800.
....	....	....	....	Died Oct. 31, 1814, at Macassar.
....	....	....	....	{ Died Jan. 23, 1823, on board the L. S. "Hope," on passage to England.
Jan. 31, 1821	....	....	....	Died July 25, 1826, at Madras.
....	....	....	....	Died Dec. 16, 1813.
....	....	....	....	Died Aug. 27, 1821, at Bangalore.
....	....	....	....	Died April 19, 1810.
....	....	....	....	Died June 8, 1825, at Naickanary.
....	....	....	....	Died April 2, 1802.
....	....	....	....	Died Oct. 16, 1819, at Vizianagrum.
....	....	....	....	{ Dismissed April 5, 1810. Restored Mar. 30, 1814. Died June 10, 1820, at Jaulnah.
....	....	....	....	Died Dec. 19, 1812.
....	....	....	....	Died Nov. 23, 1804.
....	....	....	....	Died April 7, 1804.

MADRAS

NAMES.	Cadet.	Cornet, Ensign, or Second Lieutenant.	Lieutenant.	Captain.	Major.
Palk, Charles	1799	....	Dec. 15, 1800	....	....
Porter, John Young	,,	....	Dec. 15, 1800	Aug. 27, 1807	....
Purchas, Henry Ansley ...	,,	....	July 15, 1800	June 4, 1808	Aug. 9, 1819
Parlby, Brook Bridges (C.B)	,,	....	Dec. 15, 1800	Apr. 19, 1805	Apr. 15, 1817
Pidding, Benjamin James..	,,	....	Dec. 15, 1800	....	....
Purvis, Hugh—*artillery* ..	,,	....	Dec. 31, 1800	....	....
Pentland, Andrew	,,	....	Dec. 15, 1800	....	....
Plendeleath, Wm.—*cavalry*	1800	Sep. 15, 1801	Apr. 25, 1804	....	....
Pierie, Thomas Dundas ..	,,	....	July 20, 1801	....	....
Patteshall, Edwin Sandys .	,,	....	July 20, 1801	May 27, 1810	....
Perkins, Ambrose Bening .	,,	....	Dec. 17, 1802	....	....
Peile, Christopher F.......	,,	....	July 20, 1801	Dec. 25, 1817	....
Palmer, Thomas James....	,,	....	July 20, 1801	Sep. 29, 1808	....
Pitchford, William	,,	....	July 20, 1801	June 3, 1812	....
Patullo, A. E.—*cavalry* . ..	1802	Jan. 14, 1804	Jan. 29, 1807	Sep. 1, 1818	....
Peard, Edward—*cavalry* ..	,,	....	....	....	....
Parker, Robert—*cavalry* ..	,,	....	June 1, 1804	Oct. 13, 1817	June 17, 1820
Palmer, John Fish—*cavalry*	,,	April 14, 1804	Aug. 2, 1806	Dec. 15, 1819	Aug. 15, 1829
Pollock, William James ..	,,	....	....	....	....
Proctor, Robt. B.—*artillery*	1803	....	July 18, 1804	April 6, 1810	....
Pew, John William	,,	....	Sep. 21, 1804	Nov. 12, 1815	.... 1828 ..
Parsons, John Whitehill ..	,,	....	May 21, 1804	....	....
Pickering, William	,,	....	Sep. 21, 1804	Sep. 1, 1818	Mar. 30, 1828
Prendergast, Thomas......	,,	....	Sep. 21, 1804	Brevet June ?, 1816	....
Pagan, William	,,	....	Sep. 21, 1804	....	....
Paterson, George	1804	....	July 17, 1805	....	....
Page, William George	,,	....	July 17, 1805	Feb. 23, 1821	Aug. 7, 1828
Power, John	,,	....	July 11, 1806	....	....
Pridham, William Collins..	1805	....	Dec. 16, 1806	....	....
Parker, Henry............	,,	....	Feb. 25, 1807	....	....
Perry, James	,,	June 27, 1806	Feb. 25, 1807	Feb. 28, 1820	Jan. 3, 1826
Pratt, Benjamin	,,	June 27, 1806	Oct. 10, 1809	....	....
Paske, Thos. T.—*artillery* .	,,	....	Oct. 19, 1806	Sep. 1, 1818	Jan. 29, 1828
Poulton, Charles..........	,,	June 27, 1806	Oct. 21, 1809	Nov. 23, 1823	Dec. 16, 1832
Plunkett, James..........	,,	....	....	....	....
Peirson, John	,,	....	Nov. 14, 1807	....	....
Pearson, Henry	,,	June 27, 1806	April 7, 1810	....	....
Preston, William	1806	July 3, 1807	Jan. 5, 1810	....	....
Pringle, Francis..........	,,	July 3, 1807	....	....	....
Payne, George............	,,	July 3, 1807	Mar. 31, 1811	....	....
Payne, John	,,	July 3, 1807	....	....	....
Poole, Henry Wynne	,,	May 20, 1808	Mar. 1, 1814	May 1, 1824	Aug. 31, 1834
Peyton, William..........	,,	July 3, 1807	June 15, 1810	Aug. 31, 1822	....
Poggenpohl, Paul—*artillery*	,,	....	Feb. 17 1808	Sep. 1, 1818	....
Peake, John	1807	Nov. 24, 1808	Dec. 20, 1812	May 1, 1824	....
Pattison, Frederick Hope..	,,	....	....	....	....
Pace, William Napper	,,	Feb. 14, 1810	June 9, 1813	Sep. 8, 1826	....

PRESIDENCY.

Lieut.-Colonel.	Colonel.	Major General.	Lieut.-General.	Date of Resignation, Retirement, or Death.
....	....	....	....	Died Dec. 14, 1802.
....	....	....	....	Died Dec. 10, 1812.
May 1, 1824	....	....	....	Retired from July 13, 1827, in England.
July 17, 1823	June 5, 1829	....	....	
....	....	....	....	Died May 17, 1810.
....	....	....	....	Killed Oct. 8, 1804.
....	....	....	....	Died Feb. 25, 1804, in Ireland.
....	....	....	....	Killed Aug. 8, 1803.
....	....	....	....	Killed Sep. 23, 1803.
....	....	....	....	Died Mar. 5, 1819, at Palamcottah.
....	....	....	....	Died Apr. 25, 1814, on march from Cannanore.
....	....	....	....	Died July 14, 1824, at Bangalore.
....	....	....	....	Died Aug. 18, 1810, at Masulipatam.
....	....	....	....	{ Invalided Jan. 28, 1814. Died May 22, 1818, at Trichinopoly.
....	....	....	....	Died Sep. 23, 1824, at Madras.
....	....	....	....	Died Oct. 4, 1804.
....	....	....	....	Died Mar. 11, 1826, on board the "Triumph."
....	....	....	....	Invalided Jan. 26, 1830, in India.
....	....	....	....	Died Aug. 11, 1804, at Ganjam.
....	....	....	....	Died May 23, 1813.
....	....	....	....	Retired April 10, 1829, in England.
....	....	....	....	Resigned Mar. 25, 1805.
....	....	....	....	Died Apr. 27, 1834, at Secunderabad.
....	....	....	....	Dismissed Mar. 12, 1817, in India.
....	....	....	....	Resigned June 6, 1807.
....	....	....	....	Died Mar. 23, 1817.
....	....	....	....	Died Oct. 16, 1830, at Vellore.
....	....	....	....	Died June — 1820.
....	....	....	....	Died July 21, 1815, at sea.
....	....	....	....	Resigned Mar, 23, 1813.
July 13, 1831	....	....	....	{ Struck off in 1818, having exceeded his period of furlough.
Jan. 2, 1833	....	....	....	
....	....	....	....	Invalided Feb. 19, 1833, in India.
....	....	....	....	Resigned June 6, 1807.
....	....	....	....	{ Killed Feb. 18, 1812, by the blowing down of the mess room at Cannanore.
....	....	....	....	Died Oct. 8, 1811.
....	....	....	....	Invalided Nov. 19, 1824, in India.
....	....	....	....	Died Feb. 3, 1811.
....	....	....	....	Died Feb. 6, 1820, at Ellore.
....	....	....	....	Died Feb. 27, 1813, at Bellary.
....	....	....	....	Retired Oct. 2, 1835, in India.
....	....	....	....	Died Nov. 12, 1823, at Masulipatam.
....	....	....	....	Died July 8, 1821, at Mysore.
....	....	....	....	Died Jan. 14, 1826, at Prome.
....	....	....	....	Resigned Nov. 16, 1810.
....	....	....	....	{ Retired March 1, 1837, in India, on pay of Major.

MADRAS

NAMES.	Cadet.	Cornet, Ensign, or Second Lieutenant.	Lieutenant.	Captain.	Major.
Patton, Charles—*artillery*	1808	....	Aug. 25, 1810	May 13, 1821	....
Proby, Jn. Geo.—*engineers*	1809	July 7, 1810	Oct. 8, 1815	May 1, 1824	....
Porter, James	,,	Oct. 10, 1810	....	....	....
Pasmore, John	,,	Dec. 1, 1810	July 21, 1814	....	....
Palmer, John Freke	1810	May 8, 1811	Jan. 22, 1816	May 1, 1824	May 20, 1834
Plowden, Francis	,,	Mar. 7, 1811	Mar. 23, 1816	Feb. 15, 1825	....
Peoples, John	,,	May 25, 1811	....	....	....
Prendergast, Thomas Guy	,,	Sep. 5, 1811	....	....	....
Polwhele, Rd. G.—*artillery*	,,	July 27, 1811	Sep. 1, 1818	June 22, 1824	....
Parmeter, Francis	,,	Dec. 20, 1811	Feb. 4, 1816	....	....
Price, John—*cavalry*	1811	Jan. 30, 1815	Sep. 1, 1818	....	....
Purton, John—*engineers* ..	1812	June 11, 1812	Dec. 22, 1818	Jan. 24, 1825	Sep. 2, 1836
Prescott, William	1816	....	Mar. 31, 1818	June 29, 1825	....
Pinchard, John—*artillery*..	1817	....	June 11, 1820	....	....
Parkin, John Dickinson ..	,,	....	....	....	....
Phillimore, Charles	1818	Jan. 13, 1819	Jan. 28, 1820	May 12, 1829	....
Power, Henry............	,,	....	June 13, 1819	Nov. 9, 1828	....
Puget, Joseph Baker......	,,	....	June 13, 1819	July 7, 1826	....
Pollock, Thomas..........	,,	....	....	....	....
Parsons, John Pile........	1819	....	April 7, 1820	....	....
Pitcairn, Alexander	,,	....	April 7, 1820	....	....
Powell, William..........	,,	....	Jan. 31, 1821	Jan. 8, 1835	....
Perkes, George	,,	....	Aug. 22, 1820	....	....
Preston, Richd. Babington	,,	....	April 7, 1820	May 11, 1833	....
Powell, John Moore	,,	....	....	....	....
Pace, Horatio	,,	....	June 12, 1821	Brevet April 6, 1835	....
Perrier, Thomas	,,	April 6, 1820	Mar. 14, 1822	Feb. 24, 1833	....
Palmer, Charles Mac Evers	,,	Feb. 13, 1821	Mar. 17, 1823	May 25, 1833	....
Power, James	,,	April 6, 1820	July 1, 1823	Nov. 9, 1828	....
Powell, Charles Joseph....	,,	April 6, 1820	....	....	....
Poole, Matthew	1820	April 6, 1820	June 20, 1822	May 27, 1834	....
Panton, Thomas..........	,,	April 6, 1820	Sep. 6, 1821	....	....
Phillipson, Charles Burton	,,	Feb. 13, 1821	May 1, 1824	....	....
Pope, Peter...............	,,	Feb. 13, 1821	Jan. 20, 1824	Brevet Feb. 13, 1836	....
Pooley, Charles	,,	....	Mar. 31, 1822	June 15, 1834	....
Perreau, Montague William	,,	Feb. 13, 1821	Jan. 13, 1825	Oct. 17, 1834	....
Peel, Edmund	,,	Feb. 13, 1821	May 14, 1824	....	....
Patterson, R. D.—*artillery*	,,	....	June 10, 1821	....	....
Prescott, Stephen	1821	Apr. 27, 1822	July 15, 1824	....	....
Peshall, Sparry	,,	Apr. 27, 1822	Mar. 22, 1825	....	....
Pretyman, Richard........	,,	Apr. 27, 1822	Nov. 19, 1824	Aug. 6, 1835	....
Prior, Henry	,,	Apr. 27, 1822	Oct. 8, 1824	Feb. 6, 1830	....
Peppercorne, Edward	,,	Apr. 27, 1822	Jan. 26, 1825	....	....
Pickering, Charles........	,,	Apr. 27, 1822	Sep. 8, 1826	....	....
Patterson, Jn. C.—*artillery*	,,	....	May 11, 1822	....	....
Pears, Wm. H.—*engineers*	1822	....	....	....	....
Prescott, T. W. T.—*cavalry*	,,	May 2, 1823	June 8, 1825	....	....

PRESIDENCY.   142—143

Lieut.-Colonel.	Colonel.	Major General.	Lieut.-General.	Date of Resignation, Retirement, or Death.
....	....	....	....	Retired June 16, 1826, in England.
....	....	....	....	{ Died Aug. 8, 1825, at Shooloor, near Coimbatore.
....	....	....	....	Died May 22, 1811, at Seringapatam.
....	....	....	....	{ Invalided Jan. 4, 1822. Pensioned from Sep. 22, 1826, in India. Retired June 15, 1831, in England.
....	....	....	....	
....	....	....	....	
....	....	....	....	Died Dec. 14, 1813, at Bellary.
....	....	....	....	Resigned May 21, 1813.
....	....	....	....	
....	....	....	....	Died June 7, 1817, in England.
....	....	....	....	Died Aug. 21, 1824, at Cuddalore.
....	....	....	....	
....	....	....	....	
....	....	....	....	Died April 16, 1829, at Pundegaul.
....	....	....	....	Died Nov. 22, 1819, in camp, at Jaulnah.
....	....	....	....	Retired Nov. 9, 1831, in England.
....	....	....	....	Died Aug. 24, 1829, at Allepy.
....	....	....	....	Died May 20, 1833, in India.
....	....	....	....	Died May 22, 1821, at Paulsamoodrum.
....	....	....	....	Died July 23, 1823, at Cuddalore.
....	....	....	....	Died Dec. 4, 1825, at Arracan.
....	....	....	....	Died July 14, 1835, at sea.
....	....	....	....	Died Dec. 15, 1825, at Bellary.
....	....	....	....	
....	....	....	....	Died July 1821, at Chittledroog.
....	....	....	....	
....	....	....	....	Died Aug. 7, 1834, at Vepery.
....	....	....	....	
....	....	....	....	Died Aug. 24, 1830, at Allepy.
....	....	....	....	Died May 28, 1821, at Chunchurlay.
....	....	....	....	
....	....	....	....	Died Sep. 18, 1830.
....	....	....	....	{ Killed Feb. 22, 1825, in an attack upon Ooumrauze, near Sholapore.
....	....	....	....	
....	....	....	....	{ Invalided Sep. 13, 1831, in India. Died May 24, 1833, at Vizagapatam.
....	....	....	....	Died Dec. 20, 1828, at Quilon.
....	....	....	....	{ Died March 7, 1830, at sea, on board the "Fairlie."
....	....	....	....	Invalided Aug. 28, 1835, in India.
....	....	....	....	
....	....	....	....	{ Died Jan. 18, 1833, at sea, on board the "Morley."
....	....	....	....	Died Oct. 8, 1831, in Ireland.
....	....	....	....	Died June 1, 1824, at Masulipatam.
....	....	....	....	Struck off from Sep. 29, 1824, in England.

MADRAS

NAMES.	Cadet.	Cornet, Ensign, or Second Lieutenant.	Lieutenant.	Captain.	Major.
Power, John Connor	1822	May 27, 1823	Mar. 1, 1829	....	....
Pinchard, George Thomas	1823	May 14, 1824	Dec. 11, 1826	Dec. 22, 1832	....
Prichard, Henry Marriott	,,	May 14, 1824	Sep. 17, 1827	....	....
Pocock, R. T.—*cavalry*	,,	May 14, 1824	....	....	....
Piper, William Henry	1824	May 6, 1825	....	....	....
Philpot, John Thomas	,,	May 6, 1825	June 20, 1828	Dec. 30, 1835	....
Penefather, William	1825	....	....	....	....
Pritchard Henry	,,	....	Apr. 5, 1827	....	....
Place, Thomas Longden	,,	Jan. 8, 1826	July 19, 1834	....	....
Penny, Peter	,,	Jan. 8, 1826	Aug. 7, 1828	....	....
Pigott, William Henry	,,	Jan. 8, 1826	May 11, 1828	....	....
Pogson, Beddingfield	,,	Aug. 23, 1826	....	....	....
Powys, Philip A. S.	,,	Jan. 8, 1826	Mar. 11, 1831	....	....
Pender, Thomas	,,	Jan. 8, 1826	....	....	....
Pears, T. T.—*engineers*	,,	....	June 17, 1835	....	....
Pellowe, William Osborne	,,	Jan. 8, 1826	Sep. 2, 1828	....	....
Pinnock, George	,,	Jan. 8, 1826	July 26, 1828	....	....
Pope, Hillyar Young	1826	Jan. 8, 1826	Aug. 9, 1836	....	....
Pearson, David	,,	Feb. 27, 1827	May 2, 1833	....	....
Patrickson, G.—*engineers*	,,	....	Nov. 4, 1826	....	....
Prescott, Richard—*cavalry*	,,	May 8, 1827	May 26, 1832	....	....
Paterson, Angus	,,	Mar. 23, 1828	Dec. 27, 1832	....	....
Peacock, Thomas E. D.	,,	May 13, 1828	....	....	....
Patch, Thomas Lodge	,,	May 24, 1828	Oct. 30, 1836	....	....
Porter, John F.—*cavalry*	1827	Mar. 3, 1828	Apr. 26, 1829	....	....
Paton, Robert	,,	Mar. 7, 1829	....	....	....
Pears, Arnold C.—*artillery*	,,	June 12, 1828	Aug. 5, 1835	....	....
Patrickson, J.—*artillery*	1828	June 12, 1828	May 28, 1834	....	....
Plees, Charles Gidley	,,	Mar. 23, 1831	June 19, 1836	....	....
Pereira, Edward	,,	June 3, 1831	Jan. 1, 1836	....	....
Power, John P.—*engineers*	,,	Dec. 13, 1827	....	....	....
Plummer, Charles Turner	,,	....	....	....	....
Phillott, Henry R.	,,	Dec. 1, 1831	Sep. 11, 1834	....	....
Pattison, H. J.—*cavalry*	,,	May 9, 1829	....	....	....
Pitcairn, William—*artillery*	,,	Sep. 1, 1831	....	....	....
Pettigrew, T. L.—*cavalry*	1829	Sep. 10, 1831	Dec. 9, 1832	....	....
Pitcher, St. V.—*cavalry*	1830	May 2, 1832	Apr. 5, 1837	....	....
Purvis, George John	1832	Dec. 27, 1832	....	....	....
Prendergast, J. A.—*artillery*	1833	....	....	....	....
R					
Russell, William	....	....	....	Appointed by the Court in 1770	....
Read, Andrew	....	July 3, 1771	....	Nov. 2, 1783	....
Read, Alexander	1770	May 18, 1772	July 31, 1778	Nov. 2, 1783	June 1, 1796
Rodgers, James	1778	Apr. 16, 1779	Dec. 13, 1783	June 1, 1796	Dec. 10, 1799
Riddle, Thomas	,,	May 16, 1779	May 20, 1784	June 1, 1796	June 17, 1800
Robertson, Alexander	,,	May 12, 1779	Jan. 1, 1786	June 1, 1796	June 17, 1800
Read, John	....	July 2, 1779	Apr. 17, 1786	June 1, 1796	June 23, 1802

PRESIDENCY.

Lieut-Colonel.	Colonel.	Major-General.	Lieut.-General.	Date of Resignation, Retirement, or Death.
....	....	....	....	
....	....	....	....	
....	....	....	....	Died Jan. 11, 1834, at Cannanore.
....	....	....	....	{ Died July 29. 1827, on board the "Sophia," on passage to England.
....	....	....	....	Dismissed Dec. 23, 1826, in India.
....	....	....	....	
....	....	....	....	Died Aug. 9, 1826, at Secunderabad.
....	....	....	....	
....	....	....	....	
....	....	....	....	
....	....	....	....	Resigned Sep. 8, 1831, in England.
....	....	....	....	
....	....	....	....	Cashiered Oct. 27, 1828, in India.
....	....	....	....	
....	....	....	....	
....	....	....	....	
....	....	....	....	Retired March 18, 1837, in India.
....	....	....	....	Died July 22, 1829, at Cheltenham.
....	....	....	....	
....	....	....	....	Died Dec. 21, 1834, at Sea.
....	....	....	....	Died July 24, 1830, at Secunderabad.
....	....	....	....	
....	....	....	....	Died June 8, 1831, at Nugger.
....	....	....	....	
....	....	....	....	
....	....	....	....	
....	....	....	....	Died April 5, 1834, at Kimedy.
....	....	....	....	Died 1831-32, at sea, on board the "Madras."
....	....	....	....	{ Pensioned Apr. 9, 1833, in India. Died Feb. 6, 1834, at Madras.
....	....	....	....	Died May 24, 1837, at Trichinopoly.
....	....	....	....	Died April 5, 1837, at Bangalore.
....	....	....	....	
....	....	....	....	
Aug. 15, 1785	....	....	....	Resigned 1789.
....	....	....	....	Died February, 1794.
July 27, 1796	May 1, 1804	....	....	Died May 19, 1804, at Malta.
....	....	....	....	Died May, 28, 1800.
....	....	....	....	Died Feb. 20, 1802.
Aug. 20, 1805	....	....	....	Retired Feb. 28, 1809.
....	....	....	....	Invalided Jan. 10, 1804. Died Oct. 9, 1806.

MADRAS —— U

MADRAS

NAMES.	Cadet.	Cornet, Ensign, or Second Lieutenant.	Lieutenant.	Captain.	Major.
Reilley, Edward O.	1799	Oct. 13, 1780	Apr. 17, 1786	Mar. 4, 1797	Aug. 27, 1800
Roth, John	1780	Dec. 13, 1780	Apr. 17, 1786	....	....
Reilley, Leeson	,,	Dec. 14, 1780	Apr. 17, 1786	Brevet, Jan. 7, 1796	....
Rebotier, Henry..........	,,	Oct. 31, 1781	....	....	....
Robinet, Rouliston	1781	Jan. 8, 1782	Feb. 15, 1789	Oct. 12, 1798	....
Ridge, Robert............	,,	Oct. 13, 1782	Feb. 24, 1790	Oct. 12, 1798	Sep. 21, 1804
Rhodes, William	,,	Oct. 15, 1782	Feb. 24, 1790	....	....
Rand, Charles............	,,	Oct. 22, 1782	April 3, 1790	Oct. 12, 1798	....
Reid, James..............	,,	Nov. 1, 1782	Aug. 21, 1790	Dec. 22, 1798	....
Roberts, Hadder	....	Jan. 2, 1783	Aug. 21, 1790	April 6, 1799	....
Roberts, John	....	Jan. 3, 1783	Aug. 21, 1790	....	....
Radcliffe, H. W.	1782	Apr. 28, 1783	Aug. 21, 1790	June 20, 1799	Dec. 12, 1804
Rae, John Mac	,,	May 17, 1783	....	....	....
Rind, Burnett............	,,	May 25, 1783	Aug. 21, 1790	....	....
Richardson, Plampin......	....	Sep. 5, 1786	June 7, 1792	Dec. 10, 1799	Dec. 12, 1804
Ross, Patrick—*engineers* ..	....	....	....	....	....
Russell, M.—*engineers*	....	Oct. 10, 1781	Apr. 17, 1786	Feb. 23, 1793	....
Rumley, Charles—*cavalry*	1781	Sep. 13, 1782	June 18, 1785	June 1, 1796	Sep. 4, 1799
Rideout, Richard—*cavalry*	1782	July 2, 1783	....	....	....
Roberts, George..........	....	June 17, 1770	July 1, 1771	June 18, 1781	Jan. 30, 1791
Russell, James	....	Nov. 27, 1770	Feb. 7, 1776	Nov. 2, 1783	....
Richardson, John	1770	Mar. 14, 1772	July 29, 1778	Nov. 2, 1783	Mar. — 1794
Rolliston, Arthur—*cavalry*	....	....	May 25, 1784	....	....
Rossbotham, Samuel......	....	Aug. 29, 1783	....	....	....
Ryland, Wm. W.	....	Oct. 14, 1780	Apr. 17, 1786	....	....
Rowles, James—*cavalry* ..	1790	June 4, 1792	Nov. 1, 1798	May 20, 1801	May 1, 1804
Russell, James—*artillery*..	....	Sep. 11, 1791	June 1, 1796	....	....
Redman, John............	1789	....	Oct. 9, 1792	....	....
Robinet, William	....	Sep. 29, 1791	Aug. 6, 1794	....	....
Ross, David—*artillery*	1791	April 2, 1793	June 1, 1796	April 4, 1804	Mar. 9, 1810
Ryves, Charles	,,	June 19, 1793	Aug. 6, 1794	....	....
Ravenhill, John	,,	June 20, 1793	Aug. 6, 1794	....	....
Ryan, Nicholas	,,	June 21, 1793	Aug. 6, 1794	...1802....	....
Rand, Charles	1794	Jan. 18, 1796	June 1, 1796	Sep. 21, 1804	....
Ravenshaw, W.—*engineers*	1795	Jan. 30, 1796	Aug. 12, 1802	Nov. 15, 1810	....
Russell, Sir J. (K.C.B.)—*cavalry*	,,	Feb. 22, 1796	Sep. 4, 1799	May 1, 1804	Mar. 26, 1808
Rochead, Andrew	,,	....	Nov. 29, 1797	Sep. 21, 1804	Mar. 3, 1813
Rowley, George—*engineers*	1796	Aug. 12, 1797	....	....	....
Randall, John............	,,	Aug. 3, 1797	Aug. 2, 1798	....	....
Reid, John	1797	Aug. 12, 1798	Dec. 26, 1798	....	....
Reynolds, Edmund	1795	Feb. 7, 1796	July 27, 1796	....	....
Read, Garrick—*cavalry* ..	1797	Dec. 27, 1799	Aug. 24, 1800	....	....
Remmington, John	1798	....	Jan. 1, 1800	Feb. 8, 1809	....
Robertson, Wm. M.	,,	....	Feb. 19, 1800	May 22, 1807	May 1, 1824
Rimington, J.—*artillery* ..	1799	....	....	....	....
Ross, James—*artillery*	,,	....	....	....	....
Robinson, J.—*artillery*	,,	....	....	....	....

PRESIDENCY.

Lieut.-Colonel.	Colonel.	Major-General.	Lieut.-General.	Date of Resignation, Retirement, or Death.
Sep. 21, 1804	....	....	....	Died March 22, 1816, at Samulcottah.
....	....	....	....	Died June 1, 1796.
....	....	....	....	Died in 1797.
....	....	....	....	Invalided March — 1789. Died 1791.
....	....	....	....	Died 1800.
....	....	....	....	Retired April 29, 1805.
....	....	....	....	Died in 1798.
....	....	....	....	Retired 1802.
....	....	....	....	Died 1804.
....	....	....	....	Killed July 24, 1799, at Ghooty Fort.
....	....	....	....	Died March — 1794.
...1809...	....	....	....	Retired March 6, 1810.
....	....	....	....	Died April — 1789.
....	....	....	....	Not to be traced.
Nov. 29, 1809	....	....	....	Died May 9, 1813, on his route from Goa.
Sep. 15, 1770	Mar. 1, 1794	May 3, 1796	....	Died 1804.
....	....	....	....	Died 1793.
May 20, 1801	July 25, 1810	June 4, 1813	May 27, 1825	
....	....	....	....	Not to be traced. [shire.
June 1, 1796	Oct. 12, 1798	Jan. 1, 1805	June 4, 1813	Died Feb. 24, 1831, in Buckingham-
....	....	....	....	Resigned Jan. — 1790.
June 1, 1796	Jan. 1, 1803	July 25, 1810	June 4, 1814	Died June 4, 1828, in London.
....	....	....	....	Died 1787.
....	....	....	....	King's Service, 1789.
....	....	....	....	Died 1791, in Bengal.
Mar. 26, 1808	....	....	....	Invalided Jan. 16, 1810. Retired Sep. 22, 1813.
....	....	....	....	{ Pensioned Oct. 1800. Died July 3, 1820, at Madras.
....	....	....	....	Died May 1, 1796.
....	....	....	....	Died 1796.
....	....	....	....	{ Died Oct. 21, 1814, having fallen overboard from the "Asia," on his passage to England.
....	....	....	....	Resigned Oct. 24, 1795.
....	....	....	....	Died Aug. 9, 1799, at Palamcottah.
....	....	....	....	Died July 14, 1804, at Dindigul.
....	....	....	....	Died Aug. 21, 1808, at Bangalore.
....	....	....	....	{ Died Jan. 5, 1825, on the H. C. S. "Astell," in the Madras roads.
Oct. 13, 1817	Commt. May 1, 1824 Col. June 5, 1829.	Jan. 10, 1837	....	
Oct. 2, 1818	....	....	....	Retired May 15, 1822.
....	....	....	....	Died June 28, 1803, in camp near Ahmednaghur.
....	....	....	....	Died Aug. 1, 1802.
....	....	....	....	Died Oct. 18, 1803.
....	....	....	....	Not to be traced.
....	....	....	....	Died Aug. 14, 1807, in camp, near Seroor.
....	....	....	....	Died May 22, 1817, in England.
....	....	....	....	Died April 24, 1825, at Nilgherry.
....	....	....	....	Died March 30, 1803.
....	....	....	....	Died Aug. 29, 1803, at Canton.
....	....	....	....	Died Nov. 29, 1800.

MADRAS

NAMES.	Cadet.	Cornet, Ensign, or Second Lieutenant.	Lieutenant.	Captain.	Major.
Robertson, Patrick	1799		Dec. 15, 1800	Dec. 4, 1809	
Reynolds, Lewis C.	,,				
Rivett, James (see Carnac)	,,				
Russell Samuel—*engineers*	1800	Nov. 18, 1801	July 14, 1808		
Rundall, Charles	,,		July 20, 1801	Jan. 1, 1819	May 11, 1824
Rand, J. Dennet Webber	,,		July 20, 1801	Dec. 11, 1813	
Ryder, Henry	,,	June 7, 1802			
Raynsford, H.—*cavalry*	,,		Aug. 11, 1801	May 20, 1813	Sep. 1, 1818
Rose, George	,,		July 20, 1801	Sep. 11, 1813	
Roebuck, Thomas	,,		July 20, 1801	Apr. 11, 1815	
Robertson, William	,,		July 20, 1801		
Ross, David	1801		July 2, 1803	Jan. 4, 1815	Aug. 1, 1825
Reid, James F.—*cavalry*	1802	Jan. 14, 1804	May 3, 1805		
Reid, John	,,		Sep. 21, 1804		
Richardson, Edward	,,		Sep. 21, 1804	Nov. 28, 1816	
Ross, Hugh	,,	Apr. 17, 1803	Jan. 10, 1804	Jan. 1, 1819	Feb. 21, 1826
Russell John	,,				
Rollestone, Stephen	,,		Sep. 21, 1804		
Rashleigh, Robert—*cavalry*	1803	July 18, 1804			
Roberts, Thomas—*artillery*	,,		Sep. 21, 1804		
Rigaud, C. John—*artillery*	,,		Sep. 21, 1804		
Riddell, Michael—*cavalry*	,,		Feb. 21, 1808	Sep. 10, 1817	July 15, 1819
Richardson, Robert	,,		Sep. 21, 1804	Nov. 5, 1817	
Raester, John Charles	,,		Sep. 21, 1804		
Roberts, Allen	,,		Sep. 21, 1804	Feb. 28, 1819	May 20, 1828
Ryan, John	,,		Sep. 21, 1804		
Reed, Stewart	,,		Sep. 21, 1804		
Rudyerd, H. T.—*artillery*	,,		July 18, 1804	Mar. 9, 1810	
Rolleston, Robert	,,		Sep. 21, 1804		
Reid, William	1804		July 17, 1805		
Riddell, John	,,		July 17, 1805		
Russell, Robt. H.—*cavalry*	,,	July 7, 1806	Apr. 30, 1818	May 1, 1824	Sep. 12, 1827
Robson, Felix	,,		July 17, 1805	May 1, 1819	
Robertson, Walter	,,				
Ridley, George	,,		Aug. 18, 1805		
Robinson, C. Burgoyne	1805		Sep. 9, 1806	Sep. 22, 1818	
Roberts, George	,,		Oct. 15, 1807		
Rowley, William Horsley	,,	June 27, 1806	May 23, 1808	Feb. 11, 1823	Jan. 10, 1829
Richardson, William	,,		June 24, 1807		
Reilly, Edward	,,	June 27, 1806	Dec. 29, 1808		
Rodger, James	,,		June 7, 1807	June 26, 1819	
Reid, Hugh	,,	June 27, 1806	July 28, 1808		
Ross, John (25 N. I.)	,,	June 27, 1806	Dec. 9, 1809	Apr. 11, 1821	Sep. 11, 1834
Ridding, William Henry	,,	June 27, 1806	Mar. 20, 1809		
Ritchie, Walter K.	,,	June 27, 1806	Jan. 27, 1812	Dec. 29, 1822	May 26, 1830
Robinson, Henry	1806	July 3, 1807	Aug. 26, 1810		
Robson, Thomas	,,	July 3, 1807	June 24, 1812	May 1, 1824	

PRESIDENCY.

Lieut.-Colonel.	Colonel.	Major General.	Lieut.-General.	Date of Resignation, Retirement, or Death.
....	....	....	....	Died Jan. 3, 1816, at Seringapatam.
....	....	....	....	Dismissed Aug. 7, 1801, by Court Martial.
....	....	....	....	Retired — 1822, on Half Pay.
....	....	....	....	Resigned Jan. 12, 1810.
Feb. 6, 1830	....	....	....	Died July 12, 1831, at Madras.
....	....	....	....	Died July 11, 1824, at Quilon.
....	....	....	....	Died Nov. 15, 1803.
May 1, 1824	Brevet June 5, 1829	....	....	Retired from Sep. 11, 1834, in England.
....	....	....	....	Died Sep. 5, 1820, at Chicacole.
....	....	....	....	Died Dec. 8, 1819, at Bengal.
....	....	....	....	Pensioned March 4, 1807, on Lord
June 2, 1831	....	....	....	Retired Sep. 11, 1834. [Clive's Fund.
....	....	....	....	Died Sep. 9, 1805, at Bangalore.
....	....	....	....	Died Sep. 13, 1805, at Vizagapatam.
....	....	....	....	Died Dec. 10, 1824, at Cannanore.
Aug. 6, 1831	....	....	....	"Wexford."
....	....	....	....	Died Aug. 1, 1803, on board the
....	....	....	....	{ Invalided Nov. 30, 1810; died June 22, 1817, at Vizagapatam.
....	....	....	....	Resigned Sep. 18, 1811.
....	....	....	....	{ Pensioned Mar. 10, 1809; invalided Feb. 15, 1822; died Sep. 14, 1824, at Guntoor.
....	....	....	....	Died July 18, 1807.
Dec. 18, 1826	Brevet June 18, 1831	....	....	
....	....	....	....	Retired March 6, 1822.
....	....	....	....	Died June 5, 1810, at Rodriguez.
....	....	....	....	Died Feb. 2, 1832, at Masulipatam.
....	....	....	....	Died March 13, 1807.
....	....	....	....	Died Oct. 18, 1808, at Bangalore.
....	....	....	....	Died June 24, 1824, at Bangalore.
....	....	....	....	Died Oct. 23, 1811.
....	....	....	....	Died Nov. 18, 1817, at Nagpore.
....	....	....	....	Died Sep. 1, 1818.
May 11, 1833	....	....	....	Died May 4, 1836, at Bangalore.
....	....	....	....	Died June 1, 1825, at Madras.
....	....	....	....	Resigned Oct. 9, 1807.
....	....	....	....	Died Feb. 8, 1813, at Secunderabad.
....	....	....	....	Died June 18, 1824, at Madras.
....	....	....	....	Died Oct. 13, 1819, at Tallygaum.
Apr. 27, 1834	....	....	....	Died July 20, 1836, at Kamptee.
....	....	....	....	Died July 6, 1807, at Vizagapatam.
....	....	....	....	Died Feb. 2, 1818, at Hindiah.
....	....	....	....	Died Sep. 22, 1823, off Fulta.
....	....	....	....	Died Sep. 15 1815, at Bangalore.
....	....	....	....	
....	....	....	....	Died June 14, 1810, in India.
April 1, 1835	....	....	....	Died Jan. 1, 1836, in India.
....	....	....	....	Died Oct. 22, 1824, at Vellore.
....	....	....	....	Died June 2, 1831, at Errode.

MADRAS

NAMES.	Cadet.	Cornet, Ensign, or Second Lieutenant.	Lieutenant.	Captain.	Major.
Robinson, Thomas........	1806	July 3, 1807	Dec. 1, 1810	....	....
Robinson, Geo. T·--*cavalry*	,,	....	....	....	....
Rule, Edward............	,,	July 3, 1807	May 19, 1812	....	....
Roy, James	,,	July 3, 1807	Jan. 23, 1811	May 1, 1824	....
Rankin, Archibald........	,,	July 3, 1807	June 27, 1811	....	....
Russell, Alexander Pringle	1807	Mar. 18, 1809	Dec. 17, 1813	....	....
Reid, Andrew	,,	Jan. 23, 1810	....	....	....
Rehe, Samuel Adolphus ..	,,	Jan. 8, 1810	May 11, 1813	June 26, 1824	Jan. 1, 1836
Rorison, John Gordon	,,	Feb. 24, 1810	Dec. 27, 1812	May 1, 1824	May 25, 1833
Robinson, John Sextie	,,	April 6, 1810	....	....	....
Roper, William	,,	April 6, 1810	....	....	....
Robertson, C. Macdonald..	,,	May 26, 1810	Apr. 28, 1815	May 1, 1824	....
Richardson, John Lowry ..	1809	Aug. 17, 1810	....	....	....
Rickard, Joseph..........	1810	Apr. 13, 1811	Nov. 27, 1815	April 4, 1825	....
Robertson, George	,,	June 6, 1811	Dec. 1, 1817	....	....
Robins, James—*engineers*..	1811	June 11, 1812	Sep. 12, 1815	....	....
Ross, Alexander—*artillery*	1812	June 11, 1812	May 30, 1818	Oct. 23, 1824	Mar. 4, 1832
Ronald, Basil	,,	July 6, 1813	....	....	....
Rose, Charles Price	1817	....	June 4, 1818	...1827....	....
Rogers, Edward..........	,,	....	June 4, 1818	Oct. 16, 1827	....
Ruddiman, Thomas	,,	....	June 4, 1818	Jan. 3, 1826	....
Rawstone, (now Howard) T. A. H.	,,	....	June 4, 1812	Dec. 5, 1829	....
Randall, John	,,	....	Oct. 2, 1818	....	....
Rooke, Thomas	1818	....	June 13, 1819	Feb. 3, 1832	....
Roworth, John William ..	,,	....	June 13, 1819	June 18, 1828	....
Richardson, Charles	,,	....	June 13, 1819	....	....
Rose, William **(43 N. I.)** ..	1819	....	June 13, 1819	July 11, 1827	....
Ross, John Maitland......	,,	....	June 13, 1819	Dec. 16, 1832	....
Rochfort, Cowper	,,	....	April 7, 1820	Oct. 6, 1832	....
Roberts, Emmanuel	,,	....	Aug. 6, 1820	Dec. 19, 1835	....
Roebuck, Benjamin-*cavalry*	,,	April 6, 1820	....	....	....
Raymond, E. H.—*cavalry*	,,	April 6, 1820	Aug. 8, 1821	June 12, 1827	....
Russell, John Abraham ..	,,	....	July 22, 1820	....	....
Reid, Francis Archibald ..	,,	....	Aug. 12, 1820	Nov. 17, 1834	....
Ricketts, Richard R.......	,,	....	June 30, 1821	Oct. 17, 1830	....
Ritchie, Patrick	,,	....	Apr. 11, 1821	....	....
Richardson, Gilbert James	,,	....	Feb. 13, 1821	July 18, 1832	....
Ross, John **(15 N. I.)**	,,	....	July 6, 1821	May 29, 1829	....
Ranken, John Campbell ..	,,	....	Feb. 15, 1821	....	....
Reece, William	,,	April 6, 1820	Feb. 13, 1821	July 6, 1833	....
Reid, Patrick	,,	April 6, 1820	....	....	....
Roy, William	1820	....	....	....	....
Robertson, Finlay Ferguson	,,	Feb. 13, 1821	....	....	....
Risdon, Peter—*cavalry* ..	,,	Feb. 13, 1821	May 1, 1824	....	....
Rowlandson, Michael John	,,	Feb. 13, 1821	May 1, 1824	Brevet Feb. 13, 1836	....
Richardson, Jas. **(16 N. I.)**	,,	Feb. 13, 1821	Nov. 23, 1822	Apr. 27, 1829	....
Richardson, R. H.--*cavalry*	,,	Feb. 13, 1821	May 1, 1824	Brevet, Feb. 13, 1836	....

PRESIDENCY.

Lieut.-Colonel.	Colonel.	Major-General.	Lieut.-General.	Date of Resignation, Retirement, or Death.
....	....	....	....	Died May 7, 1818, at Bellary.
....	....	....	....	Died Feb. 13, 1809.
....	....	....	....	Died Jan. 20, 1820, at Bombay.
....	....	....	....	Died Sep. 11, 1825, at Sompitt.
....	....	....	....	Died June 24, 1819, at Negapatam.
....	....	....	....	{ Died Jan. 23, 1818, on board the "Minerva," in Madras Roads.
....	....	....	....	{ Appointed a writer on the Bengal Establishment, April 7, 1811.
....	....	....	....	
....	....	....	....	Died Feb. 15, 1812.
....	....	....	....	Resigned Oct. 7, 1812.
....	....	....	....	Died June 7, 1836, at Kamptee.
....	....	....	....	Died Sep. 4, 1811.
....	....	....	....	Died June 29, 1829, in Scotland.
....	....	....	....	Admitted on Lord Clive's Fund, Aug. 12, 1819.
....	....	....	....	Resigned June 21, 1825, in India.
....	....	....	....	
....	....	....	....	Resigned Feb. 10, 1818, in India.
....	....	....	....	Died May 28, 1827, at Mangalore.
....	....	....	....	Died Feb. 2, 1829, at Secunderabad.
....	....	....	....	Retired July 17, 1832, in England.
....	....	....	....	
....	....	....	....	Died July 20, 1825, at Mahatee.
....	....	....	....	
....	....	....	....	Retired Feb. 8, 1832, in England.
....	....	....	....	Died Dec. 27, 1823, at Bellary.
....	....	....	....	Died March 1, 1836, at Masulipatam.
....	....	....	....	
....	....	....	....	
....	....	....	....	Died Sep. 20, 1822, at Jaulnah.
....	....	....	....	Died Sep. 28, 1828, at Omrah.
....	....	....	....	Retired Jan. 31, 1835, in England.
....	....	....	....	
Lieut.-Colonel.	....	....	....	
....	....	....	....	Died Jan. 4, 1824, at Bangalore.
....	....	....	....	
....	....	....	....	
....	....	....	....	Died Nov. 17, 1825, at Prome.
....	....	....	....	
....	....	....	....	Died April 17, 1822, at Mangalore.
....	....	....	....	Died Apr. 16, 1821, at Ryaccottah.
....	....	....	....	Died July 3, 1824, at Rangoon.
....	....	....	....	Died March 31, 1827, on his passage [to Penang.
....	....	....	....	
....	....	....	....	
....	....	....	....	

MADRAS

NAMES.	Cadet.	Cornet, Ensign, or Second Lieutenant.	Lieutenant.	Captain.	Major.
Roberts, Howland	1820	Feb. 13, 1821	May 27, 1823	Dec. 8, 1833	....
Rochfort, G. Cowper	,,	Feb. 13, 1821	Oct. 23, 1824	Brevet, Feb. 13, 1836	....
Russell, Henry	,,	Feb. 13, 1821	....	....	....
Robertson, Alexander	,,	Feb. 13, 1821	....	....	....
Robertson, J. R.—*cavalry*	,,	Feb. 13, 1821	May 1, 1824	Mar. 20, 1831	....
Rudd, Launcelot	,,	Feb. 13, 1821	Nov.13, 1823	....	....
Rawlins, William	,,	Feb. 13, 1821	Apr. 19, 1823	Aug.16, 1830	....
Reynolds, P. Alexander	,,	Feb. 13, 1821	Nov. 30,1823	Brevet Feb 13, 1836	....
Roberts, Claude Adolphus	1821	Apr. 27, 1822	Aug. 25,1826	April 1, 1836	....
Reynolds, Owen	,,	Apr. 27, 1822	Nov. 30,1824	....	....
Robertson, James (9 N. I.)	,,	Apr. 27, 1822	Oct. 4, 1825	Aug. 3, 1837	....
Rand, George Charles C.	1822	May 2, 1823	May 9, 1825	....	....
Rickards, John Wetherston	,,	May 2, 1823	Sep. 8, 1826	....	....
Ravenscroft, Edward W.	,,	May 11, 1824	Dec.30, 1825	....	....
Ross, Walter William	,,	May 2, 1823	Apr. 14, 1828	....	....
Rippon, Thomas Davis	1823	May 14, 1824	Jan. 4, 1826	Dec. 23, 1829	....
Rowlandson, Charles	,,	May 14, 1824	June 3, 1826	....	....
Read, John R. G.—*cavalry*	,,	....	....	....	....
Robertson, Robert Henry	,,	May 14, 1824	Oct. 15, 1826	....	....
Rumsay, John William	,,	May 14, 1824	Aug. 16,1825	....	....
Rose, John—*cavalry*	,,	May 14, 1824	....	....	....
Roberts, Thomas Digby	,,	May 14, 1824	Nov. 21,1829	....	....
Russell, William (18 N. I.)	,,	May 14, 1824	May 2, 1826	Dec. 9, 1836	....
Rolland, C. W.—*artillery*	1824	....	July 26, 1824	....	....
Rattray, James	,,	May 6, 1825	....	....	....
Rumsey, Herbert—*artillery*	,,	....	Oct. 8, 1826	....	....
Rishworth, George T.	,,	May 6, 1825	....	....	....
Russell, Francis	1825	Jan. 8, 1826	Aug.23, 1834	....	....
Robley, John Horatio	,,	....	Nov. 21,1826	Feb. 1, 1836	....
Rose, Alexander Robert	,,	Jan. 8, 1826	Mar. 23,1828	Aug. 6, 1836	....
Ryves, Thomas James	,,	....	July 11, 1827	....	....
Reade, George	,,	Jan. 8, 1826	....	....	....
Ramsden, Richard	,,	...1827...	....	....	....
Rowlandson, G.—*artillery*	,,	June 16,1826	April 6, 1831	....	....
Russell, Augustus	1826	Jan, 7. 1827	May 31, 1833	....	....
Roper, Philip Banister	,,	Feb. 8, 1827	....	....	....
Reynaud, Sydenham G. C.	,,	Mar. 5, 1827	Mar. 27,1832	....	....
Ricketts, W. H.—*cavalry*	,,	Sep. 4,1827	....	....	....
Rickards, Peter Eyles L.	,,	Mar. 5, 1827	Apr. 17, 1835	....	....
Ritchie, William	,,	Oct. 24, 1827	....	....	....
Redmond, John Joseph	,,	Jan. 5, 1828	....	....	....
Robertson, J. B.—*artillery*	1827	Dec. 12, 1827	....	....	....
Richmond, Alexander	,,	Jan. 5, 1828	May 20, 1835	....	....
Robertson, William S.	,,	....	....	....	....
Rollo, Roger	,,	June 2, 1829	Oct. 12, 1833	....	....
Rait, Alexander—*cavalry*	,,	....	....	....	....
Robertson, John (9 N. I.)	1828	June 2, 1829	....	....	....

PRESIDENCY.

Lieut.-Colonel.	Colonel.	Major General.	Lieut.-General.	Date of Resignation, Retirement, or Death.
....	....	....	....	
....	....	....	....	
....	....	....	....	Died May 27, 1824, at Hydrabad.
....	....	....	....	Died April 5, 1824, at Jaulnah.
....	....	....	....	
....	....	....	....	Died Nov. 23, 1831, at Nagpore.
....	....	....	....	
....	....	....	....	
....	....	....	....	
....	....	....	....	
....	....	....	....	
....	....	....	....	Died Apr. 20, 1827, at sea, on board [the "Norfolk."
....	....	....	....	Died Apr. 24, 1833, at Bowerpelly.
....	....	....	....	
....	....	....	....	
....	....	....	....	
....	....	....	....	Drowned May 6, 1824, off the Cape [of Good Hope.
....	....	....	....	
....	....	....	....	Died June 9, 1831, at Kamptee.
....	....	....	....	
....	....	....	....	
....	....	....	....	Died July 31, 1831, at Vellore.
....	....	....	....	Died Mar. 6, 1830, at St. Thomas's Mount.
....	....	....	....	Resigned Dec. 31, 1825, in India.
....	....	....	....	
....	....	....	....	Retired July 12, 1837, in England.
....	....	....	....	
....	....	....	....	Pensioned Oct. 4, 1831, in India.
....	....	....	....	Died April 13, 1827, at Secunderabad.
....	....	....	....	
....	....	....	....	{ Pensioned Feb. 5, 1833, in India. Died Oct. 1, 1833, at Berhampore.
....	....	....	....	
....	....	....	....	Died July 5, 1830, at the Presidency.
....	....	....	....	
....	....	....	....	Invalided Jan. 21, 1831, in India.
....	....	....	....	Died Dec. 9, 1834, at Madras.
....	....	....	....	Died Sep. 19, 1831, at Octacamund.
....	....	....	....	
....	....	....	....	Died May 18, 1829, at Bangalore.
....	....	....	....	
....	....	....	....	Died April 25, 1830, in Europe.
....	....	....	....	Killed April 3, 1234, in Coorg.

MADRAS

NAMES.	Cadet.	Cornet, Ensign, or Second Lieutenant.	Lieutenant.	Captain.	Major.
Reddie, Andrew J.—*cavalry*	1828	April 2, 1830	....	....	....
Roper, Edward Dacre	1829	Feb. 3, 1832	Feb. 24, 1836	....	....
Robertson, Edwin	,,	June 2, 1832	....	....	....
Rundall, I. W.—*engineers*..	1830	Feb. 19, 1832	....	....	....
Renwick, James	1832	Nov. 24, 1832	....	....	....
Rose, James F.—*cavalry* ..	,,	Feb. 17, 1834	Nov. 9, 1835	....	....
Robertson, John (15 N.I.)	,,	Feb. 1, 1834	....	....	....
Robertson, Alaric	,,	Feb. 1, 1834	....	....	....
Robinson, Arthur	1833	Feb. 15, 1834	....	....	....
Rees, John Mitford	,,	Mar. 1, 1834	....	....	....
Richardson, J. (43 N. I.) ..	,,	June 13, 1834	May 5, 1836	....	....
Roberts, C. H. G.	1834	Dec. 13, 1834	....	....	....
Russell, G. I.—*cavalry*....	,,	Nov. 16, 1834	Dec. 12, 1836	....	....

S

NAMES.	Cadet.	Cornet, Ensign, or Second Lieutenant.	Lieutenant.	Captain.	Major.
Short, John	....	Oct. 7, 1760	....	Nov. 12, 1765	July 30, 1778
Sale, Robert..............	....	....	Aug. 30, 1770	July 7, 1779	Jan. 24, 1788
Scouler, Robert	1767	Oct. 26, 1768	Sep. 12, 1770	July 16, 1779	....
Stewart, Arthur	1769	Nov. 13, 1770	Oct. 21, 1775	Nov. 2, 1783	....
Stewart, George	,,	Nov. 28, 1770	Mar. 6, 1776	Nov. 2, 1783	.. .1794...
Smith, Thomas	,,	Dec. 25, 1770	Nov. 18, 1776	Nov. 2, 1783	....
Swain, Stephen	1770	Feb. 17, 1772	May 18, 1778	Nov. 2, 1783	....
Smart, Charles	1771	Nov. 14, 1772	Nov. 14, 1778	Dec. 23, 1783	June 1, 1796
Smith, Eccles	....	Jan. 1, 1774	....	Brevet May 9, 1784	....
Stevens, William	1776	Mar. 31, 1778	Jan. 3, 1782	Feb. 4, 1794	....
Smith, George............	,,	Apr. 4, 1778	Jan. 5, 1782	Feb. 17, 1794	Dec. 21, 1797
Shippey, Thomas William..	,,	Apr. 14, 1778	Jan. 9, 1782	Aug. 6, 1794	Sep. 29, 1798
Sundt, Toachin	1777	Apr. 26, 1778	Jan. 16, 1782	Aug. 6, 1794	....
Sundt, Ludwick	,,	Apr. 29, 1778	Jan. 18, 1782	....	....
Salmon, George	,,	May 17, 1778	Jan. 31, 1782	....	....
Sampson, John	,,	June 29, 1778	Mar. 4, 1782	...1796....	....
Small, Lewis	,,	July 16, 1778	Mar. 11, 1782	....	....
Stuart, Hope	1778	Apr. 19, 1779	Jan. 21, 1784	....	....
Sheppard, William	,,	May 2, 1779	May 20, 1784	June 1, 1796	June 17, 1800
Sober, Elliston	,,	May 17, 1779	Jan. 4, 1786	....	....
Stevenson, Thomas	,,	May 25, 1779	Mar. 18, 1786	June 1, 1796	....
Symons, John Hilly	1779	Aug. 24, 1780	Apr. 17, 1786	June 1, 1796	Feb. 21, 1802
Seale, Benjamin	1780	Dec. 19, 1780	Apr. 17, 1786	....	....
Simons, Jeremiah	,,	Sep. 29, 1781	Sep. 6, 1788	Dec. 21, 1797	Dec. 8, 1801
Stevenson, John	,,	Oct. 15, 1781	....	....	....
Shaw Pagan	1781	Jan. 12, 1782	....	....	....
Schoy, Michael	....	Jan. 13, 1782	Mar. 6, 1789	Oct. 12, 1798	....
Sloper, Granby	1781	Sep. 26, 1782	....	....	....
Sommers, Richard	,,	Oct. 5, 1782	....	....	....
Stevenson, Roger	,,	Oct. 27, 1782	....	....	....
Simpson, Charles	,,	Nov. 24, 1782	Aug. 21, 1790	Dec. 26, 1798	....
Sherridan, Charles	1782	Dec. 16, 1782	Aug. 21, 1790	....	....
Shaw, Robert	,,	Jan. 4, 1783	Aug. 21, 1790	Apr. 18, 1799	Sep. 21, 1804

PRESIDENCY.

Lieut-Colonel.	Colonel.	Major-General.	Lieut.-General.	Date of Resignation, Retirement, or Death.
....	....	....	....	Died Feb. 6, 1831, at Bangalore.
....	....	....	....	
....	....	....	....	Discharged Feb. 13, 1833, in India.
....	....	....	....	
....	....	....	....	Died June 15, 1836, at Ganjam.
....	....	....	....	Died April 20, 1837, at Kamptee.
....	....	....	....	
....	....	....	....	
....	....	....	....	
....	....	....	....	
....	....	....	....	
....	....	....	....	
....	....	....	....	
....	....	....	....	Invalided in India, and died Feb. 6, 1803.
Dec. 11, 1793	June 1, 1796	....	....	Died May 11, 1799, at Vellore.
....	....	....	....	Died June 22, 1789.
....	....	....	....	Died 1793.
June 1, 1796	....	....	....	Died Mar. 17, 1797.
....	....	....	....	Died Oct. 6, 1789.
....	....	....	....	Died 1790.
....	....	....	....	Died Oct. 2, 1798.
....	....	....	....	King's Service 1789.
....	....	....	....	Not to be traced.
Jan. 16, 1800	....	....	....	Died May 10, 1803.
....	....	....	....	Died Sep. 24, 1799.
....	....	....	....	{ Invalided Sep. 27, 1794. Died Aug. 8, 1795, at Vellore.
....	....	....	....	Died Jan. 1791.
....	....	....	....	Died 1788.
....	....	....	....	Died 1797.
....	....	....	....	Died 1790.
....	....	....	....	Not to be traced.
May 26, 1804	....	....	....	Retired Feb. 27, 1807.
....	....	....	....	{ Invalided July — 1791. Died Oct. 8, 1814, at Negapatam.
....	....	....	....	Died Jan. 14, 1799.
Dec. 12, 1804	Oct. 9, 1818	Aug. 12, 1819	....	Died June 1, 1831.
....	....	....	....	Died 1793.
Sep. 21, 1804	Aug. 18, 1818	Aug. 12, 1819	....	Died July 27, 1826, at Worcester.
....	....	....	....	Pensioned July — 1788. Died Feb. 10, 1804.
....	....	....	....	Died 1791.
....	....	....	....	Died Oct. 21, 1803.
....	....	....	....	Not to be traced.
....	....	....	....	Died 1791.
....	....	....	....	Not to be traced.
....	....	....	....	Died Mar. 3, 1799, at Kistnagherry.
....	....	....	....	{ Invalided May — 1791. Died July — 1818, at Madras.
....	....	....	....	Retired Feb. — 1807.

MADRAS

NAMES.	Cadet.	Cornet, Ensign, or Second Lieutenant.	Lieutenant.	Captain.	Major.
Strutt, John.............	1782	Apr. 25, 1783	....	....	....
Sharpe, John	,,	Apr. 26, 1783	....	....	....
Smith, Harry	,,	May 23, 1783	Aug. 21, 1790	....	....
Speering, Thomas	1783	Sep. 6, 1783	....	....	....
Sydenham, Wm.—*artillery*	....	Oct. 15, 1768	....	....	....
Smith, David—*artillery*....	....	Jan. 20, 1772	May 2, 1777	Dec. 6, 1780	....
Slipper, John—*artillery* ...	....	Nov. 22, 1772	....	Sep. 15, 1781	....
Sutcliffe, Thomas—*artillery*	....	Aug. 8, 1774	....	Sep. 16, 1781	....
Saxon, George—*artillery*..	....	July 27, 1778	Nov. 30, 1780	Feb. 18, 1782	Apr. 22, 1793
Saunderson, John—*artillery*	1782	Feb. 20, 1782	Apr. 30, 1785	....	....
Scott, James Geo.—*artillery*	1781	Apr. 20, 1783	July 22, 1788	May 5, 1799	Sep. 21, 1804
Saunter, Samuel—*engineers*	....	Oct. 19, 1782	....	....	....
Stevenson, James—*cavalry*	....	....	....	Apr. 21, 1784	Aug. 15, 1788
Sulivan, Philip—*cavalry* ..	....	Jan. 3, 1778	....	....	....
Sentleger, Hon. A.—*cavalry*	1779	...1781....	May 4, 1783	June 1, 1796	....
Sheriffe, William—*cavalry*	....	....	Apr. 22, 1784	June 1, 1796	Sep. 4, 1799
Stuart, John—*cavalry*	1780	....	June 30, 1785	....	....
Stretch, William—*cavalry*	1782	July 6, 1783	July 22, 1786	Sep. 4, 1799	....
Strahan, Alexander—*cavalry*	,,	Nov. 29, 1785	Dec. 8, 1791	Sep. 4, 1799	Aug. 29, 1801
Smith, George...........	....	July 29, 1765	Apr. 12, 1773	Sep. 12, 1773	....
Speediman, Robt.—*artillery*	....	Jan. 11, 1775	Oct. 18, 1780	Oct. 13, 1781	....
Stockwell, Charles	....	Aug. 25, 1778	June 13, 1783	....	....
Swain, H. M. W.	1782	June 14, 1783	Aug. 21, 1790	....	....
Sinclair, Sir J. (Bt.)—*artillery*	1787	....	Apr. 22, 1793	Dec. 25, 1800	Feb. 14, 1805
Skinner, James—*artillery*	1790	July 15, 1791	....	....	....
Sinclair, John (Junr.)	....	Sep. 24, 1791	June 1, 1796	June 21, 1803	....
Shadwell, Thomas	....	....	June 7, 1792	....	....
Steele, Thomas	1789	....	Oct. 3, 1792	May 1, 1800	Sep. 18, 1807
Smith, Nicholas Mathew	1790	June 5, 1791	May 9, 1793	June 17, 1800	July 11, 1806
Stewart, Mathew	,,	June 14, 1791	June 6, 1793	June 17, 1800	Nov. 22, 1806
Spence, John	,,	July 8, 1791	Sep. 18, 1793	June 17, 1800	....
Street, John Richard......	,,	Aug. 4, 1791	....	....	....
Shaw, William	,,	Aug. 7, 1791	Feb. 17, 1794	Oct. 16, 1800	Jan. 21, 1808
Smith, Peter.............	....	Sep. 10, 1791	Aug. 6, 1794	....	....
Sheppard, Robert Robinson	1791	Apr. 29, 1793	Aug. 6, 1794	....	....
Storey, Joseph	,,	Apr. 30, 1793	Aug. 6, 1794	July 25, 1801	Aug. 2, 1806
Stonard, Joseph	,,	April 1, 1793	Aug. 6, 1794	Feb. 1, 1802	....
Stone, Webb—*artillery*	,,	June 14, 1793	Aug. 30, 1796	Aug. 17, 1804	....
Steel, George—*artillery* ..	,,	June 17, 1793	Apr. 17, 1797	Dec. 25, 1800	....
Savoct, Charles	,,	June 22, 1793	Sep. 28, 1794	....	....
Scott, Sir H. S. (K. C. B.)..	,,	June 24, 1793	Oct. 3, 1794	Sep. 13, 1804	Aug. 15, 1805
Stewart, Thomas..........	1792	Sep. 25, 1793	Oct. 14, 1794	Sep. 17, 1804	Sep. 11, 1813
Strange, Robert Montague	1777	Jan. 2, 1778	May 5, 1781	Dec. 5, 1793	Nov. 29, 1797
Seton, Thomas	1792	Sep. 30, 1793	Oct. 15, 1794	Nov. 18, 1802	....
Showers, Nathl. Thornton	....	....	Aug. 6, 1794	Dec. 15, 1801	....
Smith, Hen. Francis (C. B.)	1793	....	Dec. 12, 1794	Sep. 8, 1803	Oct. 15, 1811
Slingsby, John Henry	,,	....	Mar. 18, 1795	....	....

PRESIDENCY.

156--157

Lieut.-Colonel.	Colonel.	Major-General.	Lieut.-General.	Date of Resignation, Retirement, or Death.
....	....	....	....	Not to be traced.
....	....	....	....	Died April 10, 1789.
....	....	....	....	Blown up April 25, 1801.
....	....	....	....	Died 1791.
July 22, 1786	June 1, 1796	....	....	Died June 13, 1801.
Mar. 7, 1791	Dec. 25, 1800	....	....	Retired on the off reckoning fund, July 19, 1809. Died April 7, 1818.
....	....	....	....	Died 1791.
....	....	....	....	Died 1788.
...1796....	....	....	....	Retired Oct. 15, 1801.
....	....	....	....	Resigned 1787.
July 4, 1807	June 4, 1814	July 19, 1821	....	Died Jan. 1, 1833, in London.
....	....	....	....	Died 1789.
June 1, 1796	Sep. 4, 1799	Jan. 1, 1805	....	Died Feb. 14, 1805.
....	....	....	....	Died Oct. 1793.
Sep. 4, 1799	Oct. 25, 1809	Jan. 1, 1812	....	Died July 6, 1823, in London.
June 17, 1800	....	....	....	Died April 7, 1802.
....	....	....	....	Died 1789.
....	....	....	....	Died 1800.
June 27, 1804	....	....	....	Died Nov. 24, 1805, at Adjuntah.
May 2, 1786	....	....	....	At home, 1787. Out of the service.
....	....	....	....	Not to be traced.
....	....	....	....	Resigned 1788.
....	....	....	....	Died Aug. 19, 1794.
Mar. 9, 1810	May 1, 1824	July 22, 1830	....	
....	....	....	....	Died Sep. 1, 1795, at the Mount.
....	....	....	....	Died Feb. 15, 1807.
....	....	....	....	Europe for health, Feb. — 1795. Recommended for Lord Clive's bounty.
May 6, 1813	Commt. 1824	....	....	Died Oct. 13, 1824, at Bath.
Nov. 8, 1810	....	....	....	Died Dec. 28, 1811.
Apr. 16, 1812	....	....	....	Died Oct. 1, 1818, in camp, near Cassarbarry Ghaut.
....	....	....	....	Retired on half pay, May 8, 1804.
....	....	....	....	Died 1793.
Aug. 27, 1813	....	....	....	Died May 18, 1814, at Gollampollam.
....	....	....	....	Struck off March 10, 1801.
....	....	....	....	Died Nov. 10, 1800.
Apr. 16, 1812	....	....	....	Died Oct. 13, 1818, at Samulcottah.
....	....	....	....	Died Oct. 19, 1804.
....	....	....	....	Retired May 5, 1809.
....	....	....	....	Killed Sep. 23, 1803.
....	....	....	....	Died 1795, at Vellore.
Mar. 7, 1810	Aug. 12, 1819	July 22, 1830	....	
Jan. 27, 1819	Commt. Apr. 17, 1826. Col. June 5, 1829.	Jan. 10, 1837	....	
Dec. 10, 1799	Oct. 25, 1809	....	....	Died Nov. 29, 1811, at Ryacottah.
....	....	....	....	Cashiered June 23, 1807.
....	....	....	....	Died June 23, 1803.
Feb. 24, 1818	Commt. May 1, 1824. Col. June 5, 1829.	....	....	Died Feb. 21, 1834, at Pondicherry.
....	....	....	....	Killed by a Malay Chieftain, April 28, 1799, at Amboyna.

MADRAS

NAMES.	Cadet.	Cornet, Ensign, or Second Lieutenant.	Lieutenant.	Captain.	Major.
Scot, Sir Robert (K. C. B.)	1793	....	Aug. 5, 1795	April 8, 1803	Nov. 9, 1805
Stewart, John	,,	....	Jan. 8, 1796	Sep. 23, 1803	....
Spencer, Thomas	,,	....	Oct. 3, 1795	....	....
Sydenham, Thomas	1794	....	Dec. 5, 1794	Mar. 26, 1802	....
Sydenham, Benj.—*engineers*	,,	....	June 1, 1796	....	....
Stokoe, John Cook	,,	Jan. 8, 1796	June 1, 1796	Sep. 21, 1804	Mar. 20, 1814
Seward, Joseph Breton	,,	Jan. 21, 1796	June 1, 1796	Aug. 13, 1801	.... 1809...
Sherer, William	,,	Jan. 1, 1796	June 1, 1796	....	....
Smith, James	,,	Dec. 24, 1795	Feb. 10, 1796	....	....
Sinclair, George	,,	Jan. 15, 1796	June 1, 1796	....	....
Smith, William	1795	Feb. 5, 1796	June 28, 1796	....	....
Stevenson, Edw. Pennyman	,,	Mar. 8, 1796	Aug. 17, 1797	Sep. 21, 1804	Mar. 16, 1813
Saltwell, Charles	1797	Aug. 2, 1798	Dec. 26, 1798	Apr. 30, 1805	May 26, 1814
Stanley, Richard	1795	....	Nov. 29, 1797	Sep. 21, 1804	....
Simpson, James—*cavalry*	,,	Sep. 4, 1799	Nov. 29, 1797	June 1, 1804	Sep. 13, 1813
Smith, J.—*cavalry* (6 Rgt.)	1796	Sep. 17, 1797	May 12, 1800	Jan. 17, 1810	July 7, 1823
Smith, Thomas Hatcher	1797	Aug. 1, 1798	Dec. 26, 1798	July 2, 1806	Sep. 1, 1818
Shute, Thomas	,,	Aug. 13, 1798	Dec. 26, 1798	....	....
Skinner, Joseph H.—*cavalry*	,,	Aug. 7, 1798	Sep. 4, 1799	....	....
Smith, Walter	,,	Aug. 23, 1798	Dec. 26, 1798	....	....
Smith, Sydenham	1796	Sep. 13, 1797	Oct. 12, 1798	Sep. 21, 1804	.... 1814...
Spry, George	1795	Mar. 6, 1796	Aug. 5, 1797	....	....
Smythies, Edmund Walcot	1797	Sep. 2, 1798	Dec. 26, 1798	Jan. 27, 1806	....
Snow, E. Winterton (C. B.)	,,	Aug. 6, 1798	Dec. 26, 1798	Jan. 31, 1806	Mar. 24, 1815
Stevenson, Thos. Thompson	1798	....	Jan. 1, 1800	Mar. 18, 1809	....
Smythe, Edw. L.—*cavalry*	,,	....	June 17, 1800	July 29, 1815	Dec. 15, 1819
Smith, Thomas (14 Rgt.)	,,	....	Jan. 1, 1800	July 11, 1806	July 12, 1819
Stewart, Francis Philip	,,	....	Jan. 1, 1800	May 27, 1806	Feb. 24, 1818
Saunders, Erasmus—*cavalry*	,,	....	June 17, 1800	....	....
Stewart, Charles	,,	....	Jan. 1, 1800	April 6, 1810	....
Strange, Thomas	1799	....	....	....	....
Steuart, William Fordyce	,,	....	Dec. 15, 1800	....	....
Smith, Michael	,,	....	Dec. 15, 1800	....	....
Sampson, Francis—*cavalry*	,,	July 25, 1801	May 1, 1804	....	....
Sadler, James	,,	....	Dec. 15, 1800	Mar. 1, 1809	....
Scott, Robt. Bigo—*artillery*	,,	....	....	....	....
Shepherd, George	,,	....	Dec. 15, 1800	Brevet Nov. 7, 1810.	....
Simons, John	,,	....	Dec. 15, 1800	Feb. 24, 1810	....
Sanford, George	,,	....	Dec. 15, 1800	Feb. 24, 1808	....
Stewart, Alexander (3 Rgt.)	,,	....	Dec. 15, 1800	Mar. 18, 1809	....
Smith, Lewin Scott	,,	....	Dec. 15, 1800	Jan. 9, 1808	....
Sale, Henry Wallace	,,	....	Dec. 15, 1800	Oct. 2, 1808	Oct. 16, 1818
Simpson, Thomas	,,	....	....	....	....
Smithwaite, Thomas	,,	....	Dec. 15, 1800	Mar. 20, 1809	May 5, 1821
Somerville, Henry Erskine	,,	....	Dec. 15, 1800	Nov. 16, 1809	....
Scott, William	,,	....	....	....	....
Smith, Charles	,,	....	July 20, 1801	....	....

PRESIDENCY.

Lieut.-Colonel.	Colonel.	Major General.	Lieut.-General.	Date of Resignation, Retirement, or Death.
Oct. 4, 1810	May 1, 1824	July 22, 1830	....	Died Dec. 21, 1832, at Haddington, N. B.
....	....	....	....	Died June 26, 1804.
....	....	....	....	Died 1800.
....	....	....	....	Resigned May 4, 1810.
....	....	....	....	Resigned July 13, 1808.
....	....	....	....	{ Invalided July 16, 1819. Died Sep. 7, 1819, at Madras.
....	....	....	....	Died Oct. 9, 1810, at Ramnad.
....	....	....	....	Resigned April — 1798.
....	....	....	....	Resigned Jan. 8, 1800.
....	....	....	....	Died Nov. 9, 1802.
....	....	....	....	Died April 5, 1802.
....	....	....	....	{ Invalided Nov. 30, 1817, in India. Died Aug. 5, 1819, at Dindigul.
....	....	....	....	{ Invalided Jan. 3, 1815, in India. Died Dec. 18, 1816, at Baiswarrah.
....	....	....	....	Cashiered March 4, 1808.
....	....	....	....	{ Invalided Jan. 11, 1815, in India. Retired Feb. 11, 1829, in India.
....	....	....	....	Retired Dec. 31, 1826, in England.
May 1, 1824	June 5, 1829	....	....	
....	....	....	....	Not to be traced.
....	....	....	....	Died Nov. 4, 1801.
....	....	....	....	Died June 19, 1802.
....	....	....	....	Died Jan. 28, 1815, at Goa.
....	....	....	....	Struck off Dec. 26, 1803.
....	....	....	....	{ Died May 26, 1810, on board the "Lord Eldon."
Aug. 6, 1820	June 5, 1829	....	....	Died April 4, 1831, at Bellary.
....	....	....	....	{ Died April 3, 1816, in camp, at the north bank of the Tomboodrah.
Aug. 15, 1829	....	....	....	
....	....	....	....	Died Aug. 14, 1824, at Madras.
May 1, 1824	Feb. 15, 1832	....	....	Died Aug. 23, 1834, at Inveresk, N. B.
....	....	....	....	Died Oct. 27, 1804.
....	....	....	....	Retired Feb. 15, 1815, in England.
....	....	....	....	Died Feb. 28, 1802.
....	....	....	....	Died Dec. 28, 1802.
....	....	....	....	Died June 7, 1810, at Bangalore.
....	....	....	....	Died Dec. 31, 1810, at Seroor.
....	....	....	....	Killed Nov. 27, 1817, in action near Nagpore.
....	....	....	....	Died Oct. 5, 1801.
....	....	....	....	Killed Aug. — 1811, at Java.
....	....	....	....	Died Sep. 16, 1815, at Madras.
....	....	....	....	Retired Sep. 1, 1815, in India.
....	....	....	....	Died June 9, 1820.
....	....	....	....	Retired March 1, 1819, in England.
May 1, 1824	....	....	....	Died Dec. 11, 1828, at Wallajahbad.
....	....	....	....	Died Dec. 1, 1800.
Oct. 14, 1824	....	....	....	Died Feb. 26, 1827, at Vizianagrum.
....	....	....	....	Retired April 8, 1815, in England.
....	....	....	....	Died Dec. 3, 1800.
....	....	....	....	Died May 19, 1805.

MADRAS

NAMES.	Cadet.	Cornet, Ensign, or Second Lieutenant.	Lieutenant.	Captain.	Major.
Swayne, Henry	1799	....	Dec. 15, 1800	Nov. 17, 1812	Jan. 24, 1820
Scott, Archibald—*cavalry*	....	....	Aug. 11, 1801	Jan. 1, 1819	....
Spry, William Bach	1800	....	July 20, 1801	Oct. 25, 1815	May 1, 1824
Sweetland, Edward Seore..	,,	....	July 20, 1801	....	....
Showers, E. M. G.—*artillery*	,,	....	Dec. 12, 1800	Sep. 21, 1804	Nov. 1, 1819
Scouler, J. Braithwaite	,,	....	June 3, 1802	....	....
Spinks, George	,,	....	July 20, 1801	Mar. 1, 1815	Jan. 8, 1826
Smith, William Stewart	,,	....	July 20, 1801	....	....
Smith, James	,,	....	July 20, 1801	Mar. 24, 1815	....
Smyth, John Wickens	,,	....	July 20, 1801	....	....
Stewart, Josiah	,,	....	July 20, 1801	June 12, 1813	Sep. 8, 1826
Stock, Arthur	,,	....	Dec. 29, 1802	June 4, 1817	Apr. 25, 1824
Stone, William	,,	....	July 20, 1801	Aug. 28, 1814	....
Spears, Robert	,,	....	July 20, 1801	Sep. 1, 1818	....
Shaw, James	,,	....	Dec. 22, 1802	....	....
Smyth, Charles Fynch	,,	....	July 20, 1801	April 6, 1810	....
Skene, John	,,	....	July 20, 1801	....	....
Seton, William	,,	....	July 20, 1801	Mar. 16, 1813	....
Short, Robert	,,	....	Mar. 26, 1802	Feb. 24, 1813	May 1, 1824
Seymour, Robert	,,	....	July 20, 1801	....	....
Smith, Charles Wallace	,,	....	July 20, 1801	....	....
Sydenham, George	1801	....	July 2, 1803	May 22, 1813	....
Shairp, Walter *artillery*	,,	....	May 22, 1803	....	....
Salvin, Thomas—*cavalry*	1802	....	May 1, 1804	....	....
Saunders, Thomas	,,	Apr. 17, 1803	Sep. 21, 1804	....	....
Stewart, Duncan	,,	....	Nov. 16, 1803	Dec. 1, 1817	....
Shawe, Geo. Augustus	,,	Apr. 17, 1803	Aug. 9, 1803	....	....
Saunders, Francis David	,,	Apr. 17, 1803	June 1, 1804	Jan. 29, 1814	....
Stewart, Geo. Mackenzie	,,	....	Jan. 1, 1807	Jan. 19, 1816	Oct. 14, 1823
Scott, Hugh	,,	....	Jan. 10, 1804	June 1, 1814	....
Saunders, Wm. Thomas	,,	....	May 1, 1804	July 19, 1817	....
Shirley, Henry	,,	....	Dec. 5, 1803	....	....
Sweetland, Alexander	,,	....	May 1, 1804	....	....
Swan, John Thomas	,,	....	Aug. 28, 1804	April 9, 1815	....
Stewart, David	,,	Apr. 17, 1803	Sep. 25, 1803	....	....
Smyth, Edwin Robinson	,,	....	May 26, 1804	....	....
Scoones, George	,,	....	May 18, 1804	....	....
Smyth, D. Crommelin	,,	....	Mar. 1, 1804	Mar. 23, 1816	Mar. 31, 1822
Swaffield, Henry	,,	....	....	....	....
Stanley, Charles Duplan	1803	....	Sep. 21, 1804	....	....
Smith, H. B.—*cavalry*	,,	Mar. 7, 1805	Oct. 6, 1810	Sep. 1, 1818	Oct. 29, 1833
Smith, G. Fordyce—*cavalry*	,,	Mar. 7, 1805	Oct. 24, 1811	....	....
Scott, John (Senr.)	,,	....	Sep. 21, 1804	....	....
Stewart, Joseph	,,	....	Sep. 21, 1804	....	....
Swinton, James	,,	....	Sep. 21, 1804	....	....
Slade, John	,,	....	Sep. 21, 1804	....	....
Story, William	,,	....	Sep. 21, 1804	....	....

PRESIDENCY.

Lieut.-Colonel.	Colonel.	Major General.	Lieut.-General.	Date of Resignation, Retirement, or Death.
May 6, 1824	....	....	....	Invalided July 31, 1825. Died July 26, 1826, at Armee.
....	....	....	....	Retired Oct. 15, 1823, in England.
Jan. 23, 1830	....	....	....	
....	....	....	....	Died July 28, 1809, at Chittledroog.
May 1, 1824	Jan. 2, 1833	....	....	
....	....	....	....	Died Aug. 13, 1812, at St. Thomé.
....	....	....	....	Retired Sep. 12, 1829, in England.
....	....	....	....	{ Retired Nov. 16, 1810, in India. Died Aug. 14, 1823, at Negapatam.
....	....	....	....	{ Invalided April 13, 1818, in India. Retired May 31, 1833, in India.
....	....	....	....	Died April 18, 1812.
Feb. 4, 1832	....	....	....	
....	....	....	....	Died Aug. 5, 1831, at Ispahan.
....	....	....	....	Retired May 26, 1823.
....	....	....	....	Died May 1, 1829.
....	....	....	....	Died Jan. 24, 1811, at Trichinopoly.
....	....	....	....	{ Died June 6, 1813, with the Field force under Colonel Dowse.
....	....	....	....	Cashiered Aug. 19, 1806.
....	....	....	....	Died May 21, 1813.
May 24, 1828	....	....	....	Retired Sep. 9, 1830, in England.
....	....	....	....	Died Oct. 31, 1809, at Goa.
....	....	....	....	Died July 18, 1808.
....	....	....	....	Resigned Mar. 16, 1822, in England.
....	....	....	....	Died May 25, 1809, at Mysore.
....	....	....	....	Died Oct. 30, 1804.
....	....	....	....	Died Feb. 9, 1806, at Cannanore.
....	....	....	....	Died Aug. 26, 1819, on board the "Richmond."
....	....	....	....	Resigned Oct. 2, 1804.
....	....	....	....	Retired July 28, 1819.
Apr. 11, 1826	Brevet, June 18, 1831	....	....	
....	....	....	....	Died May 11, 1818, at Bombay.
....	....	....	....	Died Oct. 17, 1819, at Sinde Warrah.
....	....	....	....	Died March 22, 1808.
....	....	....	....	Resigned Sep. 24, 1805.
....	....	....	....	Retired Dec. 17, 1824, in India.
....	....	....	....	Died Aug. 17, 1805.
....	....	....	....	Died Nov. 23, 1813, at Masulipatam.
....	....	....	....	{ Died March 17, 1814, on board the "Lord Melville."
May 5, 1825	....	....	....	Died May 23, 1828, at Vellore.
....	....	....	....	Died Oct. 9, 1804.
....	....	....	....	Died Nov. 11, 1810.
....	....	....	....	Died Oct. 27, 1817, at Guntoor.
....	....	....	....	Died June 2, 1818, at Cannanore.
....	....	....	....	Resigned Aug. 11, 1812.
....	....	....	....	Died Nov. 2, 1813, at Fort St. George.
....	....	....	....	Died May 16, 1814, at Trichinopoly.
....	....	....	....	Struck off, in England.

MADRAS.——Y

MADRAS

NAMES.	Cadet.	Cornet, Ensign, or Second Lieutenant.	Lieutenant.	Captain.	Major.
Smart, Charles Kenworthy	1803	....	Sep. 21, 1804	....	....
Stuart, John	,,	....	Sep. 21, 1804	....	....
Say, John Alfred	,,	....	Sep. 21, 1804	Mar. 31, 1818	May 1, 1824
Smith, J. (2nd L.C.)—cavalry	,,	Jan. 19, 1805	Aug. 3, 1809	Feb. 1, 1818	May 20, 1827
Shawe, Richard—cavalry	,,	Mar. 7, 1805	Jan. 22, 1812	Oct. 20, 1823	Feb. 26, 1829
Shakespear, J. N.—cavalry	,,	Mar. 7, 1805	Jan. 17, 1810	....	....
Savery, John—cavalry	,,	July 10, 1804	Mar. 5, 1806	....	....
Spankie, James Shiells	,,	....	Sep. 21, 1804	Sep. 1, 1818	....
Still, William George	,,	....	Sep. 21, 1804	....	....
Sneyd, William Thomas	,,	....	Sep. 21, 1804	Mar. 2, 1819	June 7, 1830
Scott, John (38 N. I.)	,,	....	Sep. 21, 1804	Nov. 5, 1817	April 4, 1825
Sheen, Henry	,,	....	Sep. 21, 1804	....	....
Stewart, Alexander (16 N.I.)	1804	....	July 17, 1805	Sep. 1, 1818	....
Simpson, Robert	,,	....	July 17, 1805	Jan. 1, 1819	....
Smyth, John	,,	....	July 17, 1805	....	....
Stopford, Edward	,,	....	July 17, 1805	....	....
Swanston, Charles	,,	....	July 17, 1805	Apr. 23, 1824	....
Smith, Henry (1 N. I.)	,,	....	Aug. 21, 1805	Feb. 14, 1821	April 2, 1828
Swain, Henry	,,	....	July 17, 1805	....	....
Saunders, Richard	,,	....	....	....	....
Sinclair, James	,,	....	July 17, 1805	....	....
Stewart, James	,,	....	July 17, 1805	....	....
Steel, Scudamore Winde	1805	....	Sep. 11, 1806	May 1, 1824	Dec. 15, 1832
Snowden, Peter	,,	....	Sep. 5, 1806	....	....
Scoones, Thomas Walmore	,,	June 27, 1806	Oct. 21, 1808	....	....
Samuel, E. P.—cavalry	,,	Oct. 9, 1806	Oct. 21, 1812	Sep. 1, 1818	....
Stacey, John Ellis	,,	June 27, 1806	....	....	....
Scott, Gilbert	,,	June 27, 1806	Mar. 5, 1808	....	....
Stuart, William	,,	....	....	....	....
Smith, Clement Fitzwalter	,,	....	Oct. 10, 1807	Oct. 29, 1823	Feb. 3, 1832
Swyer, Robert	,,	June 27, 1806	Mar. 1, 1809	....	....
Sutherland, Eric	,,	....	....	....	....
Sinnock, Charles	,,	June 27, 1806	Dec. 21, 1809	May 1, 1824	....
Strachan, George	,,	June 27, 1806	May 27, 1809	....	....
Shaw, William	,,	June 27, 1806	Mar. 18, 1809	Mar. 17, 1824	July 20, 1836
Scott, William	1806	July 3, 1807	.... 1813...	....	....
Shirriff, Robert Williams	,,	July 3, 1807	June 3, 1812	May 1, 1824	....
Stott, George	,,	July 3, 1807	Nov. 12, 1810	May 27, 1823	Apr. 27, 1834
Storer, Charles	,,	July 3, 1807	Nov. 1, 1809	....	....
Story, George	,,	July 3, 1807	....	....	....
Street, J. C.—cavalry	,,	June 22, 1808	Sep. 7, 1811	July 15, 1819	....
Smithson, Samuel	,,	July 3, 1807	Aug. 17, 1812	....	....
Smyth, Henry—cavalry	,,	Nov. 15, 1809	....	....	....
Stokoe, William	,,	Aug. 3, 1808	Sep. 28, 1812	May 1, 1824	Brevet, Jan. 10, 1837
Shordich, Paul Rycaut	,,	July 3, 1807	....	....	....
Sibbald, Andrew	,,	July 3, 1807	Mar. 28, 1813	July 12, 1824	....
Sharp, Granville	,,	July 3, 1807	Jan. 29, 1810	....	....

PRESIDENCY.

Lieut.-Colonel.	Colonel.	Major General.	Lieut.-General.	Date of Resignation, Retirement, or Death.
....	....	....	....	Died July 10, 1806, at Vellore.
....	....	....	....	Died Dec. 8, 1809, at Chittledroog.
....	....	....	....	Retired from Sep. 16, 1827, in England.
....	....	....	....	Retired May 31, 1833, in India.
....	....	....	....	Died Oct. 9, 1833, at Bellary.
....	....	....	....	Retired May 29, 1818.
....	....	....	....	Retired Oct. 23, 1811.
....	....	....	....	Died Jan. 1, 1821, at Madras.
....	....	....	....	Died Dec. 28, 1808.
Dec. 24, 1835	....	....	....	Died May 11, 1836, at Goondapandy.
Sep. 10, 1830	....	....	....	Retired May 4, 1833.
....	....	....	....	Died May 2, 1818, at Asha.
....	....	....	....	Died May 4, 1824, at Nagpore.
....	....	....	....	Died Sep. 13, 1819, at Madras.
....	....	....	....	Died March 4, 1819, at Palamcottah.
....	....	....	....	Retired Feb. 26, 1816, in England.
....	....	....	....	Retired Jan. 1, 1833, in England.
June 15, 1833	....	....	....	
....	....	....	....	Died July 15, 1817, in camp.
....	....	....	....	Resigned Oct. 9, 1807.
....	....	....	....	Died June 25, 1813, at Nundydroog.
....	....	....	....	Died June 16, 1811, at Madras.
....	....	....	....	Died July 25, 1819, at Bimlipatam.
....	....	....	....	Died Feb. 3, 1813, at Bangalore.
....	....	....	....	Retired May 30, 1824, in England.
....	....	....	....	Died Jan. 8, 1808, at Samulcottah.
....	....	....	....	{ Admitted pensioner on Lord Clive's Fund, July 27, 1814.
....	....	....	....	Resigned Sep. 29, 1807.
April 3, 1837	....	....	....	
....	....	....	....	Died July 11, 1821.
....	....	....	....	{ Died Nov. 10, 1806, at Prince of Wales's Island.
....	....	....	....	Retired Feb. 23, 1833, in India.
....	....	....	....	Died April 6, 1818.
....	....	....	....	Invalided Dec. 9, 1836.
....	....	....	....	Resigned Nov. 12, 1813.
....	....	....	....	Died May 20, 1834, at Russapettah.
....	....	....	....	Died Sep. 27, 1812, at Vizianagrum.
....	....	....	....	Died July 28, 1810, at Cannanore.
....	....	....	....	Pensioned Jan. 2, 1833, in England.
....	....	....	....	Died Mar. 26, 1814, at Jaulnah.
....	....	....	....	Retired April, 1818.
....	....	....	....	Resigned Sep. 26, 1809.
....	....	....	....	Died Aug. 2, 1830, at Vellore.
....	....	....	....	{ Struck off Feb. 6, 1819, having been from India beyond 5 years.

Y 2

MADRAS

NAMES.	Cadet.	Cornet, Ensign, or Second Lieutenant.	Lieutenant.	Captain.	Major.
Smith, George M.—*cavalry*	1806	July 22, 1808	....	....	....
Spicer, Alexander Edwards	,,	July 3, 1807	Aug. 13, 1809	May 1, 1824	....
Smith, Freeman Elton	,,	July 3, 1807	Apr. 6, 1810	May 1, 1824	....
Slade, William H.	,,	July 3, 1807	Oct. 21, 1811	....	....
Snell, Charles	,,	Aug. 27, 1807	Apr. 19, 1810	Mar. 17, 1822	Brevet an. 10, 1837
Seward, Richard	,,	July 3, 1807	Feb. 3, 1813	....	....
Sweetenham, William	,,	....	....	....	....
Scott, James	,,	July 19, 1808	....	....	....
Sergeant, Henry	1807	Aug. 22, 1808	Mar. 27, 1814	Dec. 5, 1824	Nov. 24, 1833
Stockdale, Thomas Richard	,,	Dec. 29, 1808	....	....	....
Smith, Samuel Oliver	,,	Oct. 21, 1808	Jan. 6, 1813	....	....
Stewart, David Carnegie	,,	Feb. 24, 1809	Apr. 29, 1813	....	....
Sinclair, John	,,	Mar. 7, 1809	Feb. 23, 1811	May 1, 1824	....
Strahan, William	,,	Oct. 19, 1808	Apr. 20, 1814	May 1, 1824	June 17, 1830
Spence, Nicol	,,	Mar. 18, 1809	May 7, 1816	....	....
Salmon, Harry	,,	Feb. 2, 1809	Mar. 3, 1813	May 1, 1824	....
Shanahan, Richard	,,	Mar. 18, 1809	April 9, 1812	....	....
Syme, Nichcolas	,,	Dec. 4, 1809	Mar. 23, 1816	....	....
Short, Charles	,,	Aug. 13, 1809	Dec. 9, 1813	....	....
Smith, John Stanley	,,	Jan. 17, 1810	....	....	....
Skinner, David	,,	Nov. 15, 1809	....	....	....
Scott, James	,,	Dec. 14, 1809	Mar. 24, 1815	....	....
Skipp, Geo. Wm. Shaw	,,	Sep. 27, 1809	Feb. 28, 1813	....	....
Sharpe, Samuel Packman	,,	....	....	....	....
Shedden, Robert	,,	Jan. 21, 1810	Jan. 5, 1814	Sep. 8, 1826	....
Searanke, George	,,	Jan. 29, 1810	Mar. 25, 1814	....	....
Scott, William	,,	Mar. 2, 1810	May 17, 1815	Jan. 1, 1825	....
Stewart, James	,,	....	....	....	....
Stuart, Henry—*artillery*	,,	....	Feb. 28, 1810	....	....
Stewart, William	1808	Apr. 7, 1810	May 17, 1814	....	....
Strong, Henry	,,	May 23, 1810	Jan. 4, 1815	....	....
Simpson, James—*cavalry*	,,	....	....	....	....
Stuart, William	1809	Feb. 4, 1811	Mar. 24, 1817	Sep. 12, 1825	June 19, 1835
Sinclair, Charles	1808	May 27, 1810	Sep. 16, 1815	Sep. 8, 1826	....
Slade, William Thomas	1809	June 27, 1810	Sep. 27, 1813	May 1, 1824	....
Stiggall, John	,,	Nov. 7, 1810	....	....	....
Sim, Duncan—*engineers*	,,	July 7, 1810	Dec. 7, 1813	May 9, 1821	Nov. 4, 1826
Sandby, Thos. M.—*artillery*	,,	July 7, 1810	....	....	....
Sweny, Wellbore	,,	Oct. 9, 1810	....	....	....
Stuart, Samuel	1810	Apr. 3, 1811	Oct. 25, 1815	Brevet Apr.—1826.	....
Swaine, Thomas	,,	Aug. 27, 1811	Nov. 11, 1814	Dec. 18, 1824	....
Straton, Francis—*cavalry*	,,	Jan. 17, 1814	Sep. 1, 1818	Feb. 21, 1825	....
Smart, Hamilton Edmund	,,	Oct. 17, 1811	July 24, 1815	....	....
Stodart, John	1811	June 11, 1812	Sep. 10, 1813	....	....
Smith, J. (2 Rgt.)—*cavalry*	,,	Jan. 16, 1816	Sep. 1, 1818	Dec. 21, 1825	May 13, 1837
Symes, Geo. F.—*artillery*	1812	July 6, 1813	Sep. 1, 1818	May 23, 1825	....
Sandys, George—*cavalry*	,,	July 29, 1815	Oct. 18, 1818	Jan. 2, 1826	May 11, 1833

PRESIDENCY.

Lieut.-Colonel.	Colonel.	Major General.	Lieut.-General.	Date of Resignation, Retirement, or Death.
....	....	....	....	Died Sep. 14, 1819, at Madras.
....	....	....	....	Died Dec. 25, 1833, at Masulipatam.
....	....	....	....	Retired July 9, 1834, in England.
....	....	....	....	Retired May 12, 1817, at St. Thomé.
....	....	....	....	
....	....	....	....	Died April 17, 1816.
....	....	....	....	Died 1807, on his passage to India.
....	....	....	....	Died May 22, 1810.
....	....	....	....	
....	....	....	....	Resigned Dec. 1, 1809.
....	....	....	....	Died April 19, 1822, at Bengal.
....	....	....	....	Died Sep. 30, 1823.
....	....	....	....	Died Aug. 12, 1827, near Buzuah.
Dec. 24, 1835	....	....	....	
....	....	....	....	Died Sep. 18, 1818, at Hydrabad.
....	....	....	....	Invalided May 21, 1833, in India.
....	....	....	....	{ Died Jan. 2, 1818, of wounds received in action, on Dec. 21, 1817.
....	....	....	....	Died July 6, 1819, at Mundlasir.
....	....	....	....	{ Invalided Oct. 31, 1818. Died Feb. 7, 1820, at Bangalore.
....	....	....	....	Died June 26, 1811, at Haliburton's Gardens.
....	....	....	....	Resigned May 16, 1815, in England.
....	....	....	....	Died Dec. 28, 1815, at Seringapatam.
....	....	....	....	Struck off, April 14, 1817.
....	....	....	....	Retired April 15, 1809.
....	....	....	....	Died July 25, 1828, at Vizianagrum.
....	....	....	....	Struck off, beyond the period.
....	....	....	....	Died Sep. 27, 1828, at Anantopore.
....	....	....	....	Died Mar. 18, 1809, at St. Thomas's Mount.
....	....	....	....	Died Nov. 29, 1811.
....	....	....	....	Died May 13, 1820, at Madras.
....	....	....	....	Retired Sep. 26, 1822, in England.
....	....	....	....	Resigned April 24, 1810.
....	....	....	....	Retired Jan. 25, 1836, in India.
....	....	....	....	
....	....	....	....	{ Died May 5, 1826, on board the "Neptune," for England.
....	....	....	....	Struck off, in England.
Sep. 2, 1836	....	....	....	
....	....	....	....	Died Oct. 24, 1812, in camp, near Hubely.
....	....	....	....	Resigned Aug. 13, 1813.
....	....	....	....	Invalided Aug. 1. 1828, in India.
....	....	....	....	Died Dec. 19, 1835, at Berhampore.
....	....	....	....	
....	....	....	....	Died Mar. 12, 1826, at Madras.
....	....	....	....	Died May 13, 1818, at Jaulnah.
....	....	....	....	
....	....	....	....	Retired May 28, 1832, in England.
....	....	....	....	
....	....	....	....	

MADRAS

NAMES.	Cadet.	Cornet, Ensign, or Second Lieutenant.	Lieutenant.	Captain.	Major.
Sewell, Richard—*artillery*	1812	July 6, 1813	Sep. 1, 1818	....	....
Seton, R. Somner—*artillery*	,,	July 6, 1813	Sep. 1, 1818	June 10, 1825	....
Stiell, J. Henry—*artillery*	1813	July 4, 1814	Sep. 1, 1818	....	....
Shirreff, Eneas—*artillery*	1814	July 11, 1815	Oct. 25, 1818	May 8, 1827	....
Storey, George	1816	....	April 6, 1818	Oct. 14, 1824	Dec. 24, 1835
Stedman, John Cambridge	,,	....	Dec. 2, 1816	Oct. 8, 1824	....
Scott, Francis Charles	1817	....	June 4, 1818	Dec. 24, 1831	....
Stockwell, Thomas	,,	....	June 4, 1818	July 19, 1828	....
Sutton, John Dilnot	,,	....	....	....	....
Smyth, M. W. C.—*cavalry*	,,	June 3, 1818	July 5, 1819	Jan. 1, 1827	....
Stokes, John Day	,,	....	Oct. 28, 1818	Aug. 18, 1827	Apr. 10, 1836
Smith, Richard	,,	....	Oct. 1, 1818	June 20, 1824	....
Smith, Frederick	1818	....	June 13, 1819	....	....
Simons, D. H.—*cavalry*	,,	....	Oct. 26, 1819	....	....
Smith, William Hope	,,	....	June 13, 1819	Jan. 7, 1828	Feb. 20, 1836
Stewart, Richard	,,	....	June 13, 1819	....	....
Sandys, James	1819	....	June 13, 1819	Oct. 8, 1829	....
Servante, Edward	,,	....	April 7, 1820	June 30, 1829	....
St. John, Oliver	,,	....	April 7, 1820	July 13, 1831	....
Scot, William C.	,,	....	....	....	....
Seale, Francis	,,	....	Aug. 21, 1820	....	....
Shee, Benjamin Basil	,,	....	April 7, 1820	July 13, 1831	....
Seddon, James Holland	,,	....	April 7, 1820	....	....
Sparrow, Henry William	,,	....	April 7, 1820	....	....
Sheil, John	,,	....	Oct. 1, 1820	May 25, 1833	....
Short, Hubert	,,	....	June 10, 1820	....	....
Scott, Carteret George	,,	....	June 5, 1820	Jan. 23, 1830	....
Shepherd, John	,,	....	April 7, 1820	.... 1837 ..	....
Sturrock, Henry	,,	April 6, 1820	....	....	....
Sandford, John Robert	,,	....	Jan. 17, 1821	May 9, 1832	....
Symons, Thomas Edward	,,	April 6, 1820	....	....	....
Sherman, J. Standiver	,,	April 6, 1820	Oct. 14, 1821	Brevet, Apr. 6, 1835.	....
Stinton, Thomas Colley	,,	April 6, 1820	Dec. 1, 1821	....	....
Stephenson, Mowbray	,,	....	Apr. 25, 1821	....	....
Senior, Francis Stephen	,,	April 6, 1820	Apr. 24, 1823	Brevet, Apr. 6, 1835.	....
Stapylton, Bryan	1820	April 6, 1820	Dec. 4, 1823	....	....
Sinclair, William—*cavalry*	,,	Feb. 13, 1821	May 1, 1824	Apr. 9, 1830	....
Steinson, Peter	,,	....	June 20, 1822	Feb. 5, 1833	....
Sotheby, George Hull	,,	Feb. 13, 1821	Dec. 25, 1822	June 5, 1830	....
Short, William Holwell	,,	Feb. 13, 1821	Dec. 28, 1823	May 17, 1829	....
Stevenson, James	,,	Feb. 13, 1821	May 1, 1824	....	....
Setree, Thomas	,,	Feb. 13, 1821	Mar. 17, 1824	....	....
Shaw, Joseph Edmund B.	,,	Feb. 13, 1821	....	....	....
Shelley, William	,,	Feb. 13, 1821	July 17, 1824	Brevet, Feb. 13, 1836.	....
Sayers, James Robert	,,	Feb. 13, 1821	Nov. 23, 1823	....	....
Shennon, John Aylmer	,,	Feb. 13, 1821	May 19, 1825	....	....
Symes, Richard Henry	,,	Feb. 13, 1821	Apr. 4, 1825	....	....

PRESIDENCY.

Lieut.-Colonel.	Colonel.	Major-General.	Lieut.-General.	Date of Resignation, Retirement, or Death.
				Died Nov. 5, 1824, at Dharwar.
				Died Dec. 1, 1825, at Cuddalore.
				Discharged the Service, Jan. 31, 1837, in India.
				Killed Jan. 11, 1826, at Setoun.
				Died July 22, 1819, on his way to Jaulnah.
				Retired June 12, 1832, in England.
				Died June 19, 1828, on board the "Lady Faversham," off the Cape.
				Resigned Dec. 21, 1827, in India.
				Died Sep. 8, 1822, in England.
				Died Dec. 25, 1820, at Trichinopoly.
				Dismissed May 24, 1830, in India.
				Died Jan. 17, 1821, at Trichinopoly.
				Died Feb. 20, 1823, at Nundydroog.
				[the "Warrior." Died June 22, 1832, at sea, on board
				Died Dec. 25, 1825, on board the "Cambridge," for England.
				Died Nov. 30, 1821, at Nagpore.
				Retired Mar. 27, 1835, in India.
				Died Dec. 12, 1821, at Jaulnah.
				Died May 5, 1821, at Chichacole.
				Invalided Dec. 4, 1829, in India. Died Sep. 18, 1831, at Vizagapatam.
				Died July 30, 1826, at Madras.
				Resigned Jan. 4, 1828, in India.
				Retired Jan. 1, 1833, in England.
				Retired Sep. 10, 1830, in England.
				Died June 17, 1831, on board the "Georgiana."
				Died Oct. 30, 1828, at Kulladgee.
				Died Sep. 23, 1824, at Cuddapah.
				Died July 20, 1834, at Madras.
				Died Feb. 7, 1832, at Penang.
				Died April 2, 1835, on board the "Madras."

MADRAS

NAMES.	Cadet.	Cornet, Ensign, or Second Lieutenant.	Lieutenant.	Captain.	Major.
Scott, Walter	1820	Feb. 13, 1821	Sep. 24, 1824		
Shirrifs, Alexander	,,	Feb. 13, 1821	April 10, 1824	Brevet Feb. 13, 1836	
Simpson, Edward	,,		Sep. 21, 1823	June 19, 1835	
Sparrow, Richard Wheeler	,,	Feb. 13, 1821	Oct. 30, 1823	Apr. 24, 1834	
Scotland, David	,,	Feb. 13, 1821	Jan. 8, 1826	Mar. 31, 1836	
Stokes, William	1821	Apr. 27, 1822	May 11, 1824		
Symons, John	,,	Apr. 27, 1822	Mar. 31, 1824		
Sturt, Oliver Frederick	,,	Apr. 27, 1822	Aug. 19, 1824		
Stuart, Jas. Chas. G.	,,	Apr. 27, 1822	Dec. 6, 1824	Jan. 10, 1837	
Stewart, Alexander	,,				
Simpson, Wm. Hervey	,,	Apr. 27, 1822	May 1, 1826	April 1, 1833	
Sewell, Thomas	,,	Apr. 6, 1820	Feb. 8, 1825	Nov. 23, 1831	
Stirling, Peter Murdoch	,,	Apr. 27, 1822	Jan. 2, 1826		
Smith, Thos. Richmond	,,	Apr. 27, 1822	July 2, 1825		
Smyth, Jas. Watson	,,	Apr. 27, 1822	Oct. 8, 1824	May 2, 1833	
Smith, Geo. F.—*engineers*	,,		May 1, 1824		
Smith, Henry (2 N. I.)	,,	Apr. 27, 1822			
Stafford, Conway	,,	Apr. 27, 1822	Jan. 3, 1825		
Smith, Geo. Atwell	,,	Apr. 27, 1822	Sep. 8, 1826		
Saxon, Wm. Augustus	,,	Apr. 27, 1822			
Simpson, Edmund Jas.	,,	Apr. 27, 1822	Sep. 8, 1826		
Spry, George	,,	Apr. 27, 1822	Oct. 16, 1824		
Smithwaite, G. P. C.	,,	Apr. 27, 1822			
Sprye, Rich. Sam. Mare	1822	May 2, 1823	Mar. 15, 1827		
Sinclair, James	,,	May 2, 1823			
Strettell, Dashwood	,,	May 2, 1823	Jan. 18, 1826		
Smith, John	,,	May 2, 1823	Jan. 4, 1826		
Snow, Edw. Winterton	,,	May 2, 1823	Sep. 8, 1826		
Shairp, Walter—*cavalry*	,,		Nov. 6, 1824		
Savage, James R.	1823	May 14, 1824			
Sherriff, Robert	,,	May 14, 1824	April 4, 1827	Jan. 9, 1836	
Seagram, Edgar	1824				
Scutt, Ralph R.	,,	May 6, 1825	May 27, 1827		
Silver, Thos. Goldie	,,	May 6, 1825	May 31, 1827		
Strettell, John W.—*cavalry*	,,	May 6, 1825	Dec. 5, 1826	Feb. 24, 1836	
Smith, Geo. T.—*engineers*	,,		June 18, 1824	Mar. 5, 1835	
Strickland, William	,,	May 6, 1825	Dec. 21, 1830		
Simpson, G. W. Y.—*artillery*	,,		June 28, 1824		
Stackpoole, Thomas	,,	June 8, 1826	June 19, 1828		
Sharp, Thomas	,,	May 14, 1824	July 10, 1826	Jan. 24, 1835	
Stoddart, John Alfred	,,	Jan. 8, 1826	Dec. 16, 1832		
Strange, W. R.—*cavalry*	,,		July 30, 1827		
Smith, H. S. O.	1825	Jan. 8, 1827	Sep. 28, 1828		
Spence, Nicholas	,,	Jan. 8, 1826			
Steele, Thos. William	,,	Jan. 8, 1826	Sep. 5, 1834		
Sullivan, B. S.—*cavalry*	,,	Jan. 8, 1826	July 19, 1828		
Sherwood, Jas. Isaac	,,	Jan. 8, 1826	Nov. 1, 1828		

PRESIDENCY.

Lieut.-Colonel.	Colonel.	Major-General.	Lieut.-General.	Date of Resignation, Retirement, or Death.
....	....	....	....	Invalided Aug. 14, 1832, in India.
....	....	....	....	
....	....	....	....	
....	....	....	....	
....	....	....	....	
....	....	....	....	Died May 22, 1825, at Prome.
....	....	....	....	Died March 24, 1835, at Salem.
....	....	....	....	
....	....	....	....	
....	....	....	....	{ Died March 13, 1822, on board the "Duchess of Athol," on passage to India.
....	....	....	....	Died Aug. 2, 1836, at Goomsoor.
....	....	....	....	{ Pensioned on Lord Clive's Fund, Apr. 23, 1826, in England.
....	....	....	....	Resigned March 3, 1827, in England.
....	....	....	....	Resigned June 19, 1836, in India.
....	....	....	....	Died Aug. 21, 1824, at Madras.
....	....	....	....	Resigned June 3, 1825, in India.
....	....	....	....	
....	....	....	....	{ Died Apr. 6, 1825, at Kutgoondah, near Hydrabad.
....	....	....	....	Died Nov. 30, 1830, at Fort William.
....	....	....	....	Died Nov. 9, 1825, at Prome.
....	....	....	....	
....	....	....	....	Died June 20, 1826, in England.
....	....	....	....	
....	....	....	....	{ Pensioned Aug. 2, 1830, in India. Died May 13, 1831.
....	....	....	....	{ Invalided July 21, 1826, in India. Pensioned Jan. 30, 1829, in India. Died Aug. 16, 1830, at Ellore.
....	....	....	....	Died Nov. 10, 1825, at Mahutte, in Arracan.
....	....	....	....	{ Died Feb. 6, 1825, on board the "Lady Campbell," on his passage to India.
....	....	....	....	
....	....	....	....	
....	....	....	....	Died March 13, 1832, at Palamcottah.
....	....	....	....	Died July 11, 1834.
....	....	....	....	Retired Feb. 1, 1836, in England.
....	....	....	....	
....	....	....	....	
....	....	....	....	Died Feb. 12, 1328, in Koolapore.
....	....	....	....	
....	....	....	....	
....	....	....	....	

MADRAS.—Z

MADRAS

NAMES.	Cadet.	Cornet, Ensign, or Second Lieutenant.	Lieutenant.	Captain.	Major.
Stewart, James (7 N. I.) ..	1825	Jan. 8, 1826	Apr. 28, 1830	....	....
Smythe, John Groome	,,	Jan. 8, 1826	Nov. 6, 1835	....	....
Stokes, Oliver Day........	,,	Jan. 8, 1826	Mar. 19, 1831	....	....
Showers, E. S. G.—*artillery*	,,	....	Dec. 21, 1828	....	....
Shaw, Ponsonby	1826	Jan. 8, 1826	Nov. 26, 1828	....	....
Salter, John H.—*artillery*..	,,	June 16, 1826	....	....	....
Salmon, James Charles	,,	Jan. 8, 1826	Nov. 8, 1831	Apr. 28, 1836	....
Stewart, Hopton	,,	Jan. 8, 1826	Apr. 3, 1833	....	....
Stephenson, Edward Boyd	,,	....	Nov. 27, 1828	....	....
Starkey, John William C. ..	,,	Jan. 5, 1827	Oct. 17, 1834	....	....
Salmon, Arthur	,,	Jan. 16, 1827	Apr. 17, 1834	....	....
Stevenson, Edward........	,,	....	July 6, 1831	....	....
Sanson, Francis Henry....	,,	Mar. 5, 1827	Feb. 10, 1837	....	....
Stapleton, John Harrison ..	,,	Nov. 7, 1827	....	....	....
Smith, Josiah	,,	May 29, 1827	....	....	....
Sherard, Caryer	,,	Dec. 15, 1827	....	....	....
Sharp, George William....	,,	Oct. 22, 1827	Dec. 12, 1831	....	....
Sibbald, John	,,	Nov. 2, 1827	Apr. 1, 1835	....	....
Starke, James Ravenscroft	,,	Oct. 11, 1827	....	....	....
Stephenson, E. J.—*cavalry*	,,	May 20, 1827	....	....	....
Seager, John	,,	Nov. 24, 1827	Apr. 13, 1833	....	....
Sibbald, John	,,	Nov. 2, 1827	April 1, 1835	....	....
Slack, Edward............	,,	Oct. 16, 1827	....	....	....
Short, Edward Holwell	,,	June 21, 1828	Mar. 31, 1832	....	....
Shairp, Stephen William ..	1827	Oct. 28, 1828	....	....	....
Singleton, George	,,	Nov. 27, 1828	Sep. 26, 1835	....	....
Stephenson, John Lionel ..	,,	Apr. 29, 1830	May 8, 1835	....	....
Spry, Philip Lane	1828	May 18, 1831	Apr. 11, 1837	....	....
Seppings, William Lawless	,,	Mar. 19, 1831	....	....	....
Snow, Raymond Torin	,,	Apr. 29, 1829	Nov. 16, 1836	....	....
Shaw, John C.—*engineers* ..	,,	Dec. 13, 1827	Mar. 5, 1835	....	....
Stuart, Ferdinand Stuart S.	,,	Oct. 12, 1831	....	....	....
Scafe, William............	,,	Jan. 4, 1832	May 25, 1835	....	....
Smythe, Thomas—*engineers*	,,	July 23, 1829	Oct. 2, 1836	....	....
Simpson, Francis—*cavalry*	,,	Oct. 29, 1830	Oct. 27, 1834	....	....
Stewart, John	1829	May 16, 1832	Dec. 19, 1835	....	....
Snell, Thomas—*cavalry* ...	,,	Feb. 7, 1832	Apr. 25, 1834	....	....
Saunders, W. W.—*engineers*	,,	....	....	....	....
Selby, George—*artillery* ..	,,	July 29, 1833	....	....	....
Stevens, W. B.—*artillery* ..	1830	Feb. 2, 1836	....	....	....
Snow, Percy T.	,,	July 14, 1832	June 20, 1837	....	....
Studdy, Frederick—*cavalry*	1831	Feb. 17, 1834	May 2, 1835	....	....
Strettell, George James....	,,	....	....	....	....
Snow, William Stephen....	,,	Nov. 24, 1832	....	....	....
Sibley, Edward Reynolds ..	1832	Jan. 1, 1833	Jan. 31, 1837	....	....
Stevens, Josiah Fisher	,,	Feb. 3, 1833	May 31, 1836	....	....
Seton, Fredrick B.—*cavalry*	,,	Mar. 17, 1834	....	....	....

PRESIDENCY.

Lieut.-Colonel.	Colonel.	Major-General.	Lieut.-General.	Date of Resignation, Retirement, or Death.
				Died Aug. 8, 1831, at Nugger.
				Died Oct. 16, 1836, in camp, at [Goomsoor.
				{ Invalided Mar. 12, 1833, in India. Died June 2, 1834, at Vizagapatam.
				Died Feb. 22, 1831, at Salem.
				Killed Jan. 12, 1834, in Kemedy.
				Resigned Dec. 10, 1833, in England.
				Discharged Sep. 9, 1831, in India.
				Died April 28, 1830, at Trikmullah.
				Died Nov. 24, 1835, at Secunderabad.
				[of Malown."
				Died Dec. 12, 1836, on board the "Hero
				Resigned Feb. 8, 1832, in England.
				{ Died Oct. 28, 1833, on board the "Lord William Bentinck."
				Died Oct. 18, 1834, at Bangalore.

Z 2

MADRAS

NAMES.	Cadet.	Cornet, Ensign, or Second Lieutenant.	Lieutenant.	Captain.	Major.
Scott, John D.—*artillery*	1832				
Strettell, Edw.—*artillery*	,,				
Sellon, Edward	,,	Feb. 8, 1834			
Siddons, H. F.—*cavalry*	,,	Feb. 1, 1834	Jan. 5, 1836		
Steer, H. Ratbray Hall	,,	Dec. 13, 1833	Sep. 22, 1835		
Spottiswoode, M. Capel	1833	Feb. 15, 1834			
Sturrock, George	,,	Dec. 13, 1833	June 7, 1836		
Scott, F. H.—*cavalry*	,,		Feb. 14, 1835		
Skelton, J. W.—*cavalry*	,,	April 3, 1834			
St. George, William	,,	June 14, 1834			
Strange, Alex.—*cavalry*	,,	June 22, 1834	May 10, 1837		
Shawe, Robert	1834	Dec. 13, 1834			
T					
Trent, Thomas	1766	Nov. 14, 1767	July 27, 1769		Apr. 17, 1786
Tolson, Richard			July 22, 1770		July 22, 1786
Taylor, John	1768	Aug. 6, 1770		Jan. 7, 1782	
Towns, Stephen	1769	Nov. 4, 1770	June 5, 1775	May 29, 1783	
Torrens, Francis	,,	Dec. 10, 1770	Sep. 10, 1776	Nov. 2, 1783	...1794...
Turing, James	1771	May 1, 1773		Nov. 16, 1783	
Taylor, Aldwell	1775	Aug. 26, 1776	Nov. 12, 1780	Sep. 28, 1791	June 1, 1796
Tolfrey, Edward	,,	Aug. 31, 1776	Nov. 15, 1780	July 16, 1792	June 1, 1796
Turing, Robert	1778	Apr. 24, 1779	May 9, 1784	June 1, 1796	Dec. 17, 1799
Tyrrell, James	,,	May 6, 1779	Nov. 19, 1784	June 1, 1796	
Turner, James	1779	July 31, 1779	Apr. 17, 1786		
Taylor, John, Junr	,,		Apr. 17, 1786	June 1, 1796	
Taylor, John	1780	Oct. 30, 1781			
Trotter, Charles	1781	Nov. 16, 1782	Aug. 21, 1790	Dec. 26, 1798	Sep. 21, 1804
Tanner, Edward—*artillery*		Jan. 4, 1768			
Tutt, Robert—*artillery*	1771		July 25, 1778	Aug. 1, 1781	Feb. 4, 1791
Tonyn, J. C.—*cavalry*				July 3, 1770	Sep. 26, 1785
Trapaud, Elisha—*engineers*	1778	Apr. 14, 1779		May 16, 1784	Aug. 16, 1793
Tanner, John A.—*artillery*	1799	Mar. 20, 1781	June 2, 1783	Mar. 18, 1791	April 4, 1804
Taylor, John, Sen	1778	Sep. 11, 1778	Oct. 31, 1783	June 1, 1796	Dec. 10, 1799
Taynton, John—*artillery*	1789	May 11, 1790	May 18, 1794	Oct. 5, 1801	July 19, 1809
Tichborne, Thomas	,,		Oct. 2, 1792	Jan. 16, 1800	Apr. 23, 1806
Thompson, Francis	1790	July 21, 1791	Dec. 5, 1793	Aug. 27, 1800	Nov. 22, 1808
Tunston, James		Sep. 19, 1791	Aug. 6, 1794		
Torin, John—*cavalry*			Jan. 19, 1782	June 1, 1796	Nov. 1, 1798
Torriano, Hilary Harcourt	1794	Dec. 22, 1795	May 29, 1798	Jan. 1, 1806	
Taylor, Sutton	,,	Jan. 5, 1796	June 1, 1796	July 11, 1802	
Taylor, Joseph	1795	Mar. 1, 1796	July 13, 1797		
Torriano, Charles	,,		Nov. 29, 1797		
Turner, John	1796	Aug. 21, 1797	Oct. 12, 1798	Dec. 12, 1804	
Temple, John Jas.—*cavalry*	1797	Aug. 25, 1798	Sep. 4, 1799		
Taylor, Robert—*artillery*	1795	Mar. 16, 1796	May 5, 1799	May 29, 1806	Sep. 1, 1818
Turner, Robert Cantley	1796	Sep. 19, 1797	Oct. 12, 1798		
Taylor, Hen. Geo. Andrew	1798		Dec. 15, 1800	June 24, 1807	Nov. 28, 1816
Townsend, Henry	,,		Jan. 1, 1800	Dec. 18, 1805	

PRESIDENCY.

172—173

Lieut.-Colonel.	Colonel.	Major-General.	Lieut.-General.	Date of Resignation, Retirement, or Death.
●	....	....	....	
....	....	....	....	
....	....	....	....	Pensioned May 31, 1836, at Cuddalore.
....	....	....	....	
....	....	....	....	
....	....	....	....	
....	....	....	....	
....	....	....	....	
....	....	....	....	Died June 27, 1837, at Arcot.
....	....	....	....	Died Sep. 2, 1836, at Goomsoor.
....	....	....	....	
....	....	....	....	
Feb. 6, 1787	June 1, 1796	Jan. 1, 1798	....	{ Retired April 8, 1808, on the Off-Reckoning Fund. Died May 22, 1825, in London.
Dec. 29, 1789	June 1, 1796	Jan. 1, 1798	....	{ Retired Nov. 22, 1808, on the Off-Reckoning Fund. Died June 14, 1815, in England
....	....	....	....	Died Aug. 31, 1789.
....	....	....	....	Invalided 1789. Dismissed 1793.
June 1, 1796	June 17, 1800	Apr. 25, 1808	June 4, 1813	Died Aug. 5, 1820, at Fort St. George.
....	....	....	....	Died 1793.
May 19, 1799	Commt. June 21, 1807. Col. Oct. 25, 1809.	Jan. 1, 1812	....	{ Died Dec. 6, 1817, on board the "Boyne," on his passage to England.
July 31, 1799	....	....	....	Died March 26, 1801.
....	....	....	....	Died June 5, 1801.
....	....	....	....	Died Nov. — 1796.
....	....	....	....	Not to be traced.
....	....	....	....	Died 1796.
....	....	....	....	Pensioned. Died Jan. 17, 1792, at Trivatore.
Sep. 29, 1808	Brevet June 4, 1814.	....	....	Died June 11, 1819, at Cotallum.
Apr. 17, 1786	....	....	....	Died 1789.
....	....	....	....	{ Invalided. In Europe on health, 1795. Retired 1796.
....	....	....	....	Resigned Jan. — 1791.
Aug. 12, 1802	Jan. 1, 1803	July 25, 1810	June 4, 1814	Died March 24, 1828, in England.
Sep. 21, 1804	....	....	....	Died July 3, 1807.
Jan. 2, 1804	....	....	....	Retired March 15, 1805.
Sep. 1, 1818	....	....	....	{ Invalided Oct. 16, 1821. Died June 9, 1831, at Madras.
Dec. 11, 1813	....	....	....	{ Invalided July 22, 1814. Died Nov. 2, 1818, at Chicacole.
Feb. 20, 1815	....	....	....	Died Sep. 28, 1817, at Mulliot.
....	....	....	....	Died Oct. 17, 1797.
Sep. 4, 1799	....	....	....	{ Died May 10, 1801, on board the "Prince William Henry," coming home.
....	....	....	....	Resigned Apr. 12, 1797. Died Feb. 7, 1815, at Ennore.
....	....	....	....	Died June 30, 1803, at Nellore.
....	....	....	....	Died Dec. 14, 1800.
....	....	....	....	Died June 28, 1801.
....	....	....	....	Died Oct. 23, 1809, at Seringapatam.
....	....	....	....	Not to be traced.
Jan. 26, 1822	....	....	....	{ Invalided May 20, 1823, in India. Died Aug. 4, 1825, in London.
....	....	....	....	Died May 17, 1804, at Fort St. George.
Jan. 24, 1823	Commt. June 18, 1825 Col. June 5, 1829	....	....	
....	....	....	....	Lost in a Dow in the Persian Gulph, 1812.

MADRAS

NAMES.	Cadet.	Cornet, Ensign, or Second Lieutenant.	Lieutenant.	Captain.	Major.
Taggart, John	1799	....	Dec. 15, 1800	....	....
Trewman, John Turner	,,	....	Dec. 15, 1800	Mar. 14, 1813	May 1, 1824
Tichborne, B. E.—*cavalry*	,,	Sep. 30, 1801	May 1, 1804	April 6, 1810	....
Tolfrey, Charles Frederick	1800	....	July 15, 1800	June 27, 1811	Feb. 14, 1821
Tucker, George—*cavalry*	,,	Aug. 17, 1801	....	Oct. 2, 1803	....
Tytler, William	,,	....	....	Sep. 23, 1802	....
Tagg, James	,,	....	July 20, 1801	May 1, 1815	....
Turner, Alexander	,,	....	July 20, 1801	Nov. 24, 1812	Nov. 2, 1824
Thompson, Thomas	,,	....	July 20, 1801	....	....
Turner, Charles—*cavalry*	,,	Feb. 10, 1802	May 1, 1804	....	....
Townsend, John William	1802	....	....	....	....
Tabois Richard John	,,	....	May 9, 1804	Aug. 1, 1817	....
Taylor, William	,,	....	Sep. 21, 1804	....	....
Tichborne, John Michael	1803	....	Sep. 21, 1804	....	....
Talbot, John Henry	,,	....	Sep. 21, 1804	Oct. 10, 1819	....
Tullock, Alexander	,,	....	Sep. 21, 1804	July 22, 1820	Nov. 20, 1830
Trotter, John Spottiswoode	,,	....	Sep. 21, 1804	Mar. 14, 1822	....
Turton, Henry—*cavalry*	,,	....	Sep. 4, 1805	....	....
Temple, Charles—*cavalry*	1804	July 7, 1806	Jan. 17, 1814	Dec. 3, 1820	....
Trewman, Zachary Turner	,,	....	July 17, 1805	....	....
Tweedie, Maurice	,,	....	July 17, 1805	May 1, 1824	May 15, 1833
Torriano, Josias	,,	....	July 17, 1805	Nov. 11, 1818	....
Taylor, James	,,	....	July 17, 1805	Jan. 26, 1822	....
Tocker, Hannibal	,,	....	July 25, 1805	May 28, 1820	....
Tocker, John	,,	....	July 17, 1805	Nov. 29, 1821	July 1, 1833
Townesend, Stephen	1805	....	Aug. 20, 1806	Dec. 10, 1817	Feb. 24, 1828
Tennent, James	,,	....	Dec. 26, 1806	Dec. 10, 1819	Aug. 8, 1829
Tristram, W. B.—*cavalry*	,,	June 27, 1806	....	....	....
Taylor, John Keating	,,	....	....	....	....
Thompson, William	,,	June 27, 1806	Oct. 10, 1810	Nov. 28, 1823	....
Thomson, William Richard	,,	June 27, 1806	Apr. 13, 1810	....	....
Tolson, George Buchan	1806	July 3, 1807	Nov. 1, 1809	May 1, 1824	July 6, 1833
Taylor, Joseph	,,	July 3, 1807	June 29, 1810	....	....
Thompson, John	,,	July 3, 1807	Mar. 9, 1811	....	....
Tulk, John	,,	July 3, 1807	Oct. 9, 1810	....	....
Tombs, Richard	,,	July 3, 1807	June 29, 1810	....	....
Ternan, Richard	,,	July 3, 1807	June 26, 1813	....	....
Turner, Charles	,,	July 3, 1807	May 9, 1811	....	....
Thompson, H. Alexander	,,	June 23, 1808	Mar. 31, 1813	....	....
Taylor, Richard	,,	July 3, 1807	Nov. 20, 1813	Jan. 13, 1825	....
Taylor, William	,,	July 3, 1807	Aug. 27, 1811	May 1, 1824	Sep. 26, 1835
Travis, Thomas Hardy	,,	July 3, 1807	May 9, 1812	....	....
Tweedie, Alexander	,,	Aug. 19, 1808	June 23, 1811	....	....
Thuillier, Thomas	1807	Nov. 22, 1808	Aug. 30, 1814	Apr. 11, 1826	....
Thoresby, T. H.—*artillery*	,,	....	Mar. 18, 1809	May 26, 1819	....
Truman, Avery	,,	Dec. 15, 1808	Oct. 4, 1813	....	....
Tod, John (33 N. I.)	,,	Aug. 28, 1808	Nov. 8, 1812	May 1, 1824	Jan. 21, 1835

PRESIDENCY.

Lient.-Colonel.	Colonel.	Major-General.	Lieut.-General.	Date of Resignation, Retirement, or Death.
....	....	....	....	Died July 13, 1803.
Feb. 27, 1827	Brevet June 18, 1831	....	....	
....	....	....	....	Died Oct. 5, 1810.
....	....	....	....	Died Oct. 13, 1823.
....	....	....	....	Died Aug. 14, 1804, in camp, near Poonah.
....	....	....	....	Retired April 8, 1815, in England.
....	....	....	....	Died Dec. 13, 1825, at Kamptee.
....	....	....	....	{ Invalided Sep. 19, 1826, in India; died March 6, 1832.
....	....	....	....	Died Sept. 3, 1808, at Bangalore.
....	....	....	....	Died Dec. 17, 1808, at Mysore.
....	....	....	....	Died Mar. 10, 1804, at Gooty.
....	....	....	....	Retired June 19, 1828, in England.
....	....	....	....	Died Aug. 20, 1808, at Wallajahbad.
....	....	....	....	Died July 10, 1806, at Vellore.
....	....	....	....	Died July — 1821.
Mar. 31, 1836	....	....	....	
....	....	....	....	Died Aug. 18, 1824, at Rangoon.
....	....	....	....	Retired Aug. 1, 1815, in England.
....	....	....	....	Died Nov. 5, 1824, in camp, at Gooty.
....	....	....	....	Died Dec. 1, 1811.
....	....	....	....	Resigned Feb. 27, 1820, in England.
....	....	....	....	Died Dec. 28, 1822, at Secunderabad.
....	....	....	....	Retired Oct. 24, 1826, in England.
....	....	....	....	Died June 5, 1837, at Bolarum.
June 6, 1833	....	....	....	
....	....	....	....	Retired May 17, 1831, in India.
....	....	....	....	Died June 20, 1807.
....	....	....	....	Resigned June 6, 1807.
....	....	....	....	{ Died April 13, 1828, at sea, on board the " Upton Castle."
....	....	....	....	Died Oct. 23, 1816, in camp, near [Ellichpore.
....	....	....	....	Died March 3, 1818, in camp, near Poonah.
....	....	....	....	Died March 16, 1814, at Fort St. George.
....	....	....	....	Died March 27, 1821, at Cuddalore.
....	....	....	....	Died Nov. 7, 1812.
....	....	....	....	Died May 6, 1822, at Vellore.
....	....	....	....	{ Struck off from Apr. 14, 1812, having been from India beyond the period prescribed by Act of Parliament.
....	....	....	....	Died July 15, 1824, at Tarband.
....	....	....	....	Retired Feb. 21, 1830, in India.
....	....	....	....	Died Aug. 12, 1812.
....	....	....	....	Died Nov. 19, 1818, at Ellichpore.
....	....	....	....	Resigned Oct. 18, 1820, in England.
....	....	....	....	Died Nov. 16, 1816, in camp at Kottora.
....	....	....	....	Retired Feb. 14, 1836, in India.

MADRAS

NAMES.	Cadet.	Cornet, Ensign, or Second Lieutenant.	Lieutenant.	Captain.	Major.
Taylor, James William....	1807	....	June 27, 1812	....	....
Trotter, Lionel	,,	Jan. 5, 1810	Sep. 21, 1813	....	....
Tucker, John	,,	Feb. 28, 1810	Apr. 30, 1814	May 1, 1824	....
Trapaud, C. E.—*engineers*..	,,	....	Jan. 13, 1810	....	....
Tait, William	,,	April 6, 1810	Nov. 24, 1813	....	....
Taylor, William Rainsforth	1808	May 5, 1810	....	....	....
Tulloh, Alexander	1809	Jan. 25, 1811	July 28, 1814	May 1, 1824	....
Thomas, John (42 N. I.) ..	1810	June 23, 1811	Oct. 27, 1815	Feb. 21, 1826	Jan. 10, 1837
Taylor, John—*cavalry*	,,	Dec. 2, 1812	Sep. 1, 1818	May 26, 1825	....
Trimmer, George	1812	June 12, 1812	June 11, 1816	....	....
Taylor, Cortlandt—*artillery*	1813	July 4, 1814	Sep. 1, 1818	June 17, 1826	....
Thomas, Edmund—*artillery*	1816	June 26, 1817	Nov. 1, 1819	....	....
Thompson, Thomas	,,	....	Dec. 3, 1817	Nov. 21, 1829	....
Thomas, Geo. H.—*cavalry*	1817	....	Sep. 1, 1818	Feb. 7, 1832	....
Turner, Charles (35 N. I.)..	,,	....	June 4, 1818	May 18, 1831	....
Thorpe, Robert	,,	....	June 4, 1818	July 2, 1829	....
Thomson, Patrick	,,	....	June 4, 1818	Jan. 3, 1825	....
Trollope, William Henry..	1818	....	June 13, 1819	Aug. 4, 1829	....
Tyndale, Abraham	1819	....	....	....	....
Thwaits, Charles—*cavalry*	,,	....	June 17, 1820	....	....
Taylor, Henry—*cavalry* ..	,,	....	July 29, 1820	Nov. 10, 1831	....
Taylor, Alex^r. R.—*cavalry*	,,	April 6, 1820	June 21, 1822	....	....
Taylor, Peter, Alexander ..	,,	....	....	....	....
Turnour, Arthur Edw. Geo.	1820	....	Oct. 3, 1822	Brevet, April 6, 1835	....
Torriano, Charles James ..	,,	Feb. 13, 1821	Sep. 1, 1822	....	....
Thompson, George Earles	,,	Feb. 13, 1821	May 1, 1824	....	....
Trotter, Arthur	,,	Feb. 13, 1821	Feb. 22, 1825	Brevet, Feb. 13, 1836	....
Todd, Frederick William..	,,	Feb. 13, 1821	May 1, 1824	Brevet, Feb. 13, 1836	....
Thompson, A. P.—*cavalry*	,,	Feb. 13, 1821	May 1, 1824	Sep. 6, 1829	....
Thursby, Charles	,,	Feb. 13, 1821	Apr. 25, 1824	....	....
Tollemache, Charles Wm.	1821	Apr. 27, 1822	Nov. 10, 1824	....	....
Tranchell, George	,,	Apr. 27, 1822	Dec. 11, 1824	....	....
Thomas, James	1822	May 2, 1823	Sep. 8, 1826	....	....
Taylor, Thos. Jas.—*cavalry*	,,	May 2, 1823	Dec. 21, 1826	....	....
Taylor, Charles (47 N. I.)	1823	May 14, 1824	May 26, 1829	....	....
Trevor, Saml. S.—*artillery*	,,	....	May 1, 1824	....	....
Taylor, Charles (48 N. I.)	1824	May 6, 1825	Oct. 11, 1826	....	....
Tudor, William	,,	....	June 15, 1826	....	....
Taynton, Montague Ross..	,,	....	Sep. 12, 1826	....	....
Taylor, John—*artillery*....	,,	....	...1827....	....	....
Talman, Samuel	,,	....	Nov. 11, 1826	Nov. 4, 1836	....
Trewman, Fidelio Robert..	1825	Jan. 8, 1826	Feb. 3, 1829	....	....
Taylor, Robert—*cavalry* ..	,,	Jan. 8, 1826	Nov. 24, 1827	....	....
Taylor, George Phillips ..	,,	Jan. 8, 1826	....	....	....
Trapaud, John Ladwese P.	,,	....	July 7, 1827	....	....
Taynton, Edwin George ..	,,	....	May 13, 1827	....	....
Taylor, John Henry	,,	Jan. 8, 1826	Mar. 22, 1834	....	....

PRESIDENCY.

Lieut.-Colonel.	Colonel.	Major-General.	Lieut.-General.	Date of Resignation, Retirement, or Death
. . . .	. . . .	. . . .	. . . .	Resigned July 20, 1818, in India.
. . . .	. . . .	. . . .	. . . .	Died June 11, 1821.
. . . .	. . . .	. . . .	. . . .	Invalided Jan. 19, 1830, in India.
. . . .	. . . .	. . . .	. . . .	Died Dec. 6, 1813, at Bellary.
. . . .	. . . .	. . . .	. . . .	Died Jan. 16, 1815, at Rajapore.
. . . .	. . . .	. . . .	. . . .	{ Removed to the Madras Civil Establishment, Dec. 31, 1812.
. . . .	. . . .	. . . .	. . . .	Died May 25, 1833, at Masulipatam.
. . . .	. . . .	. . . .	. . . .	{ Invalided Feb. 10, 1837, and posted to 2nd N. V. Battalion.
. . . .	. . . .	. . . .	. . . .	Retired Nov. 29, 1828, in England.
. . . .	. . . .	. . . .	. . . .	Died Dec. 4, 1817, at Vizagapatam.
. . . .	. . . .	. . . .	. . . .	
. . . .	. . . .	. . . .	. . . .	Died Nov. 27, 1824, at Secunderabad.
. . . .	. . . .	. . . .	. . . .	{ Invalided July 15, 1831, in India. Retired Dec. 19, 1833, in England.
. . . .	. . . .	. . . .	. . . .	
. . . .	. . . .	. . . .	. . . .	
. . . .	. . . .	. . . .	. . . .	
. . . .	. . . .	. . . .	. . . .	Retired Feb. 8, 1836, in England.
. . . .	. . . .	. . . .	. . . .	Died Sep. 29, 1820, at Cannanore.
. . . .	. . . .	. . . .	. . . .	Died Aug. 27, 1826, at Arcot.
. . . .	. . . .	. . . .	. . . .	
. . . .	. . . .	. . . .	. . . .	Resigned July 18, 1828, in India.
. . . .	. . . .	. . . .	. . . .	Died Oct. 9, 1820, near Madras.
. . . .	. . . .	. . . .	. . . .	Retired April 7, 1835, in England.
. . . .	. . . .	. . . .	. . . .	Invalided Sep. 16, 1831, in India.
. . . .	. . . .	. . . .	. . . .	Retired Oct. 28, 1833, in England.
. . . .	. . . .	. . . .	. . . .	
. . . .	. . . .	. . . .	. . . .	Retired Jan. 20, 1835, in England.
. . . .	. . . .	. . . .	. . . .	Resigned Jan. 2, 1826, in England.
. . . .	. . . .	. . . .	. . . .	Died Sep. 19, 1834, at Trichinopoly.
. . . .	. . . .	. . . .	. . . .	Died Dec. 4, 1825, at Prome.
. . . .	. . . .	. . . .	. . . .	Died Feb. 20, 1833, in England.
. . . .	. . . .	. . . .	. . . .	
. . . .	. . . .	. . . .	. . . .	
. . . .	. . . .	. . . .	. . . .	
. . . .	. . . .	. . . .	. . . .	Died Sep. 29, 1826.
. . . .	. . . .	. . . .	. . . .	Cashiered Oct. 27, 1828, in India.
. . . .	. . . .	. . . .	. . . .	Died Feb. 24, 1828, at Belgaum.
. . . .	. . . .	. . . .	. . . .	
. . . .	. . . .	. . . .	. . . .	
. . . .	. . . .	. . . .	. . . .	{ Died April 15, 1829, on board the "Hercules," on his passage to England.
. . . .	. . . .	. . . .	. . . .	
. . . .	. . . .	. . . .	. . . .	Died Sep. 19, 1834, at Cannanore.

MADRAS.—2 A

MADRAS

NAMES.	Cadet.	Cornet, Ensign, or Second Lieutenant.	Lieutenant.	Captain.	Major.
Tulloch, Geo. Alexander ..	1825	....	June 6, 1827	....	....
Thomson, John (5 N. I.) ..	,,	Jan. 8, 1826	Feb. 20, 1833	....	....
Tainsh, John	,,	....	July 16, 1828	....	....
Taylor, William (7 N. I.)..	1826	Feb. 28, 1827	Nov. 20, 1830	....	....
Thompson, H. A. (50 N. I.)	,,	Jan. 8, 1826	June 2, 1829	....	....
Tremlet, H. Augustus	,,	July 8, 1827	Feb. 21, 1834	....	....
Turnbull, John Christie....	,,	Oct. 24, 1827	....	....	....
Thatcher, Henry	,,	Jan. 5, 1828	Feb. 21, 1834	July 12, 1837	....
Trench, Fred. F.—*cavalry*	,,	....	Oct. 6, 1828	....	....
Taylor, David G.—*cavalry*	1827	June 27, 1828	Oct. 29, 1833	....	....
Timins, J. K. B.—*artillery*	,,	June 12, 1828	Feb. 2, 1836	....	....
Thomson, David Taylour ..	1828	Feb. 13, 1831	Sep. 19, 1834	....	....
Tupper, John	1831	....	....	....	....
Templer, Frederick	,,	July 14, 1832	....	....	....
Tottenham, A.—*cavalry* ..	,,	Feb. 21, 1833	July 4, 1837	....	....
Tyler, Henry —*artillery* ..	1832	....	....	....	....
Taylor, Henry Corbett	,,	Dec. 13, 1833	....	....	....
Tod, Alexander (42 N. I.)..	,,	Feb. 15, 1834	Jan. 10, 1837	....	....
Tombs, J. Wood—*engineers*	1833	....	....	....	....
Thorne, Peregrine Francis	1834	June 3, 1834	Sep. 6, 1836	....	....

U V

NAMES.	Cadet.	Cornet, Ensign, or Second Lieutenant.	Lieutenant.	Captain.	Major.
Vigors, Urban............	1768	Aug. 2, 1770	Feb. 17, 1772	Jan. 4, 1782	Oct. 3, 1792
Ure, George.............	1771	Dec. 13, 1773	Sep. 27, 1780	...1784....	June 1, 1796
Vesey, Poole H.	1780	Sep. 1, 1781	June 4, 1787	Nov. 29, 1797	May 1, 1804
Vigors, Bartholomew......	1768	Aug. 15, 1770	Apr. 11, 1773	June 10, 1782	Mar. 11, 1794
Vernon, J. Mortimer......	1788	....	June 7, 1792	Jan. 1, 1800	July 25, 1805
Vaughan, Thomas........	1790	Aug. 9, 1791	Feb. 17, 1794	Aug. 5, 1801	....
Vaughan, Wm. Henry	,,	Sep. 22, 1791	Apr. 19, 1793	Feb. 11, 1800	Oct. 2, 1808
Vivion, J................	....	....	....	....	....
Vernon, John	1793	....	Sep. 7, 1795	June 6, 1804	April 4, 1808
Venables, Daniel	1797	Aug. 26, 1798	Nov. 27, 1798	....	....
Vicq, John	1795	Feb. 24, 1796	May 8, 1797	Sep. 21, 1804	Jan. 8, 1813
Vincent, Thomas	1799	....	Dec. 15, 1800	....	....
Vincent, Henry	1800	....	July 20, 1801	....	....
Varty, William	1802	....	Sep. 21, 1804	....	....
Utterson, John James	1803	....	Sep. 21, 1804	....	....
Vaughan, William........	,,	....	Sep. 21, 1804	....	....
Uhthoff, Gerard—*cavalry*..	,,	Mar. 7, 1805	Jan. 1, 1811	....	....
Van Heythuysen, H. I. ..	1810	May 25, 1811	Feb. 14, 1815	Apr. 25, 1825	....
Underwood, J. J.—*engineers*	1816	May 2, 1817	Aug. 4, 1821	Apr. 21, 1825	....
Underwood, C.—*cavalry* ..	1817	....	Sep. 12, 1818	....	....
Vivian, Robert John H. ..	1818	....	June 13, 1819	Aug. 1, 1825	Dec. 9, 1836
Underwood, G.A.—*engineers*	,,	Dec. 18, 1817	May 1, 1824	Nov. 4, 1826	....
Ure, John................	1819	....	April 7, 1820	....	....
Vanderzee, Henry	1821	Apr. 27, 1822	Sep. 8, 1826	....	....
Vallancy, Geo. Preston....	1823	May 14, 1824	Sep. 8, 1826	Oct. 2, 1835	....
Ussher, Edward	1825	Jan. 8, 1826	May 2, 1829	....	....

PRESIDENCY.

Lieut.-Colonel.	Colonel.	Major-General.	Lieut.-General.	Date of Resignation, Retirement, or Death.
				Died Aug. 26, 1835, at Kamptee.
				Died Feb. 28, 1830, at Trichinopoly.
				Resigned June 16, 1832, in England.
				Resigned Nov. 1, 1833, in India.
				{ Name removed from the Army List, Jan. 18, 1837, in England.
June 1, 1796	Dec. 26, 1798	Jan. 1, 1805	June 4, 1813	Died April 11, 1815, in England.
July 29, 1798				Died Jan. 22, 1802.
Nov. 29, 1809				Retired June 2, 1812.
				{ Dismissed the Service, Dec. 2, 1794, by sentence of a Court Martial.
Mar. 15, 1810				Died Oct. 14, 1811, at the Isle of Bourbon.
				Lost May — 1804, in the "Prince of Wales."
				{ Invalided Nov. 7, 1811, in India. Died Sep. 23, 1824, at Chicacole.
				Home, 1793. Struck off, Dec. 17, 1799.
Sep. 29, 1813				Died Nov. 29, 1817, at Fort St. George.
				Died May 14, 1799.
Sep. 1, 1818	June 5, 1829			Died Feb. 3, 1832, in England.
				Died Feb. 6, 1809.
				Died Feb. 24, 1807.
				Died Oct. 26, 1815, at Berhampore.
				Invalided Sep. 15, 1809. Struck off, in England.
				Killed Nov. — 1817.
				Died May 2, 1811, at Seroor.
				{ Invalided March 6, 1829, in India. Retired June 24, 1836.
				Died June 12, 1821.
				Died May 24, 1833, in England.

MADRAS

NAMES.	Cadet.	Cornet, Ensign, or Second Lieutenant.	Lieutenant.	Captain.	Major.
Vardon, Stafford—*engineers*	1826	....	Nov. 4, 1826	....	....
Vosper, James Hen. Alfred	1828	Nov. 28, 1830	Nov. 23, 1836	....	....
Vincent, John Francis	,,	Sep. 16, 1830	April 1, 1836	....	....
Vardon, Fred. C.—*artillery*	1830	Aug. 5, 1835	....	....	....
Vardon, Frank	1832	Dec. 22, 1832	May 25, 1837	....	....
W					
Wragg, Francis	....	Jan. 16, 1768	Sep. 3, 1770	Dec. 10, 1779	....
Wynch, Alexander	1767	Oct. 20, 1768	Sep. 8, 1770	Dec. 14, 1779	May 3, 1788
Wahab, George	1769	Nov. 9, 1770	July 28, 1775	June 25, 1783	June 23, 1795
Waight, George	,,	Nov. 12, 1770	Sep. 21, 1775	Nov. 1, 1783	Aug. 5. 1795
White, Edward	,,	Dec. 15, 1770	Sep. 11, 1776	Nov. 2, 1783	....
Westroppe, Lionel	1771	May 17, 1773	Nov. 26, 1778	Dec. 10, 1783	....
Willson, John	....	Aug. 19, 1777	May 4, 1781	....	....
Willson, William	1777	June 2, 1778	Feb. 19, 1782	Nov. 23, 1795	May 4, 1799
Willson, Walter	,,	July 30, 1778	Nov. 10, 1782	June 1, 1796	Dec. 10, 1799
White, Alexander	1778	Aug. 21, 1778	Apr. 15, 1783	....	....
Watkins, John	,,	May 11, 1779	Dec. 27, 1784	June 1, 1796	....
Warne, Roger.............	1779	Aug. 7, 1780	Apr. 17, 1786	June 1, 1796	May 28, 1800
Webber, Henry	,,	Aug. 16, 1780	Apr. 17, 1786	June 1, 1796	Dec. 24, 1800
Wright, Richard..........	1780	Aug. 16, 1781	Jan. 23, 1787	....	....
Watson, Lilly.............	,,	Sep. 30, 1781	Oct. 20, 1788	....	....
Willson, Thomas	,,	Oct. 23, 1781	Nov. 1, 1788	Sep. 29, 1798	Apr. 24, 1804
Wilks, Mark	1781	Sep. 25, 1782	Mar. 6, 1789	Oct. 12, 1798	Sep. 21, 1804
Walton, John	,,	Oct. 9, 1782	....	....	....
Wynn, Nanny Robert	,,	Oct. 18, 1782	Feb. 24, 1790	Oct. 12, 1798	....
Ward, Francis	,,	Nov. 12, 1782	....	....	....
Wright, Charles (Sen.)....	,,	Nov. 20, 1782	Aug. 21, 1790	....	....
Wright, Charles (Jun.)....	1782	May 19, 1783	....	....	....
Walker, Joseph	,,	May 20, 1783	Aug. 21, 1790	June 17, 1800	Sep. 21, 1804
Wooley John William	....	Sep. 8, 1783	...1792....	....	....
Willison, David —*artillery*	....	Oct. 22, 1780	Nov. 6, 1781	....	....
Wright, Nathaniel-*artillery*	....	Dec. 5, 1782	....	....	....
Wickens, John—*engineers*..	....	Aug. 19, 1778	Jan. 15, 1784	....	....
Watson, Alex.—*cavalry* ..	1779	....	May 5, 1783	June 1, 1796	May 7, 1799
Willson, Cuthbert—*cavalry*	....	....	Apr. 24, 1784	....	....
Wellwood, James — *cavalry*	....	....	July 31, 1786	....	....
Williamson, Hen.—*cavalry*	....	June 17, 1785	Aug. 12, 1788	....1796...	....
Walker, Patrick—*cavalry*..	1780	Dec. 3, 1785	Jan. 7, 1792	Sep. 4, 1799	May 1, 1804
Willcox, William	1779	Sep. 18, 1780	Apr. 17, 1786	....	....
Walcott, Thomas—*cavalry*	1790	July 5, 1792	May 7, 1799	....	....
Wilson, James	1789	....	June 7, 1792	Dec. 10, 1799	....1804...
Whittle, Thomas..........	,,	....	June 2, 1792	June 17, 1800	Sep. 21, 1804
Welsh, James	,,	....	Nov. 1, 1792	June 17, 1800	May 22, 1807
Wright, Peter	1790	June 12, 1791	June 6, 1793	....	....
Wallace, James	,,	June 22, 1791	June 6, 1793	....	....
Wahab, George	,,	July 2, 1791	June 29, 1793	June 17, 1800	Feb. 8, 1809
Willman, George Frederick	....	Sep. 28, 1791	....	....	....

PRESIDENCY.

Lieut.-Colonel.	Colonel.	Major General.	Lieut.-General.	Date of Resignation, Retirement, or Death.
....	....	....	....	
....	....	....	....	
....	....	....	....	
....	....	....	....	
....	....	....	....	
....	....	....	....	Died Sep. 9, 1789.
Aug. 6, 1794	July 27, 1796	....	....	Retired Jan. 21, 1800.
June 1, 1796	Dec. 10, 1799	....	....	Died Dec. 26, 1808.
June 1, 1796	....	....	....	Retired on full pay. Nov. 28, 1798.
....	....	....	....	Resigned 1790.
....	....	....	....	Died 1791.
....	....	....	....	Died 1792.
Feb. 1, 1802	....	....	....	Retired April 3, 1807.
Oct. 13, 1804	....	....	....	Retired July 24, 1805.
....	....	....	....	Died 1792. [1804.
....	....	....	....	Pensioned Nov. 5, 1799. Died Dec. 9,
....	....	....	....	Retired Feb. 28, 1805.
Sep. 21, 1804	June 4, 1813	Aug. 12, 1819	....	Died Aug. 8, 1833, in England.
....	....	....	....	Pensioned May — 1788.
....	....	....	....	Died 1793.
Feb. 25, 1807	....	....	....	Died Feb. 8, 1818, at Masulipatam.
Apr. 4, 1808	....	....	....	Retired Oct. 15, 1818.
....	....	....	....	Died 1791.
....	....	....	....	Died March 23, 1803
....	....	....	....	King's Service 1789.
....	....	....	....	Not to be traced.
....	....	....	....	King's Service 1789.
....	....	....	....	Died June 11, 1806, at Chatterpore.
....	....	....	....	Died 1792.
....	....	....	....	Died June — 1789.
....	....	....	....	Died June — 1789.
....	....	....	....	Died July — 1789.
....	....	....	....	Died 1800.
....	....	....	....	Died Oct. 1792.
....	....	....	....	Died 1791.
....	....	....	....	Died June 5, 1799.
May 23, 1807	Brevet June 4, 1814	....	....	Died Oct. 12, 1817.
....	....	....	....	At home 1787. Out of the service.
....	....	....	....	{ Invalided Dec. 17, 1801. Died Aug. 5, 1802, at Nellore.
....	....	....	....	Died Nov. 8, 1805, at Bangalore.
....	....	....	....	Died Mar. 19, 1809, at Seringapatam.
Feb. 20, 1813	Commt. May 1, 1824 Col. June 5, 1829	Jan. 10, 1837	....	
....	....	....	....	Died April 22, 1796, at Ramnaud.
....	....	....	....	Died March — 1794.
Oct. 25, 1815	Commt. May 1, 1824 Col. June 5, 1829	Jan. 10, 1837	....	
....	....	....	....	Died April — 1794.

MADRAS

NAMES.	Cadet.	Cornet, Ensign, or Second Lieutenant.	Lieutenant.	Captain.	Major.
Wood, Thomas—*engineers*	1790	....	May 25, 1792	Brevet June 1, 1796	....
Ward, Francis Swain......	....	....	....	Sep. 6, 1773	....
Walter, J.	....	....	Apr. 15, 1777	....	....
Wilson, Edward Buckley ..	1790	...1792...	....	....	....
Wissett, John	1795	....	Jan. 8, 1796	Sep. 21, 1804	June 28, 1814
Wakefield, Henry White ..	„	Feb. 9, 1796	Aug. 17, 1796	Sep. 21, 1804	....
Winfield, John Philip	„	Mar. 23, 1796	Nov. 29, 1797	Sep. 21, 1804	Mar 15, 1810
White, John.............	„	Feb. 28, 1796	June 27, 1797	....	....
Warburton, Garnett	„	Mar. 29, 1796	Nov. 29, 1797	Sep. 21, 1804	....
Wright, John	1794	Jan. 26, 1796	June 1, 1796	Sep. 21, 1804	....
Wright, Thomas F.	1795	....	Jan. 8, 1796	Sep. 21, 1804	Feb. 3, 1808
Waugh, Henry	„	Feb. 12, 1796	Dec. 2, 1796	....	....
Waugh, William George ..	„	Feb. 13, 1796	Jan. 5, 1797	Sep. 21, 1804	Sep. 8, 1818
Wilson, George	1796	Aug. 31, 1797	Oct. 12, 1798	Nov. 15, 1804	....
Webster, Thomas	„	Sep. 1, 1797	Oct. 12, 1798	Mar. 1, 1805	Dec. 7, 1817
Walker, John	„	Aug. 20, 1797	Oct. 12, 1798	Oct. 16, 1805	....
West, Montague H.-*cavalry*	1795	Aug. 25, 1797	Sep. 4, 1799	June 4, 1807	....
Willison, David	1796	Sep. 7, 1797	Oct. 12, 1798	July 7, 1805	....
Weldon, Anthony—*artillery*	1795	....	Jan. 8, 1796	May 11, 1806	Sep. 1, 1818
Woodhouse, William......	1798	....	Jan. 21, 1800	Dec. 19, 1804	Oct. 19, 1817
Walker, Francis—*cavalry*	„	....	June 17, 1800	Mar. 5, 1806	Jan. 13, 1816
Waugh, Gilbert	1797	July 21, 1798	Oct. 12, 1798	Dec. 22, 1804	Oct. 31, 1818
Wood, Patrick	1798	....	Dec. 15, 1800	May 16, 1805	....
Wilson, Francis W. (C. B.)	„	....	Jan. 1, 1800	May 27, 1809	May 30, 1818
Willett, A. Saltren	„	....	....	....	....
West, Mark—*cavalry*	„	....	June 17, 1800	May 1, 1804	Oct. 13, 1817
Woulfe, John	„	....	Jan. 1, 1800	June 27, 1805	July 19, 1817
Wren, Thomas	„	....	Jan. 1, 1800	June 21, 1809	Dec. 10, 1817
Wainhouse, John Brudenell	„	....	Jan. 1, 1800	June 10, 1806	....
Whyte, John William	„	....	Jan. 1, 1800	Feb. 2, 1809	....
Wulbin, Charles	1799	....	Dec. 15, 1800	Oct. 21, 1809	....
Waters, Henry James	„	....	Dec. 15, 1800	Feb. 7, 1809	....
Walker, Charles Augustus	„	....	Dec. 15, 1800	Mar. 18, 1809	Aug. 30, 1819
Wight, James	„	....	July 15, 1800	Mar. 31, 1813	July 13, 1821
Woodward, Benjamin	„	....	Dec. 15, 1800	....	....
Walker, J. (formerly of the 3d N.I.)	„	....	Dec. 15, 1800	Mar. 18, 1809	Jan. 31, 1821
Williamson, John Carmalt	„	....	Dec. 15, 1800	Nov. 30, 1811	....
West, Richard............	„	....	Dec. 15, 1800	Oct. 4, 1810	April 8, 1819
Wooldridge, Richard......	„	....	....	....	....
Williams, Hugh A. Preston	„	....	Jan. 1, 1800	....	....
Williams, C. A.—*cavalry* ..	„	....	Dec. 30, 1800	....	....
Wier, John	„	....	Dec. 15, 1800	....	....
Ward, Arthur	„	....	....	....	....
Woodhouse, John—*cavalry*	„	July 17, 1801	May 1, 1804	Sep. 6, 1810	....
Williams, R. H.	„	....	....	....	....
Wakeman, Henry	1800	....	July 20, 1801	....	....
Wilkinson, Henry John ..	„	....	July 20, 1801	Mar 27, 1816	....

PRESIDENCY.

Lieut.-Colonel.	Colonel.	Major General.	Lieut.-General.	Date of Resignation, Retirement, or Death.
....	....	....	....	Died 1800.
Apr. 17, 1786	....	....	....	Pensioned 1787. Died 1794.
....	....	....	....	Pensioned Sep. 23, 1785. Died Nov. 3, 1804.
....	....	....	....	Died 1792.
Oct. 10, 1819	....	....	....	Died Oct. 3, 1825, at Bombay.
....	....	....	....	Died May 22, 1806.
....	....	....	....	Died June 11, 1813, near Quilon.
....	....	....	....	Invalided June 29, 1804. Died July 5, 1806.
....	....	....	....	Retired May 5, 1812.
....	....	....	....	Died Oct. 21, 1807, at Masulipatam.
....	....	....	....	Died Oct. 8, 1810, at Jaulnah.
....	....	....	....	Died April 3, 1802.
....	....	....	....	{ Invalided Oct. 30, 1818. Died Jan. 11, 1820, at Mauritius.
....	....	....	....	Lost March 14, 1809, in the "Jane, Duchess of Gordon."
May 1, 1824	Feb. 4, 1832	....	....	
....	....	....	....	Died Feb. 24, 1812, at Quilon.
....	....	....	....	Died Oct. 26, 1808, at Jaulnah.
....	....	....	....	Died July 10, 1806, at Vellore.
Oct. 17, 1821	....	....	....	Retired Jan. 16, 1824.
May 1, 1824	June 5, 1829	....	....	
July 29, 1820	....	....	....	Died Feb. 25, 1829, in India.
May 1, 1824	June 5, 1829	....	....	
....	....	....	....	Retired Feb. 1, 1814.
May 1, 1824	June 5, 1829	....	....	
....	....	....	....	Resigned Oct. 10, 1801.
....	....	....	....	Died June 16, 1820, at Arcot.
Apr. 10, 1824	June 5, 1829	....	....	
....	....	....	....	Retired March 16, 1822.
....	....	....	....	{ Invalided Sep. 19, 1806. Died Aug. 13, 1813, at Ganjam.
....	....	....	....	Died July 8, 1814, at Cocanada.
....	....	....	....	Died Aug. 27, 1814, at Secunderabad.
....	....	....	....	Died July 30, 1811, at Jaulnah.
May 1, 1824	June 5, 1829	....	....	["Horatio."
Dec. 6, 1824	....	....	....	Died May 15, 1833, on board the
....	....	....	....	Died Dec. 15, 1806. [Rangoon.
Nov. 1, 1824	....	....	....	Killed Dec. 5, 1824, in action at
....	....	....	....	Died Oct. 3, 1813.
May 1, 1824	June 5, 1829	....	....	
....	....	....	....	Resigned Feb. 24, 1801.
....	....	....	....	Died Nov. 26, 1804.
....	....	....	....	Died Oct. 18, 1804.
....	....	....	....	Died Sep. 2, 1802.
....	....	....	....	Dismissed July 1, 1801.
....	....	....	....	Died Sep. 9, 1817, at Larwar.
....	....	....	....	Died May 4, 1802.
....	....	....	....	Lost in the "Prince of Wales."
....	....	....	....	Died May 10, 1819, at Bellary.

MADRAS

NAMES.	Cadet.	Cornet, Ensign, or Second Lieutenant.	Lieutenant.	Captain.	Major.
Wilson, Richard Greathead	1800	....	July 20, 1801	Feb. 25, 1812	May 1, 1824
Williams, Henry Robert ..	,,	....	July 20, 1801	....	....
Wilson, John	,,	....	July 20, 1801	May 1, 1815	July 7, 1827
Wilson, Charles	,,	....	Sep. 3, 1802	Mar. 24, 1815	....
Ward, William	,,	....	July 20, 1801	May 19, 1814	....
Warburton, John	,,	....	July 20, 1801	June 15, 1815[5]	....
Wahab, George Lancelot..	,,	....	Dec. 15, 1800	Oct. 21, 1808	Sep. 1, 1818
Wahab, James (C. B.)	....	....	Dec. 15, 1800	Dec. 27, 1808	Dec. 25, 1822
Whitehead, Fred. Molloy..	1802	....	July 3, 1803	Nov. 28, 1816	....
White, Bernard	,,	Apr. 17, 1803	July 13 1803	....	....
Watson, James	,,	....	Sep. 21, 1804	Mar. 31, 1818	....
Williams, John Stratford..	,,	....	May 23, 1804	April 3, 1813	....
Wright, Harry—*cavalry* ..	,,	....	June 1, 1804	Nov. 5, 1814	....
Wiltshire, George	,,	....	Sep. 21, 1804	....	....
Wilkinson, J.—*artillery* ..	,,	Apr. 27, 1803	July 18, 1804	July 19, 1809	....
Watson, T. W.—*artillery*..	,,	....	July 18, 1804	Brevet Apr. 20, 1810	....
White, Henry C.—*cavalry*	1803	July 21, 1804	Nov. 25, 1805	....	....
Wallace, E.—*cavalry*	,,	July 31, 1804	Aug. 15, 1807	Jan. 13, 1816	July 29, 1820
Willock, Sir H. (K.L.S.)—*cavalry*	,,	July 31, 1804	Oct. 27, 1808	Oct. 31, 1817	Mar. 20, 1831
Woolf, Robert—*cavalry* ..	,,	Mar. 7, 1805	Aug. 2, 1815	Oct. 16, 1823	....
Walpole, Henry	,,	....	Sep. 21, 1804	June 25, 1814	Jan. 3, 1825
Wynne, Julius	,,	....	Sep. 11, 1804	....	....
Winship, Phillip	,,	....	Sep. 21, 1804	....	....
Waddell, Charles	,,	....	Sep. 21, 1804	July 17, 1819	....
Watson, T. S.—*artillery* ..	,,	....	July 18, 1804	Apr. 20, 1814	May 23, 1825
Williams, William........	,,	....	Sep. 21, 1804	....	....
Wilson, John, Senr	,,	....	Sep. 21, 1804	....	....
Walker, Hugh............	,,	....	Sep. 21, 1804	Oct. 17, 1819	....
Walker, Andrew	,,	....	Sep. 21, 1804	Aug. 9, 1819	....
Wood, Jonathan..........	1804	....	....	....	....
Watson, John	,,	....	July 17, 1805	Sep. 15, 1818	....
Willows, Jeffery J. A.	,,	....	July 17, 1805	Nov. 15, 1818	Sep. 17, 1827
Wahab, Henry	,,	....	June 12, 1806	May 23, 1819	....
Wright, John Hairby	,,	....	July 17, 1805	April 8, 1818	....
Woodward, H. Courthorpe	,,	....	Apr. 23, 1806	....	....
Webb, John James	,,	....	Sep. 15, 1806	May 1, 1824	....
Wilkins, Thomas John....	,,	....	Dec. 8, 1805	Oct. 17. 1819	....
Whannell, Peter..........	,,	....	July 17, 1805	Apr. 11, 1821	July 4, 1832
Wigan, Thomas William ..	,,	....	May 28, 1806	Sep. 1, 1819	....
White, Edward Skeate	1805	....	Sep. 16, 1806	....	....
Webster, James	,,	....	Oct. 10, 1807	Aug. 23, 1822	....
Woolcock, Thomas	,,	June 27, 1806	Oct. 2, 1808	....	....
Willows, John............	,,	....	Dec. 27, 1806	....	....
Walker, Thomas..........	,,	June 27, 1806	April 1, 1809	May 1, 1824	....
Wood, Joseph	,,	June 27, 1806	Jan. 1, 1807	....	....
Williamson, W. (27 N. I.)	,,	....	Mar. 25, 1807	Jan. 31, 1821	Mar. 21, 1827
Wilson, Robert Scott	,,	June 27, 1806	April 6, 1810	Apr. 10, 1824	....

PRESIDENCY. 184—185

Lieut-Colonel.	Colonel.	Major-General.	Lieut.-General.	Date of Resignation, Retirement, or Death.
....	....	....	....	Died May 10, 1824, at Madras.
....	....	....	....	Not to be traced.
May 25, 1833	....	....	....	
....	....	....	....	Died Oct. 13, 1824, at Calcutta.
....	....	....	....	Died May 17, 1820.
....	....	....	....	Died Feb. 18, 1821, on passage to
May 1, 1824	July 5, 1829	....	....	[England.
July 2, 1825	Brevet, June 18, 1831	....	....	
....	....	....	....	Died Jan. 24, 1824, at Trevandrum.
....	....	....	....	Died Jan. 26, 1810, at Bath.
....	....	....	....	Died Feb. 22, 1821, at Madras.
....	....	....	....	Died Oct. — 1817.
....	....	....	....	Invalided Jan. 31, 1818, in India.
....	....	....	....	Retired Oct. 24, 1809.
....	....	....	....	Died Nov. 11, 1825, at Paungill.
....	....	....	....	{ Invalided June 19, 1812, in India; died Aug. 1, 1815, at Vizagapatam.
....	....	....	....	Resigned Feb. 20, 1808.
....	....	....	....	Killed May 19, 1827, at Secunderabad.
....	....	....	....	Retired Oct. 29, 1833, in England.
....	....	....	....	Died Sep. 29, 1825, at Jaulnah.
June 7, 1830	....	....	....	
....	....	....	....	Resigned Jan. 2, 1806.
....	....	....	....	Died July 10, 1806, at Vellore.
....	....	....	....	Died Aug. 22, 1822, at Masulipatam.
....	....	....	....	Died July 17, 1830, at Madras.
....	....	....	....	Died Feb. 13, 1815, in England.
....	....	....	....	Died July 9, 1817, at Vizagapatam.
....	....	....	....	Died May 13, 1821.
....	....	....	....	Died Nov. 22, 1831, at Bangalore.
....	....	....	....	Resigned Jan. 28, 1806.
....	....	....	....	Died Jan. 25, 1830, at Mangalore.
....	....	....	....	{ Invalided Dec. 18, 1829, in India, and Retired June 28, 1832.
....	....	....	....	Died June 16, 1830.
....	....	....	....	{ Invalided Aug. 11, 1818; died Jan. 4, 1820, at Trichinopoly.
....	....	....	....	Resigned Jan. 22, 1811.
....	....	....	....	Died May 5, 1825, at Trevandrum.
....	....	....	....	Died May 29, 1821, at Nagpore.
....	....	....	....	Invalided Nov. 20, 1829, in India.
....	....	....	....	{ Pensioned May 20, 1814, on Lord Clive's Fund.
....	....	....	....	Resigned Dec. 31, 1824, in India.
....	....	....	....	Died April 22, 1810. [France.
....	....	....	....	Died Aug. 21, 1817, at the Isle of
....	....	....	....	Died June 23, 1830, at Palaveram.
....	....	....	....	Died April 14, 1819, at Bangalore.
Dec. 22, 1832	....	....	....	[" Sesostris."
....	....	....	....	Died March 17, 1832, on board the

MADRAS—2 B

MADRAS

NAMES.	Cadet.	Cornet, Ensign, or Second Lieutenant.	Lieutenant.	Captain.	Major.
Williamson, Wm. (9 N. I.)	1805	....	Aug. 27, 1807	....	....
White, Henry (7 N. I.)....	,,	June 27, 1806	Feb. 28, 1810	May 1, 1824	....
Wallis, Henry............	,,	June 27, 1806	Mar. 16, 1811	May 1, 1824	....
Williams, Chas. Sawkins ..	,,	June 27, 1806	Dec. 9, 1809	....	....
Wilson, Archibald	,,	June 27, 1806	Sep. 29, 1808	July 21, 1823	....
Weir, James—*cavalry*	,,	....	Nov. 23, 1809	Sep. 1, 1818	....
Waters, Rrbert	,,	July 3, 1807	Jan. 10, 1809	....	....
Watson, Thomas..........	,,	June 27, 1806	Jan. 11, 1812	July 26, 1826	....
Watkins, J. (5 Lt. C.)—*cavalry*	,,	July 7, 1807	May 3, 1811	Mar. 9, 1820	Jan. 27, 1830
Wakefield, Thomas	1806	July 3, 1807	Dec. 4, 1809	....	....
Woodhouse, Edward	,,	July 3, 1807	Mar. 8, 1810	....	....
Williams, John	,,	July 3, 1807	Dec. 19, 1810	May 1, 1824	....
Ward, Benjamin S........	,,	....	Aug. 25, 1811	Mar. 27, 1825	Feb. 21, 1834
Woodcock, Wm.—*cavalry*	,,	Oct. 8, 1807	Sep. 6, 1810	....	....
Wiggins, Henry	,,	July 3, 1807	Aug. 4, 1812	May 1, 1824	April 1, 1833
Willock, Fred.—*artillery* ..	,,	....	Feb. 17, 1808	....	....
Winchester, Edward	,,	July 3, 1807	....	....	....
Watson, Lewis Wentworth	,,	July 3, 1807	Nov. 20, 1813	May 1, 1824	Feb. 21, 1834
Worthy, George	,,	May 23, 1808	....	....	....
Warden, John............	,,	July 3, 1807	....	....	....
West, John	,,	....	Sep. 12, 1811	....	....
Williams, Richard	,,	June 4, 1808	June 17, 1811	....	....
Wootton, Wm. Henry	1807	Dec. 29, 1808	June 21, 1812	....	....
Williams, Raymond-*cavalry*	,,	June 27, 1808	....	....	....
Ward, John (39 N. I.)	,,	Nov. 24, 1808	June 25, 1814	May 1, 1824	....
Wheeler, F. Hugh Massey	,,	April 1, 1809	Apr. 3, 1813	Sep. 8, 1826	....
Wilson, John, Junr. (30 N. I.)	,,	Mar. 7, 1809	Oct. 24, 1811	May 1, 1824	....
Welch, Robert............	,,	....	....	....	....
Watkins, Arthur—*cavalry*	,,	April 6, 1810	Sep. 1, 1818	Dec. 18, 1826	....
Wright, John (40 N. I.) ..	,,	Nov. 15, 1809	Sep. 27, 1815	Nov. 14, 1825	Feb. 11, 1835
Williames, Edward........	,,	Nov. 1, 1809	Nov. 25, 1812	....	....
Watson, John	,,	Apr. 10, 1809	Aug. 13, 1812	....	....
Willock, George—*cavalry*	,,	Sep. 6, 1810	Sep. 1, 1818	Feb. 10, 1827	....
Webb, James Taylor	,,	April 6, 1810	Feb. 2, 1814	Sep. 8, 1826	....
Williams, Andrew	1808	May 12, 1810	....	....	....
Walker, George	1809	June 27, 1810	Feb. 11, 1813	....	....
Walker, David—*cavalry* ..	,,	Nov. 9, 1812	Oct. 21, 1813	Oct. 26, 1819	....
Watkins, Westropp	1810	June 27, 1811	Oct. 8, 1814	Sep. 27, 1829	Oct. 2, 1835
Williams, Hen. B.—*cavalry*	,,	Nov. 22, 1812	Jan. 7, 1818	May 1, 1824	....
Walker, Thomas..........	,,	Feb. 27, 1811	....	....	....
Wotherspoon, W.-*engineers*	,,	July 27, 1811	....	....	....
Wallace, John............	,,	Jan. 2, 1812	Mar. 11, 1815	May 19, 1825	Dec. 6, 1834
Winbolt, John Hill	1811	June 11, 1812	April 2, 1817	May 23, 1825	Feb. 24, 1833
Watson, David	,,	June 11, 1812	Aug. 15, 1816	....	....
Warre, John T.—*artillery*	,,	June 11, 1812	....	....	....
Warre, Chas. H.—*artillery*	,,	June 11, 1812	Sep. 1, 1818	.... 1825...	....
Walters, Thomas	,,	June 11, 1812	May 13, 1817	....	....

PRESIDENCY.

Lieut-Colonel.	Colonel.	Major-General.	Lieut.-General.	Date of Resignation, Retirement, or Death.
				Struck off.
				Died May 20, 1835, at Madras.
				Died May 28, 1829.
				Resigned Jan. 5, 1813.
				Died July 31, 1831, at Madras.
				Died Feb. 15, 1824, at Bellary.
				Died June 18, 1820, at Sankerrydroog.
				Retired Mar. 18, 1831, in India.
				Discharged Oct. 27, 1834, in India.
				Struck off, April 14, 1817.
				Died Nov. 23, 1820, at Arcot.
				Died July 18, 1828, at Cootallnm.
				Died June 19, 1835, at the Cape of Good Hope
				Died Mar. 25, 1815, at Dewulwara.
				Died Aug. 31, 1834, at Yelwall.
				Died Mar. 28, 1815, at St. Thomas's Mount.
				Died Mar. 29, 1811, at Madras.
				Died April 12, 1811, at Negapatam.
				Died Oct. 12, 1812, at Jaulnah.
				Invalided 1812. Died Nov. 23, 1830.
				Struck off, Aug. 20, 1823, in India.
				Died July 23, 1820, at Vizianagrum.
				Resigned Nov. 14, 1809.
				Died June 29, 1808.
				Died Aug 1, 1833, at Bangalore.
				Retired Dec. 30, 1818, in England.
				Died May 10, 1817, at Bangalore.
				Retired Oct. 29, 1833, in England.
				Invalided Feb. 15, 1833, in India.
				Resigned Oct. 1, 1813.
				Died Mar. 15, 1819, at Baggracottah.
				Invalided Feb. 28, 1821.
				Died May 8, 1830, at Kamptee.
				Died May 10, 1813, at Bangalore.
				Died Jan. 15, 1817, near Nagpore.
				Died Dec. 11, 1820, at the Cape of Good Hope
				Killed April 16, 1817, near Sonai.
				Died Aug. 2, 1825, in camp, at Belgaum.
				Died April 22, 1819, in camp, near Guddock.

MADRAS

NAMES.	Cadet.	Cornet, Ensign, or Second Lieutenant.	Lieutenant.	Captain.	Major.
Whinyates, F. F.—*artillery*	1812	July 6, 1813	Sep. 1, 1818	Oct. 24, 1824	....
Wilkinson, Wm. John	,,	July 6, 1813	Mar. 27, 1816	....	....
Warrand, Robert	,,	July 6, 1813	....	....	....
Wardell, George Best	,,	July 6, 1813	June 4, 1817	May 6, 1825	....
Williams, George	1813	....	Sep. 2, 1815	....	....
Wynch, John—*artillery*	,,	July 4, 1814	Sep. 1, 1818	Aug. 13, 1825	....
White, Wm. George	,,	July 4, 1814	Mar. 30, 1816	Sep. 27, 1829	....
West, T. J.—*artillery*	,,	July 4, 1814	....	....	....
Westfold, Thos. Cockburn	1814	....	....	....	....
Welland, Frederick	,,	May 24, 1816	June 8, 1817	Sep. 8, 1826	....
Wyllie, James Shaw	1816	....	April 7, 1818	Aug. 13, 1827	April 1, 1836
Williams, George	,,	....	April 6, 1818	....	....
Wallace, Rob\(^t\). Tierney....	,,	....	Mar. 19, 1817	Aug. 8, 1833	....
Woodburn, Archibald	1817	....	June 4, 1818	Sep. 8, 1826	....
Wyllie, James............	,,	....	June 4, 1818	June 13, 1828	....
Woodward, James	,,	....	June 4, 1818	Dec. 19, 1829	....
Weller, William	,,	....	Sep. 18, 1818	....	....
Whitlock, Geo. Cornish ..	,,	....	Dec. 20, 1818	July 16, 1831	....
Wilkinson, Thomas	1818	....	....	....	....
Waymouth, John	,,	....	June 13, 1819	....	....
Whistler, Godfrey W.	,,	....	June 13, 1819	June 17, 1829	....
Woodward, Jas. Palmer ..	,,	....	June 13, 1819	July 6, 1831	....
Wynter, Wm. John Moad..	,,	....	June 13, 1819	....	....
Williams, Watkin Lewis ..	,,	....	June 13, 1819	Mar. 21, 1827	....
Wallace, Thomas	1819	....	Apr. 1, 1820	Sep. 23, 1832	....
Warner, Thos. Styan......	,,	....	Dec. 2, 1820	June 20, 1828	....
Wilford, Charles..........	,,	....	Apr. 7, 1820	Apr. 1, 1829	....
Wright, George	,,	....	Aug. 10, 1820	Aug. 1, 1831	....
Wahab, Charles	,,	....	Apr. 18, 1821	Aug. 10, 1825	....
Walter, Henry	,,	....	Apr. 18, 1820	Mar. 20, 1828	June 9, 1833
Watts, Harry Hall........	,,	....	May 21, 1820	Jan. 1, 1836	....
Waymouth, George	,,	....	Feb. 13, 1821	....	....
Williams, Jas. Edwin	,,	April 6, 1820	June 25, 1821	Feb. 22, 1830	Feb. 10, 1836
White, Fred. Broadhead ..	,,	Apr. 6, 1820	Apr. 30, 1822	Apr. 22, 1826	....
Warrand, Hugh	,,	....	....	....	....
Wallace, John C.—*cavalry*	1820	April 6, 1820	Mar. 26, 1823	Sep. 29, 1828	....
Wilford, Lucius B.........	,,	....	Mar. 3, 1824	....	....
Watts, Robert............	,,	Feb. 13, 1821	June 23, 1822	Nov. 17, 1831	....
Warren, Fred. John	,,	Feb. 13, 1821	Apr. 8, 1822	....	....
Wright, Francis..........	,,	....	....	....	....
Watson, Richard	,,	Feb. 13, 1821	May 5, 1824	....	....
Woodgate, John..........	,,	Feb. 13, 1821	July 7, 1824	....	....
Wright, Henry	,,	Feb. 13, 1821	May 21, 1823	....	....
Whitlock, Charles James..	,,	....	Apr. 17, 1824	....	....
Whitcombe, T. D.—*artillery*	,,	....	June 8, 1821	Mar. 16, 1831	....
Watson, Geo. Wm.	,,	Feb. 13, 1821	June 15, 1824	....	....
Wilkinson, Geo. Sidney ..	,,	Feb. 13, 1821	Apr. 19, 1823	Brevet, Feb. 12, 1836	....

PRESIDENCY.

Lieut.-Colonel.	Colonel.	Major-General.	Lieut.-General.	Date of Resignation, Retirement, or Death.
				Killed May 29, 1818, at Mallegaum.
				Resigned May 10, 1814, in India.
				Died Sep. 18, 1826, at Quilon.
				Died July 14, 1823, in England.
				Died Feb. 1, 1819, at St. Thomé.
				Resigned Sep. 19, 1815, in India.
				Retired March 26, 1827, in England.
				Dismissed June 30, 1823, in India.
				Died July 27, 1819, in camp, near Arcot.
				Died Aug. 3, 1829, at Gooty.
				Resigned April 18, 1823, in India.
				Died April 12, 1835, at Bangalore.
				Died Jan. 27, 1837, in camp, at [Vistnoochettrum.
				Died May 11, 1827, at Trichinopoly.
				[Kulladjee.
				Died May 9, 1823, in camp, at
				Died Feb. 13, 1826, in England.
				[Hooghley.
				Drowned July 4, 1827 in the River
				Lost Aug. 11, 1821, in the " Lady Lushington."
				{ Invalided Dec. 4, 1829, in India. Died Jan. 19, 1830, at Jaulnah.
				Died Oct. 14, 1826, in Amherst Town.
				{ Drowned March 2, 1829, on his passage to England, per " Charles Kerr."
				Died Oct. 17, 1826, at Prome.
				Retired Nov. 16, 1831, in England.
				{ Invalided July 12, 1831, in India. Died Feb. 22, 1832, at Vizagapatam.

MADRAS

NAMES.	Cadet.	Cornet, Ensign, or Second Lieutenant.	Lieutenant.	Captain.	Major.
Wallace, James	1820	Feb. 13, 1821	May 20, 1824	Nov. 25, 1829	
Wilkinson, B. C.—*artillery*	,,				
Weir, Robert Dundas	,,	Feb. 13, 1821	Aug. 15, 1824	Mar. 27, 1832	
Woodfall, Charles	,,	Feb. 13, 1821	Aug. 10, 1824	Brevet, Feb. 13, 1836	
Walker, William (1. L. C.)	1821	Feb. 13, 1821	June 28, 1824	Nov. 6, 1832	
Wakeman, Thomas (20 N.I.)	,,	Apr. 27, 1822	Feb. 15, 1825		
Willis, Edward	,,	Apr. 27, 1822	May 23, 1825	May 25, 1835	
Wall, Martin	,,	Apr. 27, 1822	Mar. 17, 1824		
Wilson, Frederick	,,				
Wingfield, Watkin	,,				
Willis, James	,,	Apr. 27, 1822	July 3, 1824		
Wilkie, Patrick	,,	Apr. 27, 1822	Sep. 8, 1826		
Wight, Andrew	,,		May 1, 1824		
Walker, Hugh	,,	Apr. 27, 1822	Apr. 20, 1826		
Woodfall, George	,,	Apr. 27, 1822	Sep. 8, 1826		
White, Thomas (41 N.I.)	,,	Apr. 27, 1822			
White, Matthew	1822	Apr. 27, 1822	Aug. 1, 1825	May 31, 1836	
Wynter, Daniel	,,	May 2, 1823	Mar. 13, 1826	Aug. 7, 1835	
Walker, Patr^k. A.—*cavalry*	,,	May 1, 1824	Aug. 6, 1825	Feb. 14, 1835	
Watts, John Edw.—*cavalry*	,,	May 2, 1823	Feb. 21, 1825		
White, William (34 N.I.)	1823	May 14, 1824	Apr. 13, 1826	Jan. 19, 1837	
Welbank, Richard Thomas	,,	May 14, 1824	July 7, 1826		
White, James	,,	May 14, 1824	Aug. 13, 1827		
Wakeman, Henry	,,	May 14, 1824	Feb. 21, 1826		
Wilkinson, Josiah	,,		Jan. 7, 1826		
Whistler, T. K.—*artillery*	,,		May 1, 1824		
West, Charles M.	,,	Sep. 14, 1824	Mar. 11, 1833		
Watkins, Henry—*artillery*	1824		Aug. 25, 1824		
Watts, Montague—*artillery*	,,		May 23, 1825		
Welch, Henry—*cavalry*	,,	May 6, 1825	June 18, 1828		
Wardroper, Edward	,,	May 6, 1825	Mar. 3, 1826		
Ward, William—*artillery*	,,		Nov. 12, 1825		
Welch, William H.	1825	Jan. 8, 1826	June 3, 1831		
Wallace, Alexander	,,		June 30, 1827		
Whistler, James—*cavalry*	,,	Jan. 8, 1826	Sep. 12, 1827		
Walsh, Thomas Prendergast	,,	Jan. 8, 1826	Apr. 24, 1832		
Wight, Arthur Cleghorn	,,		Feb. 28, 1827	Jan. 15, 1834	
Woodhouse, Thomas Henry	,,	Jan. 8, 1826	June 28, 1834		
Warren, Charles Hotson	,,	Jan. 8, 1826	Dec. 22, 1827		
Wilkinson, John	,,	Jan. 8, 1826			
Wilson, Henry	,,	Jan. 8, 1826			
Willins, Henry James	,,	Jan. 8, 1826	May 23, 1828		
Wilkinson, John Young	,,	Jan. 8, 1826			
Wright, Joseph	,,	Jan. 8, 1826	Feb. 24, 1833		
Walker, Charles Wake	,,	Jan. 8, 1826			
Wood, Herbert William	,,	Jan. 8, 1826	Aug. 18, 1827		
Wilder, Charles P.—*cavalry*	,,	Jan. 8, 1826	Oct. 19, 1831		

PRESIDENCY.

Lieut.-Colonel.	Colonel.	Major General.	Lieut.-General.	Date of Resignation, Retirement, or Death.
....	....	....	....	Died May 19, 1831, at Palaveram.
....	....	....	....	Died June 10, 1823, at Bellary.
....	....	....	....	
....	....	....	....	Died Feb. 24, 1836, at Madras.
....	....	....	....	Discharged Aug. 18, 1835, in India.
....	....	....	....	
....	....	....	....	Died Feb. 9, 1828, in England.
....	....	....	....	Died Feb. 28, 1823, at Cuddalore.
....	....	....	....	Transferred to Bengal.
....	....	....	....	Died June 29, 1827, at Masulipatam.
....	....	....	....	Died Feb. 20, 1828, at Secunderabad.
....	....	....	....	Died Dec. 24, 1825, at Arracan.
....	....	....	....	
....	....	....	....	{ Died June 5, 1825, at Kamptee, near Nagpore.
....	....	....	....	
....	....	....	....	Died Oct. 5, 1827, at Kamptee.
....	....	....	....	
....	....	....	....	Resigned Feb. 21, 1834, in England.
....	....	....	....	Killed in action near Malacca, April 20, 1831.
....	....	....	....	
....	....	....	....	Pensioned June 21, 1836.
....	....	....	....	{ Retired on Lord Clive's Fund, April 5, 1831 in England.
....	....	....	....	Resigned May 20, 1833, in England.
....	....	....	....	
....	....	....	....	
....	....	....	....	
....	....	....	....	{ Lost at sea Oct. 30, 1836, by wreck of the cutter "Sea Gull," at Vizagapatam.
....	....	....	....	Died March 12, 1830, at Penang.
....	....	....	....	Died Feb. 25, 1828, at Jaulnah.
....	....	....	....	Dismissed July 9, 1830, in India.
....	....	....	....	Dismissed March 3, 1828, in India.
....	....	....	....	

MADRAS

NAMES.	Cadet.	Cornet, Ensign, or Second Lieutenant.	Lieutenant.	Captain.	Major.
Wilkinson, Alfred	1825	Jan. 8, 1826	June 4, 1832		
Wilson, Thomas Seymour	,,	Jan. 8, 1826			
Waters, Henry S.—*cavalry*	,,	Jan. 8, 1826	June 10, 1831		
Wilson, Charles H.	1826	Jan. 8, 1826	Aug. 4, 1834		
White, Robert (35 N. I.)	,,	Jan. 8, 1826	Oct. 1, 1836		
Wilson, John	,,	Jan. 8, 1826	May 23, 1832		
Whitlock, John—*cavalry*	,,		Oct. 6, 1827		
Wyndham, William—*cavalry*	,,	Feb. 27, 1827	Sep. 29, 1828		
Willis, Charles T.—*cavalry*	,,	Feb. 27, 1827	May 7, 1832		
Wroughton, N.—*cavalry*	,,	Mar. 5, 1827	Oct. 29, 1830		
Willisford, Richard Vyvyan	,,	July 2, 1827			
Whitty, John Charles	,,	Jan. 5, 1828	Nov. 28, 1830		
Wake, C. Spedding Arden	1827	Aug. 7, 1828			
Wahab, James George	,,	Dec. 12, 1828	Aug. 16, 1830		
Worster, W. K.—*artillery*	,,	Dec. 13, 1827	May 1, 1833		
Woods, Wm. Geo.—*cavalry*	,,	Mar. 4, 1828	Jan. 30, 1834		
Wahab, William Morrison	,,	Dec. 12, 1828			
Walker, Lewis William	,,	Dec. 31, 1828			
White, Henry Puget	,,	May 26, 1827	May 23, 1835		
Worsley, Arthur	,,	June 2, 1829	April 3, 1834		
Wood, Alexander	,,	June 21, 1829	Apr. 16, 1834		
Walker, Godfrey F.	1828	Nov. 24, 1830	Nov. 26, 1834		
Warington, John Norris	,,	June 6, 1831	Feb. 3, 1835		
Watts, Henry—*engineers*	,,	Dec. 13, 1827	Sep. 2, 1836		
Walker, W. L.—*cavalry*	,,	July 6, 1830	Apr. 12, 1834		
Walker, George H.	1830				
Wyndham, Arthur	1831	Nov. 24, 1832	Jan. 9, 1836		
Williams, William James	1832				
Western, William Charles	,,	Nov. 24, 1832	June 21, 1836		
Welpdale, William Walter	,,	Dec. 15, 1832	Aug. 28, 1835		
Worsley, Charles	,,	Mar. 11, 1833			
Wilson, John (26 N. I.)	,,	Jan. 1, 1832			
Whapshare, William H.	,,	Feb. 25, 1833	July 26, 1836		
Watt, James	,,	Jan. 19, 1833	Dec. 20, 1836		
Wade, Henry C.—*artillery*	,,				
White, John	,,	June 11, 1833			
Wood, Matthew	,,	Dec. 13, 1833	Aug. 3, 1837		
Webb, Edward A. Henry	1833	Dec. 13, 1833			
Wilson, William John	1834	June 13, 1834	Apr. 28, 1836		
Winfield, C. H.	,,	Feb. 24, 1835	Dec. 9, 1836		
Walker, A. (Eur. Reg^t.)	,,		Jan. 25, 1836		
Y					
Youngson, William	1780	Oct. 16, 1781	Nov. 1, 1788	Aug. 2, 1798	Sep. 8, 1803
Young, Nicol	,,	Dec. 8, 1782			
Young, John	,,	Dec. 9, 1782	Aug. 21, 1790		
Younge, W. A.—*cavalry*	....		April 5, 1773	Jan. 10, 1782	Dec. 25, 1787
Young, Thomas	1790	Aug. 12, 1791	Feb. 19, 1794	Dec. 10, 1801	

PRESIDENCY.

Lieut.-Colonel.	Colonel.	Major General	Lieut.-General.	Date of Resignation, Retirement, or Death.
....	....	....	....	Resigned July 12, 1835, in England.
....	....	....	....	Died Apr. 19, 1829, at Jaulnah.
....	....	....	....	
....	....	....	....	{ Invalided Apr. 11, 1837, in India. { Died June 28, 1837, at Wallajahbad.
....	....	....	....	
....	....	....	....	Died Sep. 23, 1833, in England.
....	....	....	....	
....	....	....	....	Died May 29, 1830, at Colar.
....	....	....	....	{ Pensioned Dec. 28, 1830, in India. Died { Sep. 6, 1833, at Condapilly.
....	....	....	....	Died Dec. 5, 1831, at Trichinopoly.
....	....	....	....	
....	....	....	....	
....	....	....	....	Died Feb. 21, 1833, at Bangalore.
....	....	....	....	
....	....	....	....	
....	....	....	....	
....	....	....	....	
....	....	....	....	Killed May 3, 1832, in action, in Malacca.
....	....	....	....	Discharged Aug. 15, 1834, in India.
....	....	....	....	
....	....	....	....	Died March 28, 1836, at Gullery.
....	....	....	....	
....	....	....	....	
....	....	....	....	
....	....	....	....	
....	....	....	....	
Sep. 20, 1805	....	....	....	Retired Sep. 9, 1807.
....	....	....	....	Died 1792.
....	....	....	....	Died November, 1793.
Dec. 18, 1794	....	....	....	Died Dec. 30, 1796, at Arcot.
....	....	....	....	{ Lost in the "Jane, Duchess of Gordon," { March 14, 1809.

MADRAS——2 C

MADRAS

NAMES.	Cadet.	Cornet, Ensign, or Second Lieutenant.	Lieutenant.	Captain.	Major.
Yarde, Henry	1794	Jan. 20, 1796	June 1, 1796	Jan. 2, 1804	Feb. 9, 1818
Young, James............	1797	Aug. 26, 1798	Dec. 26, 1798	....	....
Yates, Richard Hassels ..	1798	....	Jan. 1, 1800	May 11, 1807	Nov. 12, 1815
Young, George	1799	....	Dec. 15, 1800	....	....
Yates, Charles Watson....	1802	....	Sep. 23, 1803	Sep. 29, 1817	June 20, 1824
Youngson, Thomas	,,	Apr. 17, 1803	Sep. 21, 1804	Sep. 1, 1818	Sep. 27, 1826
Young, Robert	1805	Jan. 1, 1807	June 4, 1808	Brevet, Mar. 28, 1821	....
Yates, Samuel............	1806	July 3, 1807	Oct. 7, 1809	....	....
Young, Marshall K.	1809	Oct. 10, 1810	.... 1817...	....	....
Young, Andrew	1810	Aug. 13, 1811	....	....	....
Younge, W. H. Nassam ..	1815	....	Sep. 19, 1816	....	....
Yolland, R. S.—*artillery* ..	,,	July 11, 1815	Nov. 6, 1818	June 12, 1827	....
Young, Charles Wallace ..	1818	....	June 13, 1819	Feb. 21, 1832	....
Yaldwin, John	,,	....	June 13, 1819	Feb. 4, 1832	....
Yonge, Henry William ..	1819	....	May 15, 1820	....	....
Yates, Charles	1822	May 2, 1823	May 6, 1826	....	....
Yarde, Henry Thomas	,,	May 2, 1823	June 21, 1826	Jan. 11, 1836	....
Yarde, William Hugh	1825	Jan. 8, 1826	....	....	....
Yarde, Walter George	,,	Jan. 8, 1826	Mar. 21, 1827	....	....
Young, Charles Raitt	1826	Jan. 16, 1827	Feb. 21, 1834	....	....
Younghusband, Robert....	,,	Aug. 18, 1827	Dec. 13, 1832	....	....
Young, Peter Brockhurst ..	,,	Feb. 21, 1828	Feb. 16, 1833	....	....
Yates, George Hay Smith	1827	June 2, 1829	....	....	....
Young, Archibald Goldie ..	1832	....	Jan. 24, 1835	....	....
Yates, Henry Whannel ..	,,	Feb. 11, 1834	....	....	....
Zouch, Thomas Henry	1820	Feb. 13, 1821	July 3, 1824	Feb. 8, 1836	....
Zouch, Charles S.—*cavalry*	,,	Feb. 13, 1821	....	....	....

PRESIDENCY.

Lieut.-Colonel.	Colonel.	Major-General.	Lieut.-General.	Date of Resignation, Retirement, or Death.
....	....	....	....	Invalided Sep. 7, 1818. Retired Jan. 27, 1826, in England.
....	....	....	....	Died Sep. 28, 1806.
Jan. 26, 1822	June 5, 1829	....	....	
....	....	....	....	Killed Dec. 16, 1803, at Ghyall Ghur.
....	....	....	....	Died March 12, 1825, at Sernay, on the banks of the Irrawaddy.
....	....	....	....	Retired Aug. 6, 1828, in England.
....	....	....	....	Died July 2, 1823, at Masulipatam.
....	....	....	....	Died May 6, 1813, in India.
....	....	....	....	Died May 25, 1818, on board the "Rose," on his passage to England.
....	....	....	....	Resigned Feb. 23, 1816, in India.
....	....	....	....	Died Oct. 2, 1818, in camp, near Ellichpore.
....	....	....	....	
....	....	....	....	
....	....	....	....	
....	....	....	....	Died May 13, 1824, at Jaulnah.
....	....	....	....	
....	....	....	....	
....	....	....	....	Died April 9, 1829, at Bangalore.
....	....	....	....	
....	....	....	....	Died May 8, 1835, at Sindoe.
....	....	....	....	
....	....	....	....	
....	....	....	....	
....	....	....	....	
....	....	....	....	
....	....	....	....	
....	....	....	....	Died Aug. 15, 1823, at Madras.

ERRATA.

Page 6—7.—Adams, Thomas John, for Setorin *read* Setoun.

Page 12—13.—Burton, W. M. (artillery), *read* Brevet, Col. June 18, 1831.

Page 14—15.—Beaumont, John, *read* Capt. April 6, 1816.

———————Berrie, William, for artillery *read* infantry.

———————Brett, William T., *read* Invalided March 13, 1829.

Page 28—29.—Boulderston, W. Levell, *read* Ensign Oct. 12, 1831. Lieut. April 2, 1835.

Page 34—35.—Cunningham, Henry P. *read* William P.

Page 36—37.—Colberg, Ambrose Herue, *read* Ambrose Hervey.

Page 38—39.—Campbell, Edw. Charles, *read* Died at Jaggapet.

Page 44—45.—Campbell, James, *read* Ensign May 23, 1828.

Page 56—57.—Evans, R. Lacy (C.B.), *read* Brevet June 18, 1831.

Page 70—71.—Godfrey, John Race, Major, for Jan. *read* June 15, 1833.

Page 82—83.—Hopkinson, Sir C., for B. B. *read* C. B.

———————Hadgson, Samuel Irton, *read* Hodgson.

Page 84—85.—Hevey, T., *read* Ensign June 27, 1806.

———————Henderson, Wm., *read* Ensign July 3, 1807.

———————Harrison, Henry, *read* Died April 15.

Page 100—101.—Kaye, John H., cavalry, *read* Died Dec. 6.

Page 112—113.—Maddes, B., *read* Madder.

———————Maccally, Andrew, see Cally, Andrew Mc. p. 30—31.

———————Marricott, Thomas, *read* Marriott.

Page 124—125.—Mayo, Francis Charles, *read* Lieut. May 1, 1824.

———————Macleod, Coll, *read* Cadet 1821.

Page 128—129.—McDermott, J. P., for cavalry *read* infantry.

Page 140—141.—Pickering, William, *read* Lieut. May 21, 1804.

———————Ritchie, Walter K. *read* Lieut. Jan. 27, 1810.

Page 144—145.—Read, John, *read* Ensign July 23, 1779.

Page 150—151.—Rawstone, T. A. H., *read* Lieut. June 4, 1818.

Page 152—153.—Rose, Alex. R., *read* Capt. Aug, 2, 1836.

Page 162—163.—Shakespear, J. N., *read* J. M.

Page 164—165.—Slade. Wm. H. for Retired *read* Died May 12, 1817, at St. Thomé.

Page 168—169.—Smith, Geo. T., engineers, *read* John T.

Page 182—183.—Wulbin, Charles, *read* Wulber.

Page 184—185.—Wahab, Geo. Launcelot, *read* Colonel June 5, 1829.

Page 192—193.—Wilson, John, *read* Wilton.

www.ingramcontent.com/pod-product-compliance
Lightning Source LLC
Chambersburg PA
CBHW080548230426
43663CB00015B/2760